Also by Robert M. Gates

A Passion for Leadership:
Lessons on Change and Reform from
Fifty Years of Public Service

Duty: Memoirs of a Secretary at War

From the Shadows:
The Ultimate Insider's Story of Five Presidents
and How They Won the Cold War

EXERCISE of
POWER

EXERCISE of
POWER

American Failures,
Successes, and a
New Path Forward in the
Post–Cold War World

Robert M. Gates

ALFRED A. KNOPF
New York · 2020

THIS IS A BORZOI BOOK
PUBLISHED BY ALFRED A. KNOPF

www.aaknopf.com

Library of Congress Cataloging-in-Publication Data
Names: Gates, Robert Michael, [date]- author
Title: Exercise of power : American failures, successes, and a
new path forward in the post–Cold War world / Robert M. Gates.
Other titles: America and the post–Cold War world
Description: First Edition. | New York : Alfred A. Knopf, 2020. |
Includes bibliographical references and index.
Identifiers: LCCN 2019057305 (print) | LCCN 2019057306 (ebook) |
ISBN 9781524731885 (hardcover) | ISBN 9781524731892 (ebook)
Subjects: LCSH: United States—Foreign relations—1989– |
United States—Politics and government—1989– |
United States—Military relations.
Classification: LCC E840 .G38 2020 (print) |
LCC E840 (ebook) | DDC 973.929—dc23
LC record available at https://lccn.loc.gov/2019057305
LC ebook record available at https://lccn.loc.gov/2019057306

Jacket photograph: Cultura Creative/Alamy
Jacket design by Chip Kidd
Book design by Betty Lew

Manufactured in the United States of America
First Edition

To Becky

We married young and have lived happily ever after

Contents

Contents

EXERCISE of
POWER

Prologue

On Christmas Day, 1991, the hammer-and-sickle flag of the Union of Soviet Socialist Republics was lowered for the last time over the Kremlin, and Soviet communism passed into history. On that day, the United States of America stood alone, unchallenged, at the pinnacle of global power. A mighty empire had fallen, the first in history to do so without a major war, leaving America in a position of power unique in modern history.

A year later, I stood at the wall of windows in my office on the seventh floor at CIA headquarters looking out at the Virginia countryside. It was cold and overcast. I was reflecting on my imminent retirement, stepping down as director of central intelligence in less than a month, twenty-six years after joining the agency as a rookie analyst working on the Soviet desk. I had lived through the many crises of the last half of the Cold War, never expecting to witness that conflict's end. On that wintry day in 1992, I thought about all I had seen and done working for six presidents, and wondered about the shape of the world to come. For someone *The Washington Post* had once characterized as the Eeyore of national security, able to find the darkest cloud in a silver lining, I was uncharacteristically optimistic.

As Bill Clinton raised his right hand to take the oath of office as our forty-second president on January 20, 1993, the United States singularly dominated the world militarily, economically, politically, and culturally—in every dimension of power. Not since the apogee of the Roman Empire had one country been in that position.

A quarter century later, the United States, while still the planet's most powerful country militarily and economically, is challenged on every front. China is ascending and likely at some point to surpass the United States economically in terms of gross domestic product; Russia, modernizing its military apace, is aggressively threatening and attempting to destabilize Western democracies and dominate its neighbors; North Korea has become a wild-card nuclear power; the Middle East remains a sinkhole of conflict and terrorism. A savage civil war in Syria and the war against the Islamic State of Iraq and the Levant (ISIL) and its "caliphate" brought troops from Russia, Iran, Turkey, and the United States to the battlefield. After a military intervention led by the United States in 2011, Libya remains divided and engulfed in violence, and Iraq, invaded by the United States in 2003, still strives to create a sustainable, multiethnic government amid the ruins of most of its cities. Iran continues to strengthen its military capabilities, including ballistic missiles, sophisticated drones, cyber threats, and nuclear research, and intensifies its meddling from Lebanon and Syria to Yemen even as its ramps up its contest for religious and regional supremacy with Saudi Arabia. The war in Afghanistan seems endless. Our closest ally, Britain, is leaving the European Union, and authoritarian governments rule our NATO ally Turkey and are rising in Hungary and Poland. The multilateral institutions, alliances, and trade arrangements the United States created in its own self-interest in the decades after World War II have been weakened, in no small part by the very hand that created them, albeit by a president unlike any other. At home, our government is polarized, paralyzed, and seemingly incapable of addressing the manifold problems facing the country.

How did our country go so quickly from unique global power to a country that is widely perceived as no longer willing to bear the costs or accept the responsibility of global leadership—or even capable of governing itself effectively?

Answering how we got to where we are today internationally requires understanding the multiple forms of power that contributed to our achievement of historical singularity, and our earlier leaders' skill in using those many and diverse forms of power along the road to that high point. The answer lies also in the mistakes of post–Cold War presidents and Congresses and, in particular, their failure to recognize, resource, and use the arsenal of nonmilitary assets that proved of critical importance in the long contest with the Soviet Union. It lies as well in their failure to understand that our place in the world in the decades ahead will depend for certain on a strong military but also on reimagining and rebuilding those nonmilitary tools. The answer is, essentially, the failure of too many of our recent political leaders to understand the complexity of American power, both in its expansiveness *and* in its limitations.

Dwight D. Eisenhower became president on January 20, 1953. During his two terms, the Soviet Union acquired the hydrogen bomb; there were repeated crises with China over Taiwan and the Taiwan Strait; the Joint Chiefs of Staff twice recommended using nuclear weapons—once to help the French at Dien Bien Phu and once against the Chinese; there was a major war in the Middle East involving three of our closest allies (Britain, France, and Israel). There were revolutions in Soviet-dominated East Germany, Poland, and Hungary; a revolution in Cuba; and many lesser crises. The period was one of great tension in the Cold War with the Soviets. And yet, from the moment Eisenhower signed the armistice agreement ending the Korean War in July 1953 until he left office in January 1961, not one American soldier was killed in combat. American prestige stood high around the world. How did he manage that feat?

Eisenhower was the only post–World War II president who was a career military officer, a five-star general who became commander in chief. He brought to the presidency great personal strengths, strategic insight, and leadership skills. He understood the uncertainties and risks always attendant to military operations. He knew the limits of military power in the nuclear age. He had the experience and confidence—and rank—to tell his generals no. Above all, he grasped the importance of diplomacy, economics, communication, and the many other tools of influence. He understood and wielded power in all its dimensions.

Ronald Reagan was routinely underestimated. Yet, as the Soviet Union began to falter internally in the 1980s, Reagan effectively used every instrument of American power to push the Soviets over the edge, from crisis to collapse. Upon taking office, he began the largest American military buildup in decades. He mobilized the CIA to covertly challenge Soviet adventurism and activities around the world, arming foes of Cuba—which acted as a surrogate for the USSR—in Angola, Ethiopia, and Central America; challenged the Soviets directly in Afghanistan by arming the mujahedin; and supported anticommunist movements such as Solidarity in Poland. Reagan brought economic pressure to bear on the USSR through sanctions and unprecedentedly aggressive efforts to block its acquisition of Western technology and know-how that might assist their weapons programs and their economy. Not since Eisenhower's and Kennedy's time did the United States Information Agency and its many channels of communication have such strong presidential support in sending America's message abroad—a message about the United States and what it stood for, and blunt talk about Soviet tyranny. Reagan also understood the importance of diplomacy and so, in 1984–85, he pivoted, offering an outreached hand to Mikhail Gorbachev. Despite ups and downs, they reached an agreement on eliminating intermediate-range nuclear weapons from Europe and overall dramatically eased tensions. Most important, Reagan's outstretched hand gave Gorbachev the political space at home to continue his reforms, which were destroying the Soviet Union.

There is no precedent in history of a great empire collapsing without a major war. Yet, through extraordinary diplomacy, George H. W. Bush (Bush 41) facilitated the liberation of Eastern Europe and managed to end the Cold War—and the Soviet Union—without violence. He orchestrated the reunification of Germany inside the NATO alliance, assembled a coalition of three dozen countries to reverse Saddam Hussein's aggression against Kuwait, and used that victory to begin a peace process in the Middle East. Building on and broadening what Reagan achieved, through skilled diplomacy and the judicious use of force, Bush 41 brought the United States out of the Cold War to a place of unparalleled dominance in every measure of national power.

Eisenhower, Reagan, and Bush, three presidents with very different backgrounds, wielded all the instruments of American power with extraordinary skill. This book assesses their post–Cold War successors' decisions in fifteen critical places, the effectiveness of their use of the instruments of American power, and the lessons we must learn for the future.

They are vital lessons because a quarter of a century after the collapse of the USSR a new rival for global influence and power has emerged, one far more formidable in the breadth and scale of its nonmilitary achievements and instruments of power than the Soviet Union. The USSR in its last decades was purely a military peer to the United States. As it degenerated into a paralyzed political gerontocracy and economic shambles, Moscow held little appeal around the world as a model to emulate.

China, by contrast, has a huge and growing economy and in recent decades has lifted hundreds of millions of its people out of poverty. It has built new cities and an enviable modern infrastructure. Its educational and technological achievements—and potential—are daunting. It has undertaken vast new initiatives to build infrastructure in countries throughout Asia, Africa, and the Middle East, and is expanding its economic and trading relationships globally. Xi Jinping, China's leader for life, now touts his country as a model for governance, independence, rapid economic development, and technological achievement—an attractive alternative to the liberal democracies' political dysfunction, economic crises (as in 2008–9), and disparities between rich and poor. China is beset by many difficult problems of its own, but it is also a multidimensional power eager to challenge the United States in every sphere. While both sides continue to build military power, they recognize that a military conflict between them, nuclear or not, would be catastrophic. And so, as in the Cold War with the Soviet Union, this rivalry in the years to come is most likely to play out in the nonmilitary arenas of national power, in which China has been investing and which the United States has neglected since the collapse of the Soviet Union.

Whether the perception, and in some cases the reality, of America pulling back from global leadership can be reversed, whether America will reassert its willingness to bear the mantle of such leadership, whether America has the will and the creativity to cope with China's global ambitions and those of other authoritarian regimes—not to mention other international challenges—depends upon a better understanding of what constitutes American power, how to revitalize it, and how to wield it more effectively.

Throughout history, power has most commonly been defined in terms of the ability to coerce obedience or submission by force of arms. But it is a mistake to think of power only in those terms. Think of the power of patriotism to inspire military service; of ideology and faith to evoke sacrifice; of government to protect the weak and disadvantaged; of a military to provide relief after a natural disaster; of peaceful resistance to oppression. From ancient times, there have been noncoercive, intangible forms of power that have changed history, such as the idea of democracy in Greece; Roman law and broadly offered Roman citizenship to conquered peoples; religion; the concepts that fueled the American and French revolutions; the Napoleonic Code; Marxism; and nationalism.

I argued as secretary of defense that the American government had become too reliant on the use of military power to defend and extend our interests internationally, that the use of force had become a first choice rather than a last resort. It is time to look afresh at the many forms of power available to America (and others as well) and then assess how well—or not—we have done since the end of the Cold War in resourcing, integrating, and using those tools. We can then draw conclusions about our approach to the world now and in the future.

A fundamental question about American power is: To what end do we use it? What *are* our purposes and goals in the world beyond protecting our own interests, particularly when it comes to advancing freedom and democracy? This question has dominated American foreign policy during the first quarter century after the Cold War, and it has been debated since the first days of the republic. How should we incorporate America's democratic ideals and aspirations into our relations with the rest of the world? When should we try to change the way other nations govern themselves? Should America's mission be to make the world "safe for democracy," as President Woodrow Wilson said, or, in the words of John Quincy Adams, should America be "the well-wisher to freedom and independence of all" but the "champion and vindicator only of her own"? Of our post–Cold War presidents, Bill Clinton and George W. Bush came down on the side of Wilson as interventionists, with long-term consequences for us and the world; Barack Obama tried to play it both ways; and Donald Trump has been all about minding our own business—both literally and figuratively—and being silent about the internal affairs of other countries, especially authoritarian ones. His and Obama's actions, both much closer to Adams's than Wilson's, have also had significant consequences.

Their varied responses demonstrate that once we get beyond broad agreement on protecting the country from foreign threats, the answer to the question of American purposes and goals in the world is not a simple one. But, based on our history and our experience during the Cold War and since, we must define our role and the means to fulfill it in ways that can win broad support in this splintered republic and among its leaders. Drawing on more than fifty years in the national security arena serving eight presidents, I intend to make a stab at it.

There are many studies and books on how the United States has applied its power since 1993 and should apply it in the future. Few of those authors, however, have actually had power and exercised it; only a handful have been firsthand witnesses to history making, and then nearly always under just one or two presidents. The authors are mostly foreign policy mavens, historians, and political scientists who write from think tanks, universities, institutes, and other such perches. Only a small number have written about the multiple forms of power usable in international affairs, particularly those beyond the military, diplomatic, and economic spheres.

Leaders who have held power have not written about power per se. They wrote about their own experience, policies they favored or opposed, challenges they faced, and the decisions they made (as well as writing to shape their legacies). This is true of all U.S. presidents in modern times. In their memoirs and other books, they didn't write about power as a concept or about its many different forms. The presidents I worked for just didn't think that way. National Security Advisers Henry Kissinger, Brent Scowcroft, and Zbigniew Brzezinski were world-class geostrategists, but even they didn't write or think about the different forms of power—and none of them paid much attention to economic and financial tools. I know, because I worked for all three. Nor did various secretaries of state and defense in their memoirs address the wide range of instruments of power available to them. The leaders who came closest to a comprehensive approach to power were probably Secretaries of State Dean Acheson and George Shultz, but even those two tended to view the various forms of power in relation to specific situations and not as part of the universe of instruments of power beyond military, diplomatic, and economic leverage. Historical figures writing about power, such as Machiavelli, focus primarily on how to get it and how to keep it.

I believe that each of the fifteen significant post–Cold War challenges I will examine in the pages to follow must be addressed in its own narrative as it has evolved over time. This will provide the continuity—the story line—essential to understanding the response by successive presidents, and why those challenges remain before us in every instance. Accordingly, I address the challenges separately and roughly chronologically, dating from when each first confronted post–Cold War American leaders. I will also deal with the reality that all the presidents had to confront many of these problems simultaneously and that, routinely, each problem impacted and influenced U.S. decisions on other problems—a sort of three-dimensional chess.

There are, finally, the diverse personalities and decision-making styles of presidents. I served as deputy director (and acting director) of central intelligence for Reagan and deputy national security adviser and director of central intelligence for Bush 41, the last two Cold War presidents. I was secretary of defense for two of the four post–Cold War presidents. I worked on the National Security Council staff for three other presidents, spending three years working just down the hall from the Oval Office for one of those. I witnessed and participated in decision making under more presidents of both parties than any other contemporary senior official. And so a critical component of this book is my effort to explain how and why presidents made the decisions they did, who most influenced them, and the style unique to each.

There have been U.S. successes in the international arena during the past quarter century, but the overall trend for us in the global arena has been negative, despite our braggadocio. To deal with the diverse challenges America faces, America must lead. But to lead, to achieve its purposes and goals, it must strengthen all the instruments of power and apply them with greater wisdom. We must use the American symphony of power to ensure that authoritarianism, twice defeated in the twentieth century, does not prevail in the twenty-first.

CHAPTER 1

The Symphony of Power

MILITARY

A weak military power during the eight and a half decades after our War of Independence, the United States avoided involvement in the Napoleonic Wars and other European conflicts. We became a continental power through negotiated acquisition and purchase, cession, annexation, settlement, conquest of overmatched indigenous peoples, and one relatively brief—and highly unpopular—war, against Mexico. In the European and global scheme of things, what modest influence the United States possessed beyond our borders was economic, cultural, and ideological, not military.

The American experience beginning with the Civil War, however, narrowed our view of power. The dramatic growth and use of our military power in the Civil War, the Spanish-American War, and both world wars culminated in complete victory in each case for the United States, all but one of those wars seeing the adversary crushed by overwhelming military force leading to formal, abject surrender. Coming out of World War II, this was how Americans thought every war we fought should end.

Even so, in 1945, Americans, tired of war, had no interest in a conflict with the Soviet Union to prevent its takeover of Eastern Europe (or in China a few years later to prevent Mao from taking control), and, beginning in 1946, a Democratic president and Republican Congress together dramatically cut the size of the U.S. military. By early 1947, President Harry Truman had cut the defense budget from $91 billion to around $10 billion and wanted to reduce it further, to between $6 billion and $7 billion. Truman turned to nonmilitary forms of power to thwart further communist expansionism.

Relying initially on our nuclear monopoly and subsequently on our nuclear deterrent, during the first dozen or so years of the Cold War Presidents Truman, Eisenhower, and Kennedy approved assistance to Greece and Turkey, the Marshall Plan, the creation of NATO and other alliances, and a strategy of containing the USSR. They also promoted the establishment of international financial institutions at Bretton Woods, the formation of the United States Information Agency and the United States Agency for International Development, and the use of CIA covert actions around the world—all nonmilitary "big ideas" to prevail in the global struggle against Soviet communism.

When North Korea invaded the South in 1950, our military response was characterized as a "police action," as though we were repelling some miscreants who had wandered across the DMZ. And when General Douglas MacArthur's counterattack pushed north to the Yalu River, prompting the Chinese to enter the war, neither Truman nor most Americans were prepared to launch an all-out war—or risk a nuclear conflict with the Soviets—to defeat the communist Chinese. Our political leadership, reflecting public opinion, ultimately settled for an armistice that essentially reestablished the status quo as it existed before the North Korean attack. American casualties were 33,686 killed and 92,134 wounded. We had repelled an aggression in a faraway land, but there was no sense of victory.

With the USSR's explosion of its first nuclear device in 1949, one lesson of the Korean War was that the kind of all-out war we had waged in World War II had become impossible without the likelihood of catastrophic destruction at home. Total military victory in war ran counter to the realities of the nuclear age. Americans still wanted to win our wars, but not at any cost. Political realities at home and nuclear weapons abroad imposed very real limits on our vast military power.

Nowhere was this clearer than in Vietnam, where we fought from the mid-1950s to 1975, suffered nearly 50,000 killed in combat and more than 150,000 wounded, and lost the war. We were defeated not militarily but because we were unwilling to wage all-out war—and risk confrontation with China and/or the Soviet Union—to destroy the regime in Hanoi. Critically, support evaporated at home for continuing a protracted conflict, particularly in partnership with a deeply flawed ally.

In both Afghanistan and Iraq overwhelming initial military victories were followed by political decisions that expanded the mission beyond purely military objectives to ambitious and, I believe, unrealistic nation-building. We failed to provide the much larger military forces and nonmilitary forms of power required to achieve those objectives—if they were achievable at all. With politically imposed limits on the size and duration of our deployed military forces, the obvious shortcomings (as in Vietnam) of our indigenous allies in both countries, and mounting costs in blood and treasure, once again domestic support for continuing these conflicts—especially in Iraq—plummeted. American casualties in the two wars included more than 5,000 killed and 50,000 wounded for, at best, inconclusive outcomes. In both conflicts, the United States ignored Machiavelli's warning that wise leaders should be content with victory.

There are two exceptions to this post–World War II record of the use of constrained military force. The first was our military intervention in Panama in December 1989 to remove the regime of Manuel Noriega and restore democracy. The operation was completed in a month, at a cost of 23 American lives, with 324 wounded. It was noncontroversial because Noriega was a detestable drug thug and despot, the operation ended successfully and quickly, the cost in lives and treasure was low, and it led to a restoration of democracy. It was regime change in a sovereign state (if one long an American protectorate) carried out by U.S. forces.

The second success was the Gulf War that reversed Saddam Hussein's invasion of Kuwait in 1990. It was a war that was fought to achieve very specific military objectives, ended when those objectives were achieved, and accomplished through a protracted air attack followed by a ground campaign that lasted roughly four days. Overall, the conflict lasted about six weeks and resulted in 149 Americans killed and 849 wounded. Many criticized the president's unwillingness to go on to Baghdad and "finish the job" by bringing regime change. Leaving Saddam in power and U.S. forces in the region, especially in Saudi Arabia, did have their own future consequences.

While the forty-five-year-long Cold War against the Soviet Union involved the creation and maintenance of massive military establishments and nuclear arsenals in both the United States and the USSR, because of the nuclear standoff, it never broke into direct military conflict. The Cold War certainly created the circumstances leading to the wars in Korea and Vietnam, and our leaders at the time assuredly saw both conflicts as necessary to resist the advance of Soviet-supported communism. Still, most histories report that there were probably fewer than fifty and no more than one hundred U.S. military casualties due to direct Soviet action between 1947 and 1991. The outcome of the Cold War was determined by other forms of power. Our military played a big role, but it was primarily in deterring and containing the Soviets—and forcing them to spend more money on their military than they could afford in order to keep pace with us. Because nuclear stockpiles on both sides prevented the direct use of military force, the Cold War became our only post–World War II conflict in which other forms of power were fully mobilized and exploited. Economic measures, strategic communications (propaganda), a technological contest, diplomacy, development (foreign assistance), carrying on the ideological struggle, scientific and cultural outreach, and covert operations—along with the use of armed surrogates around the world—all were expanded and applied strategically and globally against communism and its Soviet propagator. And we won.

In sum, in the nearly seventy-five years since World War II, we have fought five major wars, with one win (Iraq, 1991), one partial success (Korea, 1953), one loss (Vietnam, 1975), and two inconclusive outcomes (Iraq and Afghanistan). Four of those five were protracted conflicts, ranging from three to fifteen or more years. In Vietnam, Iraq, and Afghanistan, Americans saw the limits of military power when applied with politically determined constraints and unrealistically expansive nonmilitary goals. The outcome of those wars was influenced by—and fed—public frustration and impatience with the use of military power and the politicians who wielded it, and with an American role in the world many came to believe cost too much in lives and treasure.

So America now stands in an awkward place when it comes to military power. We face major powers like Russia, China, North Korea, and Iran that are steadily improving their military capabilities and showing a willingness to use them. We must deal with a Middle East in the midst of a long-term conflict involving numerous powers, including Turkey, Saudi Arabia, and Iran, and where Islamic extremist groups still recruit from and carry out terrorist operations against many countries, including the United States.

As a result of American presidential policies since 1993, public loss of patience with interventionism and internationalism, congressional paralysis, and two successive presidents who have signaled an American withdrawal from global leadership, potential adversaries perceive new opportunities to expand their own reach, presence, and influence. President Obama foreshadowed a shrinking American role in the world through his policies in Iraq, Afghanistan, and Libya; his unwillingness to carry out real freedom-of-navigation missions and otherwise challenge China's territorial claims in the South China Sea; his failure to enforce his own red line in Syria or become otherwise involved there; and his deep cuts to the U.S. defense budget. That message was strongly reinforced by President Donald Trump's disputes with longtime U.S. allies; criticism of NATO and initial refusal to reaffirm the U.S. commitment to defend our allies under Article V of the NATO charter; criticism of economic ties with close allies, including Canada, Mexico, Japan, South Korea, and nearly all of Europe; and his withdrawal from trade arrangements such as the Trans-Pacific Partnership. Even though Trump initially obtained significant increases in military spending, ten years of budgetary cuts and uncertainty will take time to overcome, even in the unlikely event those increases are sustained. All things considered, it is not surprising that allies and friends have begun to look elsewhere for collaboration and protection.

Under these circumstances, how then do we deter military challenges from large state actors, constrain adversaries, reassure allies, protect our country, and advance our interests? How do we achieve our purposes or goals militarily?

There are two dimensions to the challenge. The first is how we shape our military forces for the future. There is no doubt that needed resources were diverted from our current and future military capability to confront advanced great powers by our wars in Iraq and Afghanistan. We find ourselves for the first time since the 1950s in a race for technological superiority in military capabilities with Russia (and China). Addressing the consequences of that reality has properly been the highest priority for the president, Congress, and the Department of Defense in recent years. But there is another reality too. A consistent thread connects every use of American military power around the world since Vietnam: in only one case did we have any idea even a few months beforehand that we would be engaged militarily—not in Grenada, Lebanon, Panama, Iraq (1991), Somalia, Bosnia, Kosovo, Haiti, Afghanistan, or Libya (twice). Only in Iraq in 2003 was it clear war was coming, and that was because we were going to start it. Since we rarely know where and when we will next use military force, our military forces must be trained and equipped to have the greatest possible versatility across the broadest possible spectrum of conflict. They must be able to defeat the most technologically advanced nation-states as well as nonstate actors (such as ISIL, al-Qaeda, and the Taliban) and still provide security assistance and training in underdeveloped countries. As we learned in Iraq, a conventional force trained and equipped only to take on a large nation-state cannot necessarily effectively defeat lesser adversaries, such as insurgents. When we tell ourselves, especially after both Vietnam and Iraq, we won't fight that kind of war again, we forget that the bad guys have a vote on that decision, as do future presidents.

The second challenge is closing the communication and cultural gap between civilian leaders, presidents in particular, and military leaders. Presidents need to assign missions to the military that it can actually accomplish. An always, "can-do" military leadership must be willing to tell the commander in chief that a given mission cannot be accomplished with the resources and/or timetable the civilian leadership is prepared to provide. On occasion, military leadership must assert that what he or she asks is not a military mission. Based on the history of the last five decades, presidents need to be mindful that every war is predicted to be short, and that prediction is almost always wrong. There is therefore the need to carefully define the mission, always bearing in mind Machiavelli's warning to "make the war short and sharp." As a number of the most senior Defense officials, both civilian and military, have urged, presidents should have specific achievable goals, apply overwhelming force, and then stop, as did Bush 41 in 1991. Otherwise, as I will discuss in specific cases, a president is likely to find himself, as Pete Seeger sang in 1967, "waist deep in the Big Muddy."

The only near-peer military powers the United States faces are Russia and China. As I said, both are greatly strengthening their militaries, but in highly focused ways. After the collapse of the Soviet Union, Russian military spending dropped by nearly 90 percent in the 1990s, with predictable consequences for Russian capabilities and manpower in all branches of the military. As the Russian economy began to recover in the 2000s, thanks mostly to the rising price of oil and some reforms undertaken during the previous decade, President Vladimir Putin placed a high priority on revitalizing the military. Unlike the tsars and commissars, though, Putin pivoted away from a huge army to a smaller, far more proficient ground force (especially special forces) along with modernization of the navy, air force, and nuclear forces, including investments in new weapons systems, such as combat aircraft, drones, and new ballistic missiles. Russia's improved ground, naval, and air capabilities contributed to the quick seizure of Crimea in 2014 as well as intervention in eastern Ukraine and, of course, in Syria in September 2015. The credibility of Russian military power—and willingness to use it—was restored.

China's military modernization and expansion has followed a path similar to Russia's by focusing on a smaller and more effective army (including dramatic reorganization of command structures) but emphasizing growth of naval and air power—including, as in Russia, significant investment in advanced technologies. China is determined to achieve military dominance in Asia, including in the Sea of Japan and the South China Sea, and is developing the capabilities to hold U.S. naval power there (especially aircraft carriers) at risk through antiship cruise and ballistic missiles and other new capabilities. I suspect China also intends to deploy a sufficiently sizable "blue-water" navy so as to project influence and power as well as safeguard shipping lanes through the Indian Ocean and Arabian Sea to ensure its supply of oil. This objective also involves the establishment of China's first overseas base in Djibouti, another in Pakistan, and perhaps more to come—a "string of pearls," as they say, from Asia to the Middle East and Africa.

For decades, we believe China has been content with a relatively small, survivable ICBM force. We don't know with certainty the actual size of that force, however, because a substantial part of it is hidden in caves and tunnels. As the United States, South Korea, and Japan increase their antiballistic missile capabilities to counter the growing threat from North Korea, China may see these capabilities as threatening its own nuclear forces and thus opt to further expand its nuclear strike forces.

North Korea is a wild card among military (and nuclear-armed) powers given the unpredictable nature of its leader, Kim Jong-un. The regime has been relentless for some two decades in developing nuclear weapons and the means to deliver them. From Kim's perspective, Muammar Qaddafi gave up his nuclear weapons program and is dead, his regime gone; Saddam Hussein never got nuclear weapons and he is dead, his regime gone. Ukraine gave up 1,500 nuclear weapons in 1994 based on the pledge by the United States, the United Kingdom, and Russia (and separately, France) to guarantee its territorial integrity; it has since lost Crimea and the eastern part of its country. Kim is smart enough to understand these lessons.

Despite the fervent wishes of many, military power remains the most formidable asset available for a larger state to impose its will on a smaller one, such as in the U.S. invasion of Iraq and regime change by force of arms in Panama, Afghanistan, and Libya; Russia's land grab in Georgia, annexation of Crimea, and intervention in Syria and Ukraine; and China's occupation and militarization of disputed islands—and creation of others—in the South China Sea.

DIPLOMACY

Often disparaged and consistently underfunded, diplomacy is, like a strong military, an indispensable instrument of national power. Preventing and ending wars; creating and sustaining alliances; settling economic and trade disputes; limiting arms races; establishing the rules for international political, economic, and military affairs; containing and getting rid of malevolent actors on the global stage; assembling coalitions of nations to join us in military operations or to impose sanctions on aggressors and oppressors; negotiating limits on nuclear weapons; keeping conflicts from spreading; containing disease; helping new and inexperienced foreign leaders try to build democratic governments; keeping rivalries with powers such as Russia and China peaceful; ousting vicious dictators; and conducting the day-to-day business of nations interacting with one another: all these and more are the province of diplomacy. The effective use of every other instrument of power depends upon or involves, in one way or another, at one time or another, diplomacy. Caricatures of the striped-pants diplomat notwithstanding, the work is, in reality, laborious and often sweaty and dirty and conducted in dangerous places. It requires not only negotiating skill but knowledge of languages and locales—as well as patience and courage. In considering the life of a diplomat, instead of London, Paris, or Rome, think Beirut, Baghdad, Kabul, or Addis Ababa. At least 250 diplomats have died in the line of duty. It is not a role for the faint of heart.

Each of the four post–Cold War presidents, like their predecessors, engaged in personal diplomacy, in some instances with skill and success, in others, not so much. Day to day, it is the secretary of state who routinely engages the governments of other countries on major issues and oversees the ambassadors and foreign service officers doing the nation's business—and helping American citizens—all over the world. I have known and worked with many senior American diplomats over the decades, and as a group they are public servants of extraordinary quality, effectiveness, and toughness.

For many years now, our diplomatic establishment—the State Department—has been consistently starved of resources by Congress (except for brief periods under George W. Bush) and too often sidelined by the White House. I agree with critics, including inside the department, that it is stunningly bureaucratic and very much in need of reform and restructuring. But, for the most part, its human capital—the diplomats themselves—constitutes a remarkable instrument of national power. Any effort to strengthen America's nonmilitary tool kit must, of necessity, have strengthened diplomacy at its core.

ECONOMIC LEVERAGE

Economic power is second only to military power in enabling a state to achieve its goals or purposes. It is a truism that a strong economy is required to underpin a strong military. In the history of warfare, measures to weaken the domestic economy of an adversary have been an integral component of a strategy for victory. From Spartan attacks on Athenian agriculture during the Peloponnesian War to Napoleon's "continental system" aimed at ending Britain's trade with Europe to modern times, various measures have been employed to apply economic pressure on an adversary.

Probably the most comprehensive and long-lasting of these were applied by the United States against the Soviet Union over the four-and-a-half-decade-long Cold War. The United States began to encourage its Western European allies as early as 1948 to join a coordinated embargo policy against the Soviet Union and its minions in Eastern Europe, and in late November 1949 a formal organization, the Coordinating Committee for Multilateral Export Controls, was established and began operation on January 1, 1950. While the embargo list initially included about 130 items deemed strategically important, the list would at times exceed 2,000 products and technologies. The list also included "selected items in key industrial areas contributing substantially to war potential." There were periodic revisions to the list, alternately shrinking and expanding it depending on the president at the time and his foreign policy aspirations with the USSR. The United States was willing to sell the Soviets agricultural products, especially grain, during years of bad harvests (which were fairly routine in Soviet days), but for more than four decades anything that might remotely help advance military programs or systemic improvement in the Soviet economy was blacklisted.

The KGB had elaborate covert schemes for getting around these restrictions and clandestinely acquiring highly sought-after technologies. The most sophisticated of these operations was uncovered by the French in the early 1980s, and for the remainder of the Reagan administration denying the Soviets any technology or products of strategic value was a high priority. Indeed, not since the late 1940s had the United States more strategically and effectively used its economic power for the achievement of political purposes than it did during the Carter and Reagan administrations against the Soviet Union.

The effectiveness of the embargo and denial of technology in worsening Soviet economic problems and slowing modernization of its military forces was hotly debated throughout the Cold War—and after. As head of intelligence analysis at the CIA during the first half of the 1980s, I oversaw the effort by U.S. agencies to monitor the effectiveness of the export restrictions, and would occasionally complain to the Reagan White House and Defense Department that it seemed kind of silly to have export controls on an item the Soviets could buy at RadioShack. Still, I believe the full range of economic pressure applied against the Soviets over time exacerbated their deepening economic problems and contributed to slowing both economic modernization and weapons development.

China has been even more predatory—and strategic—than was the USSR in acquiring technologies and equipment that can contribute to its weapons development programs and its economy. There are multiple lines of attack against the United States, Japan, and Europe, including acquisition of companies with useful or cutting-edge technologies; agreements requiring foreign companies wanting to manufacture or do business in China to share sensitive processes and technology; hacking foreign companies' and governments' computer systems; planting moles in foreign companies; and outright theft. The United States and others have had great difficulty stemming this outward flow, with substantial economic consequences. From the business interests of companies in the United States and elsewhere to the sophistication and breadth of the Chinese effort, developed countries have struggled in vain to constrain China from vacuuming up whatever it wants.

During and after the Cold War, the United States has applied economic sanctions against dozens of countries as punishment, to get them to stop doing things we dislike or to get them to alter policies or behavior. Sanctions generally fall into two broad categories: (1) trade restrictions, including embargoes on specific goods such as arms and/or technology or more broadly on nearly all U.S. exports; and (2) financial restrictions, which can affect everything from economic assistance to denial of access to concessionary loans and/or the international banking system, a freeze on assets held abroad, denying access to dollar accounts in the United States, or simply scaring off bankers and investors.

The record of effectiveness of economic sanctions is mixed. Broad restrictions affecting an entire economy work only if there is widespread international support and enforcement. Such sanctions probably had a significant impact in bringing regime change in both South Africa and Rhodesia, in getting Qaddafi to give up his nuclear weapons program (although the U.S. invasions of both Iraq and Afghanistan surely got his attention), and in bringing Iran to the bargaining table on its nuclear ambitions. In 1956, when Britain, France, and Israel invaded Egypt, President Eisenhower conditioned a loan to save the British pound on a U.K. cease-fire and withdrawal from Suez. Ike also threatened to cut off the supply of oil to both the British and the French from Western Hemisphere sources if they didn't withdraw. On the other hand, the U.S. embargo on Cuba has been in place since 1962 and has had no discernible effect on its policies or its leadership. Punitive sanctions on Saddam Hussein failed to induce him to readmit UN inspectors in 2002–3, and severe sanctions have failed to get the North Korean regime to stop its ballistic missile and nuclear programs.

Members of Congress love to impose sanctions on countries whose actions they object to, even though usually the only effect is to make the members feel righteous and look tough to their constituents. In fact, all too frequently, the imposition of sanctions is simply a political gesture, intended mainly to show that the United States is doing something in response to another country's bad behavior without much expectation of success. For example, economic sanctions were imposed on China in 1989 after the brutal suppression of demonstrators at Tiananmen Square in Beijing and on Russia in 2014 after the seizure of Crimea and intervention in eastern Ukraine because no one was prepared to support a military response. The sanctions had little impact on China, and while the post-Crimea sanctions hurt the Russian economy, President Putin would not consider taking the actions required to get them lifted (although they may have constrained him from other acts of aggression).

Broad economic sanctions are a powerful nonmilitary instrument of power, but presidents need to understand that, nearly always, the greatest impact of effective sanctions falls mainly on ordinary people. During the period of most-severe sanctions, Saddam built nearly two dozen new palaces and lived his sybaritic lifestyle uninterrupted—as did his senior lieutenants and regime officials. Similarly, Kim Jong-un lives supremely well while his countrymen starve. The situation in Iran is the same. In fact, in most cases, regime black marketers get very rich when their country is heavily sanctioned.

Two kinds of sanctions seem effective in producing changes in policy or forcing a government to the negotiating table. One is such draconian sanctions as to create the risk of a popular uprising (as in Iran between late 2009 and 2013 and beginning again in 2017), thus prompting the regime to make concessions. Another is to shape the sanctions so they primarily impact the leadership elites directly—seizing or freezing personal assets abroad, prohibiting travel, targeting their business interests, and other highly personal measures.

I have described the use of economic power to impose pain on other countries, but there are positive economic policies and actions that have strengthened America's international influence (and power) and encouraged governments we wish to see succeed or rewarded for their assistance to us. Foremost among these was the creation of institutions designed to strengthen international economic cooperation, largely on American terms. The agreements at Bretton Woods, New Hampshire, in 1944 began this process, creating the International Monetary Fund (IMF) and the International Bank for Reconstruction and Development, later part of the World Bank. The Marshall Plan, announced in 1947, was aimed at helping Europe rebuild after the war. The plan was born out of deep concern that an economically ravaged Europe might fall prey to communist electoral victories or Soviet-inspired revolutions. At the same time, all these initiatives were seen realistically as serving America's own political and economic national self-interest.

Similarly, reflecting a broad belief that trade and tariff wars in the 1920s and 1930s dramatically worsened the Depression and helped bring on World War II, American statesmen of both major political parties after the war were committed to international economic cooperation and free trade. "Any gain for free trade anywhere was a gain for the Western world in its bid to win the Cold War," one expert wrote afterward. In the first years after World War II, the United States went beyond promoting free trade, offering concessionary trade terms to our European allies, Germany, Japan, and later South Korea. We opened our borders to their exports and companies even as they denied reciprocal concessions to us. Lingering aspects of these one-sided arrangements remained in place long after those nations had recovered economically, and would become an issue in the 2016 presidential election.

There are other economic tools in the U.S. foreign policy kitbag, ranging from loans through the Export-Import Bank to encouraging overseas investment by U.S. companies through insurance arrangements offered by the Overseas Private Investment Corporation (OPIC) and its successor organization; extension of Most-Favored-Nation treatment (resulting in significantly reduced tariffs on goods coming to the United States); financial assistance; currency stabilization; debt refinancing; and support of loans through both the IMF and the World Bank.

The post–World War II emphasis on developing and supporting international instruments of economic cooperation and the use of American economic power for geopolitical purposes began to wane as early as the 1960s. While the pursuit of international trade agreements continued, until the election of President Trump the agreements were sought primarily for economic purposes and not to achieve foreign policy or national security ends except in the broadest sense. Since the early 1990s, nearly all negotiated trade agreements submitted for Senate ratification have encountered tough opposition. Neither labor unions nor environmentalists nor economic nationalists—both Republicans and Democrats—much like them, and the political climate in the United States for such agreements has steadily worsened. For decades now, the application of American geo-economic power—"the use of economic instruments to promote and defend national interests, and to produce beneficial geopolitical results"—has become increasingly rare. American presidents have come to see our economic power principally as a punitive instrument globally.

As U.S. political leaders lost their enthusiasm for multilateral trade and economic partnerships, the Chinese saw an opportunity and grabbed it with both hands. President Xi Jinping in 2013 launched the Belt and Road Initiative (comprising the Silk Road Economic Belt and the Twenty-First Century Maritime Silk Road) designed to build infrastructure tying together Central and West Asia, the Middle East, Europe, and East Africa. To help fund the projects, China in 2015 created the Asian Infrastructure Investment Bank (AIIB), which more than seventy countries had joined as of 2019. In a major policy mistake, President Obama tried to block creation of the bank, failed, and then refused to join even though many of our closest allies did so. Through these initiatives, China potentially will enjoy significant geostrategic and economic benefits. Meanwhile, China's Export-Import Bank in 2015 lent over $80 billion whereas the Asian Development Bank lent just $27 billion that year. When the United States in 2017 declared it was ending its participation in the Trans-Pacific Partnership trade agreement, another major U.S. mistake, this time by President Trump, Xi Jinping immediately picked up the baton and—shamelessly—declared at Davos that China would lead the effort for freer trade. In short, China seems to be playing the same kind of long game using its economic power for strategic purposes as America did after World War II. Can the United States get its game back? Can a democracy, unable to compel its companies to invest abroad, compete in this arena with authoritarian state capitalism?

On a much smaller scale, other countries use their economic clout more obviously in pursuit of geopolitical purposes. Saudi Arabia, the United Arab Emirates, Qatar, Iran, and—when it was rich—Venezuela, all have done so. Think of the OPEC oil embargo in 1973 to punish the United States for its support of Israel in the Yom Kippur War. All countries seek economic advantage in their dealings with others. The defining question is which of them also try to translate economic power into the achievement of their geopolitical and geostrategic goals.

CYBER CAPABILITIES

Until recent times, the use—or threat—of military force and economic leverage was the most intimidating instrument of power. Today, however, cyber warfare has arguably become the most powerful weapon in a nation's arsenal, giving the possessor the ability to penetrate another country's military structures and weapons systems to disable or redirect them; to paralyze civil infrastructure, financial systems, and communications; to wreak havoc through seizing control of or destroying networks by implanting destructive codes, launching denial-of-service attacks, and more; and to interfere with democratic processes and aggravate domestic divisions. The more developed the economy and infrastructure of the target and the more sophisticated its weapons and communications, the more vulnerable it is to cyber assault.

A conventional military attack is guaranteed to provoke prompt retaliation. Proving beyond a doubt the origin of a cyber attack, however, is both difficult and time-consuming. Perversely, the broader the attack and thus the more lethal the presumed retaliation, the greater the need for the victim to be certain who actually fired the ones and zeroes.

Cyber has long been an instrument in the hands of governments, mainly for collecting intelligence information on an adversary's military and civilian technological advances, stealing corporate technology or financial information (such as bids), and counterintelligence. Dozens of countries have been doing this for a very long time. Beginning early in the 2000s, cyber attacks targeted American defense contractors' computer systems to steal technological information, especially on weapons development. Experts concluded that the Chinese military was the likeliest source of most of the attacks, but corporate espionage or hackers could not be ruled out. The Pentagon faces thousands of cyber attacks daily, most aimed at gathering information. The hack of the United States Office of Personnel Management yielded personal information on some 21.5 million government employees, past and present. China was suspected of being the culprit and, in August 2017, a Chinese national was arrested by the FBI in connection with the hack. Of course, criminal hackers have long used cyber to steal money or hold companies or individuals at ransom.

The expanding use of cyber capabilities for destructive and political purposes is relatively new. The Russians have been especially aggressive, launching a cyber attack in the spring of 2007 that targeted the Estonian parliament, banks, ministries, newspapers, and broadcasters. More than two weeks before Russian troops invaded Georgia in August 2008, a number of Georgian websites were hacked, including that of the Georgian president, which was reprogrammed to compare him to Adolf Hitler. Cyber attacks were widely used by the Russians when they invaded Crimea and attacked eastern Ukraine in 2014. The Iranians launched a number of cyber attacks against the Saudi national oil company, Aramco, in 2017, with one attack burning the hard drives of tens of thousands of computers.

Even more dangerous is the ability of multiple nations to implant code in key infrastructure and economic institutions that, if activated, could wreak havoc on an adversary's economy and daily life. It is reasonable to assume that a number of countries have this capability and have implanted code for future potential use. While I believe the big powers—above all, the United States, China, and Russia—would refrain from any such large-scale attacks on each other short of a major war, the same cannot be said for North Korea or Iran if faced with a threat to the regime. Nor can any country expect restraint in the use of cyber threats by nonstate entities, such as terrorist groups, should they acquire the capability. While we worry about nuclear proliferation, in truth, cyber weapons are more likely to be used than nuclear weapons because they are potentially more damaging, much less risky for the attacker, and tougher to trace to the aggressor.

Cyber is the most versatile instrument of power because it can be used overtly or covertly and with great effect against military and economic targets. It can also accomplish political objectives, recruit adherents, undermine confidence in institutions, affect decision making, and impact the personal lives of millions of people. While it can be used as a force for democratization and reform, as discussed below, it is also an exceptionally powerful tool in the hands of governments and nongovernmental organizations (NGOs) with malignant intentions.

There are a number of noncoercive options in a nation's tool kit that can contribute to accomplishing its purposes and advancing its national interests. These instruments of power influence the attitudes and perceptions of other societies and governmental decision making in ways that help a country win support for its own objectives. Characterized both appreciatively and derisively as "soft" power, and more recently as "smart" and even "sharp" power, most of these tools have been around and used by every form of government (and religion) for millennia. Only the technology has changed.

For much of the period from World War II through the end of the Cold War, the United States was overwhelmingly the most successful country in using this array of instruments of influence. Yet, at the pinnacle of our success—following the collapse of the USSR and victory in the Cold War—we began to dismantle these capabilities only to watch others, especially China, begin to compete in this arena.

DEVELOPMENT ASSISTANCE

After World War II, most U.S. economic assistance was focused on rebuilding Europe. As the Cold War heated up, the Truman administration concluded that America needed to demonstrate to "third world" countries that democratic and market-oriented programs could help them develop their economies and societies. This initiative was formally announced by Truman in his 1949 inaugural address outlining his foreign policy in four points. His fourth objective was to embark on a bold new program for making the benefits of our scientific advances and industrial progress available for the improvement and growth of underdeveloped areas. More than half the people of the world are living in conditions approaching misery. Their food is inadequate. They are victims of disease. Their economic life is primitive and stagnant. Their poverty is a handicap and a threat both to them and to more prosperous areas. . . . The material resources which we can afford to use for assistance of other peoples are limited. But our imponderable resources in technical knowledge are constantly growing and are inexhaustible.

U.S. government development assistance continued through a variety of organizational entities until Congress passed the Foreign Assistance Act of 1961, with President Kennedy's support. The act created the United States Agency for International Development which, known as USAID, continues to exist. Over the decades, USAID supported many initiatives in developing countries, focused on health, family planning, and the delivery of medicines. It also promoted teacher training, curriculum development, the providing of textbooks and materials, and the broadening of access to schools for the poor. USAID has offered assistance with developing political institutions, conducting elections, organizing political parties, and creating civil society organizations. It supported economic initiatives such as efforts to improve agricultural techniques and marketing, development of microfinancing, and infrastructure projects dedicated to building roads and power plants and providing clean water.

At home, development assistance always has been the most unpopular of all U.S. foreign policy instruments. Many Americans believe "foreign aid" dollars should be spent on needs at home, and there is wide overestimation of how much the United States actually spends. In fact, the United States ranks twenty-first in the world in development assistance spending as a percentage of GDP, with countries such as New Zealand, Portugal, and Greece ranking ahead of us. As a result of the domestic unpopularity of its mission, USAID has had a checkered history, with the House of Representatives voting to abolish the agency in 1995. While that failed, in 1997 President Clinton agreed to consolidate USAID more fully into the State Department. Another act of Congress the next year authorized Clinton to abolish the agency, but he declined to do so.

When I retired as director of central intelligence in 1993, USAID had more than 15,000 employees. Most were dedicated and skilled career professionals, many of them working in developing countries in inhospitable and often insecure environments. When I returned to government as secretary of defense in 2006, I was told USAID had been cut to about 3,000 employees, most of them managing contractors. As far as I was concerned, we had unilaterally disarmed in an important arena we had long dominated. I spoke out publicly and critically in a speech on November 26, 2007, at Kansas State University: "One of the most important lessons of the wars in Iraq and Afghanistan is that military success is not sufficient to win: economic development, institution-building and the rule of law, promoting internal reconciliation, good governance, providing basic services to the people, training and equipping indigenous military and police forces, strategic communications, and more—these, along with security, are essential ingredients for long-term success." I complained about the "gutting of America's ability to engage, assist and communicate with other parts of the world."

The USAID budget was dramatically reduced during the Clinton administration, with funding plummeting to its lowest level in the agency's history in 2000. However, during the Bush 43 years, assistance was seen as an important instrument in the war on terror in Afghanistan, Iraq, and Pakistan; USAID's funding more than doubled in real terms from 2001 to 2009. Under Obama, the assistance budget continued to grow modestly through 2011, then stabilized in 2014–16 at about $18 billion to $20 billion—more than half of all U.S. government foreign assistance. (Food aid comes out of the Department of Agriculture budget.) Often the effectiveness of USAID is inhibited by congressional restrictions and "earmarks"—significant sums are routinely set aside for Israel, Egypt, and a handful of other countries, leaving other needs unmet. In a major reversal, President Donald Trump's first budget slashed the State Department and USAID budgets by some 30 percent. Development assistance was clearly not one of his priorities. Congress blocked this draconian cut but made no effort to increase available funding.

Unfortunately, Trump's decision came not long after China's leadership had figured out more ambitious and sophisticated ways to use this policy tool. The Chinese development program of greatest potential importance is the Belt and Road Initiative, potentially a multitrillion-dollar undertaking that involves infrastructure and economic development projects—road and rail routes, airports, oil and natural gas pipelines, bridges, ports—in as many as sixty countries. No other country, including the United States, has the capacity or is structured to undertake such an ambitious program, which requires the ability to direct state-owned enterprises to invest in such projects.

The European Union, individual European governments, and Japan all have robust development assistance programs. In 2013, the EU and its member states spent €56.5 billion on development assistance in 150 countries. Japan's focus initially was on assistance in the Asia-Pacific area but now includes significant assistance to Africa in the form of yen loans, grant aid, and technical cooperation. In 2014, Japan was the largest contributor to the Asian Development Bank.

The most consequential new U.S. programs for development assistance since 1971 were created under Presidents George W. Bush and Donald Trump. The Millennium Challenge Corporation, created by Congress in 2004 to provide financial assistance to countries selected for good performance in socioeconomic development and to finance some USAID-administered development programs, was established as an entirely new agency. The President's Emergency Plan for AIDS Relief (PEPFAR), established by Bush in 2003, was placed under the direction of a new office in the State Department. The United States International Development Finance Corporation (USIDFC) was established in 2018 under President Trump, replacing OPIC to better counter China's investments in other countries by providing financially sound alternatives to state-led projects such as those funded by China's Belt and Road Initiative. The legislation creating the USDFC doubled the total investment limit from $29 billion to $60 billion. Remarkably, all of these programs had broad bipartisan support against a long history of congressional skepticism of development assistance, that is, foreign aid.

Because most development assistance goes to the poorest nations and those who deliver the programs tend to be highly idealistic, such assistance is difficult to translate into influence or leverage for the donor country. There is no question, though, that such efforts have intrinsic value and offer opportunities to build goodwill. While Bush's PEPFAR initiative received broad recognition and praise in Africa, it is a rarity in that respect. Unfortunately, the United States does little to publicize its development assistance efforts, either in the recipient country, regionally, or globally. By contrast, China seems especially adept at using its development projects to cultivate (and reward) the leaders of recipient countries and convert assistance into access and influence. The boldness and scope of the Belt and Road Initiative is an example of the potential power of development assistance.

A subset of development assistance is humanitarian assistance and disaster relief. The overall scale of humanitarian assistance by the United States to other countries after natural disasters has no parallel in human history. In 2016 alone, the United States provided nearly $6.5 billion in aid to some fifty countries. Between 1975 and 2013, the U.S. military was deployed for humanitarian purposes more than 175 times. We have been doing this for a long time—the American Relief Administration and U.S. charities provided food aid to Belgium and Hungary after World War I, and in 1921, we even sent a famine-stricken Soviet Russia enough food to feed 11 million people. Because of the crisis atmosphere associated with natural disasters, the appearance of U.S. military assets bringing relief often generates more goodwill than longer-term development assistance. Four examples demonstrate the unique capabilities America can bring to bear.

On December 26, 2004, a devastating earthquake and tsunami hit Southeast Asia, affecting fourteen countries and killing perhaps a quarter of a million people. By early January, the U.S. aircraft carrier *Abraham Lincoln* and nearly two dozen other ships, as well as the 1,000-bed hospital ship *Mercy*, 75 aircraft, and 12,000 sailors and Marines were on the scene providing relief, rescue, and medical care. The magnitude of the effort had a significant impact on public opinion in Indonesia, where positive attitudes toward the United States rose from 15 percent to 38 percent—not great in absolute terms but, relatively speaking, a big improvement.

Local Pakistanis were deeply grateful for U.S. military relief assistance after an October 2005 earthquake took approximately 80,000 lives and left about 4 million homeless in Pakistani Kashmir. However, relations between the United States and Pakistan deteriorated so badly over the next few years that when we provided relief after floods that left a fifth of Pakistan under water in July 2010, I had to insist that Pakistani military officers accompany each of our helicopters flying in supplies to explain to the locals that we were only there to help.

After the Haiti earthquake in January 2010 we sent 17 Navy ships, 48 helicopters, and some 10,000 military personnel to bring food, reopen the port and roads, and provide other assistance. When Japan suffered a historic earthquake and tsunami (including a major nuclear accident) in March 2011, the aircraft carrier *Ronald Reagan* and 23 other ships, 189 aircraft, and 24,000 sailors and Marines responded, earning extraordinary gratitude from the Japanese.

The United States provides such disaster relief all the time, worldwide. With few exceptions, such as in Pakistan, our efforts earn gratitude and respect, although both are often transitory. Our capabilities and experience in providing humanitarian assistance are worthy on their own merits, but the power inherent in such endeavors could be enhanced by better communicating about them to the recipients—and to the rest of the world, which often remains blissfully unaware of our unique contributions. Our failure to publicize and capitalize on our good deeds is a significant missed strategic communications opportunity.

COMMUNICATIONS

Important to the outcome of the Cold War was the massive effort by both the United States and the Soviet Union to communicate their points of view on global events and the nefariousness of the other side while simultaneously advocating the superiority of their own political and economic systems to a worldwide audience. The focal point for

these endeavors in the United States was the United States Information Agency (USIA), created by President Eisenhower in 1953. USIA
encompassed and built on programs and organizations originating
in World War II and the early years of the Cold War; its motto was
"Telling America's Story to the World." Through its overseas arm, the
United States Information Service, USIA established a global network
of libraries and outposts stocked with books and magazines about
democracy, history, American culture, and a broad array of other subjects. A Pakistani general once told me he had learned English in a
USIA library in Karachi. Under USIA auspices, American musical
groups, entertainers, lecturers, and researchers traveled the world as
part of cultural exchanges. Exchange programs for students to come
to the United States and for Americans to study abroad reached into
scores of countries. The Voice of America (VOA) broadcast news
and entertainment around the world, presenting an objective view of
the news to millions who would otherwise have been dependent on
government-controlled outlets. With leaders such as Edward R. Mur-
row (under President Kennedy) and Charles Z. Wick (under President
Reagan), USIA and America's message reached every corner of the
planet. It was sophisticated, it was effective, and it was a powerful
instrument.

The CIA in the early years had its own broadcast stations, Radio
Free Europe and Radio Liberty, both of which later were moved out
of the agency to an independent oversight organization. Through
clandestine means, the CIA also smuggled millions of books, magazines, recordings, and audiotapes behind the Iron Curtain, all focusing a spotlight on the repressive nature of the Soviet system, Russian
history, and Western democracy and freedom. A prime example was
smuggling into the Soviet Union countless copies of a miniaturized
edition of Alexandr Solzhenitsyn's *Gulag Archipelago,* a graphic por-
trayal of the Soviet political prison system. Other information operations publicized the Soviets' sordid human rights record at home and
in Eastern Europe and their efforts in support of surrogates in the
Third World. The agency also supported a range of journals and other
publications disseminating ideas about the importance of open societies, free markets, and free discussion of ideas. During the mid-1980s,

the CIA sponsored many press articles, television shows, and exhibitions on what the Soviets were doing in Afghanistan.

U.S. communications efforts during the Cold War had power because, when it came to the Soviets and their activities, we just told the truth. And outlets like VOA were willing to address problems in America as well (sometimes to the consternation of the White House), lending credibility to its broadcasting.

Of course, the Soviets had their own global communications apparatus, and just like the United States, they had their own broadcast capabilities, sent cultural groups and athletic teams around the world, circulated slick publications touting the superiority of the Soviet system, and invited exchange students to study in the USSR. The KGB was busy as well. In Africa, it broadly spread accusations that the CIA had created the AIDS epidemic. In South Asia, the KGB spent much time and money trying to blame the United States for the assassination of Prime Minister Indira Gandhi. Throughout the Third World, they spread the story that the United States was kidnapping babies there to use their body parts in transplant operations. Some of these tales would take on a life of their own and continue long after the Soviet Union had collapsed.

After the Cold War ended, the powerful foreign policy instruments for communications in both Russia and the United States were dramatically weakened: in Russia, because the government largely collapsed; in the United States, because budget cuts and bureaucratic and political machinations resulted in the elimination of USIA in 1999 and its residual efforts being folded into a small part of the State Department. By 2001, U.S. international communications capabilities—"public diplomacy"—were a pale shadow of what had existed during the Cold War.

The importance of communicating America's message as a critical element of foreign policy became all too clear after al-Qaeda's attacks on the United States on September 11, 2001, and the subsequent wars in Afghanistan and then Iraq. Incredibly, by 2005–6, the terrorists seemed to have a better and more effective communications strategy than we did. Shortly after I became secretary of defense, in reference to Osama bin Laden, I asked, "How can a guy in a cave out-communicate the country that invented public relations?" It would only get worse over time as al-Qaeda and then ISIL increasingly used the internet to communicate their message, to terrorize, and to recruit.

Countries have always used the various forms of communication to try to influence the internal politics and foreign policies of friends and adversaries alike, but the advent of the internet has taken such "information operations" to an entirely different level of potential effectiveness. The most obvious instances have been the Russians' use of social media and other internet applications to interfere with the Brexit election in the United Kingdom, the U.S. presidential election in 2016, and the French presidential election in 2017. While much remains to be investigated and reported, the possible avenues of interference include hacking into electronic voting rolls and machines, gathering voters' personal information, implanting fraudulent information and advertising about one candidate to advantage another, or simply planting false information that will stir partisan or racial passions and increase internal divisiveness. Another purpose is to delegitimize elections in the West more generally, thus working to undermine confidence in democratic institutions. Interfering in other nations' elections is not new, but the tools available today are qualitatively an order of magnitude more pervasive and effective.

Of course, the United States faces a different kind of challenge in communicating its message today than during the Cold War. In those days, the peoples of the Soviet Union and Eastern Europe trusted channels such as VOA and Radio Free Europe to tell them the truth, and they generally hated their communist masters while seeing the United States as a standard-bearer for freedom. In the post–Cold War, post-9/11 world, a lot of audiences, particularly in the Middle East, neither like nor trust us. This may also be true of a growing number of Chinese as their government casts the United States as an adversary. This makes getting our message through all the more difficult.

In an era of 24/7 cable, instant news and communication, smartphones, the internet, and other technological advances, information operations have become far more sophisticated and much easier to disguise. The Russians have developed diverse techniques for planting their stories and bogus information on foreign cable and internet networks, injecting bots that proliferate provocative and divisive messages, and manipulating Western sources of information and news. The Chinese have the capacity to do all that the Russians have been doing but, more strategically, have invested in media companies around the globe, especially in the developing world, to gain influence if not control over content. They have also invested in Western research centers and created others—such as the hundreds of Confucius Institutes in educational institutions worldwide, including in the United States—to shape their message about China and to propagandize Chinese policies. They have also developed partnerships with other media and cultural organizations that expand China's reach.

By contrast, the United States—which invented modern communications, public relations, and the internet itself—still lacks an effective information operations strategy, policies, and proper capabilities to communicate our message, counter that of our adversaries and competitors, defend our institutions, and go on the offensive. The United States has made use of some of these tools against ISIL and other terrorists, but has not yet figured out how to counter the Russians and Chinese, especially on their home turf. We have taken on individual hackers in Russia and China and their connections and sponsors, but lack a strategy for turning their tactics back on them more broadly at home. This lag in offensive information warfare capabilities (and counterattack) has been exacerbated by the Russian and Chinese exploitation of new technologies to control access by their own people to the internet and social media and, especially in the case of China, the development of techniques using artificial intelligence to exercise ever more complete control over their own citizens.

Most governments are challenged by now-ubiquitous social media. In some respects, the entire Arab Spring phenomenon was a product of it, as young people in Egypt in January 2011 read Facebook pages and blogs about the turmoil in Tunisia and organized their own demonstrations in Cairo's Tahrir Square. Demonstrations followed in Oman, Yemen, Jordan, Bahrain, and Saudi Arabia—and in Tripoli, Libya, where demonstrators emboldened by what they had seen elsewhere in the region on Facebook and other social media resisted the ruthless efforts of the Qaddafi regime to suppress the unrest.

Despite China's and Russia's success in blocking foreign-sourced internet outlets and social media, even they—and many others—are challenged by the ability of their citizens to use these means of communication to expose unflattering developments. In China, news of environmental disasters, epidemic diseases such as the coronavirus, horrific train wrecks, factory explosions, the inoculation of hundreds of thousands of children with tainted vaccines, rural unrest, and repressive measures is impossible to bury as photos and information circulate nationwide instantly.

Communication is a powerful weapon in the hands of a government, especially where it has a monopoly, but new forms of communication are a powerful weapon also for freedom-loving people, as well as terrorists and all nongovernmental entities. Since the end of the Cold War, as governments have been increasingly challenged to fully control their message internally, communications remain a vital and powerful strategic instrument of power. What is relatively new is the ability of governments to use new technologies to attack their adversaries and rivals. Governments' attempts to interfere in the affairs of other countries is as old as recorded history. Both sides worked hard at that during the Cold War. What is new is the availability of technologies that make earlier tools for such activities seem prehistoric. The United States has the technologies; it just lacks a strategy and policies to apply them.

INTELLIGENCE

It will not be a surprise to learn that I believe intelligence capabilities can be an important instrument of power.

First and foremost, intelligence agencies provide leaders with what I have long referred to as the daily "river of information" about what is going on around the world. The U.S. intelligence community (some fifteen agencies) has long been the best in the world at this, but its counterparts in Britain, Israel, France, China, and Russia also provide quality information. The Western agencies (including Israel's) do this best because they have a long tradition of not letting their analysis be colored by the policies of their political bosses. When it comes to troop movements or buildups, weapons deployments and capabilities, and internal political fights or unrest in other countries, most of these organizations do a good job of reporting the facts. So when it comes to monitoring what is going on around the world, their governments are reasonably well served. Most intelligence services, however, need to be much more modest about their ability to predict the intentions of foreign leaders or future events.

Intelligence agencies can be a useful diplomatic asset as well. The CIA played a central role over the decades in supporting U.S. arms control negotiations with the Soviet Union, providing much of the technical weapons information on which agreements were based and then providing the capability to monitor compliance. Intelligence also supports peacekeeping operations. It shares its information and analysis with other governments. In 1962, President Kennedy's envoys, including photo interpreters, shared U-2 photographs of Cuba to persuade other leaders that Soviet missiles were actually on the island. The United States shared satellite photography with the UN Security Council in the run-up to the first Gulf War, although a similar intelligence briefing before the invasion of Iraq in 2003 became an embarrassment when some of the information provided proved wrong. The United States shares intelligence information on a one-to-one basis with scores of countries, either to prove a point or to enhance cooperation.

Cooperative intelligence relationships among allies—especially the United States, United Kingdom, Canada, Australia, and New Zealand—have long strengthened ties between governments and helped the United States ensure that its allies would view international challenges in similar terms. A close intelligence relationship between the United States and Israel has enhanced the security of both countries while being largely immune to political ups and downs in the relationship. One extraordinary intelligence relationship for years was that between the United States and China, which began with an agreement between President Carter and Chinese leader Deng Xiaoping to establish a joint radar facility in western China to monitor Soviet missile tests. That cooperation lasted until the end of the Cold War and remained unaffected by tense times in the political relationship.

Intelligence is also a source of power through covert operations. From secret CIA funding for noncommunist parties in the French and Italian elections in the late 1940s, to helping Solidarity in Poland and the anti-Soviet resistance in Afghanistan in the 1980s, to playing a part in ridding Afghanistan of the Taliban in 2001 and helping democracy movements in multiple countries, covert action has served as the secret hand of American presidents. It works best when it provides a complement to an overt U.S. strategy and is given enough time to work. Using it in ways counter to U.S. public policy or throwing it into the breach at the last minute in the absence of any better solution nearly always ensures failure.

ALLIANCES

An often undervalued instrument of power, especially for the United States since World War II, is a system of alliances with other countries that are bound together by common strategic objectives and values. Over the years, many American officials—including me—have complained about the failure of allies to carry their fair share of the burden, especially in military spending. At last count, only nine of the twenty-nine NATO countries spend the agreed-upon minimum threshold of 2 percent of GDP on their military forces. The NATO members' commitment to a common defense—an attack upon one is considered an attack on all (Article V)—arguably played a role in deterring Soviet aggressiveness in Europe and keeping the peace there during the Cold War. The alliance does not mean that all members agree with each other on everything, but they do tend to stick together on the big issues. Nearly all the allies joined the coalition against Saddam in 1991, and the only time the alliance actually invoked Article V was to support the United States after the attacks on 9/11. As Russia has become more aggressive, beginning in 2007, the alliance has stood together and significantly expanded its military presence in Poland and the Baltic states. Similarly, U.S. alliances with Japan, South Korea, Australia, and others in Asia have proved a significant source of strength and solidarity in dealing with China. And although we have no formal alliances in the Middle East, there are close relationships with several countries, including Israel, Saudi Arabia, the United Arab Emirates, Jordan, Egypt, and, until recently, Turkey.

Often overlooked in the United States is that while we have many allies, Russia and China have none, only clients, giving the United States a unique advantage. With regard to NATO, South Korea, and Japan (absent invocation of Article V or an outbreak of war), nothing compels these countries to support the United States. They do so because it is in their interest or they share our objectives. The long duration of most of our alliances is rare in history. Most are short-lived and for a specific purpose, as with the USSR in World War II. For alliances to endure, common objectives and values must endure, so sustaining those fragile relationships requires continuing effort. They cannot be taken for granted. Every post–World War II president has understood that until Donald Trump. It would be a tragedy, not to mention a colossal strategic mistake, to weaken or lose this instrument of power unique to America.

SCIENCE AND TECHNOLOGY

Technological and scientific achievements are important instruments of power whether or not directly wielded by a government. I was in high school when the Soviet Union launched the first space satellite, Sputnik, in 1957. The achievement immensely boosted the international prestige and position of the USSR. Their launch of the first man into space in 1961 had a similar positive effect. In turn, the United States got a boost around the world when we became the first nation to land a man on the Moon in 1969. While companies like Apple, Google, Microsoft, and Facebook operate globally, everyone knows they are American companies and represent the leading edge of technology and innovation—even as concerns grow over their size and use of personal information. Every country tries to figure out how to replicate Silicon Valley.

Another measure of leadership is the number of Nobel Prize recipients, and here the United States is in a class by itself. Counting all categories (including peace, literature, economics, and the sciences), as of 2019 the United States had received 383 Nobel Prizes, the United

Kingdom 132, the USSR/Russia 31, and China 6 (counts vary slightly; these are from WorldAtlas.com). All of this contributes to an image globally of the United States as the intellectual and scientific leader. Equally impressive is the fact that more than a quarter of U.S. recipients have been immigrants. There are more concrete consequences of U.S. scientific and technical leadership than perceptions. Our country serves as a magnet, attracting the smartest and most capable professionals and young people from other countries to come here to go to school and to work in high-tech industries and companies.

For the first time since the 1950s, the United States is facing a rival bent on dominating the scientific and technological space. China's leaders have announced plans to develop by 2025 a leading role in ten new technologies, including robotics, quantum computing, space, and artificial intelligence. They and the Russians are developing new technologies, such as hypersonic flight, for military purposes, and both are devoting significant resources to these efforts. The United States, complacent for decades about our overwhelming lead in science and technology, now finds itself playing catch-up in key areas.

CULTURE

American culture has penetrated every corner of the planet. Whether clothing, music, television, movies, or social media, wherever you are, you will find it. In the remotest areas, you will encounter young people wearing T-shirts, sweatshirts, and baseball caps with the logos of American universities and professional sports teams; watching American movies; and listening to American musicians. American products appear on store shelves everywhere, and American fast-food restaurants are ubiquitous.

An American college education is a globally attractive facet of our culture. Nearly a million foreign students study each year in the United States, mainly from China, India, South Korea, and Saudi Arabia. A high percentage of graduate students in engineering in American universities are from other countries. Many U.S. colleges and universities have campuses overseas. One great benefit of having young people from other countries attending universities here is that they experience everyday life in America, including extraordinary freedom—experiences that they internalize and take home with them.

The pervasiveness of American culture does have its downside. A number of foreigners are offended by the coarseness of American culture, its excessive individualism at the expense of a sense of community, and the prevalence of drugs and alcohol. For some who come here, the freedom and endless choices are frightening. The latter is captured wonderfully in the 1984 movie *Moscow on the Hudson,* in which Robin Williams plays a Soviet defector who, confronted with dozens of choices in the coffee aisle of a U.S. supermarket, has a nervous breakdown. In more conservative societies, such as many in the Middle East, American culture is an object of condemnation, not admiration.

Still, no other country comes close to America in terms of the global penetration of its culture, and apparently many more people—especially among the young—would rather be a part of U.S. culture than not. That, added to the broad worldwide affinity for Apple products, Facebook, Windows, Starbucks, and many other distinctly American goods, suggests that the pervasiveness of American culture is an asset in the competition for influence. It is a power largely independent of government—except during the Cold War, when our culture was aggressively promoted all over the world by the State Department, USIA, and numerous NGOs. Nonetheless, the United States could do much more to promote the best aspects of our culture around the world—especially because, as noted earlier, China is investing heavily to spread its culture and control political messaging.

IDEOLOGY

A fundamental component of the Cold War was the ideological struggle between Soviet communism and Western democracy, between socialism and capitalism. It was a conflict between two fundamentally different approaches to social organization—one based on protection of the rights of the individual and the other on subordination of the individual to the interests of the masses, manifested in the state.

Soviet communism probably had its greatest appeal in the West after World War I and during the Great Depression of the 1930s: after the war, because of the carnage wreaked by capitalist nations warring with one another, and during the Depression, because it seemed capitalism no longer worked. Many in the West looked on in admiration as Soviet Russia quickly industrialized, most unaware at the time of the human cost. The Soviets' alliance with America and Britain to defeat Nazism also generated considerable sympathy and goodwill in the West.

While the Soviet takeover of Eastern Europe and the ensuing onset of the Cold War greatly weakened sympathy for Soviet communism in Europe, its ideology came to have widespread appeal in developing nations emerging from colonialism. The anticolonialist, anticapitalist themes of Soviet propaganda, not to mention Soviet support for "wars of national liberation," had real impact in Africa and Asia. Further, a highly centralized state and powerful government along Soviet lines had appeal to many rising leaders in those areas. Communist ideology continued to pack a punch in the Third World well into the 1970s.

As the Soviet economy and Soviet leaders became more sclerotic, the appeal of the USSR and its ideology faded. This process accelerated as it became clear that communist ideology had led mainly to poverty, hardship, and authoritarianism in the Soviet Union and all the countries that had followed the Soviet model in Eastern Europe, Africa, and Asia. With the collapse of the Soviet Union, ideology no longer was an instrument of power or influence for Russia.

Chinese communism never had much appeal beyond its borders, although the Beijing model of ruthlessness and authoritarianism was happily adopted in places like Myanmar and Cambodia, and some relatively small groups of Maoist extremists cropped up in a few developing countries, as well as on some American university campuses. However, after the Great Leap Forward in the 1950s and the Cultural Revolution, which began in the 1960s, and the extraordinary human and economic costs of both, and with the economic reforms begun by Deng Xiaoping in 1976, the appeal of communism weakened, even in China. While long-standing Chinese communist institutions such as the party, the politburo, and the party congresses and the pretense of ideology endure, the government's only real source of legitimacy is a steadily improving standard of living for the Chinese people. Maoism, as a practical matter, is dead. However, China's economic success—including raising hundreds of millions of people out of poverty, its rapid modernization, especially of infrastructure, and its appearance of political stability—is viewed increasingly widely as an attractive model for development. President Xi touts it as such, and as superior to Western democratic capitalism. It is not really proffered as an ideology by Xi but rather as a practical alternative to emulate.

America's ideology is encapsulated in the Declaration of Independence and the Constitution. It is based on individual freedom, democratic governance, the rule of law, and a regulated market economy. From its first days, the United States has encouraged and supported the spread of human and political rights around the world. Even as the United States worked with despotic (often murderous) governments in World War II, the Cold War, and beyond, both openly and privately it continued to be a champion of freedom, reform, democratization, and human rights. Since our earliest days, the United States has been a beacon to oppressed peoples everywhere, not necessarily for our political system but because we have been the most steadfast example and proponent of human rights and individual liberty, and defender of the repressed everywhere. The world has always known we fall short of our ideals, but we have never abandoned our aspirations. America is unique in that the only thing binding us together is ideas and ideals. Those ideas and ideals collectively represent a source of great power. To forgo our advocacy of freedom and human rights would cede not only an instrument of our strength but also our uniqueness—what truly has made America great.

I believe the power of America's ideology and its appeal as a political and economic model has diminished. Our political polarization and the inability of our government to address any of the big problems facing the country have sullied our political system in the eyes of others. The Great Recession of 2008–9 as well as the struggles of the middle class and income inequality have also led others to question our economic model. Our inability to modernize our infrastructure compares poorly to the ambitious internal improvements undertaken by the Chinese.

The appeal of our ideology was further reduced by President Trump's approach to foreign policy, in which U.S. advocacy for human and political rights was silenced and subordinated to doing deals with other governments intended to singularly advantage the United States and its economy. Trump's weakening of America's ideological power was captured in an op-ed column in *The Wall Street Journal* on May 31, 2017, by White House advisers Gary D. Cohn and H. R. McMaster, who wrote, "The world is not a 'global community' but an arena where nations, nongovernmental actors and businesses engage and compete for advantage. . . . Rather than deny this elemental nature of international affairs, we embrace it." While this Hobbesian description of the world is accurate, it is incomplete: American ideology has always aspired to more.

Warts and all, America's ideology has had power throughout our history. Our support of international rules and cooperation, freedom, and human rights has waxed and waned, but we have been their most reliable defender. Russia no longer has an ideology. For the first time in decades, though, liberal democracy as it emerged in Europe and in the United States faces a formidable alternative model, all the more challenging because it is propounded by a rich, competent, and powerful regime in Beijing. Among great powers, only the United States still has an ideology with the potential to be a useful instrument of power in a deeply unstable world, but not without serious repair work at home.

Our rivalry with China includes an intense competition of ideologies. Chinese (and Russian) leaders "view authoritarianism as a superior method for organizing society," writes historian Hal Brands, and "portray liberal political ideals as antithetical to the national strength and stability they aim to achieve." President Putin has said that the "liberal idea is obsolete." President Xi describes democracy as a "flawed alternative that would bring social chaos, moral degradation and vast human suffering." Liberal democracy "rests on a commitment to a set of key ideas: a defense of individual liberties and property rights, an appeal to reason over custom, and a demand for government limited under law and based on the consent of the governed." During the Cold War, more than a few foreign policy experts downplayed the role of ideology in Soviet decision making. They were wrong. Communist ideology was the lens through which Soviet leaders saw the world, even if it didn't affect specific decisions. We must not make the same mistake. Communism as an ideology is dead, but authoritarianism has deep roots in human history and is alive and well. Indeed, it is thriving. Ideology is a source of national power; we forget the ancient appeal of authoritarianism, and the significance of our own concepts of liberty and human rights, at our peril.

THE PRIVATE SECTOR

A distinctively American instrument of power is the broad range of nongovernmental institutions that are great assets in our interactions with the rest of the world.

The business community is probably the most significant. When most American businesses build manufacturing facilities or stores, or develop natural resources such as oil and gas abroad, they tend to hire local inhabitants, pump money into the local economy, and pay attention to local environmental and social issues. To build and sustain relationships with local and national leaders, they often will fund improvements such as construction of schools, roads, wells, and the like. They do these things not out of altruism (although there is some of that) but simply because it is good business. As a result, American business investment is broadly welcomed in other countries. There are obviously exceptions and some horror stories, but by and large U.S. investment—especially in developing countries—enhances the U.S. image and is an asset. The challenge is how the government can more effectively partner with businesses to encourage them to invest in certain countries and, once there, cooperate with U.S. government organizations in strengthening local institutions and enhancing the relationship between the host country and the United States.

American universities are another instrument of power through the foreign students they educate here and through the hundreds of thousands of U.S. students who go abroad to study. Beyond this, thousands of faculty specializing in agriculture, human and veterinary medicine, the environment, hydrology, education, and countless other fields work in developing countries not just doing research but helping to improve lives. I will refer repeatedly to the extraordinary contribution such civilian expertise could make by augmenting and improving government development assistance programs.

Private U.S. foundations and charitable and religious organizations make a difference in the lives of millions of people in developing countries. The best-known foundation is the Bill and Melinda Gates Foundation, which has had such a profound impact through its efforts to eliminate polio and malaria, as well as other programs. There are thousands of other foundations and charitable organizations engaged in improving lives through building schools and providing teachers, clinics, and more. American churches support a wide range of schools, medical facilities, and other services in some of the poorest parts of the world.

Many who work in developing countries for U.S. businesses, universities, foundations, charities, and religious organizations want nothing to do with the American government, and, too often, this attitude is reciprocated by the government. That is a mistake on all sides. The challenge for the government is to create new avenues of cooperation that maintain the independence of private sector institutions and create synergies between government and nongovernment programs that magnify the impact of both. Our government has been singularly unimaginative in figuring out how to do that.

RELIGION

When the deputy national security adviser to President Carter, David Aaron, asked the CIA in 1977 what it knew about Islamic fundamentalism, the answer, in essence, was, What's that? In a world dominated by the secular ideological struggle with the Soviet Union, religion seemed to many leaders in the West to have little relevance to international affairs, outside of Northern Ireland. The CIA, for example, did virtually no analysis on the role of religion internationally in those days. Then the Islamic revolution came along in Iran in 1979.

For most of written history, secular and religious authorities have at different times colluded and competed. Our preoccupation with Nazism and communism in the West for the last eight decades led us, I believe, to forget the power of religion in shaping history, including long and bloody wars over religion as well as the role of religion in empowering and legitimizing secular authority.

Until the nineteenth century (and for some, beyond), many European monarchs and emperors from London to Moscow believed they derived their power straight from God—they ruled by "divine right," beginning with the coronation of Charlemagne as the first Holy Roman Emperor on Christmas Day, 800. In the Middle East, fundamental to the power of the kings of Saudi Arabia is their role as Custodian of the Two Holy Mosques (in Mecca and Medina). Even in the United States, where separation of church and state is foundational, presidents take the oath of office with their left hand on a Bible, adding to the constitutionally prescribed oath the words "so help me God." Monarchs, emperors, and elected politicians all feel empowered by a divine mandate and connection to the Almighty.

Religious wars are hardly an artifact of history. Much of the conflict in the Balkans in the 1990s involved Christians versus Muslims, especially in Bosnia and Kosovo. The Protestant-Catholic conflict in Northern Ireland did not formally end until the Good Friday Agreement in 1998. The civil war in Lebanon, which raged from 1975 to 1990, began with fighting between Maronite Christians and Palestinian Muslim forces. Israel has fought four major wars with Muslim Arab states and, practically speaking, has been at war with the Palestinians, the Shia Muslim group Hezbollah, and the Sunni Muslim group Hamas for decades. The 1947 partition of British India into predominantly Muslim Pakistan and predominantly Hindu India led to at least half a million deaths and the movement of more than 14 million people from one side of the line to the other. Despite India's constitutional secularism, large-scale Muslim-Hindu religious violence continues.

Just as Christians fought each other in Europe, we see Muslims fighting Muslims throughout the Middle East. While the fights are often about political power, much of the fighting during the Iraq War pitted Sunnis against Shias. Even now, Shia militias in Iraq contend with the Iraqi army and Sunni tribes. Al-Qaeda in Iraq killed far more Iraqi Muslims than they did foreigners, and its offshoot, ISIL, directed its harshest measures toward other Muslims—although the group also enthusiastically slaughtered non-Muslims, such as the Yazidis and Christians. After taking power in Afghanistan in 1996, the Taliban imposed sharia law with severity and would do so again. The ongoing war in Yemen is but a proxy fight for the greatest contemporary struggle of all in the Middle East: between Shia Islam, led by Iran, and Sunni Islam, led by Saudi Arabia.

The Philippines have been plagued by religious conflict for more than a century. Until the conflict in Afghanistan, America's longest counterinsurgency war was waged against Muslim Moros in the Philippines from 1899 to 1913. During that war, more than 70,000 U.S. troops were engaged and more American soldiers were killed than have been lost in Afghanistan to date. More than a century later, U.S. Special Forces are back in the Philippines helping government forces battle Muslim extremists.

Who would have dreamed after a hiatus of nearly 350 years that the West would once again face a threat from the Islamic world? Nineteen seventy-nine marked the beginning of the conflict, with the revolution in Iran (February), the seizure of the Grand Mosque in Mecca (November 20), the associated burning of the U.S. embassy in Pakistan (November 21), and then the Soviet invasion of Afghanistan (December), the latter precipitating a call for holy war that recruited Muslim fighters from across the Middle East. In 1988, Osama bin Laden founded al-Qaeda and the next year the Soviets completed their withdrawal from Afghanistan. Bin Laden issued his first "fatwa," or edict, to attack American forces on the Arabian Peninsula in 1992. Al-Qaeda's first attack on the World Trade Center was in February 1993, and we have been at war with Islamic extremists ever since.

Only with the killing of thirteen soldiers and the wounding of more than thirty others at Fort Hood, Texas, in 2009 by a self-radicalized army major did Americans begin to confront the reality of religiously motivated extremists becoming an internal threat. In truth, religiously motivated terrorists—most but by no means all of them Muslim—are carrying out acts of terrorism worldwide: in Indonesia, the Philippines, China, Russia, Malaysia, Pakistan, India, France, Spain, Britain, and the United States, not to mention across the entire Middle East and Iran.

Who can doubt religion is an instrument of great power? It has infinite power to motivate and inspire people to do good in the world. But it can also be a powerful tool in the hands of governments, fanatics, cynics, the ambitious, and the unscrupulous. The United States, and its government, awoke late to the reality that religion still has the power to provoke terrorist violence and war as well as promote peace—to curdle men's souls as well as save them. The tough question is whether governments can effectively limit the appeal of violent religious fanatics and draw benefit from the power of religion for good.

NATIONALISM

Nationalism is a remarkably strong and enduring instrument of power. Nationalism was thought to be waning in Europe during the decades after World War II. Leaders throughout Europe, where warfare had been more or less constant for centuries, devoted great energy then to building a European community where nation-states would cede certain powers to a pan-European government, tying those states together economically and politically in a way that they would not—and could not—make war on one another again. Thus emerged the European Union and its centralized bureaucracy in Brussels, along with open borders and a common currency. Economic institutions such as the World Trade Organization were established to provide a common set of rules for international trade, including a mechanism for settling disputes peacefully. To deal with climate change (specifically, greenhouse gases), the Kyoto Protocol was adopted in 1997, with eventually 192 signatories. In 2015, the Paris climate agreement was signed, with 195 signatories eventually agreeing to voluntarily plan and report on their individual efforts to mitigate global warming. In each of these, as well as other alliances and agreements, governments agreed to limit their own actions and authority for a perceived greater good. All were intended to curb nationalistic policies in which one country's behavior might negatively affect others.

The problem, however, has been that until recently, elites—that is, leaders—in the West have been far more enthusiastic about curbing nationalism than their publics. In truth, nationalism remains very much alive—and kicking. Nationalism when it is most admirable is defined by patriotism, or love of country: pride in its history and accomplishments, jealous protection of its sovereignty, a shared set of principles for governance, and a belief in the uniqueness of the country and its culture. American nationalism over the years has been expressed in terms such as "American exceptionalism," characterization of the country throughout our history as "the shining city upon a hill," and by Abraham Lincoln's description of America as "the last best hope of earth."

Some leaders recognize that nationalism retains a formidable power and exploit it. In the 2016 U.S. election, Donald Trump ran on an "America First" platform—"Make America Great Again"—calling for withdrawal from a range of international trade agreements and promising to evaluate every international endeavor mainly on whether or not it brings advantage to the United States. A new generation of leaders in Europe have capitalized on resentment of the EU and its massive regulatory system and have exploited public anger over the millions of refugees fleeing to Europe from Syria, other nations in the Middle East, and North Africa. That anger is rooted in fears that the large numbers of immigrants will unalterably change their national cultures.

China's leaders often appeal to nationalism, whether defending questionable historical claims to islands in the South China Sea or ginning up xenophobic demonstrations against countries with which it has differences. Occasionally, these efforts take on a life of their own and risk spinning out of control, as happened in 2012, when demonstrations in China protesting Japanese detention of Chinese activists on a disputed island grew violent and armed troops had to be sent to restore order.

President Vladimir Putin of Russia has exploited the power of nationalism with particular effectiveness. I think the West never fully appreciated the magnitude of Russians' humiliation over the collapse of the Soviet Union, perhaps because many foreigners didn't grasp that it also represented the end of the nearly four-century-old Russian Empire. The domain ruled from Moscow shrank to the size of Russia prior to the reign of Empress Catherine the Great in the eighteenth century, and its population fell from nearly 300 million to 140 million. The 1990s were a period of great economic distress for many Russians, especially those middle-aged and older. There was also widespread dismay over the policies—and personal behavior—of the alcoholic Boris Yeltsin, and over the repeated snubbing of Russia internationally.

When Putin became president, he was determined to restore Russia's place as a world power to be feared and respected, and without which no international problem could be addressed effectively. Putin's state-of-the-nation speech in April 2005 fired a warning shot aimed at the former Soviet republics that had become independent in 1991, calling the collapse of the Soviet Union "the greatest geopolitical catastrophe of the last century." He continued ominously: "As for the Russian people, it became a genuine tragedy. Tens of millions of our fellow citizens found themselves beyond the fringes of Russian territory." In addition to restoring respect for Russia, Putin was bent on pursuing a strategy as old as the Russian Empire: establishing a buffer of friendly states or frozen conflicts on the periphery of Russia, and taking as a personal mission the protection of the roughly 25 million ethnic Russians left behind in the newly independent states of the former Soviet Union, referred to by Russians as the "near abroad."

Putin's subsequent military aggressions in Georgia, Ukraine, and Crimea—ostensibly to protect Russians and Russian interests—as well as the 2015 intervention in Syria proved highly popular in Russia, with government media hailing Putin's success in defying the West and asserting Russia's power. Putin also began to appeal to Russian nationalism on a more basic level: Western culture was decadent, Russia did not want to be like other states in Europe, and Russia has a unique historical role to play in protecting Christian values. Indeed, Putin's policies and rhetoric began to sound very much like the ideology of Tsar Nicholas I in the first half of the nineteenth century: "Orthodoxy, Autocracy, and Nationality." Even as the Russian economy declined with the price of oil, Putin's continuing appeals to Russian nationalism became critical to his political power. The average Russian may be poor but, once again, is proud.

Any leader who minimizes nationalism as an instrument of power, especially when it comes to mobilizing popular support at home, is making a big mistake. But it can also be a powerful tool for rallying audiences at home and in foreign countries to oppose outside interference.

WISE AND COURAGEOUS LEADERSHIP

Wise and courageous leadership is not, strictly speaking, an instrument of power. But it is essential to the effective exercise of *all* forms of power. Those who exercise such leadership know which instruments of power to use and when; they are maestros of the symphony. They have the courage to act in the face of opposition from senior advisers, politicians, or the public; the courage to act when the intelligence is ambiguous or there are no good options; and sometimes the courage *not* to act despite pressures to do so.

Courage alone, however, is not enough. A wise leader is just as important to national power as a courageous one. Courage must be yoked to wisdom for effective national power. America's greatest presidents have exhibited both qualities: Washington, Jefferson, Lincoln, both Roosevelts, Truman, Eisenhower, Reagan, Bush 41. I believe post–Cold War presidents at key moments have made unwise decisions and then aggravated the consequences by failing to strengthen and use all the instruments of American power in implementing those decisions.

The world today is more complicated than at any time since the end of World War II. In many respects, it resembles the international landscape before World War I, with major states vying for power, territory, and markets; nationalism feeding conflict between states; rival militaries posturing against one another, with the attendant risk of a minor incident or mistake escalating into a major conflict; economic challenges; religious strife; terrorism; separatism threatening even ancient states such as Britain and Spain. What is different about the post–Cold War world is that it is a far more complex one than the forty-five-year-long contest between two superpowers, a rivalry that both framed and dominated—and disciplined to a degree—local and regional actors and global developments.

Symptomatic of this complexity, and danger, was the terrorist attack on the United States on September 11, 2001, the first major foreign-based attack on the continental United States since the War of 1812. To deal with this new threat, the most dramatic changes to the national security structure and associated laws since 1947 were implemented with broad bipartisan support. Suddenly, threats from remote parts of the world that had been ignored during the Cold War became real. Internal developments in backward countries required American attention. No longer was the threat to America confined to one superpower, on which we could focus our resources and attention. While the new threats were not apocalyptic, as a nuclear war with the Soviets would have been, they were far more likely to be actualized, as we learned on 9/11. Thus, some sympathy is in order for the post–Cold War presidents as they have faced a very different—and in some ways more dangerous and challenging—international environment than their post–World War II predecessors.

Unlike many crises during the Cold War, few contemporary problems are susceptible to being resolved and put behind us. The history of the last quarter century is one of multiple challenges repeatedly bedeviling successive presidents, each of whom had his own way of dealing with those challenges and each applying the multiple forms of power differently and with varying degrees of comprehensiveness and success. The problems posed by North Korea and Iran are not crises that can be resolved by one president, whose successor can then move on to different problems. The same is true of challenges posed by China, Russia, Iraq, Afghanistan, and terrorism. All of these problems, and others as well, have confronted all four post–Cold War presidents and most, if not all, will confront future presidents as well.

Now that we know the principal instruments that make up the symphony of power, we need to take a look at how presidents conduct the orchestra. By what means do they actually exercise power?

CHAPTER 2

Exercising Power

He'll sit right here and he'll say do this, do that! And nothing will happen.
Poor Ike—it won't be a bit like the Army. He'll find it very frustrating.

—HARRY TRUMAN ON THE ELECTION OF
DWIGHT D. EISENHOWER

President Truman's words above capture the sentiments of the eight presidents I worked for and probably those of every incumbent: the most powerful person in the world much of the time feels like Jonathan Swift's Lemuel Gulliver, a giant tied down by a thousand strings, unable to act or move as he might wish. The Constitution, laws, Congress, bureaucracy, and the media all hem in presidents, limiting their freedom of action, preventing them from accomplishing their agenda (for good or ill). As President Obama once told me, "I'm the leader of the free world, but I can't seem to make anything happen." Yet, despite such complaints, every president in recent times has launched conventional as well as trade wars, intervened in other countries, unilaterally made and ended agreements, initiated programs that saved millions of lives, beat back terrorists, and helped others save their own countries from extremists. But how do such decisions get made and implemented?

Some observers talk about the president as being at the apex of a pyramid, sitting atop the world. I have a different perspective. I see the president sitting at the bottom of a funnel, at the wide top of which are more than 3 million men and women in and out of uniform in a dozen or more departments and agencies engaged in helping to formulate American foreign and national security policies or in implementing them. Every day, the Departments of State, Defense, Treasury, Homeland Security, and Energy; fifteen intelligence agencies (above all, the CIA); and other agencies of the government dump into that funnel hundreds of thousands of reports from all over the world that are intended to inform or shape presidential policies and decisions. Under the funnel, with the president at the table in the White House Situation Room (the National Security Council conference room/ command center in the west basement of the White House), usually are just eight people to help sort the urgent from the important, develop strategies, and make decisions: the vice president, secretaries of state and defense, chairman of the Joint Chiefs of Staff, director of national intelligence, CIA director, national security adviser, and White House chief of staff. Sometimes there are others, such as the secretaries of the treasury and homeland security, and a handful of presidential staff. That's it. Every major problem—and a lot of minor ones, too—in the world pops out of the funnel onto that table, where nearly every day that small group of people helps the president decide the fate of our country (and that of many others) and, very often, make life-and-death decisions.

Thoughtful national security advisers make sure there is a coffee cart in the Situation Room for often-needed caffeine. I once suggested a bar, but wiser heads prevailed.

Today's formal structure for deciding and implementing foreign and national security policy—for exercising power abroad—was established by the National Security Act of 1947, which created the Department of Defense, the Air Force (as a separate military service), and the CIA as well as the NSC itself. The statutory members of the NSC are just the president, vice president, and secretaries of state and defense, with the chairman of the Joint Chiefs of Staff as the senior military adviser and the director of national intelligence (as of 2005) as principal intelligence adviser. Despite the fact that this foundational national security law gives each president enormous leeway to organize the decision-making process in ways congenial to his or her style, as we will see, the structure itself is quite outdated. The NSC is served by a staff headed by the national security adviser. The size of that staff has ranged under recent presidents from fewer than a hundred under Bush 41 to more than four hundred under Obama. It is the job of the NSC staff to coordinate policy and decision recommendations from State, Defense, and others for presentation to the president, monitor implementation of presidential decisions by the bureaucracy, and provide day-to-day support for the president, such as background information for meetings with foreign leaders or overseas travel.

The national security adviser is the pivotal player. The three most influential advisers have been Henry Kissinger (under Nixon and Ford), Brent Scowcroft (Ford and Bush 41), and Zbigniew Brzezinski (Carter). I worked for all three, and no post–Cold War occupant of the job has had anything like the power and influence they wielded. He or she is the ringmaster, responsible for ensuring that the views and recommendations of various departments are coordinated and integrated into the president's decision-making process, and that the president's decisions are carried out. When it all works as designed, presidents know what their senior officials recommend and why, and can make fully informed decisions. Those officials know their views have been seriously considered, even if not adopted. When it doesn't work—either because the national security adviser cuts key departments and agencies or senior officials out of the loop, fails to inform the president of their views, one or more of the most senior advisers chooses not to cooperate; or, as we have seen under Trump, the president opts to bypass the entire process—the result is internecine bureaucratic warfare and leaks and sometimes bad decisions and inept or grudging implementation. However a president organizes the process, whether or not it works depends on how everyone works together and whether they trust each other.

Scowcroft, generally considered the model national security adviser, once observed that during the Cold War the adviser had to handle one big thing—the U.S.-Soviet competition and, at any given moment, one or two smaller matters. In the post–Cold War world, he said, the adviser has eight to ten important things on his or her plate at any given time. Stephen J. Hadley, national security adviser in Bush

43's second term, succinctly described the job as being like a plate spinner in the circus—ten plates spinning on top of ten thin poles simultaneously with the adviser running from pole to pole to keep them spinning so none stops and falls to the ground. Or, he added, the job is analogous to cooking on a ten-burner stove, with a pot on each burner, the adviser madly stirring one pot and then another, just trying to keep them from boiling over. The problem, Hadley concluded, is that the national security adviser is always moving from crisis to crisis, usually at the eleventh hour. But if all you do is manage crises, you have no time to develop and implement strategies designed to avoid them and shape events.

What people—sometimes even those at senior levels in the government—often don't understand is that all presidents go outside the formal structure for advice. Presidents talk to family, golfing partners, friends, business associates, old pals in Congress, celebrities, journalists, and others, seeking their views. Sometimes they get really bizarre information and it can be tough to convince them that it's really not true that Denmark wants to sell Greenland or that Noah's Ark has shown up or that aliens (of the outer-space variety) are among us. Over the years, I actually had to deal with those very things and more. And those outside views—stray voltage, as I like to call it—are every bit as much a part of a president's decision making as the NSC process. The wise national security adviser does not try to interfere with these informal contacts, but works to ensure they are only one—preferably minor—part of the spectrum of information the president receives.

It is also the case that all presidents from time to time disagree with all of their senior advisers and make decisions following their own instincts. Bush's decision on a troop surge in early 2007 was made against the advice of nearly all his senior-most military advisers; Obama's decision to call for Egyptian president Mubarak to leave office immediately in early February 2011 was against the unanimous advice of all eight of those senior officials at the Situation Room table. Trump, infamous for going his own way, is unique in having the most disorderly decision-making process of any modern president, but not uncommon in following his gut and overruling advisers.

As I have observed and experienced all too often, there is usually an undercurrent of discord (and sometimes open conflict) between the White House/NSC staff and the departments and agencies. Sometimes it is because there is a genuine difference of perspective and views on how to deal with a problem. But there are less lofty reasons as well. The secretaries of state and defense and others have huge organizations to run and resent being called to the White House—sometimes two or three times a day—for meetings that may or may not be productive. Further, White House and NSC staff all too often undercut the agency heads with presidents, telling them—sometimes accurately—that a particular department or agency is dragging its feet implementing a decision, has an agenda of its own, or is not on board with what the president is trying to accomplish. There are also differences because those in the White House operate in a bubble, often oblivious to the difficulty of actually implementing decisions made there, difficulties the cabinet and agency heads must deal with and work through. Moreover, no one working there ever has to testify in front of Congress to defend tough or controversial (or bad) decisions, including those they may have opposed. They are shielded from sitting in front of members of Congress, on television, taking the public slings and arrows. That is a job for other participants in the process, and never a pleasant experience.

Personalities matter hugely in decision making, even at the top. Some presidents are more manipulative than others. FDR, Nixon, Reagan, and, I suspect, Trump, knowingly fostered disagreements among their senior advisers—or at least tolerated them—because such infighting actually gives the president more latitude in making decisions. Whereas a unified front among advisers tends to box in the president, divided counsel lets him pick and choose among options. A president can stop cabinet-level infighting with a couple of phone calls; when he chooses not to do so, there usually is an ulterior motive.

Regardless of whether senior advisers are united or divided, the president will still be criticized. If there are disagreements, they will become public—they always do—and the press will report that the administration is in "disarray" and the White House is "dysfunctional." If there is a unity of views, the administration will be accused of "groupthink" and "mindless conformity" among the president's advisers. The best course for a president is to encourage senior advisers to state their views candidly, insist that their advice remain private, and make clear publicly that the president is calling the shots. While Congress and the media will obsess about what the secretaries of state and defense and the national security adviser think and whether they agree or disagree, the only thing that actually matters is what the president thinks. The president needs to reinforce that reality—and make sure his cabinet members both understand it and make the point publicly.

When it comes to implementation of presidential decisions, it matters when the secretaries of state and defense can't stand each other (more often than not during my career), or both mistrust the national security adviser (or think he or she is a dolt). If there is no trust and collegiality at the top, cooperation between departments further down the ranks is hard to come by. And every department and agency head has one or more provocateurs in his or her office trying to set the boss's hair on fire with gossip about the machinations of other agency heads or the White House, thus feeding ill will and suspicion. When I was secretary of defense, I made a deal with Secretary of State Condoleezza Rice, and then Hillary Clinton, that if one of our staff people came in with some lurid tale about dastardly plotting by the other, we would get on the phone in the presence of that staffer to confirm it was all lies and subsequently inform the provocateur that a second such offense would result in getting fired or sent to Thule.

It should come as no surprise that presidents personally like some of their senior appointees more than others, and every president finds a way to give some of their top officials "more time with their family," i.e., fire them—although only two of the eight I worked for had the guts to do it face-to-face. The others had a political executioner do the dirty work. Presidents even have favorites (and not-so-favorites) among senior military officers.

Cabinet departments like Defense and State—the permanent bureaucracy—rarely put forward bold ideas or new initiatives for a president to consider. Indeed, in my long experience, nearly all truly innovative, bold, or creative proposals in foreign policy I can remember have originated within the White House—from the president, national security adviser, or NSC staff—or from a cabinet secretary personally or his or her closest aides. The big bureaucracies offer few incentives for people at lower levels to challenge conventional wisdom or depart from long-standing practices, programs, or policies. Even if there is the germ of a good idea at lower levels, the process of working it through the many layers of the organization and getting everyone to sign on is nearly always lethal for the idea (and sometimes for the career of the originator). The drive for consensus is deep in the institutional DNA. Kissinger used to say the bureaucracy always came up with three options: option A represented virtually no change, option C called for such radical change it was sure to be rejected, and option B proposed modest modifications to existing policy—the bureaucracy's choice. All presidents complain about the limited options offered by the bureaucracy, and turn to their own staff for alternatives.

The departments and agencies outside the White House contribute to presidential policy making through interagency mechanisms run by the NSC staff and the national security adviser. These mechanisms—generally consisting of three tiers (assistant secretaries, deputy secretaries, and then the cabinet principals)—make two contributions when the system is working properly. When a new proposal is put on the table, people with experience and deep background knowledge can ensure it is not crazy or dangerous and can help the White House shape it to make it work better. The "system" is a lot better at killing bad ideas than it is at creating bold, new ones. In 1985, the NSC staff devised a plan for invading Libya. State, Defense, and the CIA all colluded to put a bullet in the proposal. Over the years, many a White House bright idea for covert action by the CIA experienced a timely death in a Situation Room meeting.

Whether this process is successful in yoking the agencies together in a broadly supported common endeavor depends predominantly on the national security adviser and his or her deputy and on the personalities and approaches of the secretaries of state and defense. The system is commonly believed to have worked best under Bush 41 when Brent Scowcroft was the national security adviser and (immodestly)

I was his deputy. When I was the chair of the Deputies Committee, no meeting lasted more than an hour, and there was always an action or decision at the end. Everyone got a say and every principal had confidence their views would be honestly reported to the president. Senior staff at State, Defense, and the NSC worked together exceptionally closely. Post–Cold War NSC advisers and their deputies who were successful in managing the process included Steve Hadley (Bush 43) and Tom Donilon (Obama). Unfortunately, they were the exceptions. Too often, "interagency" meetings would run on interminably and inconclusively, disgusting all the participants and contributing to internecine conflict.

To the outsider, this all sounds like a bunch of bureaucratic mumbo jumbo. And it is, but it is still important in understanding how decisions are made and how power is exercised. However, even a perfectly run process does not prevent bad decisions, as I will describe later. A good process does not ensure good outcomes, but it helps.

Outside of the White House, the most important player in implementing the president's foreign policy is the State Department. Under strong secretaries, who by definition have close relationships with the president—since 1991, James Baker, Madeleine Albright, Condoleezza Rice, Hillary Clinton, and Mike Pompeo—State has the lead departmental role in executing policy. That said, I don't think any of the presidents I worked for (except maybe Bush 41) ever thought the State Department really worked for them but instead viewed it as some kind of alien entity within his administration. The secretary knew he or she worked for the president, but most of the career folks considered themselves as working only for the State Department. Their attitude all too often is typified by a State desk officer I called many years ago when I was on the NSC staff to get information relating to a presidential trip overseas. Amid much heavy sighing, the guy finally blurted out, "If I could just get the goddamn president and secretary of state off my back, I could get my work done!" Many of our career diplomats are among the smartest, wisest people I have ever met, but as country and regional experts, they often disagreed with whoever was president about how to deal with this or that foreign government. Embassy officials, including ambassadorial appointees, often suffered from "clientitis," sympathy toward and support of the host government even to the point of arguing its case in the event of a dispute with the United States. According to State Department lore (meaning the story may be true), when George Shultz was secretary, he would greet new U.S. ambassadors in his office, take them over to a large globe, and ask them, "Which is your country?" They would invariably point to the country where they were to serve as ambassador. And Shultz would invariably correct them, pointing on the globe to the United States and saying, "This is your country, and don't forget it."

Sadly, many of the best people in State, including the secretary, have been as frustrated with its awful bureaucracy as presidents have been.

Modern telecommunications, together with increasingly operational presidents and NSC staffs, have diminished the role of senior State Department officials and ambassadors. In most crises, as will be described, the president, secretaries of state and defense, and national security adviser nearly always will just pick up the telephone and call their foreign counterparts, with whom they often have remarkably candid and familiar relationships. It is hard for an assistant secretary of state—or the CIA—to advise the secretary or the president about the views and personality of a foreign leader when they have a close personal relationship with that leader and talk with him or her regularly. I remember Bush 41 returning from a meeting with his foreign counterpart laughing about a briefing paper that said the man didn't drink alcohol: "He likes scotch, and a lot of it."

On routine day-to-day matters and in the interagency process, State professionals still play an important role in implementing presidential policies. Assistant secretaries also tend to regional and other issues and problems that do not rise to the presidential level. But these days the important stuff, more often than not, gets done at the top. Indeed, with modern technology, during a crisis the president can chair a meeting in the Situation Room with all key U.S. ambassadors and military commanders even when they are in a distant country or region thanks to large video screens.

Similarly, most of the time, ambassadors and embassies play little role in policy decisions, and those in important countries—Russia, China, Great Britain, France, Germany, Japan, and others—are kept on the sidelines as the president and his top advisers talk with the leaders directly. There are exceptions and they tend to be in countries where we have troops in military operations, where there is an internal crisis affecting U.S. interests, or where the relationship is important but parlous. For example, our ambassadors in Iraq, Afghanistan, Pakistan, Egypt, and Syria all were consulted directly by Bush 43 and Obama at various times, and participated (in some cases under Bush, routinely) by videoconference in NSC meetings. In each case, the ambassador was an experienced senior State Department career officer. Ambassadors who are political appointees can play an important role as well. One of my favorite examples involves a car dealer from Southern California, Robert Nesen, named by Reagan as ambassador to Australia in 1981. On the advice of his embassy senior staff, Nesen immediately began to cultivate an opposition politician, Bob Hawke, at a time when no one else was paying any attention to him. Sure enough, Hawke became prime minister in 1983, served for more than eight years, and was one of the most pro-American Australian prime ministers in recent history.

Embassies manage the day-to-day business of the United States and the president's policies in each country, and that in itself can be pretty daunting. The best ambassadors, drawing on their own experience and that of their embassy team, can help Washington understand what is going on in their country, how to think about it in relation to U.S. interests, and how best to achieve American objectives there. At the same time, as many as two dozen different agencies and departments may reside within an American embassy, and it is the ambassador's role to ride herd on what they are all doing. In 1978–79, as Brzezinski's assistant in the Carter White House, I was in the middle of negotiating with State, Defense, and the CIA the president's letter of instruction to ambassadors, spelling out their authority vis-à-vis other agencies in the embassy. Negotiating arms control treaties with the Soviet Union was easier (and, sometimes, friendlier).

All presidents wrestle with how to deal with the Defense Department and the military. As a stubborn, slow-moving bureaucracy,
the Defense Department can make the State Department look as sleek
and nimble as an America's Cup sailboat. When I was secretary, there
were twenty-seven bureaucratic layers between most action officers in
the Pentagon and me. When issues involved military operations, especially in Iraq and Afghanistan, the department could move with great
speed and agility. But dealing with internal policy issues on matters
such as personnel and acquisition was Sisyphean. In four and a half
years working on some problems, I made almost no progress—and I
was considered a very strong secretary.

With nearly 3 million people and a budget of more than half a
trillion dollars, Defense is a bloated leviathan that is saddled with
escalating health care and retirement costs, and a bunch of expensive programs forced upon it by Congress. Because members, both
Republicans and Democrats, cannot abide the thought of a single
Defense program in their state or district being cut by a dollar, the
department is also stuck with paying for a significant number of
bases and facilities—probably 25 percent of the total—it neither wants
nor needs. When presidents look at the discretionary federal budget (money left after paying for entitlements such as Social Security
and Medicare), Defense is always the elephant in the room, receiving
about 15 percent of the federal budget (it was 50 percent in the 1950s).

Senior military officers have special credibility with Congress, the
public, and even the media, and many are not shy about sharing their
views when it comes to decisions to cut programs they favor—or even
presidential decisions about operations. Senior civilians do the same,
but they lack the special cachet of a four-star officer. When officers
speak out publicly, people listen, often to the chagrin of presidents.
Repeatedly as secretary of defense, I had to chastise very senior officers for public comments that angered the president. And because,
in the confirmation process, every senior officer has to promise Congress that he or she will always provide them with his or her candid professional military opinion, testimony by senior officers often

creates tension with the White House. The military takes rightful pride in being nonpartisan (increasingly difficult over the last three decades), but that does not mean they don't have strong views on policy matters—and, privately, on an incumbent president.

Presidents get especially frustrated when asking the military for options involving the use of force. As I wrote years ago, the biggest doves in Washington wear uniforms, partly because they have seen up close the cost of war in lives broken and lost, and partly because they fear, with good reason, that if things don't go well the politicians will abandon them and whatever fight the president has started. Time and again over the years, I have seen the president ask for options for a limited military operation only to have Defense come back with a proposal that looks like D-Day. Bush 43 was frustrated with the senior military and even commanders in the field toward the end of 2006, when it was clear what we were doing in Iraq wasn't working. Obama became similarly frustrated with the limited range of military options he was offered in the review of the war in Afghanistan in late 2009. Once in a conflict, it is a very rare commander in the field who doesn't want more troops—sometimes a lot more, as Obama discovered. I have seen nearly every president disagree with his generals and admirals and chart his own path. Still, when the president does make a decision, military leaders salute and do their damnedest to make the effort successful. And they try to make decisions work even when they know they have not been given the necessary forces to ensure success.

Most of the time, senior civilian and military personnel in Defense collaborate pretty closely when policy issues are being developed and debated in the interagency process. Most of the time, but not always, the civilians and the uniforms present a united front. It is one of those quirks of the system, much to the annoyance of State, that the Defense Department has two seats at the president's table—the secretary and the chairman of the Joint Chiefs of Staff—an arrangement replicated at every level of the interagency process. The personal relationship between the secretary and the chairman obviously impacts civilian-military relationships throughout the department. I was fortunate in that I worked with two great chairmen, General Peter Pace and Admiral Mike Mullen, and I can count on the fingers of one hand the number of times we disagreed on something of consequence over nearly five years.

The role of the secretary of defense has been diminished in recent years by rapid turnover. I served for four and a half years (only four others since 1947 served longer), but since I stepped down in 2011 there have been seven secretaries or acting secretaries. Such turnover, not to mention numerous vacancies in other key civilian jobs, has weakened the role of civilian officials in the relationship with the military, in presidential decision making, and with Congress.

The third leg of the triangle of power agencies is the CIA and the other fifteen intelligence organizations. But the CIA remains preeminent and is the only intelligence agency at the president's table. The conventional wisdom is that the CIA does everything possible to please presidents, including slanting analyses on sensitive subjects to be supportive of presidential policies. In reality, nothing could be further from the truth, as every president I worked for would attest. Lyndon Johnson was once meeting with one of the post–World War II wise men, John J. McCloy, and McCloy asked LBJ how things were going with the intelligence agencies. LBJ replied by telling a story about milking his cow on the farm as a boy in Texas. He said he had gotten a full pail of milk, was distracted, and the cow "swept a shit-smeared tail through the bucket of milk, spoiling it." He concluded, "That's what these intelligence people do. You get a good policy going, and they swipe a shit-smeared tail through it." Richard Nixon once asked, "What the hell do those clowns do out at Langley [CIA's headquarters in northern Virginia]?" The only president I served who was not harshly critical at times of the CIA and its analysis was Bush 41, who had once been the agency's director.

While presidents value the CIA's covert action capabilities and the reports of some of its spies, they wonder why they can't get better information on what other leaders are thinking and planning. They often detest the intelligence assessments the agency produces. Above all, they dislike them because the reports often are implicitly critical of the president's policies, such as when he says things are going great in country X and the CIA assesses that, actually, things are awful there. That is LBJ's "shit-smeared tail." What's worse, virtually all those assessments are sent to Congress, giving the president's critics loads of ammunition. Finally, the assessments often leak, and when they do and are at odds with what the administration is saying, foreign countries are, at best, confused. In late 2007, when Bush 43 was placing heavy pressure on other countries to sanction Iran for its nuclear weapons program, U.S. intelligence published an assessment reporting that in 2003 Iran had halted its efforts to build a nuclear weapon. The pressure campaign collapsed, at least temporarily. Because very few intelligence agencies around the world have the independence of U.S. agencies in doing assessments, foreign governments couldn't figure out the Bush administration's game, conducting a pressure campaign with the right hand while totally undercutting it with the left. Presidents remember that sort of thing.

It is the analytical function of intelligence that plays the primary role in policy and decision making. The analysts provide the informational basis for the debate and, when the process works properly, ensure that everyone is working from the same set of facts and that no participant distorts them to advance his or her case. Unfortunately, there are times when directors of central intelligence (after 2005, directors of national intelligence) have strong policy views and express them at the table. When that happens, his or her role as factual referee is compromised. To avoid this, some presidents—Nixon and Bush 41 most notably—would have the director begin a meeting with an intelligence briefing and then, before beginning the policy discussion, often excuse him from the room.

In my experience, intelligence presentations in the policy-making process can be flawed in several ways. First, the agencies pretend to be able to forecast the future with far more confidence than is justified and make predictions that are really no more than educated guesses clothed as facts. Second, they can be overly confident in their analytical assessments and about the reliability and accuracy of the information they present. A good example was director George Tenet telling Bush 43 that the information about weapons of mass destruction in Iraq was a "slam-dunk case." Third, experts nearly always have a bias.

It's not necessarily political and can be as benign as judging that a dictatorial leader will remain in power simply because he's already held power for so long. Discerning such biases and trying to account for them is the responsibility of CIA managers of the process. As a longtime CIA analyst and head of the analytical directorate, and from my perch as an NSC staff member under four presidents, I saw these deficiencies all too often, and was personally guilty of them on more than one occasion.

All that said, day in, day out, and regardless of policy makers' and politicians' complaints, the U.S. intelligence agencies provide presidents and their advisers with a daily stream of information on developments around the world unparalleled in its accuracy and honesty. And, whether admiringly or begrudgingly, presidents depend on that information in making decisions. An example of historical consequence was the analytical case built by the CIA that in the spring of 2011 Osama bin Laden was in the compound in Abbotabad, Pakistan. They were honest about the lack of hard evidence and both the strengths and weaknesses of their circumstantial case. Their analysis gave Obama an option and he took it.

So, how is power actually exercised?

A critical responsibility of the national security adviser is to ensure that presidential decisions are clear and unambiguous. Once the ponderous wheels of the big departments start to turn, they damn well better be headed in the right—and same—direction. The story (likely apocryphal, but still useful) goes that many years ago FBI director J. Edgar Hoover wrote on a memo "Watch the borders." Hundreds of agents were dispatched to the Mexican border before someone thought to ask Hoover what they were to do there. He exploded, and then explained he had only been referring to the proper size of the margins of the report he had been reading.

The president and national security adviser must assign clear primary responsibility for implementation. In many instances, that responsibility is obvious. If it is a military mission, the secretary of defense and the appropriate combatant commander (Pacific Command, European Command, Africa Command, et al.) issue the relevant orders and see to their execution down the chain of command, ultimately to commanders on the front lines. (Contrary to what many think, neither the vice president nor the chairman of the Joint Chiefs of Staff nor the service chiefs are in the military chain of command—although any secretary who does not keep the chairman at his side and intimately involved is an idiot.) While Defense has the main action in military operations, the State Department will have the job of notifying other countries of what we are doing and seeking international support in capitals, at NATO, and at the UN. U.S. ambassadors in countries where we are operating must be partners of our military commanders in dealing with the local government, as worked well most of the time in both Baghdad and Kabul. And the CIA both at home and in-country will provide support to the commanders.

Without close coordination in the field and direction from the president, crossed wires and confusion follow. And that's for a simple military operation. Things get complicated once the military endeavor moves beyond defeating an enemy and turns to a broader, primarily nonmilitary mission. When military missions morph into nation-building, as happened in Somalia, Haiti, Afghanistan, and Iraq, the potential for trouble—and mistakes—increases exponentially. As I will describe, the lack of clarity on who in Washington would be in charge after the initial military mission was complete would lead to real problems in Iraq and elsewhere.

Initiatives that appear superficially to be purely diplomatic rarely are. U.S. relationships with every country are complex. As noted above, each embassy can have two dozen or more agencies represented. Arms control is the province of the State Department, which has led such negotiations for decades. But most such negotiating teams have military and secretary of defense representation, the Department of Energy is probably involved if nuclear weapons are being discussed, and many delegations have CIA experts both to inform the delegation and to facilitate the use of classified intelligence information in the negotiations. Any diplomatic action involving economic sanctions immediately broadens the circle of involved agencies to include Treasury, Commerce, the office of the U.S. Trade Representative, and others. State will take the lead in all such cases, but every negotiation involves herding the interagency cats, to ensure not only strategic coherence but day-to-day cooperation. When a delegation head does not keep other agencies informed and on board, distrust and internecine conflict in Washington inevitably follow—as we will see in the North Korean negotiations under Bush 43.

You might think that the CIA alone would be involved if the president ordered a covert action. Not so. In the normal course of affairs, State will be involved and the CIA must coordinate with the U.S. ambassador in the country where the operation is to take place. Often the military is involved in a support role, and the NSC staff is supposed to monitor such operations very closely. On the occasions when cooperation is inadequate, bureaucratic hell breaks loose.

Exercising power is complicated but manageable when a presidential decision clearly identifies a single lead department or agency. This is especially the case with military operations, intelligence operations, diplomatic initiatives, and the uses of economic instruments of power. It is in the many instances where decisions necessarily involve the collaboration of multiple agencies that the exercise of American power becomes a formidable task. Presidents, other government leaders, and experts alike speak of the need for "whole of government" efforts in different situations—for all the relevant departments and agencies to work together and contribute to a common effort. But as we will see, the U.S. government simply is not organized to exercise power effectively in areas such as nation-building, the offensive use of cyber capabilities for political purposes, strategic communications, humanitarian and development assistance, and intervention in internal conflicts in other countries.

Responsibility for nation-building—essentially development assistance against a backdrop of internal conflict—is the most complicated case and the most likely to result in bureaucratic confusion and involve a serious mismatch between responsibilities and resources. We will see this repeatedly. State nominally has the principal responsibility for the nation-building enterprise, but in Iraq, Afghanistan, Somalia, Haiti, and other places, there were far too few State Department and USAID personnel, while the military had the overwhelming preponderance of resources. As a result, men and women in uniform often were assigned to execute tasks that were civilian in nature and for which they were not trained. On the civilian side, there too often was lack of coordination and accountability, and once multiple other agencies became involved—Treasury to help set up financial systems, Justice to help with rule-of-law projects, and many others—implementation of decisions became immensely complicated and difficult. Due to the lack of structure, improvisation became the order of the day. There were too many instruments and, too often, no empowered conductor.

Time and again, I will describe the inadequacy of American efforts to harness the many instruments of communication we have for a single strategic purpose. The dismantling of USIA in the Clinton administration, the many disparate organizations with their own messaging capabilities—State, Defense, CIA, Treasury, the Agency for Global Media, and more—and the proliferation of new forms of communicating, from social media to cyber tools, have left us with massive capabilities and no way to mobilize them collectively for the exercise of power.

As we will see, Congress can be both an asset and a liability in the implementation of presidential decisions—that is, in the exercise of power. Congressional support and restrictions were vital to U.S. success in Colombia and to Bush 43's successful initiatives in Africa. Congress has been a reliable partner of most presidents in dealing with Iran, Russia, and China, often pushing presidents to be tougher. On the other hand, its failure to adequately fund the nonmilitary instruments of power over many years has significantly weakened the U.S. ability to find nonmilitary solutions to problems. How ironic that so many members of Congress who decry the use of our military to deal with problems abroad have contributed to dismantling, starving, or restricting the nonmilitary instruments of power. At one point in the Obama administration, the secretary of agriculture, Tom Vilsack, called me to offer to send seventy agricultural experts to Afghanistan to help with development assistance, but he could not spend money to send them there, and as it turned out, neither I nor the secretary of state could either because of congressional restrictions on transfers of money within the executive branch. Government leaders encounter such hobbling legislative micromanagement every day in trying to exercise American power.

I n the pages ahead, the reader will see the strengths and weaknesses in how our government exercises power, reflecting the realities I have described. What will become evident is that structures and procedures designed for the exercise of power during the Cold War and a simpler time are no longer adequate for the more complicated and more technologically advanced post–Cold War world. As we contemplate long-term rivalries and competition—if not adversarial relations—with Russia and China in the years to come, failure to remedy those deficiencies and to strengthen all of our nonmilitary instruments of power will tie one hand behind our back. We cannot afford that.

CHAPTER 3

Iran

Great Satan's Bane

U.S. presidents have been surprisingly restrained in the use of the instruments of power available to them against Iran. They have used economic and financial sanctions creatively and effectively, and kept the military pressure on through large-scale naval deployments in the Persian Gulf. But despite ample evidence of popular unrest in Iran, especially among young people, due to economic hardship and social constraints, the United States has been reluctant to use every available means to inform the Iranian population about the pervasive corruption of their leaders, aggressively promote broader exchanges, proselytize Iranian students and businessmen abroad, and create problems internally. Nor has it undertaken actions inside Iran to help opposition groups or otherwise complicate the lives of Iran's leaders. Why has the "Great Satan" been so restrained?

From my front-row seat at the White House/NSC, at the CIA, and as secretary of defense, I have watched seven presidents wrestle with Iran as an ally and then as a sworn enemy since the 1970s. For most of the Cold War, Iran was an ally of the United States. After a brief exile, in August 1953, Shah Mohammad Reza Pahlavi was returned to power in a CIA-assisted coup that ousted the elected prime minister, Mohammad Mossadeq. The shah ensured access to Gulf oil for the West as well as Israel. Tehran refused to join the Arab oil embargo against the United States after the Yom Kippur War in 1973 and even kept oil flowing to Israel—although the shah consistently worked to keep the price of oil as high as possible to fatten his bank account.

The relationship between the United States and Iran reached its apex during the Nixon and Ford presidencies. In the early 1970s, the "Nixon Doctrine" designated Iran as a regional surrogate for American military power in preserving stability in the Persian Gulf and blocking Soviet ambitions there, thus opening the floodgates to the sale of ever more sophisticated weapons and a huge Iranian military buildup. By the mid-1970s, Iran alone accounted for about half of America's annual arms sales. Human rights and democratization were not on Nixon's priority list. To the degree there was concern elsewhere in the U.S. government about the harsh treatment of the shah's opponents, it was more about stability in the country. At that point the opposition did not seem to be much of a threat. Geostrategy and national interest were paramount for Washington in those days.

As he was on so many national security challenges, Jimmy Carter was of two minds on Iran. He entered the presidency determined to make human rights and limiting arms sales to other countries high priorities. When it came to Iran, though, he hedged on both of those commitments, remaining supportive of the shah to the end. The president hosted the shah at the White House on November 15, 1977. I witnessed his arrival on the south lawn of the White House, a ceremony punctuated by anti-shah riots in the streets of Washington and teargas wafting over the official parties. I was a member of the advance party for Carter's visit to Tehran later that year. Imagine my surprise when on New Year's Eve in Tehran that year, Carter toasted the shah and described Iran as an "island of stability" in the region.

During the growing popular discontent in Iran in late 1978, there was serious conflict between Brzezinski's NSC, which wanted the shah to get tough and crack down on the opposition, and the State Department and the U.S. ambassador in Tehran, who wanted the shah to make concessions to his adversaries and move toward a constitutional monarchy—or leave. As I watched all this back-and-forth from my little office in the West Wing, I believed the time for concessions and accommodation had long passed. The measures the shah took were too little, too late, and when he was unwilling to use the kind of violence against his people that we would see in Libya and Syria many years later, he was done for.

The shah was forced from power on January 16, 1979, and fled into exile. In late October, Brzezinski was in Algiers representing Carter at the twenty-fifth anniversary of Algerian independence. The prime minister and ministers of foreign affairs and defense of the new Iranian revolutionary government, in Algiers for the same ceremony, asked to meet with him. I was Brzezinski's note taker at the meeting. He offered U.S. recognition of the revolution and even suggested we would sell them the weapons already paid for by the shah. The Iranians' sole purpose for the meeting was to demand that we return the shah to them. When Brzezinski refused, the meeting ended. On November 4, radical Iranian students seized the American embassy in Tehran and took fifty-three Americans hostage (one, who was sick, was subsequently released). The takeover of the embassy was enormously popular in Iran and soon was embraced by the "supreme leader," Ayatollah Ruhollah Khomeini, who at that point began referring to America as the "Great Satan." In fact, the ayatollah may well have known about the "spontaneous" plans to seize the embassy and in any event encouraged them, as the takeover contributed to the consolidation of power by the more radical, anti-American elements within Iran. Not surprisingly, the seizure led to a strong anti-Iranian backlash in the United States. If America had become the Great Satan in Iranian eyes, Iran would become an American nemesis.

U.S. policy toward Iran during the presidency of Ronald Reagan was dominated by four events. The first was the release of the fifty-two remaining American embassy hostages in Tehran literally minutes after Reagan was sworn in as president on January 20, 1981. The Iranians delayed release of the hostages just long enough to deny Carter any credit for the action.

The second event, the eight-year-long Iran-Iraq War, began prior to Reagan taking office, when Saddam Hussein launched a surprise attack on Iran on September 22, 1980. The war lasted until August 1988. Reagan's approach to the war was in the finest tradition of a balance-of-power strategy. We wanted the war to end but didn't want either side to win. Reagan used a variety of nonmilitary measures—instruments of power—toward that goal. The United States refused to sell weapons to either side and endeavored to stop the flow of weapons from others. When, toward the end of 1982, it looked as though Iran might win, Reagan provided Iraq with credits to purchase American wheat, rice, and feed grains; access to Export-Import Bank credits; and continued financing of agricultural sales. He also provided the Iraqis with intelligence—an often-overlooked policy tool—on Iranian force deployments. In short, the Reagan team made good use of nonmilitary measures to achieve its "no-winner" goal.

The third important development was the intensification of terrorist attacks against Americans by Iranian-sponsored groups, above all, Hezbollah in Lebanon. The president of the American University of Beirut, David Dodge, was taken hostage in July 1982. In April 1983, the U.S. embassy in Beirut was car bombed, and on October 23, a truck filled with explosives hit the U.S. Marine barracks in Beirut, killing 241 Americans. Hezbollah was responsible for all three. Then, on December 12, six targets were hit by terrorists in Kuwait, including the U.S. and French embassies. Seventeen terrorists were captured. Fourteen were members of al-Dawa, an Iranian-backed group, and the other three were Hezbollah. In March 1984, Hezbollah began an intensified campaign of kidnapping Americans, with three Americans taken hostage that spring, including the CIA station chief in Beirut, William Buckley. On September 20, the new American embassy in Beirut was severely damaged by another vehicle bomb, again Hezbollah's work. The next day, a Kuwaiti airliner was hijacked to Tehran by Shia Muslim terrorists, who killed two more Americans. The following year saw more terrorist actions, including the Hezbollah hijacking of a TWA airplane, the seizure of the cruise ship *Achille Lauro*, and a Libyan-sponsored attack on the Israeli airline El Al's ticket counter in Rome that left twenty dead, including five Americans.

Reagan's preoccupation with getting the hostages back led to the fourth major development. In 1985 and 1986, Reagan approved the sale of antitank and antiaircraft weapons to Iran in the expectation that, in exchange, the Iranians would direct Hezbollah to release all the American hostages. Both Secretary of State George Shultz and

Defense Secretary Caspar Weinberger opposed the sale of the weapons, arguing that the United States was selling arms for hostages, an act totally contrary to U.S. policy. Reagan countered that it was not arms for hostages because the weapons were going to Iran, not to Hezbollah, which held the hostages. The failed initiative morphed into a shattering scandal when a small group of people on the NSC and probably a few others, including CIA director Bill Casey, jacked up the price being charged the Iranians for the arms and siphoned off the excess funds to support the anticommunist Contra guerrillas in Nicaragua—contrary to legislation banning such support from the United States. Thus was born the Iran-Contra scandal that nearly cost Reagan the presidency.

Iran was very low on George H. W. Bush's priority list when he became president in January 1989. He shared Reagan's concern about Iran's expansionist ambitions in the Middle East, its nuclear aspirations, its support for terrorism—especially its backing of Hezbollah, which continued to hold American hostages—and the determination of its religious leaders to export their version of Shia Islamic fundamentalism throughout the Middle East. Nonetheless, alluding to possible Iranian help in getting the hostages released, Bush offered a conciliatory gesture in his inaugural address, noting: "Good will begets good will. Good faith can be a spiral that endlessly moves on." Nothing came of it, and I don't think Bush was surprised, having witnessed Reagan's repeatedly dashed hopes. The subsequent death sentence handed down in 1989 by the ayatollah against Salman Rushdie, author of *The Satanic Verses*, and the killing of longtime hostage Lieutenant Colonel William Higgins, both during 1989 (Higgins was officially declared dead by the United States on July 6, 1990), further soured any chance of a change in the U.S.-Iranian relationship.

Before Ayatollah Khomeini died on June 3, 1989, he had arranged a succession process naming President Seyed Ali Khamenei as supreme leader, ensuring a smooth transition—and a continuing hard line toward the United States. Khamenei was succeeded as president by Ali Akbar Hashemi Rafsanjani. During his two terms as president, Rafsanjani focused on rebuilding the country and the economy after the war with Iraq. He also worked to normalize relations with

Iran's neighbors, the Soviet Union, China, and Europe as a means of increasing foreign investment.

Bush 41 had the strategic sense to see that America and its allies' military victory over Iraq in early 1991 created an opportunity to advance our interests and the cause of Middle East peace through another instrument of American power, diplomacy. He announced to Congress in March 1991 that the time had come for peace in the Middle East. The Madrid Conference convened at the end of October, cohosted by Bush and Soviet president Mikhail Gorbachev. It was the first time Israel, Syria, Egypt, Lebanon, Jordan, and the Palestinians had held face-to-face talks about peace. The assemblage created a strategic challenge for Iran by helping to legitimize Israel in the Arab world, placing Iran's terrorist surrogate Hezbollah at risk, and jeopardizing Tehran's close relationship with Syria. Thus, Iran increased its support for not just Hezbollah but also Hamas and the Palestinian Islamic Jihad. The subsequent wave of new terrorist attacks in the region aimed, with some success, at derailing the Madrid process.

The Bush administration was aware that Iran was developing ballistic missiles, but the program was still in the very early stages and the missiles themselves were quite short-range. We believed Iran had aspirations for nuclear weapons, but we had no evidence they were then working on such a program. Under the shah, in 1975, the Germans had begun building a nuclear power plant at Bushehr, near the Persian Gulf, but the site was bombed repeatedly during the Iran-Iraq War. After the war, the Soviets contracted to finish the power plant. In October 1992, I was the first CIA director to visit Moscow and, in a private meeting with my counterpart, Yevgeny Primakov, urged the Russians to abandon the power plant project because of the opportunity it might provide Iran for a weapons program. Primakov bluntly told me they couldn't cancel the project because there was too much money at stake for a then-impoverished Russia.

The first post–Cold War president, Bill Clinton, faced the challenge of figuring out how the United States, now a singular superpower, should conduct itself and, more important, what America's role in the world should be. His foreign policy was reactive in some places and aggressive in others, but highly tactical in all. Clinton quickly adopted a policy of "dual containment" in the Persian Gulf area, aiming to isolate both Iraq and Iran and to deny them the opportunity to develop advanced weapons. The approach looked a lot like Reagan's and Bush 41's. There was no public signaling to the Iranian leadership of interest in a better relationship, as Bush had done in his inaugural address or as Barack Obama would later do. And while President Rafsanjani was reaching out to many countries to broaden economic and political ties—to lessen Iran's isolation and rebuild its economy—there was no outreach from Tehran to the Great Satan.

Clinton's first signal to Tehran must have puzzled the Iranians. It had to do with the civil war then raging in the former Yugoslavia. In 1994, Croatian president Franjo Tudjman asked two senior U.S. diplomats what the American attitude would be toward establishment of a secret arms pipeline from Iran through Croatia to Bosnian Muslims fighting the Serbs. At the time, there was a UN arms embargo affecting all the parties involved in the Balkan wars, an embargo the United States was obligated to uphold. Our European allies, moreover, were concerned that additional arms would escalate the conflict as well as put their peacekeepers in the region at greater risk. The Clinton administration chafed at the embargo because it tilted the conflict strongly in Serbia's favor given its access to the Yugoslav army's arsenals. So Clinton secretly gave a green light to establishment of the Iranian arms channel in contravention of the UN embargo and established U.S. policy. For the second time in eight years, a U.S. president approved a secret arms transaction involving the Iranians that was contrary to public U.S. policy.

Clinton's 1994 decision had everything to do with helping the Bosnian Muslims and not with improving relations with the Iranians. He proved that when, a year later, he signed an executive order imposing tight oil and trade sanctions on Iran because of its sponsorship of terrorism, nuclear ambitions, and opposition to the Middle East peace process. The first post–Cold War president turned to our favorite and most used nonmilitary instrument of power: economic sanctions.

The beginning of Clinton's second term in 1997 coincided with

the election in May of a new Iranian president, Mohammad Khatami, who defeated the supreme leader's candidate, the conservative
speaker of the parliament. Khatami's victory was due in no small part
to widespread fears in Iran—especially among women and young
people—that his opponent in the election would roll back Rafsanjani's
loosening of regulations governing social behavior and his economic
reforms.

Meanwhile, the first-term secretary of state, Warren Christopher,
was succeeded by Madeleine Albright, who had been Clinton's ambassador to the UN. I first met Albright when we both worked for Brzezinski. Whereas Christopher was taciturn, reserved, and cautious,
Albright was outspoken, activist, feisty, and fun. She saw in Khatami
an "avowed reformer," and she advocated a softer line toward Iran during 1997. There was a very modest increase in cultural, academic, and
athletic exchanges that year. Albright saw the possibility of a further
opening in the relationship when Khatami, in an interview with CNN
in January 1998, advocated "a dialogue of civilizations" beginning with
an exchange of artists, scholars, journalists, and tourists. She later
wrote that the same month, Palestinian leader Yasir Arafat showed the
administration a letter he had received from Khatami in which the Iranian president supported Palestinian participation in the Middle East
peace process—a reversal of Iran's previous position, acknowledged
Israel's legitimacy, and discussed the possibility of region-wide peace
if the Palestinians were allowed to establish a state on the West Bank
and in Gaza. Albright, seizing on these signals, concluded that Iran
was no longer in the same category as Iraq, and thus that the time
"was ripe to move beyond dual containment."

The following June, Albright gave a speech welcoming Khatami's
election, endorsing his call for intercultural communications, and saying that "if Iranian officials were ready, we were prepared to sit down
without preconditions and develop a roadmap to normal relations."
She was clearly prepared to employ a number of nonmilitary instruments of power, including diplomacy and cultural and educational
exchanges. She didn't have many carrots to offer, but I think she used
all she had in the hope of seizing an opportunity.

Albright, though, made a mistake U.S. officials had made before and would make again. She assumed that Iran's relatively freely elected president (the elections were open but the clerics controlled the candidate lists) had real power and that the terms "reformer" and "moderate" extended not only to internal economic and social policy but to the United States as well. As she later acknowledged, in reality the ayatollah controlled all the levers of hard power—the military, the Iranian Revolutionary Guard Corps (IRGC), police, intelligence, and judiciary. (The IRGC is an independent military force reporting directly to the ayatollah and charged with the security of the regime. It is in charge of Iranian ballistic missile and nuclear programs and the regime's external military efforts as well as support for terrorist groups such as Hezbollah. The IRGC has become a powerful political force and controls a vast business empire.) While the ayatollah might allow some loosening internally to manage widespread popular discontent, he had no interest in improving relations with the Great Satan (or with Israel). Khatami continued to talk a good game through 1998, but Clinton administration efforts to reach out to him privately were rejected. Although there was mutual interest between the United States and Iran in dealing with the ongoing civil war in Afghanistan, the ayatollah barred both Khatami and the Iranian foreign minister from any direct contact with the United States even on that subject while at the UN that fall.

Khamenei continued the pursuit of nuclear weapons, arming and financing Hezbollah, suppressing human rights at home, and supporting anti-Israel and anti-U.S. terrorist groups. Indeed, at the end of 1998, the FBI acquired information directly implicating Iran in Hezbollah's 1996 attack on the Khobar Towers in Saudi Arabia that killed nineteen American servicemen. By that time, even Khatami's domestic reform programs had been stymied by the clerics.

Still, Albright was persistent in her pursuit of a better relationship with Iran. In February 2000, she sent a memo to Clinton pointing out gains by Khatami supporters in the parliamentary elections earlier that month, as well as Iran's signing of the chemical weapons convention, efforts to fight the narcotics trade, support for a negotiated solution in Afghanistan, and interception of ships trying to smuggle Iraqi oil in violation of UN sanctions. She suggested that the administration acknowledge these positive steps while "retaining our best carrots and sticks." She was trying to straddle the political divide in Iran: "We couldn't ignore the ayatollah's hardline policies when reaching out to the Iran of Khatami, and we didn't want to ignore the promise of reform while trying to rein in the ayatollah."

With Clinton's approval, Albright gave a speech in March 2000 in which she announced that the United States was lifting import restrictions on Iran's main non-oil exports—carpets, pistachios, dried fruit, and caviar—and again invited Iran to engage in an official dialogue. Albright offered what could only be regarded as a public apology to Iran for U.S. involvement in the 1953 coup that overthrew Mossadeq, and acknowledged that the U.S.-supported shah had repressed his political opponents at home. These economic and political concessions were to no avail. Khatami responded that U.S. "deeds were insufficient for a new relationship." On that frosty note, efforts by President Clinton and his secretary of state to improve the relationship with Iran came to an end.

Containment was the U.S. strategy toward the hostile regime in Tehran, but throughout the Clinton administration and beyond, it was a curious kind of containment that in no way resembled comprehensive American containment strategy toward the USSR. Rather, it was narrowly focused on military deterrence and economic sanctions. Even the sanctions were limited because so many countries—France, Germany, Russia, and China among them—wanted to do business with Iran despite its support for terrorism. While the United States criticized the Iranian government for repression of student demonstrators and other protesters in July 1999, there was no sustained overt or covert support for the internal fight for human and political rights. Hardly any multimedia communication into Iran highlighted the corruption of the clerics, the IRGC's growing control of major parts of the economy, the clerics' distortion of Islam, and news of repression. Nor was there a concerted effort inside Iran to counter Tehran's efforts to portray the United States as anti-Islam and antireligious by communicating how the United States had stepped in to protect Muslims in Somalia, Bosnia, and elsewhere, or how we had offered massive assistance to Muslim countries such as Pakistan after natural disasters. Nor was there an attempt to highlight the deep religious beliefs of many Americans. With regard to the many instruments of nonmilitary power available to Washington in dealing with a hostile Iran, we were passive and unimaginative.

Then came 9/11.

The United States and Iran had been participating in a UN-sponsored dialogue about Afghanistan's future since the fall of 1998, the "Six plus Two" talks that included Afghanistan's neighbors as well as Russia. That dialogue continued in the new Bush administration and even improved for a few months after 9/11. Right after the attack, Friday prayers in Tehran omitted "Death to America" chants for the first time in years, sermons condemned the attacks, the Iranians agreed in October to rescue any U.S. pilots shot down over Iran. Secretary of State Colin Powell and the Iranian foreign minister met at the Six plus Two session at the UN and shook hands—a minor, but unprecedented, gesture. The Iranians had backed the so-called Northern Alliance in Afghanistan, the main opposition to the Taliban, which was the principal group the United States supported to defeat the Taliban.

Even though the Bush administration for some time continued the dialogue with Iran on Afghanistan, Iran had not actually diminished any of its activities of concern to Washington. Iran continued unabated its support for Hezbollah, Palestinian Islamic Jihad, and Hamas. On January 3, 2002, the Israeli navy captured a shipload of arms bound for Gaza, almost certainly from Iran. Tehran also continued to work on developing both ballistic missiles and nuclear weapons. It was this combination of support for terrorism and development of weapons of mass destruction that led Bush to include Iran along with Iraq and North Korea in referring to the "axis of evil" in his State of the Union speech at the end of January 2002. The following August, internal opposition sources provided evidence that the Iranians had a covert uranium enrichment facility at Natanz and a secret heavy water plant in Arak.

Still, the United States and Iran had worked together at the Bonn conference in December 2001 to create a new Afghan government led by the U.S. choice, Hamid Karzai. Bush's then deputy national security adviser, Stephen Hadley, later wrote that Iranian support had been essential in convincing the Afghan opposition to support Karzai. The U.S.-Iranian dialogue continued after the invasion of Iraq, including three meetings in 2004 in Baghdad, focused on growing terrorist and insurgent violence. But fundamental differences between the two countries remained. Iranian shock at the U.S. invasion of countries on both their eastern and western borders faded, and the dialogue ended.

There was one curious diplomatic initiative in May 2003, when the State Department received a fax from the Swiss ambassador in Iran (the Swiss looked after our interests there since we had no embassy) titled "Roadmap." It purported to be a back-channel message from unnamed officials in the Iranian government expressing an interest in exploring a "grand bargain" between the two countries. The suggested agenda was expansive, including weapons of mass destruction, terrorism, Iraq, and Middle East peace. The document purportedly had been prepared by the nephew of the Iranian ambassador and had been seen by senior Iranian leaders. This was not the first time the U.S. government had received overtures from anonymous "moderates" in Iran, and the Bush administration was skeptical. Was this genuine outreach from the Iranians or mostly freelancing by the Swiss ambassador seeking to play peacemaker? Both the White House and the State Department thought it was most likely the latter, and did not pursue it.

On December 26, 2003, the Iranian city of Bam suffered a catastrophic earthquake killing more than 26,000 and injuring as many as 30,000. Despite the fraught political relationship between the two countries, Washington offered humanitarian assistance. On December 30, an eighty-one-person U.S. emergency response team deployed to Bam via military aircraft, the first to land in Iran (with permission) in decades. In multiple flights, the United States airlifted tents, kitchen sets, blankets, and nearly seventy tons of medical supplies. In return, Iran promised to improve its compliance with International Atomic Energy Agency (IAEA) monitoring of its nuclear program. The American humanitarian assistance put the Iranian government in a quandary. They needed the help but didn't want the Iranian people to know the United States was providing assistance. Accordingly, the leadership kept quiet while Iranian state radio accused the United States of illegal interference in internal Iranian affairs. It is incomprehensible to me why we did not publicize by every means available inside Iran and worldwide our humanitarian assistance to the Iranian people despite the enmity of their government toward us. It was a big opportunity to use those instruments of power potentially to great effect.

Most of Europe, especially the leaders of France and Germany, opposed the U.S. invasion of Iraq and worried that a Bush administration they considered too aggressive was overreacting to the Iranian nuclear program and might take military action to eliminate it. They argued that Iran had a right to a civil nuclear program under the Treaty on Non-Proliferation of Nuclear Weapons (NPT), whereas the United States took the position that any Iranian nuclear program was unacceptable. Unlike in isolated North Korea, most foreign countries had embassies in Tehran and there were strong international trading relationships—Iran's largest trading partners in 2002 were Germany and Japan. For all practical purposes, when it came to the Iranian nuclear program, a number of European leaders believed the United States was as big a problem to manage as the Iranians.

When Iranian president Khatami confirmed the developments at Natanz and Arak in February 2003, Britain, France, and Germany—the EU3—seized the opportunity to forestall U.S. military action by trying to negotiate a deal with Iran that would permit it a civil nuclear program in exchange for revealing the full extent of its nuclear activities, agreeing to intrusive and no-notice inspections of its nuclear facilities by the IAEA, pledging to suspend all uranium enrichment, and providing guarantees that it would not seek to develop nuclear weapons. An agreement, with additional financial and diplomatic benefits for Iran, was reached in Tehran on October 21, 2003. Although Iran signed the agreement in December, it stalled on ratification, and the final agreement was not codified until November 14, 2004. Vice President Dick Cheney and Secretary of Defense Donald Rumsfeld were not sold, believing as early as 2002, as Condi Rice would later write, that when it came to weapons of mass destruction, Iran "would never make a deal and that any deal that could be made was not worth having." Cheney held to that view consistently for as long as he was vice president.

As though to prove Cheney's point, Hassan Rouhani, the Iranian negotiator of the EU3 deal and future president, gave a speech to the Supreme Cultural Revolution Council in 2004 in which he acknowledged the EU3 agreement was a tactical move to buy time for the Iranian enrichment program: "While we were talking with the Europeans in Tehran, we were installing equipment in parts of the [uranium conversion] facility at Isfahan, but we still had a long way to go to complete the project. In fact, by creating a calm environment, we were able to complete the work in Isfahan."

At the end of January 2005, Rice made her first trip abroad as secretary of state and realized European leaders continued to see Washington as just as much of a problem as Tehran, in no small part because the press kept harping on the possibility of the United States using military force against Iran. Upon her return, she told Bush they needed to reassure the Europeans that he was not planning anything dramatic. She suggested the administration get some leverage by allowing Iran to begin the process of negotiating membership in the World Trade Organization and allowing them to buy spare parts for American-built commercial aircraft. In this way, she argued, we could perhaps unify U.S. and European policies toward Iran and get the allies to take a tougher stand. Rice saw it all as a first step in building a stronger coalition to deal with Iran. These political and economic measures were intended primarily to pacify the Europeans, but there was always an outside chance that they might also break the ice with the Iranians.

The task of creating a stronger anti-Iranian coalition became easier when Mahmoud Ahmadinejad, prevailing in a run-off election over Rafsanjani, became president of Iran on August 3, 2005. From the outset, Ahmadinejad made clear he intended to be even more repressive at home and aggressive abroad than his predecessor. He called Israel "a stinking corpse" that should be "wiped off the map" and labeled the Holocaust a "myth." The new president was intent on creating trouble in Lebanon, the Palestinian territories, and Afghanistan, and significantly increased Iranian-backed militia attacks on U.S. troops in Iraq. He accused the Iranian officials who had negotiated the nuclear deal with the EU3, including Rouhani, of treason and moved to restart

Iranian nuclear activities. When Vladimir Putin and the Europeans both offered to support a civil nuclear program in Iran if it would stop its suspect activities, Ahmadinejad rejected the proposal.

At the end of January 2006, Rice and the French, German, and British foreign ministers met with their Russian and Chinese counterparts in London to discuss the Iranian nuclear problem. The group, consisting of the five permanent members of the Security Council plus Germany, was tagged the P5+1. They reached an agreement that the Iranians would be invited to negotiations about their nuclear program and, if they refused, would face the threat of UN sanctions. It represented progress in developing a united front to deal with Iran. Then, in April 2006, Tehran announced it had resumed uranium enrichment at Natanz.

Bush faced the same challenge as Clinton had: he characterized it as a "two-ticking-clocks" problem—how to slow down the nuclear clock and how to speed up the internal reform clock. However, while Clinton had Khatami to deal with, Bush had Ahmadinejad, a very different proposition.

On national security problems like Iran, presidents rarely have good choices; they just have to figure out the least-bad decision. Bush felt he had three options. The first was to negotiate directly with Iran, which he thought would legitimize Ahmadinejad, confuse if not demoralize Iranians seeking greater internal freedom, and, perhaps most important, probably not be successful in stopping the nuclear program. The second option was to engage in multilateral diplomacy, with incentives for Iran to stop its suspect activities and, if it refused, impose tough sanctions. The conundrum was that while sanctions would make it tougher to obtain technology for the nuclear program, they also would make economic reform more difficult. His third option was a military strike on the nuclear program, a choice he considered a "last resort."

The president wrestled with these choices through the spring of 2006, just as the situation in Iraq was deteriorating badly. He consulted intensively with his senior advisers, who were deeply divided. In April, Secretary of Defense Rumsfeld wrote a memo in which he said of the P5+1 talks, "I think they are a disaster. We are stepping on a rake." Bush also reached out to Putin, Chancellor Angela Merkel of Germany, and Prime Minister Tony Blair. In the end, he authorized Rice to announce that the United States would join the Europeans in negotiating directly with Iran if the latter agreed to verifiably suspend its enrichment and reprocessing activities.

Rice's announcement on May 31 went well beyond nuclear matters as she indicated the United States would be willing also to discuss Afghanistan, Iraq, economics, and trade. She suggested as well that the United States might end its opposition to Iran's civil nuclear program, a major shift in our position. Finally, the secretary avowed that Bush wanted a better relationship between the American and Iranian peoples, including increased travel and investment as well as educational, athletic, and cultural exchanges. This was an adroit move, potentially bringing to bear a broad range of nonmilitary instruments of power to change the direction of the relationship.

The far-reaching announcement, which included a litany of Iranian sins from supporting growing violence in Iraq to terrorism, also enabled Rice to get UN Security Council support for setting a deadline of August 31 for the Iranians to agree to cease their enrichment activities—and, if they didn't, to pursue the imposition of strong sanctions. The August date came and went without any Iranian response.

Rumsfeld would later write that the diplomatic outreach yielded no significant concessions even as Iran accelerated its illegal weapons programs, continued to fund Hezbollah, crushed domestic dissidents, escalated attacks against U.S. troops in Iraq, and continued to threaten Israel. All Rumsfeld said was true. I believe, however, that the U.S. initiative was effective win-win diplomacy: Iran would either agree to cease enrichment and accept the U.S. inducements to improve the relationship or, if it refused, give the United States leverage to get other countries to join in tougher sanctions.

Bush's strategy worked. The UN Security Council on December 23, 2006, condemned Iran for failing to stop its enrichment of uranium, and imposed new sanctions aimed at keeping Iran from importing technology and materials that could be used to advance its nuclear and ballistic missile programs as well as freezing the assets of individuals and companies in Iran associated with the nuclear program.

Embargoes, freezing assets, restrictions on trade, and other such economic sanctions were nonmilitary techniques long used by the United States and others to punish governments or get them to change their policies. But, in the fall of 2006, in addition to securing international sanctions through the UN, the Bush administration developed new methods of imposing economic pain on Iran that could be applied unilaterally. The effort, led by Stuart Levey, the undersecretary of the treasury for terrorism and financial intelligence, involved using executive orders, a section of the Patriot Act, and other measures to blacklist Iranian individuals and institutions supporting proliferation, money laundering, and terrorism. The United States pressured European and other governments as well as international financial institutions and companies to shun investments in and financial dealings with Iran. The United States also blacklisted some of Iran's biggest banks as well as individuals and companies associated with the IRGC. As Rice later wrote, "Forced to choose between their activities in Iran or access to the United States financial system, many Western institutions opted to scale back their operations in Tehran." Economic measures, once again, proved to be an important instrument of power.

Unlike Clinton before him or Obama after him, Bush also brought to bear a panoply of other nonmilitary tools in the national security kit. In 2002, the administration began a major effort to get information and news directly to the Iranian people. That year, Voice of America established the Persian News Network and, together with Radio Free Europe/Radio Liberty, created Radio Farda. The administration ratcheted up such programs in February 2006 when Rice asked for $75 million in supplemental funding to support U.S. democracy and cultural diplomacy initiatives in Iran. She told the Senate Foreign Relations Committee that the funding would be used to increase "exchanges" with Iranian professionals and students, and to increase U.S. radio broadcasting service. Cheney and Rumsfeld wanted to go even further in supporting opposition groups in Iran, but others worried that U.S. support to specific groups, even if covert, would put them at greater risk and allow the regime to label them as tools of the Americans. Even so, critics characterized the efforts Bush approved as support for "regime change" by another name. They also charged that such endeavors eliminated any chance Tehran would negotiate limits on their nuclear program. U.S. restraint from aggressively encouraging internal opposition and from publicizing the regime's corruption and repression failed to bring Tehran to the negotiating table. Only the most punishing economic sanctions by Obama would accomplish that goal.

As someone who had watched firsthand similar Cold War initiatives intended to encourage and support those in the USSR and Eastern Europe seeking observance of human and political rights and to let them know they had not been forgotten, I thought the administration's efforts were to be applauded. Inasmuch as the Iranian leaders consistently blamed the United States for any internal challenge or protest anyway, it seemed to me there was little risk in trying to do what we were already being blamed for. The key was to be cautious in the extreme about supporting any specific group, to avoid inciting people to violence, and to discourage unrealistic expectations about U.S. military help. Nearly everyone in the administration knew the United States could not, on its own, bring regime change to Iran. Such change could only come from within.

Bush did a lot more than Clinton to encourage such change, but we could and should have done more, then and later. There was still an ambitious menu of economic sanctions that might have been applied to both the country and its leaders (as would be imposed by both Obama and Trump). There was no support for opposition groups, no effort to use surrogates for sabotage or to provoke social discontent. There was no effort to send back to Iran children of regime leaders who were studying in U.S. or European universities as a means of punishing the ruling elite. Nor was there any serious effort to covertly interrupt the flow of Iranian weapons and financing to Hezbollah and Hamas. There wasn't even a global campaign to encourage our friends and allies to expand cultural, athletic, and academic exchange programs with Iran in the hope of exposing Iranian youth to the world their clerical leaders were trying to keep at bay. Each measure would have involved downsides and risks, but some should have been tried. Not to pursue every possible sanction and nonmilitary measure to stop Iran's nuclear program and every possible avenue to give moral and other support to those in Iran seeking democratic reform was contrary to our national interest.

Bush continued to tighten the economic screws on Iran for the rest of his term in office. He and Rice succeeded in getting three more UN Security Council resolutions supporting that objective, each one with the support of—or lack of opposition from—Russia and China. Rice gained Russia's support, in some measure, by approaching her counterpart, Sergei Lavrov, in September 2007 to inquire whether Putin could get the message to Khamenei that the United States was interested in solving the nuclear problem and to see whether the Iranians were interested too. According to Rice, Putin delivered the message. The failure of the Iranians to follow up in any way angered the Russians, and by late fall, Moscow's attitude toward Tehran had "soured significantly."

In the same September conversation with Lavrov, Rice also told him she was thinking about opening in Tehran a U.S. interests section, a diplomatic outpost handling routine matters with less status than an embassy, much as we had in Havana for many years. Rice saw it as an opportunity to have a presence in Iran, which we had lacked since 1979—a place where Iranians could get visas and interact with American diplomats, and for those diplomats to be visible in the Iranian capital. As an old intelligence officer, I strongly supported the idea because it would give us the opportunity both overtly and covertly to get better "ground truth" about what was actually going on inside the country, not to mention a base for operations.

Cheney was opposed, believing it sent the wrong signal—that we were interested in "normalizing" the relationship. In any event, five Iranian fast boats took aggressive action toward three American warships in January 2008, and the U.S. ships came within a hair's breadth of sinking them before they turned away. That action sunk the idea of an interests section.

Bush's efforts to strengthen the sanctions on Iran by getting other countries to cooperate suffered a terrible setback in December 2007 when, as noted previously, a National Intelligence Estimate was issued—and made public—concluding that Iran had "halted" its nuclear weapons program in 2003. The same day it was released, Chancellor Angela Merkel had a meeting scheduled with German industrial leaders to encourage them to stop dealing with Iran. After National Security Adviser Steve Hadley called his counterpart in Merkel's office, Christoph Heusgen, to forewarn him about the estimate, Merkel canceled the meeting. It took months for Secretary Rice and the rest of the administration to get the UN sanctions effort back on track. Such are the vagaries of policy making in the United States.

Because so many of Bush's critics at home and abroad regarded him as trigger-happy in light of U.S. actions in Afghanistan and Iraq, throughout 2007–8 many were alarmed that the president was considering a military attack to eliminate the Iranian nuclear program. Every time we reported some new hostile Iranian action—from providing explosively formed projectiles (a particularly deadly shell that could penetrate an Abrams tank) to Shia militias attacking our troops in Iraq to sending arms to Hezbollah and Hamas—critics at home alleged that Bush was simply building the case for an attack.

The issue of a possible attack actually came to a head inside the administration in May 2007, when the president met with his senior advisers to consider an Israeli request for military equipment that would significantly enhance their ability to strike Iranian nuclear facilities. Vice President Cheney argued strongly that if we were not prepared to take out those facilities militarily ourselves, we should enable the Israelis to do so. The rest of us were opposed to giving the Israelis the capability to take independent action that would have profound consequences for American interests both regionally and globally. Bush ultimately deflected the Israeli request but, using other tools at his disposal, directed a significant ramping up of intelligence sharing with them and joint development of nonmilitary means of slowing Iran's nuclear weapons program. We further increased our military presence and capabilities in the Persian Gulf area both to reassure our allies and to give the president options should the Iranians make military action necessary.

The Israelis weren't the only ones trying to pressure the United States to act against Iran. King Abdullah of Saudi Arabia told Rice and me in the summer of 2007 that Bush should wipe out the entire

Iranian military. The Israelis kept after us to give them the military wherewithal to go after the nuclear facilities. To show they were serious, in mid-June 2007 they held a military exercise in which they flew more than one hundred fighters to Greece and back, also deploying refueling tankers and rescue helicopters. The distance flown was 862 nautical miles. The distance from their home airfield to the Iranian nuclear facility at Natanz was 860 nautical miles.

Because Bush was personally so close to then Israeli prime minister Ehud Olmert and Saudi king Abdullah, and because Cheney offered both the Israelis and the Saudis a direct pipeline into the White House, I continued to worry that Bush might change his mind about launching a preventive attack. I was just as worried as Cheney about Iran's program. However, because congressional acquiescence in the surge in Iraq hung by a thread, I was convinced any Bush-directed attack on Iran would almost certainly provoke Congress into cutting off all funding for the war in Iraq and mandating the immediate return of all U.S. troops—which to me meant certain defeat in Iraq. I also had high hopes for the nonmilitary options against Iran the president had approved. My strongest argument with both Bush and Cheney was that taking military action against Iran would risk the improvements in security and reduction in violence we had made at great cost in Iraq by the end of 2007. Only later would I realize that Bush had already made up his mind not to act militarily unless Iran forced him to do so.

By the end of the Bush administration, through effective U.S. diplomacy, the UN Security Council had passed four separate resolutions successively tightening the sanctions on Iran. The Bush team developed and applied an array of new financial measures targeting the regime, its leaders, and key institutions such as the IRGC. Our ability to communicate our message inside Iran had been significantly improved. We also had deployed two carrier strike groups in the Gulf to demonstrate our resolve and taken other measures to slow the Iranian nuclear program. Finally, the administration took steps to strengthen the military and intelligence capabilities of our allies in the region to push back against Iranian meddling, interference, and support for terrorist groups such as Hezbollah and Hamas.

At the same time, Bush, like Clinton, authorized several serious overtures to the Iranians not just to negotiate over their nuclear program but also to discuss how to change the direction of the overall relationship. While there had been potential opportunities for progress while Khatami was president, ultimately Clinton and Bush both learned the Iranian president could not challenge the authority of the ayatollah and the clerics. The United States reached out to Ahmadinejad after the 2005 Iranian election, to no avail. Consistent with his "freedom agenda," Bush approved a much more aggressive effort than Clinton had to communicate U.S. support for reform and an authentically open democracy to the Iranian population. We could not bring about regime change, but the message was clear that America was on the side of the young people, women, and others in Iran who wanted more freedom.

Ayatollah Khamenei, like Khomeini before him, was not interested in a better relationship with the Great Satan. At the end of 2008, he was intent on pursuing Iran's nuclear weapons program and striving to expand Iranian—and Shia—influence in Iraq and throughout the Middle East. Contrary to impressions at the time, Bush reached out to Tehran at several junctures while he was president. Like Clinton, he received no positive response. Bush had been effective in bringing to bear a number of diverse instruments of American power to intensify the economic, military, and internal pressures on the clerical regime. He led the symphony well, but the ayatollah and President Ahmadinejad weren't listening.

More than either of his post–Cold War predecessors, I think Barack Obama wanted a "Nixon in China" moment—successful outreach to a longtime American adversary that changed a relationship of global importance and earned a special place in the history books. In 2009, there were only three countries that met that standard: Cuba, North Korea, and Iran. The latter two had ongoing nuclear weapons and ballistic missile development programs, and both already posed a regional security challenge. North Korea had agreed to limits on its nuclear program in 1994 but cheated and ultimately abandoned the deal. Iran, as we've seen, had rejected all proposals from Clinton and Bush that might limit its programs. As primary financial supporter and arms supplier to the terrorist group Hezbollah, a threat to both Israel and the United States, and an aggressive meddler in Sunni Arab states in the region, Iran represented the biggest potential prize for Obama. Reaching out to the Iranians was clearly on his agenda from day one of his presidency, and both diplomacy and strategic communications—the spoken word—were his chosen instruments.

Obama first signaled a willingness to engage with Iran in his inaugural address, in which he told the Muslim world that "we seek a new way forward, based on mutual interest and mutual respect." He told autocrats of all stripes that they were on the wrong side of history (a formulation he would use often in the future) and said that "we will extend a hand if you are willing to unclench your fist." A week later, on January 26, Obama made the outreach to Iran explicit in an interview with the Al-Arabiya news channel, saying, "I do think that it is important for us to be willing to talk to Iran, to express very clearly where our differences are, but where there are potential avenues for progress. And we will over the next several months be laying out our general framework and approach. And as I said during my inauguration speech, if countries like Iran are willing to unclench their fist, they will find an extended hand from us."

Twice in the spring of 2009, Obama wrote letters to the ayatollah expressing his interest in an improved relationship. Based on everything I had witnessed as secretary of defense during the Bush administration and before, I was deeply pessimistic the letters would yield any positive results. In our discussions about the letters in the Situation Room, though, I did not oppose Obama's sending them because I believed such outreach efforts, when rebuffed, would only enhance our position with other countries in applying more coercive instruments of power, such as strengthened sanctions and other nonmilitary measures. Sure enough, the responses from Khamenei were diatribes of rejection.

In March, Obama also telecast a New Year's (Nowruz) message to Iran. He was widely criticized by conservatives and others for doing so despite the fact that Bush had also sent such greetings. There was a difference, though. Bush's broadcast messages were generally quite short and aimed at the Iranian people, although his 2008 message was followed by an interview on Voice of America in which he criticized Iran's leaders for decisions that made life hard for the people, and promised that there was a way forward if only the leaders would agree to verifiably suspend enrichment of uranium. Obama's message was addressed to both the people and their leaders, and was much more forthcoming. He avowed that he was committed to diplomacy addressing the full range of issues between the two countries, pursuing constructive ties, and seeking "engagement that is honest and grounded in mutual respect."

Obama's outreach to Iran drove the Israelis and Arab states nuts. They feared that Obama might be willing to reach a "grand bargain" reconciling the United States and Iran, thus giving the latter freer rein to extend its influence and power in the region. From the early months of 2009, Obama's relationships with leaders in Israel and the Gulf states steadily deteriorated because of that.

In fact, Obama wanted to change the tone and nature of U.S. policy in the Middle East more broadly. He believed that a long history of American political, military, and, in some cases, economic support for autocratic, corrupt regimes, as well as our protracted military conflicts in Afghanistan and Iraq, had been contrary to both our values and our long-term interests in the region. He indicated soon after he became president that he wanted to make a speech in a major Middle Eastern city, and he did so in Cairo on June 4. Although criticized by some at home as an apology for previous American policies in the region, it was well received locally. I think it was one of his best foreign policy speeches—honest and forthright, and focused on the future. Sadly, because there was no policy framework or strategy underpinning or following up on the speech, its impact had the half-life of a bottle rocket.

In the exercise of power, speeches and good intentions are not enough. Strategic planning, specific measures, effective implementation, and consistent follow-through—the integrated use of multiple instruments of power—are essential to success, as we will see in the pages ahead.

Obama spoke directly about Iran in the Cairo speech, repeating and elaborating on his earlier messages. He commented on the U.S. involvement in the 1953 coup that overthrew a "democratically elected" Iranian government—as Madeleine Albright had done in 2000—as well as problems posed by Iran's nuclear program, its support for hostage taking and violence against U.S. troops and civilians, and the "tumultuous history between us." But he went on to say,

> Rather than remain trapped in the past, I've made it clear to Iran's leaders and people that my country is prepared to move forward. The question, now, is not what Iran is against, but rather what future it wants to build. I recognize it will be hard to overcome decades of mistrust, but we will proceed with courage, rectitude, and resolve. There will be many issues to discuss between our two countries, and we are willing to move forward without preconditions on the basis of mutual respect.

Eight days later, in a rigged national election, the hard-line Ahmadinejad was reelected president of Iran. Months of protests ensued by pro-democracy opponents of the regime, mainly young people who were subjected to a severe government crackdown. Known as the Green Movement, this opposition confronted Obama with a serious challenge: how far to go in denouncing the unfair election and supporting the demonstrators. Critics then and subsequently have alleged that the administration soft-pedaled its response in order not to undercut the outreach efforts to the Iranian leadership. I was in on the debate in the Situation Room and I can attest that it focused, rather, on whether aggressive American support for the demonstrators would allow the government to portray them as agents of U.S. interference. Obama ended up condemning the violence of government repression and urging that the democratic process be respected. But in general, the U.S. reaction was pretty low-key, much more muted than, say, Bush 41's imposition of sanctions in response to the repression of demonstrators in Tiananmen Square in Beijing twenty years earlier.

We should have exercised our power more aggressively. The Iranian government was unlikely to react to the demonstrators more violently than it already had, and it was going to blame the United States for instigating the protests in any case. Ironically, Iranian opposition leaders urged Obama to take a tougher line. We should have used some of the new tools at our disposal—such as the Persian-language VOA programming and other broadcast resources created during the Bush administration—to publicize both the protests and the government's repressive response. We could have found the means, clandestine or otherwise, to get our message into Iran, and we could have imposed additional unilateral economic sanctions. We missed an opportunity to send a strong message of support to advocates of democracy inside Iran—and elsewhere—with little or no military risk.

Obama underestimated just how much the clerics and Ahmadinejad loathed the Great Satan and were determined to go their own way. In September 2009, U.S. intelligence discovered a new, undeclared nuclear enrichment facility near Qom, less than eighty miles from Tehran. On September 21, the Iranian government quietly sent a letter to the IAEA admitting to the existence of a "small pilot project" at the site. Two days later, Obama and Secretary Clinton met with Russian president Dimitri Medvedev and Foreign Minister Lavrov at the UN and informed them about the facility at Qom. And on September 25, at the G20 summit in Pittsburgh, Obama, British prime minister Gordon Brown, and French president Nicolas Sarkozy made the information public, stating that the "size and configuration of this facility is inconsistent with a peaceful program. Iran is breaking rules that all nations follow." A few days later, Iran agreed to allow IAEA inspectors to visit the secret site.

The Obama administration made one further effort in 2009 to address Iran's nuclear program diplomatically. The previous summer, Iran had announced that the Tehran Research Reactor, which produced isotopes for the diagnosis and treatment of disease, was running out of fuel. Senior State Department officer Robert Einhorn came up with an ingenious proposal that Iran send 80 percent of its low-enriched uranium to Russia, where it would be further enriched and sent onward to France for conversion into fuel rods—rendering the nuclear material unsuitable for creating a bomb—and then returned to Iran to power the Tehran reactor. It was a way to get most of Iran's enriched uranium out of the country, thereby dramatically slowing, if not stopping, Iranian development of a nuclear weapon. The UK, France, Germany, China, and Russia all supported the proposal, and the Iranian negotiator did as well. Agreement was reached on October 22. But the hard-liners in Tehran prevailed once again, and Iran withdrew its agreement the next day. It had been a creative diplomatic initiative, even though it failed.

Despite using every diplomatic and rhetorical means of outreach, despite bending over backward to entice a dialogue, Obama had hit the same brick wall as Clinton and Bush before him (not to mention Carter, Reagan, and Bush 41). Khamenei—and Ahmadinejad—had no interest in engaging with the United States or in any agreement curtailing its nuclear program. Nine months of the "extended hand" had produced zero progress.

And so, in the fall of 2009, the administration pivoted to the application of different, more coercive instruments of power. For the next four years, Obama and his team built on the international sanctions regime established through four UN Security Council resolutions obtained by Bush and unilateral sanctions imposed by both Bush and Congress. Iran would be squeezed by economic instruments of power as never before, even as Obama and Secretary Clinton kept the door open to engagement.

The first step was to get another Security Council resolution, targeting the IRGC, arms sales, financial transactions, and oil exports. China relied heavily on imports of oil from Iran and, further, after a U.S. arms sale to Taiwan in January 2010, was in no mood to help Washington. Russia's behavior was mixed. Medvedev acknowledged to Obama that the United States had been right about Iran's nuclear and missile ambitions. The Russians refrained from selling the highly sophisticated S-300 antiaircraft missile system to Iran and finally broke the contract. Yet, while the Russians didn't block efforts to get new UN sanctions against Iran, they worked tirelessly to water them down. In contrast, the French were aggressively supportive of new sanctions, President Sarkozy telling me face-to-face that "Iranians are liars" and the "extended hand" was "a waste of time, a sign of weakness." Thanks to U.S. efforts, a new UN resolution imposing additional sanctions was passed on June 9, 2010. Three weeks later, Obama signed into law the Comprehensive Iran Sanctions, Account-ability, and Divestment Act, further adding to the pressure on Iran.

From 2010 to 2013, the United States went after Iran's oil industry, banks, and weapons programs with a vengeance. In an effort to fur-ther isolate Iran economically, the administration obtained the coop-eration of shipping lines, insurance companies, financial institutions, and others. The EU agreed to a full boycott of Iranian oil. Assistant secretary of the treasury for terrorist financing (later undersecretary) David Cohen, following in the footsteps of his Bush administration predecessor, Stuart Levey, developed additional instruments of eco-nomic and financial power to enforce the sanctions against Iran. The United States froze the assets of Iranian banks, made it impos-sible for Iranian oil tankers to get insurance, and cut off access to the global financial system. Individuals, companies, and countries found themselves sanctioned. It seemed like new sanctions on Iran were announced every few months, touching every part of the economy except food and medicine. Using the UN Security Council resolutions as a foundation, Washington relied on presidential executive orders, actions by the Treasury Department, and legislation. Financial institu-tions around the world were warned that they had to choose between doing business in the United States or in Iran. Predictably, they cut ties to Iran. All in all, new sanctions were imposed on Iran or those doing business with it more than two dozen times from 2010 to 2013.

By the end of 2012, the economic pressure finally began to have an impact. The previous year, the sultan of Oman had offered to broker—and host—a secret direct dialogue between the United States and Iran. Both sides were skittish and, despite several meetings, nothing of consequence emerged until late 2012, when the Omanis believed the Iranians were ready to move. Accordingly, the two sides met in March 2013 in Muscat, the United States represented by the State Department's undersecretary for policy, Bill Burns, and the Ira-nians by a deputy foreign minister. There still was no progress. As Secretary Clinton later wrote, powerful forces in Tehran seemed to be holding back the negotiations.

In the background, the ayatollah hinted publicly at growing divi-

sions in Tehran over talking with the United States, and his public remarks in February and March demonstrated a shift in his own
thinking. In early February 2013, Khamenei rejected an offer made a
few days earlier by Vice President Biden for direct talks, saying, "Some
naive people like the idea of negotiating with America. However, negotiations will not solve the problem." Nine days later, he claimed that
while Tehran had no intention of building nuclear weapons, "America
would not have been able to stop the Iranian nation in any way." Yet,
just over a month later, in a speech on the Iranian new year, Khamenei
said he wasn't opposed to direct talks with the United States but wasn't
optimistic about the prospects for success.

Those prospects changed on June 15, 2013, when Hassan Rouhani
was elected president of Iran in a landslide. Ahmadinejad's policies
and bluster, combined with the sanctions, had isolated Iran and made
the lives of ordinary Iranians even more difficult. They turned out in
droves to vote for change—for reform. Almost immediately after Rouhani took office in August, conciliatory messages began to flow out
of Tehran. President Obama sent a letter to Rouhani, and in contrast
to his previous letters to the Iranian leaders, he received a positive
response. Behind the scenes, the dormant Omani channel for direct
U.S.-Iranian talks on the nuclear problem finally became active, with
the Iranian representatives empowered to negotiate.

The election of Rouhani was important to any change of approach
in Tehran. But, as with Rafsanjani, Khatami, and Ahmadinejad, Ayatollah Khamenei continued to hold ultimate power and make the big
decisions. It seems pretty clear that by the spring of 2013 he and those
close to him feared the regime was increasingly at risk from popular
unrest as the sanctions-afflicted economy worsened. The Green Movement in 2009 had been a warning, and life in Iran in subsequent
years had gotten much more dire as the sanctions noose tightened.
Unlike North Korea, Iran's economy and its people were globally con-
nected, thus making the regime—and the general population—much
more sensitive to the impact of the sanctions. The ayatollah did not
come to the nuclear bargaining table voluntarily. He was forced there
by American economic power.

After two decades at an impasse, negotiations on Iran's nuclear program began to move during the fall of 2013. On September 26, the foreign ministers of the P5+1 countries and Iran met during the UN General Assembly session and agreed to resume negotiations in Geneva. Secretary of State John Kerry and Iranian foreign minister Mohammad Javad Zarif met on the sidelines, the first-ever meeting at that level. While Obama and Rouhani were in New York, they had a telephone conversation on September 27, another first.

Negotiators from the P5+1 and Iran met in Geneva as planned in mid-October, and a breakthrough appeared imminent during the subsequent session in early November, only to be blocked at the last minute, reportedly by French demands for tougher terms. I heard gossip in Washington that the French interceded in no small part because they were concerned that Secretary of State Kerry, desperate for a deal, was negotiating poorly. Concerns about Kerry's ardor for an agreement as his legacy appear to have been shared by Obama himself. According to Peter Baker in his book *Obama: The Call of History,* at one point Obama tried to "restrain" Kerry, saying, "It would be better to give up than to have a bad deal. 'John, I've already got my legacy,' Obama told him, referring to health care and other achievements. 'I don't need this.'"

On November 24, an interim agreement was reached. The six-month time limit in the agreement was to allow time for negotiation of a "comprehensive and permanent" settlement that would allow Iran a peaceful nuclear program, but with limits and inspections to provide assurance that any covert program would be discovered long before Iran could build a nuclear bomb.

The six-month deadline to negotiate a permanent nuclear deal was wildly optimistic. A tentative long-term agreement was not announced until April 2, 2015, and the final agreement—the Joint Comprehensive Plan of Action (JCPOA)—was signed in Vienna on July 14. The Iranians made an open-ended commitment not to "engage in activities, including at the research and development level, that could contribute to the development of a nuclear explosive device." Once Iran implemented all the provisions of the agreement, UN Security Council sanctions as well as economic embargoes imposed by the United States and the EU associated with the nuclear program would be lifted. Sanctions imposed on Iran by the United States unrelated to the nuclear programs—for example, for terrorist-related activities—would remain in place.

While Iran's ballistic missile development program was not addressed in the JCPOA, a unanimous UN Security Council resolution approved five days after the nuclear agreement was signed contained an eight-year restriction on Iranian nuclear-capable ballistic missile activities. The resolution called upon Iran "not to undertake any activity related to ballistic missiles designed to be capable of delivering nuclear weapons, including launches using such ballistic missile technology." The Iranians denied their missiles were designed for weapons of mass destruction and claimed their program was "outside the purview or competence of the Security Council resolution." The ballistic missile restriction in the resolution had no enforcement mechanism.

The JCPOA was controversial from the outset. There were two main threads to the criticism: the terms of the agreement itself and the consequences for the region. Regarding the agreement, critics pointed out Obama's statement in 2012 saying that the only deal with Iran he'd accept was "that they end their nuclear program." While the agreement purportedly increased the break-out time (how long it would take Iran to produce a bomb after abandoning the agreement) from a few months to a year, the agreement only bought time. Further, the administration had said publicly in April that "anytime, anyplace" inspections were core to effective monitoring—a U.S. position that was abandoned between April and July. Subsequent to signing, the Iranians repeatedly took the position that military sites were off-limits to the inspectors, denying them access to the most obvious sites for cheating.

Other critics were concerned that the agreement failed to address Iran's subversive activities as well as its support for Hezbollah, Syrian president Bashar Hafez al-Assad, and the Houthi rebellion in Yemen. They were outraged that lifting the sanctions might bring a windfall of as much as $100 billion to the regime in Tehran, some significant portion of which would be used to fund its military and strategic ambitions. Israel and the Gulf Arabs were especially hostile to the agreement as empowering Iran and made no secret of their views, further fueling opposition in the United States. Moreover, Obama was accused of soft-pedaling during the negotiations any criticism of the Iranian regime over its support for Assad in Syria's civil war and other actions lest he upset the Iranians and jeopardize the agreement. The observation was often made that the Iranians *needed* the agreement more, but Obama *wanted* it more.

Obama defended the agreement as a "good deal" and argued that the diplomatic solution was preferable to the use of military power to reduce or eliminate Iran's nuclear capability. In response to the criticism that the agreement failed to address Iran's imperial ambitions in the region, the administration countered that no arms control arrangement between the United States and the USSR ever addressed non-nuclear issues between the parties, and that their objective had been solely to stop Iran's march toward nuclear weapons.

The problem, of course, was that both Obama and his critics had valid points. As I had argued when I was secretary of defense, a military attack would only delay the Iranian program by one to three years and would make them all the more determined to build a nuclear weapons capability and do it all the more secretly. With Iranian agreement to the JCPOA, there was little likelihood other countries, especially Russia and China, would be willing to maintain or reimpose severe sanctions. So the alternatives to a negotiated deal were considerably less appealing than the deal that was signed. Yet, there was a lingering feeling, even among those who accepted the agreement, that Obama had been too eager to get an agreement, and that tougher negotiating on issues such as inspections would have resulted in better terms.

Obama further opened himself and his team to harsh criticism by failing to state publicly immediately after signing the agreement that the United States would use other instruments of power to resist Iranian support for terrorist groups such as Hezbollah and Hamas, and work with our friends and allies in the region to counter Iran's regional ambitions, meddling, and interference in Arab states. Moreover, while the UN Security Council resolution calling on Iran not to develop ballistic missiles capable of carrying a nuclear weapon lacked any enforcement mechanism, the United States could have used the resolution as leverage to threaten unilateral action and pressure allies to impose heavy costs on Iran for violating its restrictions. The president also had the opportunity to provide reassurance that the United States would use both military and nonmilitary means to contain Iran's imperial ambitions, and that any Iranian effort to use the vast sums of money suddenly available after the lifting of sanctions for nefarious purposes in the region would be resisted. The irony is that the ayatollah gave a speech declaring plainly that the agreement would not limit Iran's non-nuclear activities beyond its borders. Obama's silence in this regard and his soft-pedaling of criticism of Iran before and after signature of the JCPOA gave much fodder to critics at home and abroad. It was an unforced error that gave credence to the idea that a breakthrough with Iran was his top priority.

I worked closely with Barack Obama for two and a half years as his secretary of defense, and I believe his approach to the nuclear deal was driven primarily by his core beliefs and aspirations. He is, at heart, an optimistic progressive. He truly believes there is such a thing as the "arc of history" and that, in the long run, it bends toward justice and peace. I think Obama agreed to a time-limited, flawed agreement with Iran mainly because he was convinced it was better than any of the alternatives, and that a new generation of leaders over the time span of the agreement would result in an Iran open to commerce and interchange with the rest of the world—an Iran treated with respect by other nations that would dramatically change its outlook and behavior. Obama believed that Iran would become more democratic and less dominated by the conservative, harshly anti-American clerics and, over time, decide not to pursue a nuclear weapons capability. In 2015, he made a big bet based mainly on his gut feeling that by 2025 Iran would become a different country. It was a risky bet.

During Donald Trump's campaign for president, he excoriated the Iran nuclear deal, calling it the "worst deal" ever, and promised that, if elected, he would tear it up. He also accused Obama of ignoring Iranian support for terrorists and its aggressive behavior in the region in order to get the nuclear deal. Once Trump was elected, unlike Bush and Obama, there was no invitation to dialogue or expression of interest in a better relationship between the United States and Iran.

Quite the contrary. When Iran provocatively tested a ballistic missile little more than a week after Trump's inauguration, his national security adviser, Michael Flynn, on February 2 appeared before the White House press corps to announce that the administration was putting Iran "on notice" that the United States would take action against Iran unless it stopped testing missiles (as I believe Obama should have done in 2015) and supporting the Houthi rebels in Yemen. Flynn accused Iran of threatening U.S. allies and spreading instability throughout the Middle East and also criticized the Obama administration for doing too little to stop such behavior. Announcing new sanctions on Iran, Flynn said that Iran's "belligerent and lawless" behavior had only increased since signing the JCPOA in 2015, and that "the international community has been too tolerant of Iran's bad behavior." Flynn warned that "the days of turning a blind eye to Iran's hostile and belligerent actions toward the United States and the world community are over." I think Flynn was reflecting Trump's visceral loathing of everything Obama had done, especially the Iran deal. In office less than two weeks, the new administration sent a strong message that its approach to Iran would be much different and far more hard-line than its predecessor.

Trump's first foreign trip was to Saudi Arabia in May 2017, and he used the occasion to firmly align the United States with the Saudis in their regional conflict with Iran. Two days after Hassan Rouhani had won reelection as president of Iran, Trump, speaking before the leaders of fifty Muslim countries in Riyadh on May 21, reassured them that the United States would no longer condition its support on observance of human rights and progress toward democracy: "Our partnerships will advance security through stability, not through radical disruption. . . . And, wherever possible, we will seek gradual reforms—not sudden intervention. We must seek partners, not perfection."

The president reserved his strongest remarks, though, for Iran:

No discussion of stamping out this threat [terrorism] would be complete without mentioning the government that gives terrorists . . . safe harbor, financial backing, and the social standing needed for recruitment. It is a regime that is responsible for so much instability in the region. I am speaking of course of Iran. From Lebanon to Iraq to Yemen, Iran funds, arms, and trains terrorists, militias, and other extremist groups that spread destruction and chaos across the region. For decades, Iran has fueled the fires of sectarian conflict and terror. It is a government that speaks openly of mass murder, vowing the destruction of Israel, death to America, and ruin for many leaders and nations in this room. . . . Until the Iranian regime is willing to be a partner for peace, all nations of conscience must work together to isolate Iran, deny it funding for terrorism, and pray for the day when the Iranian people have the just and righteous government they deserve.

Trump faced two problems in trying to get rid of the nuclear agreement with Iran. The first was that Iran was not in violation of the JCPOA, as affirmed by both the IAEA and the other signatories of the agreement. Second, the agreement was a multilateral one supported by our closest allies in Europe as well as Russia and China. No one else was interested in "tearing up" the deal, especially inasmuch as the IAEA consistently was reporting that the Iranians were in compliance with its terms, at least with regard to its nuclear program. Unilateral action by Washington would isolate the United States, not Iran, and as long as Iran remained in compliance, the United States would have a difficult time getting anyone else to agree to reimposing economic sanctions.

Congress meanwhile had provided the president a way to demonstrate his unhappiness with the deal. Mistrusting Obama, critical of the nuclear agreement, and frustrated that the JCPOA did not require legislative approval, a Republican-controlled Congress in 2015 passed the Iran Nuclear Agreement Review Act mandating that every ninety days the president must certify to the Congress that Iran was fully implementing the JCPOA and, more vaguely, that the president believed the suspension of sanctions on Iran was appropriate and proportionate to the measures taken by Iran and vital to U.S. national security interests. Trump wanted to decertify the JCPOA from the day he became president but was persuaded by his advisers—especially Secretary of State Rex Tillerson and Secretary of Defense James Mattis—to certify it in April and July. Trump signed on through gritted teeth and made clear that he was unlikely to do so at the next required certification, in October 2017.

On October 13, the president announced that he would not certify the JCPOA to Congress. He used the occasion to make a major speech describing a new U.S. strategy toward Iran, a strategy—at least on paper—much tougher than his predecessors'. Trump reviewed the anti-American actions of the Iranian regime since the 1979 revolution and the threats posed by its support for terrorist groups, missile programs, harassment of U.S. naval ships, and cyber attacks. He spoke about Tehran's fueling of sectarian violence in Iraq and in the Syrian and Yemeni civil wars. The nuclear deal, Trump again asserted, "was one of the worst and most one-sided transactions the United States has ever entered into" and "threw Iran's dictatorship a political and economic lifeline." He recounted his view of the agreement's many deficiencies.

Trump then announced a new American strategy to address the full range of "Iran's destructive actions." We would work with allies to counter the regime's destabilizing activity and support for terrorist proxies, impose additional sanctions, address the proliferation of Iran's missiles and weapons, and deny the regime all paths to a nuclear weapon. One of the few specific steps he mentioned to implement the strategy was imposing new sanctions on the entire Iranian Islamic Revolutionary Guard Corps. Trump said his administration would work with Congress and U.S. allies to fix the many serious flaws in the agreement, including the time limits and failure to include Iran's missile programs. He warned that if these efforts failed, the United States would terminate the agreement.

Seven months later, on May 8, 2018, he did just that, announcing that the United States would withdraw from the JCPOA and reimpose sanctions on Iran. He justified the action on the grounds that the agreement didn't address the threat of Iran's ballistic missiles or its behavior in the region, and that the expiration dates opened the door to Iranian nuclear weapons in the future. He added, "It didn't bring calm, it didn't bring peace, and it never will."

Just two weeks later, on May 21, Secretary of State Mike Pompeo, in his first major speech as secretary, focused entirely on Iran. He cataloged the regime's corruption, mistreatment of its own people, widespread violation of human rights, and the economic hardship it imposed on the Iranian people. Pompeo then listed the steps the regime would need to take for a new agreement, including an end to all nuclear enrichment; admission of the military purposes of their dormant nuclear program; an end to support of Hezbollah, Hamas, and the Houthis in Yemen; withdrawal of all its forces from Syria; and an end to the production of ballistic missiles. The scope of the demands made clear there was no U.S. interest in pursuing a new agreement, and that the American attitude toward the clerical government in Iran under Trump would be one of unremitting hostility. Even more crippling sanctions aimed at cutting off all Iranian oil exports were imposed in 2019.

I n the first half of 2018, the Iranian regime was confronted with widespread protests. Protests were nothing new: university students and unemployed youth organized one in 1999 after the closure of a reform newspaper; there were more demonstrations by students in 2003 and by women in 2005–6, and in June 2009 after a rigged election. Most of these events were concentrated in Tehran. But the nationwide protests in early 2018 and the following summer, in multiple cities and towns, seemed different. They began in January in the eastern city of Mashhad and quickly spread to provincial towns across the country. Many of the demonstrations were in economically disadvantaged rural provinces. The target initially was President Rouhani's austerity budget, which included welfare cuts and price increases for fuel and basic commodities but also revealed huge sums of money being allocated to the IRGC and the military as well as organizations controlled by the clerics. The protesters also focused on the weak economy, strict

Islamist rules, water shortages, and corruption. Demonstrations against economic mismanagement swiftly expanded into denunciation of privileged elites, Rouhani and the so-called "reformers," and even the ayatollah himself. Protesters' signs for once didn't read DEATH TO GREAT SATAN but DEATH TO THE FREE-LOADING BIG-WIGS and DEATH TO UNEMPLOYMENT. I wonder how the ayatollah reacted to the signs that read DEATH TO THE DICTATOR—the same words used in demonstrations against the shah in 1978–79. Shouts of "Death to Khamenei" and "Death to Rouhani," as well as against Iranian involvement in Gaza and Lebanon, revealed an underlying lack of support for the regime and for the money it was spending on its adventures abroad. The security forces suppressed the protests within a few days but only after some two dozen demonstrators had been killed and several thousand arrested.

After the January 2018 unrest, both Khamenei and Rouhani were at pains to acknowledge publicly for the first time the legitimate grievances of the demonstrators. Khamenei said, "Their voices should be attended, heard, and responded to. We should all pursue that." Their concern presumably was heightened because most of the protesters were not political opponents in Tehran or university students, but people in rural and provincial areas who in the past had been staunch supporters of the regime. Their unhappiness at being left behind economically represented a much more serious problem for the clerics and the government.

The depth of popular discontent was exposed most dramatically in November 2019, when an increase in fuel prices provoked widespread, protracted protests across Iran that quickly turned anti-regime (and against the supreme leader) and violent. Facing the largest, longest-lasting, and most violent and widespread protests since seizing power in 1979, the regime resorted to brutal suppression.

Over the years, even if the security forces remained strong and loyal, it had become clear that the ideological foundations of the regime were weak. However, until the 2018 protests America had largely been mute with respect to internal affairs in Iran, apart from an occasional presidential remark or speech by a secretary of state, and the Bush administration's information campaign aimed at the Iranian public. Trump changed this, tweeting early in the 2018 unrest: "They are hungry for food & for freedom. Along with human rights, the wealth of Iran is being looted. TIME FOR A CHANGE!" The United States pushed for a UN Security Council resolution condemning suppression of the protesters but gained little support from the Europeans, Russians, or Chinese. Although the president was critical in his short tweets, the U.S. ambassador to the UN excoriated the Iranian regime, and some members of Congress talked about sanctioning those responsible for putting down the unrest, there was no coordinated, strategic U.S. response from the White House or the State Department.

The strong message from the top of the administration continued in late 2018 with the publication of an essay by Secretary of State Pompeo in the November/December 2018 issue of *Foreign Affairs*. In the article, Pompeo outlined a "Trump Doctrine" of "maximum pressure" in Iran. The first component was new economic sanctions against both individuals and entities, including a strategy to reduce Iranian oil exports "as close to zero as possible." In summarizing the economic measures, Pompeo went well beyond previous U.S. government statements to elaborate on the corruption of the regime, naming individual leaders who had "plundered" Iran and how. Other components of the pressure campaign, Pompeo wrote, would be deterrence—holding Tehran accountable for any attack that resulted in injury to Americans or damage to U.S. facilities; and exposing the brutality of the regime, including its "illicit revenue streams, malign activities, crooked self-dealing and savage oppression." Exposing regime abuses would be at the heart of the strategy. However, beyond tweets, speeches, and essays by Trump and Pompeo, once again there was no integrated strategy for a communications campaign or other measures inside Iran to add to pressure on the regime.

A s was the case with Obama's approach in 2010, Trump's strategy of maximum pressure on Iran was based almost entirely on more severe economic sanctions. Neither president took advantage of the range of other nonmilitary instruments of power to bring even greater pressure to bear. Neither sought to exploit domestic unrest (so evident in 2018–19), stoke resentment of widespread regime corruption and abuses as well as the costs of supporting surrogates abroad, use clandestine means to increase domestic problems, or take measures to interrupt the flow of support to proxies in the region. Economic sanctions were, of course, effective, but there was a singular lack of imagination in using other available instruments of power.

In my view, the United States was too restrained for too long in using nonmilitary instruments of power to try to weaken the Iranian regime internally; too reluctant to expose and communicate to the Iranian people the corruption, financial self-aggrandizement, power struggles, and repressive measures of the clerical leadership; too hesitant to support internal opposition. Economic sanctions could and did pressure the regime to make concessions, as in 2013, but only because they made living conditions for ordinary Iranians so difficult that the clerics feared revolt. There are many overt and covert nonmilitary instruments available to the United States to turn up the heat on the Iranian regime. The clerics control the levers of power and the guns, but so did the shah. Even though the ayatollah and his minions are far more ruthless than the shah had been, the country they rule is changing. Forty percent of the population is under twenty-five. In 1980, 37 percent of the people were literate; today 81 percent are. There are more women in Iranian universities than men. In the first Iranian parliament forty years ago, 61 percent of the members were clerics; today they make up only 6 percent.

The Trump administration's willingness to take the offensive in messaging to the Iranian people in the starkest terms specifics about the corruption and repression of the regime is long overdue, but will it be sustained? Will it be amplified by using all the means of strategic communications available to the U.S. government? Will the administration take advantage of the other nonmilitary instruments of power available to it? We need to return to the Cold War playbook if we are serious about a change in direction inside Iran. The regime is its own worst enemy. That may be our greatest leverage of all.

As long as the ayatollahs and the IRGC rule Iran, there will be no lessening of the forty-year-long enmity toward the Great Satan.

Until there is internal change in Iran, its government will remain a challenge—a bane—for its neighbors and for U.S. presidents. The U.S. goal must be a change in regime that arises from the Iranian people themselves. But we must use nonmilitary instruments of power to inform them of specific abuses by their government and to convey our support for their efforts to increase pressure on the regime. To hasten change in Iran, presidents need to be more creative about using the array of instruments of power available to them in addition to economic sanctions.

CHAPTER 4

Somalia, Haiti, and the Yugoslav Wars

Good Intentions and the Road to Hell

*H*umanitarian *assistance after natural disasters has rarely been con-troversial in the United States and has even more rarely created problems for us abroad. The same is not true, however, when we intervene for humanitarian purposes after man-made disasters. Helping out during or after such disasters usually also involves addressing root causes: internal conflict, such as ethnic, religious, or tribal violence, and/or a ruthless authoritarian government. While responding to natural disasters usually draws heavily upon military capabilities overseen by civilian experts and authorities, man-made disasters nearly always involve the use of force— a kinetic military response. That is where our good intentions have gotten us into trouble. Such was the case in Somalia, in Haiti, and in Yugoslavia during its breakup in the 1990s.*

Somalia, slightly smaller than Texas in area, is a semi-arid country with less than 2 percent arable land. In the early 1990s, the country was torn apart by rival warlords, whose conflicts produced a famine. A UN peace operation intended to deliver international relief supplies was unable to prevent those supplies from being stolen by the warring factions, thus worsening the humanitarian crisis. By late 1992, an estimated 350,000 Somalis had starved to death.

Around Thanksgiving, U.S. secretary of state Lawrence Eagleburger told UN secretary-general Boutros Boutros-Ghali that President Bush (41) had approved the U.S. military's leading an international effort to bring relief supplies to the Somalis and then quickly handing responsibility back to the UN afterward. Boutros-Ghali accepted the offer but asked that the United States also disarm warlords such as Mohamed Farrah Aidid. Eagleburger refused.

As CIA director, I participated in the White House discussions leading up to this decision. National security adviser Brent Scowcroft had serious reservations about getting involved at all, worrying about how, once in, we would get out of Somalia. I considered the operation to be the first U.S. military intervention driven by CNN, as the constant television coverage of starving Somali children blanketed the national news and had created a groundswell of political pressure for the president to do something. Rather coldheartedly, I considered it policy making by television, bringing public pressure for the government to act whether it was in America's best interest or not. Some of us worried that because the famine was caused by feuding warlords, it could not be ended without also ending the internecine conflict, and how would you do that?

Bush had just lost his bid for reelection, and the last thing he—or his closest advisers—wanted was a new foreign policy problem while he was still dealing with such a devastating personal setback and making plans to leave the White House. But he would fulfill his duties to the last day.

While Bush was primarily concerned about the potential catastrophic loss of life from the famine, he was also mindful, as he wrote in his diary on November 30, 1992, of the impression at home and abroad that the United States did not help black nations enough, and he thought that a "peripheral benefit" of the aid would be to show that we did care. Similarly, he was concerned about the feeling in the Muslim world that Americans didn't care about Muslims, and a "large U.S. humanitarian effort backed by force would help in that category." The United States would, in fact, get little credit among Muslims for its humanitarian effort in Somalia (and in Bosnia) in no small part because of a failure to harness the power of strategic communications—the absence of any concerted program to publicize our actions in the Muslim world.

When Bush addressed the nation, announcing he was sending 28,000 U.S. troops to Somalia, he warned that in the months ahead a million and a half people could starve to death as "food from relief flights is being looted upon landing; food convoys have been hijacked; aid workers assaulted; ships with food have been subject to artillery attacks that prevented them from docking. There is no government in Somalia. Law and order have broken down. Anarchy prevails." Trying to preempt criticism, he said, "I understand the United States alone cannot right the world's wrongs. But we also know that some crises in the world cannot be resolved without American involvement, that American action is often necessary as a catalyst for broader involvement of the community of nations." He reassured his listeners that once a secure environment was established, he would withdraw U.S. troops and hand the security mission back to the UN peacekeeping force. He emphasized that the mission had a limited objective: "to open the supply routes, to get the food moving, and to prepare the way for a UN peacekeeping force to keep it moving."

U.S. troops met with little resistance as they deployed into Somalia and reopened the supply lines. Consistent with Eagleburger's response to Boutros-Ghali, there was no effort to disarm the warlords. Instead, the U.S. arranged meetings with them at which they all, including Aidid, agreed to observe a cease-fire and let the food supplies flow unimpeded.

Even after security was established for providing food supplies, Boutros-Ghali opposed the withdrawal of U.S. forces from Somalia, contending that the UN was neither staffed nor equipped to take on the operation. At the end of March 1993, the new Clinton administration negotiated an agreement with the secretary-general under which the UN would recruit a peacekeeping force of 28,000 and the United States would keep 4,000 troops in the area, including a 1,300-member "quick reaction force" under U.S. command. The UN also committed to disarming the warlords, providing security, creating a long-term political process based on cooperation among local leaders, and "assisting" in rebuilding Somalia's economic, political, and social life.

It was all a pipe dream. Although the Somali problem came early in Clinton's term, he and his team should have realized these objectives were hopelessly unrealistic, and insisted on a more limited, achievable mission—one that might enhance the perception of American power rather than diminish it.

With the drawdown of U.S. forces, tensions in Somalia again grew. According to then U.S. ambassador to the UN Madeleine Albright, Aidid sabotaged efforts at reconciliation and broadcast virulently anti-U.S. and anti-UN propaganda. Then, on June 5, 1993, Aidid's forces ambushed and killed twenty-six Pakistani peacekeepers. The UN Security Council called for the apprehension of those responsible. According to President Clinton, Boutros-Ghali and his special representative for Somalia, retired American admiral Jonathan Howe (my successor as deputy U.S. national security adviser under Bush 41 and Brent Scowcroft), were "determined" to get rid of Aidid and asked for U.S. help. They believed that arresting Aidid was the only way to end the clan-based conflicts.

In August, Clinton authorized deployment of a 400-man Army Ranger team augmented with Special Forces and additional equipment with the mission of capturing or killing Aidid (later requests for more equipment were denied by the Pentagon). On October 3, the Rangers assaulted a building in Mogadishu where two top Aidid aides were reportedly holed up. By the time the battle was over, eighteen American soldiers were dead, seventy-three were wounded, and two Black Hawk helicopters had been shot down. To the horror of Americans, the corpse of the crew chief of one of the downed helicopters was dragged through the streets of the city.

How much of the Somali disaster was due to Boutros-Ghali's and Howe's—and then the United States'—obsession with getting rid of Aidid? How did the Clinton administration get co-opted into such a feckless pursuit after Secretary Eagleburger had refused to go along with it the previous December? Clinton would later pose the question, "How had our humanitarian mission turned into an obsession with getting Aidid?"

The Clinton administration made several mistakes in Somalia. The first was going along with (or perhaps leading) the UN expansion of the mission in Somalia from humanitarian relief to nation-building. "The original humanitarian mission had been broadened for good reasons but without sufficient preparation or resources," wrote Albright. It was, in fact, a colossal mistake. As Secretary Albright admitted in her memoir, "In Somalia we tried to do too much." A considerable understatement.

The second mistake was sending 400 Rangers into a hostile city to capture or kill Aidid while facing a disparity in numbers and firepower that even those skilled American warriors could not overcome. The U.S. military was given a risky mission without the resources to accomplish it, an unforgivable error. Third, Boutros-Ghali's Ahab-like obsession with Aidid left the warlord with little incentive to cut a deal. Fourth, there was a failure to rely on skilled diplomacy. Ambassador Robert Oakley early on had persuaded Aidid and the other warlords to observe a cease-fire that allowed the relief operation to proceed. After the October disaster, he was able to negotiate the release of a captured American pilot and a subsequent truce. Why weren't his talents brought to bear during the interval?

The disaster in Mogadishu is an enduring example of the failure to properly exercise both military and nonmilitary power. It would be used often in the years ahead to argue against U.S. involvement, especially military, in problems abroad. Our withdrawal, or retreat, from Somalia after the October tragedy sent a message to other governments and to terrorists such as Osama bin Laden that there was no tolerance in the United States for casualties, and thus killing American soldiers or sailors, or even seeing them at risk, would get Washington to withdraw. It was a failure that diminished both the perception and the reality of American power.

Since the U.S. withdrawal twenty-five years ago, Somalia has remained unstable, suffering from internal conflict and armed struggles for power. As a result, a terrorist threat emerged there. The country became a focus for U.S. counterterrorism operations following the 1998 bombings of the U.S. embassies in Nairobi, Kenya, and Dar es Salaam, Tanzania, because the perpetrators were suspected of operating out of

Somalia. A group called the Islamic Courts Union, with its fundamentalist militias, seized power in 2006 and was defeated the following year. One hard-line Islamist group, al-Shabaab, remains a threat. The United States continues to provide military help and equipment to African peacekeepers in Somalia. The mission is now all about security and political power. The broader, ambitious objectives of the original UN Security Council resolution have long since been abandoned.

The other threat emanating from the poverty, constant conflict, and chaos in Somalia was piracy. The problem emerged after another collapse of the central government around 2000 and the disbanding of the Somali navy. Initially, hostile action was taken by Somali fishermen in retaliation against foreign ships that invaded their fishing grounds and others that were dumping illegal waste and thus impacting fish catches. As the fishermen began to collect ransoms for ships they seized, they quickly realized that hijacking ships was dramatically more profitable than fishing. Since no foreign government wanted to intercede, the pirates operated with impunity, becoming increasingly aggressive and ranging far from the Somali coast.

In 2008, there were over a hundred attacks and forty-two successful hijackings. The rate of attacks increased dramatically in early 2009. Over time, the international community, led by NATO, assembled a substantial naval force in the region with warships from dozens of countries, including Russia and China, to deal with the pirates. Also, ship owners became smarter about protecting their ships from boarders by removing ladders, using high-pressure hoses, arming crews, and placing security teams aboard. Thanks to these measures, successful pirate attacks dropped dramatically by the end of 2011.

A quarter century after the United States first intervened in Somalia to provide humanitarian assistance because of potential famine, little has changed for the better. More than half a million Somalis have died in the country's civil wars, and USAID estimates that more than 1.5 million people are at risk of starving. Almost every military operation in Somalia in which the United States takes part receives global news coverage. Yet, the fact that America year after year is by far the largest donor of humanitarian assistance there—in 2015–16, nearly $150 million in emergency food aid alone—goes unnoticed. If effective communications—propaganda, if you will—is an important instrument of power, the country that invented public relations has forgotten how to exercise it.

The United States brought to bear in Somalia multiple instruments of power: the military, diplomacy, and development and humanitarian assistance. However, the question I and others posed in the Situation Room in late 1992 remains unanswered: Can any of these instruments of power make a difference unless and until the Somalis themselves figure out how to stop killing each other?

The larger question for the United States is how to provide humanitarian assistance to a dysfunctional country without getting drawn into its internal conflicts and politics, as happened in Haiti even as the Somali disaster was playing out.

Haiti is one of the world's poorest countries and a perennial contestant for worst governed. The United States has a history in Haiti, and it is not one that endears us to the Haitians. In 1915, amid political chaos and after six Haitian presidents in four years, not to mention Imperial Germany's domination of the country's international commerce, President Woodrow Wilson sent in 330 Marines to safeguard U.S. interests. The United States, for all intents and purposes, ran Haiti until the Marines departed in 1934.

Beginning in the late 1950s, Haiti suffered decades of dictatorial and brutal misrule under François "Papa Doc" Duvalier and subsequently his son, Jean-Claude ("Baby Doc"), during which tens of thousands were killed and hundreds of thousands either fled the island or were exiled. Baby Doc's overthrow in 1986 was followed by several years of army rule punctuated by fraudulent elections and periodic coups, until December 1990, when a leftist former Catholic priest, Jean-Bertrand Aristide, was elected president. He, in turn, was overthrown by the military in late September 1991. Led by the United States, the international community imposed severe economic sanctions on Haiti and the military junta, headed by Lieutenant General Raoul Cédras. Over the next several years, military repression, coupled with even greater economic hardship because of the sanctions, prompted more than 150,000 Haitians to flee the island, most of them desperately poor and headed for Florida in rickety boats. The Haitian "boat people" represented a humanitarian crisis of significant proportions.

In July 1993, the UN reached an agreement with General Cédras that he would "avail himself of the right of early retirement" and allow Aristide to return to Haiti. To implement the UN-brokered transition, a U.S. Navy ship, the USS *Harlan County*, was sent to Haiti on October 11 with two hundred or so American (and a couple of dozen Canadian) military, police, and governmental advisers on board. As the ship approached its berth in Port-au-Prince, it was met by a menacing crowd opposed to its docking, shouting anti-American slogans and threats. The Clinton administration, not wanting an armed confrontation, ordered the ship back to sea the next day. The incident was a humiliation for the United States, and was seen as such by governments and others around the world. Coming just a week after the disaster in Somalia, the incident reinforced the impression that the U.S. administration was weak and that Washington was loath to undertake operations that might involve casualties. Cédras had double-crossed the UN by reneging on the July agreement, and appeared to have forced an American military retreat. Subsequently, economic sanctions on the regime were reimposed and repression by the Cédras government intensified.

As the months wore on, the Clinton administration was deeply divided over the question of intervening militarily, with the White House and National Security Council staff generally in favor and the Defense Department and many in the State Department, including Secretary of State Warren Christopher, opposed. (This alignment would be repeated many times in the years to come.) Despite the fact that public and congressional opinion was strongly against U.S. action (the Congressional Black Caucus was an exception), Clinton eventually sided with the interventionists and ordered the Pentagon to proceed with military planning to forcibly remove Cédras from power. It was never clear whether Clinton's decision was influenced more by domestic politics—deference to the Black Caucus—or by Cédras's repression. At the end of July 1994, the Security Council authorized the use of all necessary means to remove Cédras.

At the president's direction, in September an American military force composed of two aircraft carriers and more than 20,000 troops prepared to invade Haiti. The first elements of the invasion force were to parachute onto Haitian targets beginning at one minute past midnight on September 19. In a last-ditch effort to avoid bloodshed, Clinton sent former president Jimmy Carter, former senator Sam Nunn, and former chairman of the Joint Chiefs of Staff Colin Powell to Port-au-Prince to try to persuade Cédras to give up without a fight. Only a few hours before the invasion was to begin, they succeeded. Fifteen thousand American troops who thought they were going into a bloody fight with the hated Haitian military went ashore without conflict and were directed to partner with the same military they had been sent to defeat. The thugs were now our friends and partners in stabilizing Haiti and bringing order.

The administration's defense of the intervention—to advance democratization and economic development in Haiti—was not credible from the beginning, but more to the point, implementation of the administration's proclaimed nation-building strategy was left almost entirely to the U.S. military, which was ill prepared and ill equipped for the task. The American military is not trained to remedy underlying political and economic problems in other countries. The U.S. Army or Marine Corps is not the Peace Corps with guns. In fact, they had been sent to fight, not to build. The reality was that only one instrument of U.S. power was put to use to any extent in Haiti—guys with guns. Clinton himself underscored that disparity when he noted in his memoir that the UN mission consisted "of more than 6,000 military personnel, 900 police officers, and *dozens* [my emphasis] of economic, political and legal advisors."

There was an emphasis on avoiding casualties, which meant our troops largely remained in their encampments with little interaction with the Haitian people; law enforcement was left to the newly formed Haitian National Police (many of whom came from the repressive former military); and, finally, many Haitians, including Aristide, were opposed to U.S. and other international proposals for economic reform. While initially most Haitians warmly welcomed U.S. troops, before too long Haitian newspapers were calling the intervention a humiliation and Haitian politicians would begin to refer to the return of American imperialism. As would be the case too often in the years to come, reasonably free and fair elections were seen in Washington as synonymous with democratization, with little attention given to the need for long-term institution-building, rule of law, accountability, and the other pillars of a truly free society. With the removal of most U.S. troops and diminished enthusiasm in Washington for nation-building, Haiti soon sank back into the mire of misgovernment, corruption, and violence that had long characterized the country.

Madeleine Albright wrote of Haiti in her memoir, "The international community, through the UN or other means, had a responsibility to help societies endangered by natural or human-caused catastrophe. It was in America's interest to ensure this responsibility was fulfilled." But how do you do that and at what cost? Solving such problems is usually the work of generations. Also, which societies suffering from human-caused catastrophes—and there are many—should we help? How should we help? For how long? Because we didn't answer these questions in the early 1990s (and before) and learn from our experiences in Somalia and Haiti, we would make the same strategic mistake again, at far higher cost.

Our experiences in Somalia and Haiti make apparent that even if all the different instruments of power—including the nonmilitary—are robust and effectively used, that often is not enough to bring success. American presidents need to be more realistic about the limits on what U.S. intervention in man-made disasters can accomplish.

In contrast, the American response to Haiti's frequent natural disasters has repeatedly demonstrated both generosity and skill in providing humanitarian assistance—the effective integration of multiple instruments of power. This assistance has been forthcoming every time Haiti has been hit by devastating hurricanes, tropical storms, and earthquakes, on average, about every other year.

One of the worst natural disasters in Haiti was a magnitude 7.0 earthquake on January 12, 2010, killing more than 300,000 people and affecting more than 3 million. As I wrote in my book *Duty*, we moved heaven and earth to get ships, aircraft, equipment, and people there immediately. I directed several Navy ships to head for Haiti, including the aircraft carrier *Carl Vinson*, which arrived on January 15, with 600,000 emergency food rations and 19 helicopters. Within days of the earthquake, the United States had 17 ships, 48 helicopters, and 10,000 sailors and Marines in Haiti or off its coast. Afterward, billions of dollars in assistance and for recovery were provided from many countries. As usual, the United States was the largest contributor, providing nearly $1.3 billion in government spending alone and feeding 3.5 million people. But Haiti just couldn't catch a break. The following October, there was a widespread cholera epidemic and then the country was hit by Hurricane Tomas.

A year after the earthquake, 80 percent of Haitians were unemployed, half were illiterate, and most still lived on less than a dollar a day. Despite the U.S. commitment of $4.2 billion in assistance between 2010 and 2016, in 2017 USAID described Haiti this way: "Although the country has the formal structures of a democracy, many of these have yet to become fully functional, as evidenced by recurring periods of political and institutional instability. Haiti's state institutions are under-resourced, and provide services to only a small percentage of the population." USAID has been engaged in Haiti for half a century, but its efforts to improve governance, access to justice, and human rights truly, and sadly, have been a Sisyphean endeavor.

Americans and the rest of the world are unaware of all the United States has done to help Haiti, as in the case of Somalia, due to the neglect and underfunding of strategic communications in our government, an important instrument of power unemployed. The world knows nearly instantly of our military actions abroad, but we seem to think the selfless actions we take aren't worth publicizing effectively. That is not how a country best builds or exercises power.

One prediction the CIA got exactly right in the late 1970s was that the Balkan country of Yugoslavia—an artificial state created in the aftermath of World War I—would probably break apart when its longtime ruthless communist dictator, Marshal Josip Broz Tito, died. In 1990, ten years after his death, the dissolution began. A National Intelligence Estimate issued on October 18 predicted: "Yugoslavia will cease to function as a federal state within a year, and will probably dissolve within two. . . . The violence will be intractable and bitter."

The disintegration of Yugoslavia in the 1990s with its attendant ethnic cleansing, forced mass relocations, and vast suffering is a sordid story of unscrupulous and power-hungry local leaders reviving and stoking age-old grievances, plus ethnic and religious conflict, horrifying violence, and European fecklessness.

Tito's new constitution for Yugoslavia in 1974 in essence provided that, after he died, power in Yugoslavia would devolve away from a centralized federal government to the six republics: Serbia, Croatia, Slovenia, Macedonia, Montenegro, and Bosnia-Herzegovina. That is what happened during the 1980s as each republic began to exercise those powers to which it was entitled by the constitution.

Yugoslavia broke up at virtually the same time as the Soviet Union. Slovenia and Croatia both declared their independence on June 25, 1991. The federal government in Belgrade resisted the action, and launched a military offensive against the Slovenes two days later. The latter prevailed in a conflict that lasted just ten days.

Croatia's initial steps toward independence in May 1990 alarmed Serbs living there (about 12 percent of the population), who began armed resistance in August. The Serbs in Croatia had reason to be alarmed. During World War II, the Nazis created an independent client state of Croatia ruled by a fascist militia known as the Ustaše, which was Roman Catholic and bitterly anti-Serb. The Ustaše murdered hundreds of thousands of Serbs, who were predominantly Orthodox Christians, expelled a quarter of a million, and forcibly converted perhaps a couple of hundred thousand to Roman Catholicism. The fighting during the summer of 1990 was sparked when the Croatians, whose forces wore uniforms remarkably similar to those worn by the Ustaše, tried to replace police in the Serb-populated area of the country. Memories are long in the Balkans, and the roughly 600,000 Serbs living in Croatia began armed resistance with the support of the Serb-dominated Yugoslav federal army.

Slobodan Milošević, the ultra-nationalistic president of Serbia since 1989, was willing to let Croatia proceed with independence, but only if Serbia could hold on to those parts of the country populated by Serbs. Full-scale war broke out in the fall of 1991, with the federal army—with its predominantly Serb officer corps—fighting on the side of the Croatian Serbs. Hundreds of thousands of Croatians fled a Serb campaign of ethnic cleansing in the areas they controlled. In January 1992, UN special envoy Cyrus Vance, a former U.S. secretary of state under President Jimmy Carter, negotiated a cease-fire that established de facto borders between Croatia and the breakaway state, the Republic of Serbian Krajina.

Where was the United States in all this? Peter Galbraith, the first U.S. ambassador to Croatia, later pointed out that, as Yugoslavia descended into war in 1991, "the Europeans told the Bush Administration that this was a European problem and that Europe would solve it." EU negotiator Jacques Poos crowed, "This is the hour of Europe." All that was music to the ears of President Bush and his team, focused at the time on the aftermath of the Gulf War, newly liberated Eastern Europe, and reunified Germany, and the impending collapse of the Soviet Union. In 1991–92, Bush no more wanted to get involved in Yugoslavia's problems than he did Somalia's—or Afghanistan's—at the time.

In the Bush 41 administration, there were three people at the center of decision making who knew a lot about Yugoslavia. National Security Adviser Brent Scowcroft had been an Air Force attaché in Belgrade, Deputy Secretary of State Larry Eagleburger had been U.S. ambassador there, and I had studied the history of the area in depth during graduate school and subsequently at the CIA. All three of us, steeped in the violent history and ethnic divisions of the area, in White House discussions urged keeping the hell out of the Balkan mess. The hatreds were so ancient, the mutual desire for revenge so deep, the leaders so nationalistic and narrow, that we were confident diplomacy and politics could not prevent conflict. We believed that if any outside powers had a direct interest in intervening, it was the Europeans. That view was widely shared among Bush's other senior advisers.

As then Secretary of State Jim Baker would write in his memoir, "unlike in the Persian Gulf, our vital national interests were not at stake." As appalled as we all were by the bloodshed and forced relocations, no one supported using the U.S. military to end the violence either. So during the latter part of 1991 and throughout 1992, the Bush administration deferred to the Europeans, supported UN-imposed economic sanctions against the Federal Republic of Yugoslavia (by then composed of just Serbia and Montenegro), and an arms embargo on all sides (which had the effect of advantaging the Serbs because they controlled the federal army and its stockpiles of weapons), and cooperated in efforts to isolate Serbia. We should have anticipated the Europeans would be overwhelmed by the crisis and be unable to "solve" it, in no small part because the EU required unanimity in everything it did, not an easy thing to arrange.

The uneasy cease-fire in Croatia lasted until 1995, when a now well-equipped Croatian army retook most of the ground earlier occupied by the Serbs.

Bosnia-Herzegovina declared its sovereignty on October 15, 1991. Its ethnic composition—43 percent Bosnian (called Bosniaks or Bosnian Muslims), 31 percent Serb, and 17 percent Croat—made such a move even more complicated than Croatia's. Accordingly, it spawned two separatist conflicts, the first by the Serb minority and the second by the Croatian minority.

In late October, the Serb members of parliament walked out, formed the Assembly of the Serb people of Bosnia and Herzegovina, and on January 9, 1992, established what would become the independent Republika Srpska. On November 18, 1991, the minority Croatian members of parliament also walked out and proclaimed the establishment of the Croatian Community of Herzeg-Bosnia. These tiny, unsustainable enclaves would have been laughable if it were not for the enormous human suffering that would follow.

Initially, the Bosniaks and the Croatian Republic of Herzeg-Bosnia (inside Bosnia) fought together against the Serbs and the breakaway Republic of Serbian Krajina in Croatia, but amid growing tension, in October 1992, local armed conflicts between them began and in early

1993 their alliance collapsed. Thus began what became known as the "war within a war." It might also have been called the "weird war," because the two parties fought viciously against each other in some places and fought together against the Serbs in other places, with the conflict punctuated by frequent cease-fires.

The nastiest fight, though, was between the Bosnian government in Sarajevo and the Serbs in Bosnia-Herzegovina (backed by Milošević's Serbia). A referendum on independence was held at the end of February 1992 and, thanks to a Bosnian Serb boycott, 99.7% of voters said yes. The Republic of Bosnia-Herzegovina was declared on March 3 and international recognition followed on April 6.

The Bosnian Serbs were ready to fight and the Bosnian government was not. As the referendum on Bosnian independence neared in early 1992, the Bosnian Serbs—with the support of Serbia and the federal army—began a brutal campaign of forced evacuation of Bosnian Croats and Bosniaks from mixed-ethnic towns and territory they considered historically Serbian.

With Bosnia-Herzegovina now a sovereign state, the Yugoslav federal army withdrew, but many soldiers simply changed uniforms and joined the army of Republika Srpska (Serbs living in Bosnia and Herzegovina). That army also was able to draw on Yugoslav army stockpiles in Bosnia and received extensive additional help from Serbia. Its offensives in 1992 captured most of the country, and in areas it occupied, ethnic cleansing of both Bosniaks and Bosnian Croats followed. The Republika Srpska army encircled the Bosnian capital of Sarajevo and on May 2 blockaded the city, a siege that would last nearly four years with untold suffering and the death of nearly 14,000 people.

The siege of Sarajevo, and accompanying graphic television images of it broadcast around the world, brought new pressure on the United States to intervene. The most Bush and Baker were prepared to do was airlift humanitarian supplies into the city after a cease-fire was established, and even that was opposed by Defense Secretary Dick Cheney and Joint Chiefs chairman Colin Powell. Nonetheless, after both a UN and European Community ultimatum led Serbia to reopen the Sarajevo airport, U.S. relief flights began in early July.

Baker summarized the outgoing national security team's views in his memoir:

> The only way that it [a humanitarian nightmare] might have been prevented or reversed would have been through the application of substantial military force early on, with all the costs, particularly in lives, that would have entailed—and, by everyone's reckoning, in that environment the casualties would have been staggering. President Bush's decision that our national interests did not require the United States of America to fight its fourth war in Europe in this century, with the loss of America's sons and daughters that would have ensued, was absolutely the right one. We cannot be, and should not be expected to be, the world's policeman.

Thus, we in the Bush 41 administration handed off the Balkan mess to Bill Clinton, who brought a different perspective. During his campaign, he had urged more aggressive action by the United States and the Europeans, from the use of NATO airstrikes against the Serbs in Bosnia to lifting the arms embargo. Once in office, though, his team was divided over what to do, because he faced some of the same constraints as his predecessor. He recalled that he didn't want to unilaterally lift the arms embargo, which would weaken the UN, and he didn't want to unilaterally bomb Serb military positions because that might weaken NATO solidarity and also endanger European soldiers on the ground with the UN peacekeeping mission. As his UN ambassador, Madeleine Albright, wrote, "At this stage, with a new President, a wary Secretary of State, a negative Pentagon, nervous allies, and crises in Somalia, then Rwanda and Haiti blowing up, we weren't prepared to run the risks of leadership on Bosnia."

Still, by the end of March 1993 the UN had imposed even stricter economic sanctions on Serbia and Clinton had convinced the UN to authorize a no-fly zone over Bosnia to keep Serb aircraft at bay. By the end of the summer, arrangements were in place for NATO to conduct airstrikes in Bosnia, but only if both NATO and the UN approved. The UN secretary-general's representative steadfastly refused to give his approval, largely out of fear of Bosnian Serb reprisals against the UN peacekeepers.

Those peacekeepers turned out to be a major impediment to Western military action. They had a very narrow mandate, mainly humanitarian, and were more observers than peacekeepers. Because of their light blue helmets and their inability to do much, they were derisively referred to as "Smurfs." The Bosnian Serbs took them as hostages in response to Western threats, sometimes handcuffing them to potential targets such as bridges and air defense sites. Places the UN designated as "safe zones" to protect civilians were hardly safe inasmuch as the peacekeepers were not allowed to use force.

Albright in those days strongly supported American intervention in the Balkans, pressing for the use of the U.S. military in liberating the besieged airport in Sarajevo. When Colin Powell objected, Albright demanded to know, "What are you saving this superb military for, Colin, if we can't use it?" But I suspect Powell was just being cautious about the exercise of military power in the absence of a clear mission and broader strategy.

Not much changed until early 1994, when Clinton's special envoy, Ambassador Charles Redman, helped the Bosniaks and breakaway Bosnian-Croats negotiate an agreement establishing the Federation of Bosnia and Herzegovina and effectively ending their war (the Washington Agreement).

As the Bosnian Serbs continued their brutal attacks on the Bosnian Muslims that year, the restrictions on NATO air operations were relaxed. As previously mentioned, Clinton secretly green-lighted an arms channel from Iran through Croatia to the Bosnian Muslims in early 1994, and then unilaterally lifted the U.S. arms embargo on November 10, 1994, allowing the Croats to acquire new weaponry and subsequently push back the Serb lines. The new American negotiator, Richard Holbrooke, managed to get agreement late that fall between the Bosniaks and the Bosnian Serbs for a four-month cease-fire, but then the violence resumed with significantly greater intensity. On July 11, 1995, the Bosnian Serbs seized the Bosniak enclave of Srebrenica, and over the next several days massacred more than 7,000 men and boys.

Even after Srebrenica, the Clinton administration remained divided over whether to act more aggressively, both militarily and diplomatically, to bring an end to the war. National Security Adviser Anthony Lake summed up the different positions: "Madeleine feels the stakes are so high, they affect the administration's leadership at home and abroad, and that we have no choice but to accept a considerable risk. [Lake agreed.] The biggest fear of State and Defense is that we will become entangled in a quagmire. They favor a more limited approach." President Clinton sided with Albright and Lake, and directed a maximum effort to get a settlement in Bosnia.

Between ever-tightening economic sanctions on Serbia, elimination of the UN veto over airstrikes and subsequent NATO aircraft pounding of Bosnian Serb positions, and Bosnian and Croatian gains on the ground, by September 1995 the percentage of Bosnia controlled by the Serbs had dropped from 70 percent to 50 percent. The stage was set for negotiations to end the conflict. Those negotiations among the Bosnians, Croatians, and Yugoslavs (Serbs) were conducted by Ambassador Holbrooke at Wright-Patterson Air Force Base near Dayton, Ohio, and resulted in a peace agreement—the Dayton Accords—on November 21, 1995. Two million Bosnians had been displaced by the war and over 250,000 killed.

Part of the agreement was a U.S. and European commitment to provide a peacekeeping force, one-third of whom (20,000) would be provided by the United States. Their mission would not end for nine years. There was little support at home for our involvement in the peacekeeping force. But American diplomacy was decisive in ending the war in Bosnia.

If the Dayton Accords brought accolades, the next chapter in the Balkans would have far-reaching, negative international impact.

Before Yugoslavia blew up in 1991, Kosovo was an autonomous province in the Republic of Serbia. Although ethnic Albanians accounted for some 90 percent of the population of the province, it occupied a singular place in Serbian history because in 1389 (as I said before, memories are long in the Balkans), an Ottoman army routed a Christian army led by Serbs in Kosovo. Serbian national culture and history are intimately tied to that disaster. Six hundred years later, Slobodan Milošević abolished the province's autonomy, integrating it into Serbia proper. He directed a pervasive campaign denying the majority-Albanian population their political and economic rights. On Christmas Day 1992, President Bush sent Milošević a secret letter warning him that Serbian aggression in Kosovo would bring a unilateral American military response. The president was concerned that such a conflict would spill over into Macedonia and potentially then drag in both Bulgaria and Turkey, thereby threatening NATO interests. Bush's warning was repeated by the new Clinton administration.

Milošević ignored the warnings, and his repressive actions in Kosovo sparked the emergence in the mid-1990s of a violent Albanian movement—the Kosovo Liberation Army (KLA)—that sought outright independence for Kosovo and was prepared to kill Kosovar Serbs to achieve it. A massacre of Kosovar Albanians by Serbian paramilitary units in early March 1998 finally galvanized international involvement, led by the United States.

Impatient with the Pentagon's reluctance to get involved in a second major military operation in the Balkans, Albright as usual was the foremost advocate of a military response to Milošević within the Clinton administration. She also advocated "that we should initiate a concerted strategy aimed at ending Milošević's rule in Belgrade"—i.e., regime change. The KLA launched its "summer offensive" against Serbs in July 1998, and Milošević responded with an overwhelming counterattack that continued into the fall and drove perhaps 1.3 million Albanian Kosovars from their homes and into the mountains.

In response to the Serb attacks, the UN, EU, and the United States all imposed a variety of additional economic sanctions on Serbia. The UN imposed an arms embargo on Serbia in 1998, and in April 1999, the EU banned oil exports to the country. The next month the United States blocked all World Bank and IMF credits, and in June the EU froze assets held by the Serbian government in member states. As in the early 1990s, during the Bosnian War the sanctions inflicted considerable economic pain on Serbia and its people, but as before, the sanctions were insufficient to cause the Serbian government to change its policies or moderate its military actions. Sanctions, in this instance, proved a useful but inadequate instrument of power to achieve U.S. objectives.

Diplomacy to stop the fighting and restore Kosovo's autonomy took place under NATO auspices and not the UN's because the Russians—linked to the Serbs by history, ethnicity, language, and religion—viewed developments in Kosovo as an internal Yugoslav matter and made clear they would veto any Security Council resolution authorizing the use of force to get the Serbs out of Kosovo. As events played out, there was another massacre of Albanians, followed by another failed diplomatic effort, NATO air operations against Serb forces in Kosovo and targets in Serbia itself, and finally Milošević's capitulation on June 3, 1999. A NATO peacekeeping force of some 50,000 troops was deployed to Kosovo, including 7,000 from the U.S.

In 2007, Finnish president Martti Ahtisaari, acting on behalf of the UN, put forward the Comprehensive Proposal for the Kosovo Status Settlement, which essentially recommended independence. The United States strongly supported the plan, as did most European governments. The Russians, however, were unalterably opposed, thus making it impossible to proceed through the UN. The U.S. government, Condoleezza Rice wrote, was convinced a decision was needed before the Kosovars became too impatient and took to the streets, and so the "only choice was to manage the problem in a way that prevented violence, convincing as many countries as possible to recognize Kosovo." On June 9, 2007, President Bush called for Kosovar independence, and on February 18, 2008, the United States recognized Kosovo. Rice later acknowledged that the United States had helped midwife another weak, unsustainable state, but admitted, "What choice did we have?" She then added, "But in time Kosovo will be alright. It was the right thing to do."

With an end to most of the fighting, the United States turned to nonmilitary instruments. USAID provided Kosovo development assistance beginning with $150 million in 2001, but the level of aid declined sharply after that. The money was a drop in the bucket compared to need, and even the small amount provided probably was largely wasted. But, as we will see, the exercise of military power to change the political situation of a country has long-lasting, and often expensive, consequences.

There is no denying that the U.S. and NATO military action ended a humanitarian disaster in Kosovo, and prevented worse. But NATO had intervened militarily in a sovereign state to end an internal conflict without UN Security Council sanction, setting the dangerous precedent that any state or states could intervene in the internal affairs of another if it could make the case that it was acting on humanitarian grounds to protect elements of the population. Russia would subsequently intervene forcibly in neighboring countries on the same pretext. Both China and Russia were concerned that the same rationale used by the West to intervene in Kosovo might be used against them in Tibet, Chechnya, or elsewhere. When Western countries recognized Kosovo's independence, they were violating the post–Cold War principle that borders in Europe could only be changed by mutual agreement. A sovereign state, however loathsome its leadership, had been dismantled without its consent.

Less than seven months after NATO peacekeepers entered Kosovo on December 31, 1999, Boris Yeltsin resigned as president of Russia. The following March, Vladimir Putin was elected Russia's new president. He would not forget what had happened in the Balkans, and the precedents the West had set.

In each case, American involvement in Somalia, Haiti, Bosnia, and Kosovo was initially characterized by the U.S. as a humanitarian mission intended to protect the inhabitants from being killed by their own government, political or ethnic conflict, warlords and bloodthirsty leaders, or starvation. In Somalia and Haiti, Washington also harbored hopes that culture and history could be overcome with American help, and the inhabitants persuaded to live in peace and develop politically and economically. In both places, as well as in Bosnia and Kosovo, we acted because we could, because there was no one to stop us, and because we were well intentioned. As one scholar put it, "The humanitarian interventions aimed not at protecting American interests, the traditional goal of foreign policy, but at vindicating American (and what the Clinton administration considered universal) values." In each case, ironically, it was the U.S. ambassador to the UN and then secretary of state Madeleine Albright who was most aggressive in wanting to intervene and to do so with American military power. As I wrote more than twenty years ago, contrary to conventional wisdom, the biggest hawks in the White House Situation Room are often the diplomats.

The lessons from Somalia and Haiti seem clear. When we limited our involvement in Somalia and Haiti to humanitarian assistance after famine and natural disasters, we exercised our power effectively, made a substantial difference, and—especially in Haiti—commendably integrated different elements of our national power, both civilian and military. We identified a problem, brought to bear our diverse capabilities, and were successful.

Our responses to man-made disasters had a different outcome. Efforts to shape the political environment through the use of military power led to failure in both Somalia and Haiti—as well as humiliation in the Battle of Mogadishu and in Haiti, with the *Harlan County* turning tail. Both episodes weakened perceptions of American power globally and, in the case of Somalia, led adversaries from Bin Laden to hostile governments to conclude the United States lacked resolve.

The Yugoslav wars provide different lessons—above all, the powerlessness of the Europeans. Here was a major political and humanitarian problem at their back door, a problem involving aggressive and eventually murderous behaviors in Serbia, Croatia, and Bosnia-Herzegovina, and Europe's governments were paralyzed. Divided over the imposition of sanctions and then over the use of force, they allowed the dissolution of Yugoslavia to become a catastrophe. The Bush administration wanted no part of the Balkan mess. President Clinton was willing for the United States to help seek solutions but initially was held at arm's length by the Europeans, who assured him they could handle the situation. When it became apparent they couldn't deliver, the Clinton team effectively applied several instruments of American power—economic and financial sanctions on Serbia, diplomacy, and limited military force. The first success was the Washington Agreement settling the conflict between Bosnia-Herzegovina and its Croat minority. The second, and greater, success was the adroit mix of air-power and diplomacy to end the Bosnian War through the Dayton Accords. These achievements did not resolve the ethnic conflicts at the root of the violence or address the longer-term consequences of ethnic cleansing and economic destruction—nor did they aspire to do so. The U.S. objective was to stop the killing, bring in the peacekeepers, and hope that over time the different ethnic groups would accommodate themselves to a new reality. In Kosovo, on the other hand, there were diplomatic initiatives to stop the killing, but they succeeded only after enough bombs had fallen on Serbia.

There is at least one other lesson from the U.S. exercise of power in Somalia, Haiti, Bosnia, and Kosovo. It involves how we should decide where to intervene to prevent widespread murder.

The UN General Assembly in 2005 unanimously agreed to Responsibility to Protect (R2P), a political commitment to protect populations "from genocide, war crimes, ethnic cleansing and crimes against humanity." Each state had primary responsibility for this purpose within its borders, but in the event a state was unable or unwilling to provide protection, R2P sanctioned the use of force by outside parties—breaching the sovereignty of the subject state—with the approval of the UN Security Council. But, even with UNSC sanction, when should the United States act? And should it act, as it did in Kosovo, without UN sanction?

Over the years, we have used our military power to stop a slaughter in some places, but not in most. The United States sat on the sidelines during the Nigerian civil war in the late 1960s, during which between 500,000 and 2 million Biafrans died of starvation brought about by a government blockade, and there was considerable slaughter of minorities by both the government and the Biafran forces. In 1971, the United States did nothing as the Pakistani military cracked down on East Pakistan (now Bangladesh), resulting in millions of refugees fleeing into India and at least 200,000 people dying in the first six months of violence. In 1994, 800,000 people were killed in the Rwandan genocide while the international community, including the United States, looked on. In Darfur, in western Sudan, in response to rebel attacks on government military posts in 2003, the government mobilized proxy militias, which by 2005 had killed some 450,000 black Africans and displaced nearly 2 million. Between 1998 and 2008, as many as 5.8 million people were killed in the Second Congo War. We intervened militarily in Libya in early 2011 (with UN, NATO, and Arab League authorization) ostensibly to forestall a massacre in Benghazi, but ultimately took the opportunity to bring regime change. However, we abstained from the Syrian civil war that began a few months later, with its massive loss of life and millions of refugees.

Why did we use our military power to intervene in Somalia, Haiti, Bosnia, Kosovo, and Libya to stop human carnage, but not in other man-made disasters? Surely there ought to be some underlying principles or strategy to guide such decisions in the future.

In Albright's memoir she refers to a 1994 report by the Stimson Center, which observed: "When the Security Council approves a peace operation with an ambiguous or impossible mandate simply as a political 'gesture' . . . it damages the United Nations as an institution and reduces its ability to act." She later wrote, "The experts had concluded, then, that the UN should refrain from intervening in circumstances precisely like those in Rwanda, where there were no security guarantees, no cooperation between the parties, and no readily achievable mandates." Perhaps those three preconditions should provide, at a minimum, a starter set of principles for American decision makers when faced with demands to intervene in man-made humanitarian disasters in other countries in the future.

The main lesson of the events in Somalia, Haiti, and Yugoslavia is that a president must not let sentiment and sympathy over great bloodshed obscure the need to ask hard questions and insist upon realistic answers. The bar for use of the U.S. military in a man-made humanitarian disaster abroad ought to be a high one.

Because power misused is power lost.

CHAPTER 5

Colombia

The Plan That Worked (Mostly)

*A*merica's record since the end of the Cold War (and often before) in rescuing failing Third World states, strengthening their institutions and the rule of law, and ending internal conflict is so bad that the very idea of trying it should give great pause to any sentient decision maker in Washington. Just look at Iraq, Afghanistan, Haiti, Somalia, Libya, and Egypt for starters. However, there is at least one success story, Colombia, and there is much to learn from that experience—above all, about the effective application and integration of multiple instruments of noncoercive American power.

Colombia is an especially intriguing story because during the first three years of our fifteen-year engagement, which began in the late 1990s, the rationale for our involvement kept changing in dramatic ways due to our domestic politics. It ranged from an initial idealistic Colombian request for a "Marshall Plan" to help wean peasant farmers away from growing coca, to a U.S.-devised, military-oriented counter-narcotics program, and, finally, to a U.S.-Colombian partnership to conduct a counterterrorism/ counterinsurgency campaign. The counter-narcotics effort largely failed, but the counterinsurgency—and the effort to pull Colombia back from the precipice of becoming a failed state—worked. The history of decisions and actions by both U.S. and Colombian leaders contributing to the success of Plan Colombia in its final form helps explain our failures elsewhere and is rich in lessons for future U.S. presidents when they are being urged to *intervene in another country to bring stability, an end to killing, the rule of law, and democracy.*

Geography was long a significant obstacle to the development of a strong central government in Colombia. The country is almost twice the size of Texas. It is trisected by three ranges of the Andean mountains, severely limiting the construction of roads and railroads. Because of the challenges of travel and communication, there was for many years little trade among towns and cities, a further obstacle to the development of a modern state. The limited reach and power of the central government meant that security historically was privatized and dispersed: "Examples include the private armies . . . that were used to settle local accounts and that were also employed in inter-party warfare, the development of peasant and community defense organizations, the proliferation of forces hired to protect a wide assortment of economic enterprises, the private forces of criminal syndicates, as well as a slew of other manifestations."

Among those other "manifestations" was the formation of left-wing armed groups, the most significant of which was an alliance in 1950 of Liberal Party guerrillas and Colombian communists to form "self-defense" units. These were largely armed groups of peasants who had lost their land. (Their numbers grew substantially during the 1960s when the government encouraged the formation of large farms growing crops for export, a policy that involved forcing poor peasants off their land.) In 1964, the leader of the Colombian Communist Party, Jacobo Arenas, formally joined with other "resistance" forces led by former Liberal Party guerrilla Manuel Marulanda to found the movement that in 1966 would assume the name Revolutionary Armed Forces of Colombia, or FARC. The FARC's political platform called for land redistribution and a more equitable division of the country's wealth. Whatever the motivations of the peasant soldiers, the leadership of the Colombian Communist Party and later the FARC itself were Marxist-Leninist, anti-imperialist, anti-capitalist, anti-American revolutionaries who sought to follow in the footsteps of Cuba's Fidel Castro.

No doubt alarmed by Castro's successful revolution in Cuba in January 1959, the U.S. Army in 1962 recommended to the Colombian government a counterinsurgency strategy encompassing both military operations and civic action in those parts of the country held by the self-defense forces in order to reestablish control. The FARC subsequently suffered significant defeats and was pushed into the interior jungles, "precisely the regions that would serve in the 1980s and beyond as the propitious economic base of coca growth and the narcotrafficking industry," wrote political science professor James Rochlin. Fueled by taxes imposed on the drug traffickers in FARC-controlled areas and funds from other crimes such as extortion and hostage taking, by the early 1980s the FARC had grown into a major irregular army willing to confront the Colombian military.

After a 1984 cease-fire, the FARC entered the Colombian political process. Its electoral success in 1986 led to a slaughter of its members by mainly right-wing paramilitary forces. Abandoning the political process, the FARC resolved to overthrow the government in Bogotá or establish their own government in the parts of the country they controlled. During the late 1980s and the 1990s they enjoyed some military successes and by 1998 had 17,000 to 20,000 fighters.

The FARC was not the only nongovernmental organization at war in Colombia. The leftist National Liberation Army (ELN) was founded in July 1964 by Fabio Vásquez Castaño, another Marxist-Leninist inspired by Castro. The ELN recruited peasants, college students, and liberal priests. In 1967, the Maoist Popular Liberation Army (EPL) was founded with predictably revolutionary and violent objectives. Then, in 1971, the left-wing M-19 guerrilla group emerged to join in the violence. In 1985, M-19 guerrillas forced their way into the Palace of Justice in Bogotá, killing eleven judges and ninety other people. M-19 became a legal party in 1990 as part of a peace agreement with the government.

The most powerful of the many nongovernment groups apart from the FARC was the United Self-Defense Forces (AUC), a right-wing paramilitary force created in 1997 through the merger of several right-wing militias. The AUC was funded primarily by landowners and businesses seeking protection from the FARC and other left-wing guerrillas, as well as by the paramilitaries' own involvement in drug trafficking. The AUC also protected local economic and political interests. At their height, the AUC paramilitaries had some 20,000 members.

All through the 1980s and 1990s, with the active support and participation of the FARC and the AUC, the cultivation of coca and poppies in Colombia expanded significantly, along with shipments of cocaine and heroin into the United States. With the success of counter-narcotics efforts in Peru and Bolivia, Andean coca growing and cocaine production shifted to the jungles of southern Colombia, where there was little government presence and the FARC could provide protection. Further, in the early 1990s, after the breakup of the Medellín and Cali drug cartels and fragmenting of the drug industry in Colombia, the smaller drug "families" and cartels that arose in their stead were substantially more dependent on the FARC for protection.

President Ronald Reagan in April 1986 signed a National Security Decision Directive declaring drug trafficking a threat to the national security of the United States. Public and congressional pressure for greater American military involvement in the war on drugs had increased, with both houses of Congress in 1988 directing the U.S. military to stop the flow of drugs into the country. One manifestation of the lack of realism—or just plain stupidity—of Congress was the provision in one House bill that the U.S. military stop all illicit drugs from coming into the U.S. within forty-five days. The proposal had no impact.

Nonetheless, there remained a pressing political necessity in the United States to do something about the drug epidemic. In August 1989, President George H. W. Bush offered $65 million in emergency military aid to Bogotá and signed a new national security directive that lifted Reagan's restriction of U.S. military advisers to base camps and allowed U.S. forces to accompany "routine" indigenous military patrols. Bush formally announced an "Andean Initiative" in a speech to the nation from the Oval Office on September 5, 1989, pledging more than $250 million in military and law enforcement assistance for Colombia, Peru, and Bolivia during the coming year, which he described as "the first part of a 5-year, $2 billion program to counter the producers, the traffickers and the smugglers." By the end of the administration in January 1993, Colombia was the largest recipient of U.S. military assistance in Latin America.

While the Bush administration claimed to have cut the quantity of cocaine coming into the United States, the purity of the product remained the same and the street price overall remained below where it had been in 1987—two strong indications of continuing ample, probably undiminished, supply.

Reagan and Bush may have described the drug problem as a national security issue, but it was dealt with in the White House mainly as a domestic problem. Under both Reagan and Bush (and later), most senior national security officials (including me) considered the U.S. drug problem more one of demand—the insatiable appetite for cocaine among Americans—than of supply. Reagan's secretary of state, George Shultz, would later advocate legalization of some drugs in light of the demand and the difficulty of curbing supply. There was a fatalistic view that, just like during Prohibition, as long as there was a huge market in the United States, foreign suppliers would find a way to meet the need, and all the border guards and interdiction planes and boats we could offer would make little difference. Domestic politics and policy necessitated efforts at home and abroad to deal with both supply and demand, but those efforts focused on largely ineffective education programs at home and whack-a-mole seizures of illegal drugs by the Drug Enforcement Agency. Most politicians found it easier to talk tough about eradication and interdiction of supply—and going after the cartels—than to come up with ways to reduce demand inside the United States.

Bill Clinton and his national security team essentially ignored Colombia and its drug industry during his first term. This was probably due to concerns in the White House—and in Congress—that the Colombian military and police were guilty of significant human rights abuses and thus were unappetizing partners; reports that officials of the Colombian government at the highest level were in league with the traffickers; information linking the brutal AUC paramilitaries with the government, military, and big business; and distractions such as Somalia, Haiti, the Balkans, Iraq, North Korea, terrorism, and the Whitewater investigation. The administration began to pay more attention to the problem with Clinton's appointment of General Barry McCaffrey, former commander of Southern Command, as "drug czar" in January 1996. McCaffrey had worked to stop the flow of cocaine from Colombia and elsewhere and brought experience, expertise, and commitment to his new position. It remained, however, a position without meaningful authority or resources.

The security situation in Colombia deteriorated to the point that, in 1998, a U.S. intelligence report forecast that the FARC and its allies would be able to defeat the Bogotá government within five years and convert Colombia into a "narco-state." By the time of Colombia's presidential election in mid-1998, the country was on the verge of becoming not only a failed state but a vast criminal enterprise. Colombia had become the world's primary producer of coca and cocaine, the export value of these drugs amounting to between one-fourth and one-third of Colombian exports. In 2000, 67 percent of the total area of coca cultivation in the world was in Colombia, with cocaine production reaching its peak of some 700 tons that year. During this period, between 80 percent and 90 percent of the cocaine consumed in the United States came from there.

The election of 1998 was a turning point. Conservative Party candidate Andrés Pastrana had promised during his campaign to begin peace talks with the FARC. On June 8, after the first round of the presidential election, Pastrana, calling to mind the massive American assistance program for Europe after World War II, said, "Developed countries should help us to implement some sort of 'Marshall Plan' for Colombia, which will allow us to develop great investments in the social field, in order to offer our peasants different alternatives to illicit crops." On August 3, just days before his inauguration, President-elect Pastrana told President Clinton in Washington that his priorities were to end Colombia's long civil conflict, end drug trafficking, and stimulate the economy. Pastrana proposed an increase in U.S. assistance for counter-narcotics efforts, sustainable economic development, protection of human rights, humanitarian aid, stimulating private investment, and joining with others to promote Colombian economic growth.

Despite Pastrana's outreach to the rebels, a few days before his August 7 inauguration the FARC launched a number of attacks on police and army bases around the country. Undaunted, and still committed to the peace process, Pastrana on November 7, 1998, granted the FARC a 17,000-square-mile safe haven in southern Colombia, a refuge the size of Switzerland. Such a demilitarized safe haven had been a FARC precondition for peace talks, and Pastrana agreed to it as a "confidence-building" measure. Pastrana soon put forward his "Plan for Colombian Peace," which he envisioned as a collaboration with multinationals and foreign governments to concentrate on economic development, human rights, and judicial reform. The original plan did not focus on either drug trafficking or military assistance, but on manual eradication of drug crops. Pastrana aimed to end the violence through peace talks with the FARC, acknowledging that Colombia's conflict was rooted in economic inequality and poverty.

Negotiations between Colombia and the United States over the plan and U.S. aid proceeded through the fall of 1998. On October 28 Pastrana met with Clinton again at the White House, where, as the communiqué stated, they "consolidated a comprehensive partnership between their two governments designed to promote democracy and economic growth, fight illicit drugs, strengthen respect for human rights, extend the rule of law, and help bring an end to Colombia's armed conflict." During the visit, Clinton pledged over $280 million in new assistance and expressed his support for the "courageous efforts to end the decades-old conflict with guerrilla groups."

In light of the broad pessimism of most experts about seriously reducing the foreign supply of illegal drugs while U.S. demand remained high, it is hard to know what motivated Clinton to participate. (He didn't write about it in his memoir.) Three possibilities seem likely. First, because of the flood of cocaine entering the United States in the late 1990s, politicians were under heavy pressure to do something to reduce the supply from abroad. The 1998 midterm elections were on November 3, less than a week after the October 28 meeting between Clinton and Pastrana. Whether or not intended to help in the midterms, agreement on Plan Colombia allowed the president to point to a strategy and a concrete plan to tackle the narcotics scourge, thereby easing the political pressure.

Second, Pastrana's August and October visits and the agreement on Plan Colombia coincided with an intense phase of the impeachment proceedings against Clinton. On August 3, the same day as Pastrana's visit, Clinton was asked to give a blood sample for DNA testing in connection with the Monica Lewinsky scandal. On October 5, the House Judiciary Committee voted to launch a congressional impeachment inquiry, and three days later, the full House voted to begin impeachment proceedings. With all this going on, the president presumably would have welcomed a foreign policy success as a distraction, all the more so because it addressed a problem of concern to politicians in both parties. Also, at a time when Washington was obsessing over the impeachment drama, Clinton could point to Plan Colombia as evidence he was still focused on the job and able to work across the aisle with the same Republicans who were trying to drive him out of office.

Third, and perhaps most important, Pastrana's Plan Colombia actually held the promise of making an impact on a serious national problem, even though it would be fundamentally revised in the months ahead. My bet is that all three factors were at play in Bill Clinton's embrace of the plan at the end of 1998.

As Pastrana's negotiating strategy produced little, U.S. officials leaned increasingly toward a more military-oriented approach. This inclination intensified in February 1999 when three American activists helping an indigenous tribe were killed by the FARC. When the FARC launched a nationwide offensive in the summer of 1999, drug czar McCaffrey offered a plan composed of mainly military initiatives that would provide Colombia with more than $1 billion in assistance. This was an approach that could be sold to Congress. The United States would support Plan Colombia, but a version intended to strengthen the Colombian military and police so they could successfully attack the drug traffickers and their FARC protectors, and thus beat back the rebel challenge to the government.

On January 11, 2000, Clinton committed $1.3 billion to the revised

Plan Colombia, in addition to $330 million already approved. He acknowledged that the funding in 2000 would focus on a "one-time infusion of funds to help boost Colombia's interdiction and eradication capabilities," but added there would also be assistance for economic development, protection of human rights, and judicial reform. The package also provided up to 500 military trainers and 300 civilians to help with coca eradication, and promised mobilization of a number of nonmilitary U.S. programs to help Colombia develop its economy and tackle drug production. With the stroke of a pen, Colombia became the third-largest recipient of U.S. foreign aid in the world. The administration was mobilizing a number of instruments of American power.

Three days after Clinton's announcement, Secretary of State Madeleine Albright flew to Cartagena, Colombia, where she promised Pastrana and Colombians that she and Clinton would fight to get congressional approval of the assistance package. Albright underscored that the assistance package supported the peace process, economic development, the defense of human rights, and the need for alternative development. She neglected to mention that Pastrana's original plan had been significantly reshaped by Washington and was now a military- and police-driven counter-narcotics strategy focused on eradication, arrests, and military action against the traffickers and the insurgents who protected them. Rhetoric about economic development, human rights, and judicial reform notwithstanding, 78 percent of the Clinton package in 2000 and nearly 98 percent in 2001 was for the Colombian army and police.

The administration wanted it both ways: credit from the left at home and abroad for taking seriously the economic and social dimensions of Colombia's crisis, and from the right for going after the FARC and traffickers militarily.

Hearings in the House of Representatives on the president's aid package began on March 9, 2000. It soon became clear that it would face a rougher road than anticipated. Both parties in Congress, while supportive of going after the drug traffickers, were leery of helping to fight a counterinsurgency in Colombia. As Condi Rice would later write, "The confusion in Plan Colombia, though, was rooted in queasiness about the degree to which the U.S. should take on the civil conflict itself and support the Colombian military in confronting the insurgents and armed groups." There was a lot of skepticism among members about a key part of the plan, the "push into southern Colombia," an army offensive to provide security for aerial and manual eradication of drug crops. The push involved driving the FARC out of areas they had controlled for some time, a very different activity for U.S. advisers than their previous support for Colombian police antidrug operations. Many members of Congress were concerned that if the operation failed, it would lead to a further escalation of U.S. military involvement, and the proposal thus raised fears about getting involved in another "quagmire," as in Vietnam. A number continued to harbor reservations about the Colombian military's abuse of human rights; were suspicious that there were continuing ties between the military, the police, and AUC paramilitaries responsible for atrocities; and worried about connections between all three and the traffickers. It was also unclear how the aid package would actually decrease the flow of drugs into the United States.

What helped carry the day for the Clinton proposal, though, was domestic politics: it was an election year—a presidential election year to boot—and no one wanted to look soft on the drug scourge. The aid proposal, with modifications, passed and Clinton signed it into law on July 13, 2000.

Pastrana's original Plan Colombia was heavily dependent on contributions from international organizations as well as Europe, Japan, Canada, and Latin America. But there was a backlash among the other prospective donors against the revised, predominantly military-directed U.S. assistance effort, coupled with their doubts about the likely success of the initiative. On June 21, 2000, an Amnesty International press release stated: "The Plan proposes a principally military strategy (in the U.S. component of Plan Colombia) to tackle illicit drug cultivation and trafficking through substantial military assistance to the Colombian armed forces and police. Social development and humanitarian assistance programs included in the Plan cannot disguise its essentially military character."

On July 5 in Madrid, and again on October 24 in Bogotá, Colom-

bian officials met with more than two dozen potential donor countries. Only Spain made a pledge, $100 million. Otherwise, the United
States and Colombia were on their own.

W hen George W. Bush became president in January 2001,
neither the United States nor Colombia had clear objectives
with respect to the FARC or Plan Colombia. Was our objective to
stop the flow of drugs into the United States, as the Clinton administration argued, or was it to help the Colombian government (and
armed forces) regain control of their country by defeating the FARC?
There had been little support in Congress or the Clinton administration for targeting the FARC insurgency except as ancillary to the
counter-narcotics strategy. Pastrana, on the other hand, continued to
believe he could negotiate a peace deal with the FARC that would
weaken the narcotraffickers they protected and allow for alternative
development away from drug crops. Condi Rice would later write
that Bush came into office believing that Plan Colombia was not sustainable without resolving the underlying question of whether the
United States should support the Colombian government in ending
the insurgency militarily.

As helicopters and other equipment provided under the Clinton
aid package began to flow into Colombia in 2001, and Bush increased
Andean Counterdrug Initiative funding by $676 million ($380 million for Colombia), Pastrana continued to negotiate with the FARC.
Finally, though, he showed some muscle, at various times mobilizing
troops, insisting on aerial surveillance of the FARC safe haven, and
pushing for military checkpoints on its periphery. Nonetheless, in
January 2002, he agreed to a FARC cease-fire timetable.

In early 2002, Bush began to consider how to use funds designated
for counter-narcotics operations to assist the Colombian government
in fighting the insurgents. After 9/11, the Bush administration had
declared the FARC to be a terrorist group. Rumsfeld recommended
that Bush provide military assistance to the Colombians to aid in
their struggle against the insurgents to underscore that the campaign
against terrorists was, in fact, global and that the United States wasn't

just attacking Islamic extremists. Congress, however, had specifically prohibited the use of any funds to help the Colombian military fight the FARC and other insurgents.

When, on February 21, 2002, the FARC, continuing a campaign of violence, hijacked an airplane carrying a senior Colombian senator, Pastrana had had enough. He ended the government's cease-fire and began military operations in the south, taking back control of several major towns. On February 23, the FARC kidnapped presidential candidate Íngrid Betancourt, who was held captive by the FARC for six years.

Bush wanted to be responsive to Pastrana's requests for military assistance, but his hands were tied by the congressional prohibition. The attacks against the United States on 9/11 and the attacks inside Colombia during February, however, changed congressional attitudes. On March 6, 2002, the House of Representatives passed a resolution inviting Bush to submit legislation that would authorize him to assist Colombia in protecting itself against U.S.-designated terrorist groups. Two weeks later, the administration asked Congress for nearly $29 billion for a global counterterrorism effort, including a request for authorization to use counter-narcotics funds for "a unified campaign against narcotics trafficking [and] against activities by organizations designated as terrorist organizations," including the FARC.

There was still hesitancy to act. At Bush's request, Rice convened the NSC principals—the vice president and secretaries of state and defense—to discuss Pastrana's request for military assistance. Secretary of State Colin Powell was skeptical of the prospects for success and of Pastrana's "willingness to stay the course against the FARC." State believed that the millions of dollars spent for alternative crop programs to wean peasants away from coca and poppies had been a failure. Rice would later write that "everyone generally agreed" with Powell's assessment. Just as had been the case under Reagan, Bush 41, and Clinton, Bush 43's senior advisers were deeply skeptical that the supply of illegal drugs could be stanched by eradication and interdiction. As Rumsfeld wrote, "stopping the flow of drugs into our country, while important, was fated to be unsuccessful as long as the powerful demand for illegal drugs persisted."

In the spring of 2002, then, the counter-narcotics-focused Plan Colombia was in trouble and there was not yet either a firm decision to shift from counter-narcotics to counterinsurgency nor congressional approval to do so.

Everything changed with the election of Álvaro Uribe as president of Colombia on May 26, 2002. I met with him on several occasions after I became secretary of defense in 2006 and was always impressed. A diminutive man, with his round spectacles he looked like a stereotypical accountant. But he was tough as nails. The FARC had killed his father, and he personally had survived more than a dozen assassination attempts. As the new president, he was determined to regain control of Colombia from terrorists, rebel insurgents, and traffickers. He would conduct the campaign using and strengthening the democratic institutions of government, reestablish government control of the countryside, carry out political reform, and demand the surrender of insurgents on both the left and right.

Uribe visited the White House on June 21, 2002, to meet with Rice. He told Rice of the need for military assistance, arguing that he couldn't fight the insurgents with just economic assistance. Bush dropped by Rice's office during the meeting and a very frank conversation ensued. According to Rice's account, Uribe told Bush he was committed to confronting the FARC and the AUC. Bush pushed him: "Do you really mean it? Because if you do, you have to be prepared for really tough action. Kill their leadership, and they will start to fold." And Uribe said he intended to do just that. He reaffirmed his commitment in an Oval Office meeting six weeks later, after new acts of violence by the FARC, including attacks during his inauguration ceremony.

Five days before Uribe's inauguration, Congress approved legislation permitting the administration to support his campaign against terrorist groups—insurgents—in Colombia. Lingering concerns about human rights abuses by the Colombian army led Congress (as it had under Clinton) to condition military assistance on certification by President Bush that the Colombian army was taking strong measures against abusers in its ranks. Such a certification was soon forthcoming. While the legislation lifted the restrictions on the use of funding for counterterrorism and for advising military units, members were deeply concerned about U.S. troops getting involved in combat and so kept a tight leash on the number of Americans permitted to provide training and support: 400 U.S. military personnel and 400 U.S. citizens working for private contractors.

Contrary to Uribe's assurances before being elected, on August 12 he declared a state of emergency and imposed a one-time tax on wealthy individuals and companies, raising $800 million to increase and improve Colombian military capabilities. Over the next several years, the Colombian military budget would triple, to nearly $12 billion, and the ranks of the military and police would grow from 279,000 in 2000 to 415,000 in 2007.

The first U.S. military counterinsurgency trainers arrived in October and November 2002, bringing with them helicopters and other materiel. In December, Secretary of State Powell visited Colombia and pledged more help. He made explicit the Bush administration's support for eliminating the security threat in Colombia by military means. By 2004, more than 30,000 Colombians had received American military and police training.

The battlefield in Colombia became less complex in November 2002, when the AUC declared a unilateral cease-fire, ostensibly because of Uribe's determination to take on the FARC and the ELN. A year later, the AUC agreed to demobilize, enabling Uribe to focus on the FARC. Military operations became more aggressive even as he held out the olive branch of reintegration into society for all illegal armed groups. In May 2006, Uribe was handily reelected as president, and several months later the United States committed to providing an additional $4 billion in assistance.

It was a measure of the progress in improving security that Bush could visit Bogotá in March 2007. Even if the visit lasted only a few hours and took place amid very heavy security, symbolically it was an important show of support for the reelected Uribe and his efforts to reestablish government control over all of Colombia.

Nevertheless, violence in Colombia escalated in 2007, with the FARC launching multiple successful attacks against the Colombian military and kidnapping more Americans along with Colombian politicians and soldiers. In June, a group of kidnapped lawmakers in FARC hands were killed. Despite these attacks, security had improved enough that, as secretary of defense, I visited Bogotá in October. I was helicoptered to a Colombian special forces training camp, where the skills that would be used in any hostage rescue mission were displayed. The carefully choreographed demonstration concluded with all the troops rushing together, half down on one knee, all pointing their rifles at me. I admit I had a few qualms as I remembered at that moment how Egyptian president Anwar Sadat had been assassinated by his own troops.

Two thousand eight would mark a turning point in the fight against the FARC. The Colombian military attacked a FARC base in Ecuador on March 1, killing the insurgents' second-in-command, Raúl Reyes, and twenty-four others. One of the FARC founders, Manuel Marulanda, died of natural causes on March 26. That same month, the youngest member of the FARC secretariat, Iván Ríos, was murdered by his bodyguard in return for a government reward. The FARC's legendary senior female commander, Elda Neyis Mosquera, also known as Karina, surrendered in May. And in July, those Colombian special forces I had watched train rescued Íngrid Betancourt and fourteen other hostages. The operation was so skillfully executed that there were suspicions U.S. troops had been involved. I told the press our only involvement had been some intelligence support and, above all, training those Colombian troops.

The U.S. contribution during these years, in addition to training, was to help improve the Colombian forces' mobility and ability to operate in difficult terrain, intelligence collection, and night fighting. Throughout, Congress kept a tight leash on the number of Americans involved, in 2004 grudgingly expanding the number of military personnel from 400 to 800 and the number of U.S. citizens working for contractors from 400 to 600, tiny increases compared to what was going on in Iraq and Afghanistan. Even with these limitations, Colombia provided a vivid demonstration of the value of U.S. military assistance, training, and supply of equipment as an effective instrument of power that enabled local forces to successfully combat threats to peace and stability.

By the end of the Bush administration, the security situation in Colombia had improved dramatically. The number of kidnappings had dropped from 2,882 in 2002 to 376 in 2008. Terrorist acts during the same period declined from 1,645 to 303, and homicides from 28,837 to 13,632. Attacks on the 500-mile-long oil pipeline that was a major source of revenue for the government dropped from 170 in 2001 to one in 2007. Colombia was no longer at risk of becoming a failed state.

To the extent that Plan Colombia was originally sold to Congress and the American people by the Clinton administration as a means to reduce the supply of cocaine to the United States, it must be judged a failure. Plan Colombia had the goal of reducing the cultivation, processing, and distribution of illegal narcotics by 50 percent by 2006. While that goal was achieved with respect to opium poppy cultivation and heroin production—despite years of crop eradication efforts, both manual and aerial—according to an October 2008 Government Accountability Office report, coca cultivation was 15 percent greater in 2006 than in 2000 and cocaine production about 4 percent higher. The Office of National Drug Control Policy in the White House estimated that cocaine production had decreased by almost 25 percent from a high of 700 metric tons in 2001 to 535 metric tons in 2007, far below the goals of Plan Colombia. More telling, during this period there was no increase in the street price of cocaine in the United States nor any crimp in availability. The counter-narcotics effort pursued by both the Clinton and the Bush administrations had an impact but fell far short of the plan's goals.

President Pastrana and his successors recognized that the only way to get peasant farmers to stop growing poppies and coca was to provide alternative means of livelihood, either by growing licit crops or by creating other jobs. Between 2002 and 2008, the United States allocated $500 million to alternative development in Colombia. However, as I would argue with respect to the counter-narcotics problem in Afghanistan, these alternatives had to be in place *before* eradication began. Unfortunately, in both countries, manual and aerial eradication usually preceded alternative development programs; moreover, the latter were quite limited relative to the scale of eradication. Alternative crops required the development of markets, means of getting those crops to market, and judicial and governmental structures to support legitimate economic activity. The substantial U.S. contribution added to Colombia's own investments in alternative development, which improved the lives of hundreds of thousands of Colombians, but in a country with some 3 million to 5 million displaced citizens, the resources fell far short of the need. The growers also became more clever about hiding their coca crops under jungle canopy and moving to even more remote areas of Colombia. There were few alternative development programs in those areas of Colombia where most of the coca was grown, and the Colombian government unwisely, I believe, prohibited such assistance projects in communities where any illicit crops were being cultivated.

On the other hand, Plan Colombia as framed by the Bush administration must be counted as mostly successful in terms of reestablishing government control over nearly all of Colombia, dramatically weakening the FARC and paramilitaries, and improving security.

NGOs and other governments continued to be critical of the revised Plan Colombia's focus on enhancing the capabilities of the military and the police to go after the traffickers and then the insurgents. But a lesson learned in Colombia that should have been applied in Iraq—before the 2007 troop surge—was that without security, economic development and institutional reform are impossible. Of the $6.1 billion the United States spent between 2000 and 2008 under Plan Colombia, $4.8 billion was mainly to build military and police capabilities and mobility.

Despite the funding imbalance between military and nonmilitary assistance, Plan Colombia drew heavily upon nonmilitary instruments of power. Led by the State Department, a number of other agencies and departments had a robust presence and engagement in Colombia. According to an October 2008 General Accounting Office report, the United States spent over $1 billion between 2000 and 2008 promoting social and economic justice and another $250 million promoting the rule of law. USAID oversaw the alternative economic development programs and provided over $150 million to support protection of human rights, creation of conflict resolution centers, and training of public defenders; $200 million to provide economic and social assistance to internally displaced persons; and nearly $30 million to support Colombian government programs to reestablish government services and presence in areas retaken from the FARC. The Justice Department provided $115 million to help Colombia build a new criminal justice system, including training over 40,000 judges, prosecutors, police investigators, and forensic experts. Different components of the State Department oversaw both the security and counter-narcotics efforts, including providing and sustaining additional helicopter assets; funding weapons, ammunition, and training to the Colombian army's counter-narcotics brigade; enabling the Colombian air force to improve its air interdiction capabilities; supporting creation of police squadrons to establish an immediate government presence in areas newly taken from the FARC; and providing humanitarian assistance to displaced persons. Throughout Plan Colombia, the State Department had the lead, with the Defense Department in support. Four years into Plan Colombia, the country was the third-largest recipient of U.S. aid and the embassy staff in Bogotá was the largest in the world (later supplanted by Baghdad).

The Bush administration recognized that trade and direct foreign investment, both important instruments of power, were key to Colombia's future, both economically and politically. Accordingly, in May 2004 the United States initiated negotiations for a free trade agreement with Colombia, Peru, and Ecuador. The treaty with Colombia was signed on November 22, 2006, and after a long delay and revisions, was ratified by Congress in 2011.

President Obama continued U.S. support for Plan Colombia and its successors, embracing both military and nonmilitary assistance, but was clearly supportive of the congressional Democrats' desire to change the balance in favor of nonmilitary instruments as the overall level of U.S. support declined. Between 2010 and 2016, annual funding of nonmilitary assistance dropped from $507 million to $300 million, and military assistance from $134 million to $58 million. Obama supported Colombia's National Consolidation Plan integrating security, development, and counter-narcotics to establish a government presence in areas newly retaken from the FARC. The counterpart U.S. program brought together the State, Defense, and Justice Departments along with USAID to help Colombia expand the government's presence and promotion of economic opportunities in vulnerable areas. The administration also signed a ten-year defense agreement with Colombia on October 30, 2009.

Such was the success of the security campaign in Colombia that the Obama administration began to address how to transfer the lessons learned there to other countries in the region, in particular, Mexico and Peru. I visited Bogotá again in April 2010. A major theme of my visit was promoting partnerships between Colombia and other Latin American governments.

Uribe was succeeded as president in 2010 by his former defense minister, Juan Manuel Santos. Santos praised Uribe's security policies, saying that "it is possible to have a peaceful Colombia" because of their success. Formal peace talks began in 2012 and dragged on for years. Opponents of the talks, led by former president Uribe, believed that Santos was too conciliatory. Running on a peace platform, Santos barely won reelection in 2014.

As the negotiations proceeded, U.S. assistance to Colombia focused increasingly on post-conflict planning and Colombia's transition to peace—specifically, strengthening democratic institutions, protecting human rights, promoting reconciliation, and improving economic opportunities. According to the State Department, assistance going forward would address drug crop eradication and interdiction, citizen participation in the licit economy, land restitution, demobilization and reintegration of ex-combatants and child soldiers, promotion of human rights, protection for and services to internally displaced persons, initiatives to address climate change, and humanitarian assistance for conflict victims.

President Obama was supportive of Santos's efforts to achieve an internal peace agreement. He and Secretary of State John Kerry appointed Bernard Aronson, assistant secretary of state for Inter-

American Affairs under Bush 41, to work with Santos and help him in any way possible. In February 2016, President Santos met with Obama in Washington. At the end of the visit, in the East Room of the White House, President Obama extolled Colombia, saying that the country "on the brink of collapse is now on the brink of peace." Obama said the United States would partner with Colombia in waging peace and announced "a new framework for the next chapter of our partnership"—he called it Peace Colombia/Paz Colombia. He pledged more than $450 million to help reinforce security gains, reintegrate former combatants into society, and extend opportunity and the rule of law into areas long lacking either.

During Obama's visit to Cuba on March 20–22, 2016, Santos asked Kerry to meet in person with the FARC negotiators. Kerry did so, telling them that "if they laid down their arms and complied with the peace agreement, the United States would see them as a legitimate actor and there would be a path for them to enter politics." The FARC representatives responded that they were worried about security and reminded Kerry of the 1986 slaughter of FARC members who had joined the political process. In the following months, Aronson would often be engaged in telephone diplomacy with Santos.

After much controversy, including rejection of the peace agreement in a national referendum, on November 29–30, 2016, the Colombian Congress approved an overall peace agreement, including amnesty for FARC fighters guilty of committing minor crimes. The demobilized FARC members subsequently began moving to the demobilization zones.

Implementation of the peace agreement was a challenge. Creating the two dozen demobilization camps, removing personal arms, setting up a "peace tribunal," instituting land reform, and going after coca farms proved a daunting task for the government. Ironically, the peace deal with the FARC made the counter-narcotics struggle even harder, as military operations were dramatically reduced from the early days of Plan Colombia. In fact, in 2016, Colombia produced 710 metric tons of cocaine—somewhat more than in 2000 before Plan Colombia and up from 235 metric tons in 2013.

As Santos's second term wound down, his approval rating plummeted to just 14 percent. Partly this was due to widespread sentiment that the peace deal with the FARC was far too generous. Perhaps even more important, though, was the public's concern over the economy and jobs, health care, and corruption. Uribe protégé Iván Duque was elected to succeed Santos in 2018.

The cost of Plan Colombia to the United States since President Clinton signed the first assistance legislation in 2000 was roughly $10 billion. Not one American soldier died.

Since the end of the Cold War, the United States has tried to help multiple countries achieve peace and stability internally and to strengthen democratic institutions. Colombia is, arguably, the only major success story. Why? What are the lessons to be learned?

First and foremost, we had a strong local partner in President Uribe. He was not only tough enough to take on the FARC and other armed groups but also, in the main, willing to do it through established government institutions and in accordance with Colombian law (despite his declaration of a state of emergency in 2002). There were many instances of human rights abuses during Plan Colombia, but Uribe was willing to jail those in the military responsible for such abuses, as well as sack generals and even his military chief of staff. If Uribe had the steel backbone to take the fight to the rebels, after considerable success in improving security had been achieved, President Santos was tough enough to pursue peace through negotiations with a hated enemy. The lesson: a tough, courageous national leader willing to use force against the bad guys yet also work with all elements of society is a precondition for American success in stabilizing a country long racked by violence, and a leader committed to democratic principles and strengthening (or creating) a country's rule of law and institutions is a huge bonus. In Colombia, we had both. Nearly everywhere else we tried to help after 1993, we had neither.

Second, Colombia had a long history as a unified, democratic nation with well-established government institutions. Those institutions—judiciary, military, police—were weak, as was the democracy itself, but there were foundations upon which to build.

Third, Plan Colombia was not driven by the U.S. Defense Department and drew on multiple nonmilitary instruments of power. The State Department took the lead in Colombia for the American government. Many departments were involved in the plan, including Defense, but in a support role coordinated by State. Though the Colombian military and police led the fight against the rebels, and improving security was central to the plan, the U.S. assistance effort was civilian managed. We were there to help Colombians fight, not to do the fighting ourselves.

Fourth, congressional limits on the size of the U.S. military and contractor presence were critically important to success. They prevented the "slippery slope" of an escalating American military role so feared in Congress at the outset of Plan Colombia. The very limited U.S. military presence forced the Colombians to do the fighting themselves, and that involved significant professionalization and expansion of both the military and the police. From the outset, the U.S. role was limited to training and advising, as well as providing some equipment, above all, helicopters. A Congress that took seriously its responsibilities—and powers—prevented mission creep.

Fifth, bipartisan support in Congress allowed the United States to support the plan over fifteen years through three presidencies. As the public rationale in the United States for Plan Colombia changed in the early years—from alternative economic development to counter-narcotics to counterterrorism/counterinsurgency—Congress continued its support. There were never expectations in Congress that the situation in Colombia could be significantly improved quickly, and so all involved in Washington took an exceptionally rare long-term view.

Sixth, Colombia wanted our help. We were neither invaders nor occupiers, and our small but critical presence was barely noticeable to most Colombians.

Bearing in mind these lessons from success in Colombia, the next time an American president is urged to intervene in a Third World country's internal conflict, stabilize the situation, or improve governance, he or she should ask these questions: Do we have a strong, competent, reasonably honest local leader committed to democracy and the rule of law with whom to partner? Are there existing indigenous institutions and capabilities on which to build? With our help, can the country's military and police be strengthened sufficiently to carry the burden of the fight? Is the effort likely to be protracted, and if so, what is the prospect for long-term U.S. public and congressional support? Can we bring to bear a wide array of U.S. instruments of power in order to achieve our objectives without American forces being directly engaged in combat? Will we have the discipline to keep the number of U.S. military in-country small, forcing the locals to carry the burden of the fight?

Unless America's vital interests are at risk, if the answer to any of these questions is no, the president should take a deep breath—and be very, very cautious about proceeding.

CHAPTER 6

Afghanistan

War Without End

What began as one of the smallest, least expensive, shortest, most successful military campaigns in American history morphed into a generation-long conflict, the longest war in our history. Things went so wrong for the same reasons other post–Cold War imbroglios did: hubris in believing we had the power to transform a country and its culture, strategic mistakes, and the weakness of our nonmilitary instruments of power that are so essential to any chance of success. There was a terrible mismatch between our aspirations to change Afghanistan and our ability to do so. And in our ambition, we lost sight of the very specific and limited reason we went to Afghanistan in the first place after the attacks of September 11, 2001: to destroy those who attacked us, al-Qaeda, and to oust the Taliban, who had sheltered them. We assumed—because of our good intentions and our unparalleled power—that our experience in Afghanistan would turn out differently and better than that of all the foreign invaders over the centuries who preceded us. We were mostly wrong, mainly because we decided the initial military victory wasn't enough.

The terrain now known as Afghanistan has been a battleground for nearly four thousand years. Over forty centuries, part or all of Afghanistan faced the armies of Persia, Alexander the Great, Parthia, Arab Islam, Genghis Khan, Tamerlane (Timur), Mughal India, Great

Britain, the Soviet Union, and us, as well as assorted lesser-known invaders.

There were two significant attempts by Afghan leaders in the twentieth century to reform and modernize the country. Both failed. After the third war with Britain and the Treaty of Rawalpindi in August 1919, King Amanullah Khan declared Afghanistan sovereign and independent. Amanullah was a reformer who made elementary education compulsory, abolished the burqa for women, developed coeducational institutions, advocated the education of women, and abolished slavery. Foreshadowing things to come, the king's reforms alienated a number of tribal and religious leaders, and he was forced to abdicate in January 1929, his reforms abandoned. In 1933, nineteen-year-old Mohammed Zahir Shah became king after considerable internal conflict, including the assassination of his father. He held the throne for forty years.

Under Zahir, Afghanistan broke out of its isolation, joining the League of Nations and establishing close relations with a number of countries, including the Axis powers: Germany, Japan, and Italy. The United States granted Afghanistan diplomatic recognition in 1934. Before World War II, Nazi Germany started commercial air service in Afghanistan and built hydroelectric plants. The king and his uncles (who really ran the show) sat on the sidelines during World War II and maintained neutrality in the Cold War while cultivating relations with both the United States and the Soviet Union. In 1963, the king fired Prime Minister Daoud Khan (his brother-in-law) and maneuvered his uncles out of power. The new constitution he proposed, approved in 1964, was intended to make Afghanistan a modern, democratic state—a constitutional monarchy with a parliament, civil rights, women's rights, and universal suffrage. His reform efforts, like those of Amanullah in the 1920s, came to naught. They had little impact outside of Kabul because of opposition from tribal and religious leaders as well as factionalism and the overall weakness of the central government.

During an overseas trip by the king in 1973, Daoud Khan carried out a successful coup and Zahir went into exile. Daoud declared himself the first president of Afghanistan. There was little popular resistance to the coup, in part because the king's government had been ineffective in dealing with a terrible three-year drought that killed more than 75,000. Zahir had given Afghans forty years of relative peace and quiet. In the decades to come, that would be considered a remarkable achievement.

Until 1989, Afghanistan was of interest to the U.S. government only in the context of the Cold War. From the late 1950s until the late 1970s, Washington provided some $500 million for education, improving government administration, and expanding agricultural production (especially through building irrigation systems). The Soviets spent about twice that in Afghanistan during the same period. The superpowers built the airports in Kabul (USSR) and Kandahar (United States), highways, and a number of other infrastructure projects. President Eisenhower made a state visit to Kabul in December 1959, and in the ensuing years Afghanistan received a steady procession of senior American leaders, politicians, astronauts, and celebrities. The U.S. Peace Corps was active in Afghanistan from 1962 to 1979. At one point, the scale and impact of the American effort led to concerns in Moscow that Afghanistan was at risk of becoming an American satellite. Taken together, U.S. programs during that twenty-year period represented an effective demonstration of the deployment of non-military instruments of national power: diplomacy, development and humanitarian assistance, the use of private sector expertise (especially in agriculture), student exchanges (one Afghan high school exchange student was Zalmay Khalilzad, who would become U.S. ambassador to Afghanistan, Iraq, and the United Nations), and strategic communications. While many of those engaged in these efforts were altruistic, for the U.S. government it was all about superpower politics.

On Christmas Eve and Christmas Day 1979, 85,000 Soviet troops poured into Afghanistan to ensure the survival of its client regime there. The Soviet leaders who supported the intervention believed the military operation would be relatively brief, a routine mistake made by leaders many times before and since when deciding to go to war.

The last Soviet soldier marched out of Afghanistan and back into the Soviet Union a decade later. During this period, 13,310 Soviet soldiers were killed and 35,478 wounded. More than a million served there. Between 500,000 and 2 million Afghans died at Soviet hands, with at least 5 million turned into refugees, mostly in Pakistan. Many experts believe the Afghan War contributed to the collapse of the Soviet Union by undermining the ideological tenet that history was on their side, giving the lie to the Brezhnev doctrine that once a country was under the Soviet heel it stayed there forever, and dramatically increasing cynicism and skepticism at home due to the leadership's pervasive lying about the war. Of course, there were also the body bags and tens of thousands of maimed soldiers.

If the invasion of Afghanistan had serious unintended consequences for the Soviets, it did for the United States as well. American assistance to the anti-Soviet resistance, the mujahedin, began during the Carter administration and ramped up dramatically under President Reagan. By 1987, the United States (including Saudi matching funds) was spending a billion dollars a year on weapons and equipment for the mujahedin, including the Stinger antiaircraft weapons that played a significant role in the outcome of the war. While the United States served as quartermaster for the resistance, Pakistan's president Muhammad Zia-al-Haq and his Inter-Services Intelligence organization (ISI) decided which resistance groups would get the lion's share of the weapons. As CIA deputy director during the period, I was deeply involved in this effort, and I can attest that neither I nor anyone else at the top of the American government fully grasped Zia's Islamist agenda and the fact that he was directing most of the weapons we provided to some of the most extreme Afghan Islamic groups. Unknowingly, we armed and strengthened those in Afghanistan who would attack us on September 11, 2001. The law of unintended consequences, indeed.

After our initial military victory in Afghanistan in 2001, the United States should have learned a lesson from how accurately Soviet leaders had eventually come to perceive their situation in Afghanistan years before, how badly they wanted out, and how they couldn't agree on a way to accomplish this. On June 2, 1986, Soviet general secretary Mikhail Gorbachev told the Politburo, "We have to get out of there." At a January 21, 1987, meeting, Politburo member Yegor Ligachev told his colleagues, "We've been defeated." Even the defense minister, Marshal

Sergei Sokolov, admitted, "We can't win this war militarily." But they also knew the Afghan government couldn't survive on its own. In late February 1987, Foreign Minister Andrei Gromyko said there was no alternative to supplying the Afghans, and Vladimir Kryuchkov, soon to be promoted to head of the KGB, argued that Moscow could not "leave, to run away, to throw away everything" and allow the country to become "a beachhead for Iran, Turkey and the fundamentalists." Gorbachev's principal foreign policy aide, Anatoly Chernyaev, wrote in his diary on August 28, 1987, "Fuck it all! We got dragged in and now we don't know how to crawl out."

The Soviets installed Mohammad Najibullah as their appointed leader in November 1986. Najibullah was still in power when the Soviets withdrew their forces in 1989, and they continued to provide economic and military assistance to him. He tried to strengthen his position with a new constitution in 1990, under which Afghanistan officially became an Islamic state. His hold on power became untenable when the Soviet Union collapsed in December 1991, and all outside assistance came to an end. He was ousted the following April. On April 24, 1992, most Afghan factions signed the Peshawar Accord, a power-sharing agreement that established the Islamic State of Afghanistan and an interim government.

One significant group that refused to sign the accord was Hezb-e Islami, led by Gulbuddin Hekmatyar, a Pashtun who had the strong support of the Pakistanis. Hekmatyar had a long and bloody history of fighting (and double-crossing) rival resistance groups, so it was consistent with past behavior that on the same day the accord was signed he attacked Kabul. Soon a full-scale civil war was under way. Kabul was a battleground for the next four years as one group and then another seized the city, but Hekmatyar caused the greatest damage and loss of life, mainly because he intentionally struck civilian targets.

During this period (and later), the Pakistanis' primary objective was to install a Pashtun-dominated government in Kabul. (The Pashtuns are the largest ethnic group in Afghanistan and the second-largest in Pakistan.) When, by 1994, it became clear that Hekmatyar would be unable to achieve this objective, the Pakistanis began redirecting their support to the predominantly Pashtun Taliban, a movement that grew out of the religious schools (madrassas) for Afghan refugees in Pakistan. With support from both Saudi Arabia and Pakistan, the Taliban seized Kabul in September 1996. After the fall of Kabul, Tajik leader Ahmad Shah Massoud joined forces with Abdul Rashid Dostum to form the Northern Alliance, but serious resistance to the Taliban ended with Dostum's defeat by the Taliban during the battles of Mazar-i-Sharif in 1997–98. The Taliban had significant support from Pakistan's chief of army staff, Pervez Musharraf. After the defeat at Mazar-i-Sharif, Dostum went into exile but Massoud continued to fight the Taliban, with support from Russia, Turkey, Iran, India, and others. On May 4, 2001, he spoke before the European Parliament in Brussels, seeking humanitarian help. I'm told that Richard Clarke, the president's counterterrorism adviser at the White House, pushed for providing support to Massoud and what was left of the Northern Alliance, but it was early days in the Bush administration, and nothing came of his effort. It is hard to see how the United States could have made a difference. Massoud was assassinated on September 9, 2001.

After the Soviets withdrew, the United States largely ignored Afghanistan, even closing our embassy in Kabul in 1989. There is a sad scene at the end of the movie *Charlie Wilson's War* in which Congressman Wilson, having been instrumental in acquiring hundreds of millions of dollars for the CIA to help the mujahedin fight the Soviets, tries and fails to get a couple of million dollars to build schools in Afghanistan after the Soviet defeat. It's a true story.

There are those who contend that U.S. neglect of Afghanistan after the Soviet withdrawal contributed to the eventual takeover of the country by the Taliban eight years later, that our lack of engagement left a vacuum the extremists exploited. Although the Bush 41 national security team was preoccupied with the liberation of Eastern Europe, the reunification of Germany, the collapse of the Soviet Union, and the first Gulf War, it is probably true that Scowcroft and I, as national security adviser and deputy, should have at least devoted some time to focusing on how the United States and others might help Afghanistan after a decade of war and destruction. We certainly sent the wrong signal when we closed our embassy so soon after the Soviets left. After helping the Afghans defeat the Soviets, we presumably had a foundation of at least some goodwill that could have been built on.

That said, there was no vacuum in Kabul in the years immediately following the Soviet withdrawal. Najibullah served as president from 1986 to 1992, and he was ousted only after the collapse of the Soviet Union ended all external help to him and his government. There was no appetite in either the executive branch or Congress to help Najibullah, who was regarded as a Soviet stooge. After his ouster, there was even less interest in picking a side during the civil war.

Hindsight provides a clarity I think was lacking in those days. The Taliban wasn't even founded by Mullah Muhammad Omar until 1994, by which time the civil war was well under way, and Bin Laden would not arrive in Afghanistan for two years after that, following the Taliban victory. Perhaps it is a rationalization, but given the situation on the ground (including large-scale Pakistani military support for the Taliban), it is hard to see how the Clinton administration could have offered anything more than perfunctory assistance, and we most assuredly could not have helped shape a better outcome.

During his first term, President Clinton continued the Bush 41 administration's neglect of Afghanistan but did confront an intensifying terrorist threat that eventually would bring the country into the American crosshairs. Five weeks after Clinton's inauguration, on February 26, 1993, terrorists attacked the World Trade Center, killing six and injuring more than a thousand. Ramzi Yousef, chief planner of the attack, had spent time in an al-Qaeda training camp in Afghanistan and received funding for the attack from his uncle, Khalid Sheikh Mohammed, an al-Qaeda member and architect of the September 11, 2001, bombing of the same target.

In late 1994, the Philippine national police thwarted an ambitious terrorist scheme (code-named Bojinka) that, once fully revealed, involved plans to kill Pope John Paul II during his visit to the Philippines in mid-January 1995, place bombs on eleven U.S.-bound airliners from Asia and kill thousands of primarily American passengers a week later, and subsequently crash a plane into CIA headquarters. Funding for the plot was provided by Osama bin Laden and several front organizations run by his brother-in-law.

Bin Laden, a wealthy Saudi, had been deeply involved in the mujahedin fight against the Soviets, primarily as a source of funding. As deputy director of the CIA between 1986 and 1989, I oversaw the covert program in support of the Afghan resistance and was briefed weekly on its progress; I do not recall hearing Bin Laden's name in connection with the fight. He and his followers remained in Afghanistan and Peshawar after the Soviets withdrew their troops and, radicalized against the West in general and the United States in particular, especially over the presence of U.S. troops in Saudi Arabia during the first Gulf War, they plotted the al-Qaeda terror campaign.

The Clinton administration, and specifically the president's counterterrorism adviser Richard Clarke, took the Bin Laden threat seriously, urging the CIA to get more information on al-Qaeda. After the 1993 attack on the World Trade Center and the revelation of the Bojinka plan, and in light of other thwarted plots, in January 1996 the CIA established a "station" within its Counterterrorism Center focused exclusively on al-Qaeda. In 1991, Bin Laden had moved his headquarters to Sudan, and in early 1996, the United States began pressing the Sudanese to expel him. That year, Bin Laden left Sudan and returned to Afghanistan, probably not because of U.S. pressure but because the Taliban seized Kabul that fall and their leader, Mullah Omar, made Bin Laden welcome. Thus began the symbiotic relationship between the Taliban and al-Qaeda.

In February 1998, Bin Laden issued a fatwa from Afghanistan calling for attacks on American military and civilian targets anywhere in the world. In May, he said his supporters would hit U.S. targets in the Gulf region, and in a June interview he threatened to shoot down our military aircraft with missiles. Less than two months later, on August 7, 1998, al-Qaeda struck the American embassies in Kenya and Tanzania. Two hundred twenty-four were killed, among them 12 Americans, and nearly 5,000 Africans and Americans were injured.

Shortly afterward, the United States learned that Bin Laden and his top assistants planned to meet at a specific site in Afghanistan on

August 20. Clinton directed cruise missile strikes on that target as well as al-Qaeda training camps in Afghanistan and a suspected VX nerve weapons storage site in Sudan. Seventy-nine missiles struck their targets, killing perhaps twenty al-Qaeda members and injuring several others. Bin Laden was not among them. Speaking to Americans from the Oval Office that day, Clinton said that Bin Laden was "perhaps the preeminent organizer and financier of international terrorism in the world today" and had vowed to wage terrorist war on the United States. Clinton subsequently signed multiple executive orders imposing economic sanctions on Bin Laden and al-Qaeda, later expanding them to include the Taliban. He also authorized the CIA to use "lethal force" to get Bin Laden. No one at the time dreamed that the August 20 cruise missile attacks would mark the beginning of America's twenty-year (and counting) military conflict in Afghanistan.

According to Madeleine Albright, two days after the U.S. attacks, Mullah Omar called Michael Malinowski, a senior State Department officer in the Bureau of South Asian Affairs, and told him the air strikes had been counterproductive and that Clinton should resign and U.S. forces should vacate Saudi Arabia. Malinowski urged Omar to turn over Bin Laden and proposed a formal dialogue. Omar agreed to talk, and a few weeks later, U.S. ambassador to Pakistan William Milam initiated a series of meetings with the Taliban that continued for two years. The U.S. message was consistent and simple: give up Bin Laden. The Taliban leaders offered excuses but refused.

Later in 1998, the administration further ratcheted up the pressure on the Taliban, declaring that its leaders would be held accountable for any future terrorist actions attributable to Bin Laden and that the United States reserved the right to use military force either preemptively in self-defense or in response to future attacks. The administration asked Pakistan, Saudi Arabia, and the United Arab Emirates to back the U.S. demand that the Taliban turn over Bin Laden and, if they refused, to deny landing rights to the Afghan airline, freeze financial assets, and prohibit Taliban leaders from traveling internationally. The United States imposed sanctions against the Taliban in July 1999, and the UN Security Council did likewise in October (by a unanimous vote). All these measures isolated the Taliban but didn't persuade them to give up Bin Laden. As Albright recounted, "We offered rewards, froze terrorist assets, tripled our counter-terrorism budget, enhanced antiterrorism training, and accelerated research into antiterrorism technology." The problem was that our economic and political instruments of power were of little use against a ruthless regime supported by neighboring Pakistan and governing an impoverished, isolated, and primitive country.

There were multiple intelligence reports in the latter half of 1999 indicating that al-Qaeda intended numerous attacks. The director of central intelligence, George Tenet, told President Clinton that Bin Laden was "planning between five and fifteen attacks around the world during the millennium and that some of these might be inside the United States." On December 14, Ahmed Ressam was arrested in Port Angeles, Washington. He had in his car materials for making one or more large bombs. It later emerged that he had been trained at an al-Qaeda camp in Afghanistan. His target was Los Angeles International Airport. Most intelligence reporting on al-Qaeda plans had focused on attacks against U.S. facilities and citizens abroad. Ressam's plan made clear that al-Qaeda was coming to America. But his arrest failed to set off enough alarm bells.

I believe the Taliban were adamant in not giving up Bin Laden to the United States in part because the Pakistani military did not want them to do so. Clinton met with Pakistani prime minister Nawaz Sharif on July 4, 1999, and reminded Sharif that he had three times previously asked for Pakistan's help in getting Bin Laden. Clinton said there were reports al-Qaeda was planning further attacks on U.S. facilities and officials around the world, including perhaps in the United States. Clinton told Sharif plainly that if he didn't do more to help, the United States would announce that Pakistan was "in effect supporting terrorism in Afghanistan." On October 12, 1999, Sharif was overthrown by General Musharraf. Shortly after the coup took place, a plan to send Pakistani commandos into Afghanistan to capture or kill Bin Laden was canceled. Then and now, it is unclear whether there was a connection.

According to Tenet, after January 1, 2000, reports of terrorist threats subsided, only to spike again in late summer. On October 12, al-Qaeda terrorists attacked the USS *Cole* in Aden harbor, killing seventeen sailors.

On December 18, 2000, Tenet wrote to Clinton and the rest of the national security team that the coming weeks would bring an increased risk of attacks on U.S. interests. "Our most credible information on bin Laden activity," he wrote, "suggests his organization is looking at US facilities in the Middle East especially the Arabian peninsula, in Turkey and Western Europe. Bin Laden's network is global however and capable of attacks in other regions, including the United States."

The incoming Bush administration took the warnings seriously. They kept in place the Clinton counterterrorism team, including its head, the irascible but capable Dick Clarke. On January 31, Bush's national security adviser, Condoleezza Rice, told Clarke he had a "green light" to develop a strategy to deal with al-Qaeda. Rice later wrote that Bush didn't want his only option in response to a terrorist attack to be using cruise missiles or bombers in retaliation: "What was needed now was a strategy not to 'roll back' al Qaeda but to eliminate the threat."

Rice and her deputy, Steve Hadley, were also convinced that the problem of Pakistan had to be addressed, along with the role of other regional actors. The best U.S. contacts inside Afghanistan were with the Northern Alliance, led by Uzbeks and Tajiks and supported by the Indians and the Russians. However, the largest ethnic group in Afghanistan (and the Taliban) were ethnic Pashtuns, who were supported by Pakistan. That support for the Pashtuns, including safe haven in Pakistan for the Taliban and its leaders, would plague four successive American presidents.

Historians, partisans, and the U.S. officials involved will argue forever over whether Clinton fumbled several opportunities to kill or capture Bin Laden and whether Bush failed to heed multiple warnings of an impending major attack on the United States. Both presidents and their senior advisers have mounted a defense of their actions, and both feel unfairly maligned by critics they accuse of benefiting from perfect hindsight. Several things are clear, however. First, by 1996, the Clinton administration was onto Bin Laden and trying to stop him; by 1998, they were trying to kill him. Second, I know from long experience that intelligence reporting is seldom as unambiguous in the moment as it is in retrospect. For example, we had many warnings of an impending terrorist attack on the Marine barracks in Beirut in 1983, but without any sense of timing or method—and even Marines can remain on full alert only for a limited time—we failed to predict the attack that cost more than two hundred lives. There were many warnings of impending terrorist attacks during the summer of 2001, but there was little specificity about where or when. And most of the U.S. officials involved believed the attacks against us would be overseas. Third, finding a bad guy on his home turf can be maddeningly difficult, whether Saddam Hussein, hostage takers in Beirut, the Unabomber in the United States (who remained at large for seventeen years), or Bin Laden in Afghanistan.

These considerations notwithstanding, it is important to note that Clinton and his team used a wide range of instruments of power to try to get Bin Laden and prevent further terrorist attacks. Through diplomacy, new cooperative counterterrorism arrangements were developed with other countries, international law enforcement was mobilized, and international sanctions were imposed on the Taliban. Economic leverage was used to try to prise Bin Laden out of Afghanistan and to enlist Pakistani assistance. Security assistance was offered to other countries to improve their counterterrorism capabilities, and intelligence sharing arrangements were greatly expanded. Covert operations were employed to stop attacks by, gather information on, and attack al-Qaeda. And when the opportunity presented itself, an overt military operation was launched to kill Bin Laden. These actions, overt and covert, continued in 2001 under President Bush. In terms of seriously damaging al-Qaeda itself, the new administration was thinking in terms of three to five years.

Tragically, all these measures failed to prevent the attack on the World Trade Center on September 11, 2001.

The post–9/11 military campaign in Afghanistan to oust the Taliban and destroy al-Qaeda was brilliantly conceived and skillfully executed. The idea of a retaliatory strike as punishment was quickly discarded; that approach had been tried after the embassy bombings in 1998 and had no impact. Bush wanted American forces on the ground: "We need to unleash holy hell." At a White House meeting just ten days after the attack, Central Command commander General Tommy Franks and Major General Dell Dailey of the Joint Special Operations Command proposed linking American Special Forces with the fighters of the Northern Alliance to attack the Taliban. They thought they could begin the campaign within two weeks. CIA officers would go in first, establish contact with the Northern Alliance, and then be joined by U.S. military Special Forces. As Rumsfeld described it, "Once embedded with the Northern Alliance, American special operations forces would upgrade their weaponry, provide supplies, and serve as on-the-ground air controllers to call in precision air strikes. The effort would combine the use of satellite communications, laser designators, GPS capability, and powerful precision munitions with friendly Afghan intelligence, language skills, cultural familiarity, and ground combat manpower."

The Bush administration was fully aware of Pakistan's support for the Taliban and, after the 9/11 attacks, quickly moved to force President Musharraf's hand. On September 13, Secretary Powell called Musharraf and told him he had to pick a side, presenting the Pakistani leader with a list of demands, including breaking relations with the Taliban. Bush spoke to Musharraf shortly afterward and the latter told him, "We are with you." Administration officials appear to have taken Musharraf at his word, even while acknowledging that others in his government, in particular the military and intelligence services, continued to help the Taliban. I have always believed Musharraf consistently spoke out of both sides of his mouth and provided support to the Taliban even while helping us. It would have been impossible for Mullah Omar and the Taliban leaders to live and operate for years in Peshawar and Quetta without Pakistani—and Musharraf's—complicity.

The first insertion of U.S. Special Forces took place on October 7, and that evening Bush told the American people that the Taliban had refused to give up Osama bin Laden and therefore the United States was at war with the Afghan regime. U.S. Special Forces linked up with Dostom and his Northern Alliance forces on October 19, and the same day two hundred U.S. Army Rangers landed in southern Afghanistan, the Taliban heartland. There they joined with an anti-Taliban Pashtun leader, Hamid Karzai. On November 9, Dostum's forces, accompanied by U.S. Special Forces—some on horseback—took Mazer-i-Sharif. Herat fell on November 11, Kabul on the 13th, Jalalabad on the 14th, and Kandahar on December 7. The Taliban and al-Qaeda were on the run, ultimately into Pakistan. The two-month campaign was successful: the U.S. achieved its objective of ousting the Taliban. Osama bin Laden had not been captured, but Afghanistan no longer would serve as a base for al-Qaeda terrorist planning and operations.

The military success story was complemented by diplomatic success in forging consensus among the Afghan factions and interested international parties on formation of an interim government in Kabul. The outcome of the military campaign and the political arrangements that followed would affect the interests of not only the multiple factions in Afghanistan but all the nations on its borders (Pakistan, Iran, China, Uzbekistan, Tajikistan, and Turkmenistan) as well as Russia and India. As the Northern Alliance campaign swept toward Kabul, there was widespread fear that the ouster of the Taliban would simply lead to a return to the civil war of the early 1990s. In particular, Pakistan saw a Northern Alliance–dominated government in Kabul as a threat given India's longstanding support for the Alliance.

It is to the credit of the Bush administration, and the State Department in particular, that as early as October, they began developing internally a policy with respect to a successor government in Afghanistan. Secretary of State Colin Powell appointed veteran diplomat James Dobbins as envoy to the Afghan opposition, and it fell to Dobbins and NSC senior director Zalmay Khalilzad to forge internal agreement on U.S. objectives and then secure both Afghan and international agreement. Given Afghan history, the magnitude of the challenge they faced is hard to exaggerate. Just inside the U.S. government,

Dobbins had to deal with four different regional bureaus at the State Department (South Asia, Europe, Middle East, and East Asia), not to mention the NSC, the Defense Department, and the CIA; the latter had positioned liaison officers with all the key warlords. In consultation with the U.S. ambassador to the UN, John Negroponte, State proposed a UN-sponsored conference to address the future governance of Afghanistan, a meeting to include all the different factions in Afghanistan as well as representatives of neighboring countries and others with an interest in the outcome.

At the UN, the secretary-general appointed Ambassador Lakhdar Brahimi as UN envoy to Afghanistan. Brahimi embraced the idea of a UN-sponsored conference but held off announcing dates until he had some assurance that all the Afghan factions would attend. He relied on the United States to get those assurances. Dobbins and Khalilzad were dispatched abroad to secure the agreement of interested governments to a conference and to sound them out on a possible new leader. Both the Turks and the Pakistanis told Dobbins that Hamid Karzai, a Pashtun, was the best candidate, the Pakistanis making clear that any government led by the Northern Alliance would be unacceptable. In Afghanistan, Dobbins met with the Northern Alliance leaders, who said they were willing to "move forward to form a broad-based government which will represent all regions and all ethnicities." Empowered by Powell to deal directly with the Iranians, Dobbins met with that delegation the night before the conference opened and they, too, indicated that Karzai would be agreeable to them as the new leader.

The conference opened in Bonn, Germany, on November 27. Twenty-five Afghans participated, representing all the major factions. On December 5, the Agreement on Provisional Arrangements in Afghanistan Pending the Re-Establishment of Permanent Government Institutions (known as the Bonn Agreement) was announced. It provided for an Afghan Interim Authority of thirty members, headed by a chairman, that had a six-month mandate, after which there would be an "emergency" *loya jirga,* or traditional assembly of Afghan worthies, to select a broad-based Transition Authority "to lead Afghanistan until such time as a fully representative government can be elected through free and fair elections to be held no later than two years from the convening of the Emergency Loya Jirga." Within eighteen months of the establishment of the Transitional Authority, a constitutional *loya jirga* was to convene to adopt a new constitution for Afghanistan. Hamid Karzai was selected as chairman of the Interim Authority and subsequently the Transition Authority. The agreement provided for the establishment, under UN auspices, of a force to "assist in the maintenance of security for Kabul and its surrounding areas. Such a force could, as appropriate, be progressively expanded to other urban centers and other areas." It was also to train Afghan forces.

The UN Security Council approved the Bonn Agreement and authorized creation of the International Security Assistance Force (ISAF) on December 20, and two days later sovereign power was transferred to the Afghan Interim Authority. Roughly ten weeks after the first American soldier set foot in Afghanistan, the Taliban and al-Qaeda were ousted, replaced by a UN-sanctioned and sovereign Afghan interim government representing all the major factions, some of which had been at war with one another for a decade, others from time immemorial. It was an amazing U.S. military and diplomatic achievement. Eleven American servicemen had been killed, thirty-five wounded. Our objective had been achieved with stunning speed, a very light American military footprint, and remarkably few casualties. Success was due to the extraordinary exercise of both military and diplomatic power.

But the seeds of unending war were sown at the very beginning. According to President Bush, "we had liberated the country from a primitive dictatorship, and we had a moral obligation to leave behind something better. We also had a strategic interest in helping the Afghan people build a free society. The terrorists took refuge in places of chaos, despair, and repression. A democratic Afghanistan would be a hopeful alternative to the vision of the extremists." According to Steve Hadley, Bush believed the fight against terrorism must involve both force and a positive, hopeful vision for the future. So, when Bush first met with Karzai in the Oval Office, they talked about not only the need to train an Afghan army and police force, but also the importance of constructing roads, health clinics, and schools. At a National Security Council meeting on September 17, six days after the attack, as Rice later wrote, "we felt an obligation to leave them better off than when we had come. Thus freeing Afghan women emerged early as a policy goal."

The Bonn Agreement set forth extraordinarily ambitious objectives. Beyond declaring that the legal framework of the country until a new constitution was approved would be King Zahir's constitution of 1964 (except for the role of the monarchy and the old executive and legislative bodies), it also stated that an independent judiciary and supreme court, a central bank, an independent civil service commission, and an independent human rights commission were to be established. The Interim Authority was charged with ensuring "the participation of women as well as the equitable representation of all ethnic and religious communities in the Interim Administration and the Emergency Loya Jirga." The agreement called as well for establishment of a "broad-based, gender-sensitive, multi-ethnic and fully representative government"; adherence by government officials to "a Code of Conduct elaborated in accordance with international standards," i.e., no corruption; declared that "all mujahedin, Afghan armed forces and armed groups in the country" would be commanded by the Interim Authority in Kabul; and required Afghanistan to adhere to "international instruments on human rights and international humanitarian law." With the help of the United States and other Western democracies, Afghanistan would be remade in their image.

I believe American decision makers that fall and winter failed to grasp the magnitude of that challenge in light of the failed reform efforts of the 1920s and 1960s in Afghanistan, including the historically limited writ in the countryside of the central government in Kabul and the enduring strength and influence of religious and tribal leaders as well as warlords and power brokers. The post-2001 president of Afghanistan, Karzai, was often derisively referred to as "the mayor of Kabul" because he had so little power beyond the city limits, but neither did King Zahir or his predecessors.

One senior American urged a very different, less ambitious approach. Defense Secretary Donald Rumsfeld on November 6, 2001, telephoned Bush and told him, "It's my view we need to limit our mission to getting the terrorists who find their way to Afghanistan.

We ought not to make a career out of transforming Afghanistan."
He would write years later that "we were not in Afghanistan to transform a deeply conservative Islamic culture into a model of liberal
modernity. We were not there to eradicate corruption or to end poppy
cultivation. We were not there to take ownership of Afghanistan's
problems, tempting though it was for many Americans of goodwill.
Instead, Afghans would need to take charge of their own fate. Afghans
would build their society the way they wanted." "It struck me," Rumsfeld added, "that sending U.S. servicemen and -women in pursuit of
an effort to remake Afghanistan into a prosperous American-style
nation-state or to try to bring our standard of security to each of that
nation's far-flung villages would be unwise, well beyond our capability,
and unworthy of our troops' sacrifice." While Rumsfeld exaggerated
Bush's aspirations for Afghanistan, I think even the more limited
goals the president had in mind—an inclusive government responsive
to and respectful of its citizens' rights and dignity—were daunting, as
we would see in the years to come. I do not know how hard Rumsfeld
pressed for limiting our objectives in Afghanistan in the fall of 2001,
but the point he made in that November 6 phone call was exactly right.

I believe the thinking in the White House about the importance of
staying in Afghanistan and bringing change in governance and culture was influenced by what it believed had happened there between
the departure of Soviet troops and the Taliban taking power: a vacuum
was created, which led to civil war and the victory of the Taliban. As
Hadley later told me, the administration thought that if the United
States were to leave Afghanistan after ousting the Taliban, that would
likely lead again to a vacuum and the return of the extremists.

I think they misunderstood the lessons from the early 1990s. In
contrast to the chaotic events of 1992–96, the 2001 expulsion of the
Taliban had led to the major Afghan factions agreeing on a political process for forming a government and who should lead it, all
thanks to the exercise of American power. That agreement was internationally sanctioned at Bonn, with all of Afghanistan's neighbors
in support. There was a significant UN and U.S. effort at the outset
to engage other countries to work in partnership with us to support
and strengthen the new government. The UN took ownership of the

Bonn conference and authorized an international peacekeeping force (the ISAF).

In all fairness, with the transfer of sovereignty back to the Afghans and to Karzai on December 22, 2001, the Bush administration tried to pull back, turning security over to the UN-mandated ISAF under NATO leadership and working with the many countries who signed up for the UN-run reconstruction and peacekeeping effort. The involvement of the United States in Afghanistan was the glue that held the entire endeavor together. But the size and shape of our involvement over time was determined by America's ambitious objectives there.

The challenges we have faced in Afghanistan over the past dozen years obscure the memory that things actually went pretty well there between 2002 and 2005. Karzai effectively brought the leaders of different ethnic groups—such as Dostum and the Tajik leader Mohammed Qasim Fahim Khan—into the government, schools were opened to girls, women began participating in both business and the political process, and a remarkably free and open media quickly emerged. Levels of violence remained low, and in 2004, millions of Afghans turned out to elect a president, Karzai. The situation in the country improved to the point that several million refugees returned home. Creation and training of a new Afghan army proceeded—with the United States providing most of the equipment and training—although the size was purposely limited to what the Afghan government could afford (under 70,000 troops) and was consistent with the security environment at the time. During this period, there were never more than 15,000 U.S. troops in the country.

U.S. intelligence agencies failed to notice, however, that after the Taliban's expulsion from Afghanistan in 2001, they had regrouped in Pakistan, reconstituting and rearming their military forces. They began to infiltrate back into eastern and southern Afghanistan, unhindered and doubtless helped by the ever-duplicitous Pakistanis. The first significant. American encounter with a revitalized Taliban came in eastern Afghanistan on June 28, 2005, when four Navy SEALs were ambushed in a well-organized attack, and a helicopter with SEAL and Army Special Forces reinforcements sent to assist them was shot down. Three of the SEALs on the ground were killed, as well as sixteen U.S. servicemen on the helicopter. American casualties that day were the worst yet in a single engagement in the Afghan War and a wake-up call that the Taliban had returned.

The level of violence, especially in the east and south, steadily increased over the ensuing months. The situation worsened dramatically in the fall of 2006, when President Musharraf cut a deal with Pakistani tribal leaders along the border with Afghanistan, promising to keep his troops out of their territory if they would prevent al-Qaeda and the Taliban from operating in their lands. The cynical deal essentially gave the Taliban safe haven on the Pakistani side of the border. By the end of 2006, the number of Taliban attacks in Afghanistan surged by more than 200 percent and, after Musharraf's deal, by more than 300 percent. Roadside bombings rose from 783 in 2005 to 1,677 in 2006; direct attacks, from 1,558 to 4,542. At the end of 2006, the number of U.S. troops had grown to about 21,000.

On the military side, the history from late 2006 until December 2009 was of one Afghan policy review in Washington after another, each followed by an increase in U.S. troops. In late 2006, President Bush ordered an increase of 10,000 American troops and authorized an increase in the size of the Afghan army. At the end of 2007, we had 31,000 troops in Afghanistan. Because of the troop surge in Iraq, during all of 2008 we were able to increase that number only modestly—to about 33,000, with several thousand more en route. By fall a request had come from our commander for 20,000 more. In light of an ever more bleak outlook in Afghanistan, the Bush administration late in 2008 reviewed the situation. Bush was willing to approve the request for 20,000 more troops but agreed to let the new administration make the call. After the new Obama team examined the situation in February–March 2009, the president approved sending 17,000 more troops and an additional 4,000 trainers. All in all, this brought the U.S. troop level in Afghanistan to 68,000. In late summer, the new U.S. commander, General Stanley McChrystal, examined what would be required to accomplish the mission he had been given and requested an additional 40,000 troops. Following another, more protracted and contentious review of U.S. strategy and aims in Afghanistan, Obama agreed to send 30,000 more American troops and ask our coalition partners to provide another 7,000–8,000. It is a measure of the deterioration in Afghanistan after 2006 that in just three years the number of U.S. military personnel in Afghanistan had more than quadrupled to nearly 100,000.

At an October 9, 2009, meeting on the strategy and troop increase, CIA director Leon Panetta observed, "We can't leave, and we can't accept the status quo"—words eerily reminiscent of Gorbachev adviser Anatoly Chernyaev's lament about Afghanistan twenty years earlier: "Fuck it all. We got dragged in and now we don't know how to crawl out."

As secretary of defense, I recommended to Bush and Obama all the troop increases in Afghanistan after 2006. Why did we at the Pentagon believe at each stage that more troops were needed or would make a difference? I think the single most important factor was the success of the troop surge in Iraq during 2007–8 in restoring security to the point where economic recovery could begin and daily life return to some semblance of normalcy. We accordingly embraced the counterinsurgency strategy that establishing security in Afghanistan was required before anything else positive could happen. To improve security in the face of a resurgent Taliban, we needed more troops. But we at Defense also were acutely aware that military power by itself could not achieve the United States' broader goals in Afghanistan, and without progress toward improved governance our gains would not be sustainable.

Taliban success in challenging the Afghan government beginning in 2005, especially in the east and south, was due in large part to their ruthlessness in killing local police and officials as well as ordinary villagers who refused to join them; safe havens in Pakistan; and the corruption, incompetence, and infighting among and between officials in Kabul, the provinces, and the districts that left many ordinary Afghans indifferent or hostile to the government. U.S. aspirations to remake Afghanistan were unrealistic even before the Taliban returned. Trying to do so as the security situation steadily deteriorated made the challenge even more difficult.

Bush's goal was to "stabilize the country and help the Afghan people build a free society," a task he acknowledged was "the ultimate nation building mission." The first review in the Obama administration, in March 2009, asserted that "a fully-resourced counterinsurgency campaign will enable us to regain the initiative and defend our vital interests." In a March 27 speech announcing his policy, Obama called for a dramatic increase in the U.S. civilian effort—involving agricultural specialists, educators, engineers, and lawyers—to advance security, opportunity, and justice, and to help the Afghan government serve its people and develop an economy not dominated by illicit drugs. Having campaigned for the presidency condemning the war in Iraq and praising the "good war" in Afghanistan, Obama embraced, and doubled down on, Bush's nation-building project. He did so again in the fall of 2009, approving a strategy that included making Karzai more effective as president, reducing corruption, and improving the capabilities and performance of the Afghan government.

On November 5, 2006, in my job interview with Bush to be secretary of defense, I told him I thought there was too much emphasis in Afghanistan on trying to build a capable central government in a country that essentially had never had one, and too little focus on the provinces, districts, and tribes. Returning from a visit to Afghanistan in December 2007, I told the president we had to transition from European-favored comprehensive nation-building toward a more focused counterinsurgency. A week after Obama was inaugurated, I told him we should have "no grandiose aspirations in Afghanistan," and just try to prevent the country from again becoming a source of threats to us or our allies, as it had been under the Taliban. The next day, I told the Senate Armed Services Committee: "If we set out to create in Afghanistan a central Asian Valhalla, we will lose. We need to keep our objectives realistic and limited, or we will set ourselves up for failure." As we debated the troop increase the following fall, I urged the president to narrow our mission. I argued that we should focus our military operations on stabilizing the situation, especially in the east and south, and buy time to expand and train the Afghan security forces. I wrote Obama a private memo on October 13 suggesting that we "quietly shelve trying to develop a strong, effective central government in Afghanistan," and focus on strengthening a few key ministries (defense, interior, finance). Our strategy should be limited so as to "*deny* the Taliban momentum and control, *facilitate* reintegration [of the Taliban], *build* government capacity selectively, *grow* the Afghan security forces, *transfer* security responsibilities, and *defeat* al Qaeda." Like Rumsfeld, I thought our strategy and aspirations unrealistically ambitious.

Bush and Obama, their advisers, and the international community would have been well served had they heeded Machiavelli: "Men always commit the error of not knowing where to limit their hopes, and by trusting to these rather than to a just measure of their resources, they are generally ruined." No one in the American government bothered to take a "just measure" of our resources for carrying out nation-building. Had they done so, they would have found such resources woefully scarce and the government poorly organized for the purpose. This was true of our ISAF allies as well. The history of American failure to accomplish more modest changes in culture and governance in Somalia, Haiti, and the Balkans in the 1990s had been forgotten.

America's singular power in every dimension after the end of the Cold War, I think, obscured for our leaders the reality of very real limitations to that power. It tempted Clinton, Bush, and even Obama to think we could change other countries, despite history and culture, and make them more like us. Contrary to Machiavelli's warning, they misjudged our power and our resources.

The growing security challenge posed by the Taliban beginning in 2005 is often cited as the main reason we could not make better progress in improving governance and helping develop a government more responsive to the needs of its people. That was certainly true in the east and south of Afghanistan but not so much in the north and west and around Kabul, where political rivalries, infighting, and plain incompetence were the main barriers to greater success. Corruption contributed significantly to the deteriorating security environment. This was especially the case with the Afghan police and army, where promotions were bought and sold, officers stole the pay of their troops, weapons disappeared into the black market, soldiers were asked to serve for the duration of the fight without returning home (and so often deserted), and nearly every unit had "ghost" soldiers—missing or nonexistent troops whose pay went into the officers' pockets. Many Afghan soldiers and police died trying to protect their country from the return of the Taliban; there was no lack of courage on their part. But for many, looking at their leaders and the condition of their families at home, there was little motivation. We knew all this.

Thanks to the "Obama surge" in 2010, we actually made significant headway in improving security in the south and east of Afghanistan. But the progress was temporary because, thanks to Obama's deadline, the Taliban knew we would begin pulling out the following year. Without the massive U.S. troop presence, there could be no long-term success in bringing security to the south and east of Afghanistan. And without security, as we also learned in Iraq, there could be little stabilization, economic development, or improved governance. As part of a vicious circle, without those benefits for the population, there was little incentive for the Afghans to contribute to improving security by enlisting, providing information, or otherwise resisting the Taliban. The only chance to break that vicious circle would have been to prolong the Obama surge of 2010–11. But that was just not acceptable to the president or, I believe, to the American people. Because our security gains could not be sustained nor the Taliban held back without a substantial U.S. military presence, the war would go on and on.

The biggest single obstacle to achieving our economic, social, and political aspirations for Afghanistan was, in fact, Afghanistan itself. It was, and remains, a staggeringly backward nation. The 2004 United Nations Development Program ranked Afghanistan, roughly the size of Texas, 173rd out of 177 countries, near or at the bottom of nearly every development indicator including nutrition, infant mortality, life expectancy, and literacy. Moreover, we Americans had little understanding of Afghanistan, its culture, its tribal and ethnic politics, and its power brokers and their relationships.

From our experience in helping the mujahedin fight the Soviets, we should have been more attuned to the deep ethnic conflicts in

Afghanistan, especially between the Pashtuns, who dominated the south and east, and the Uzbeks, Tajiks, Hazaras, and others. We especially should have anticipated continuing conflict between the political forces represented by the Northern Alliance and the Pashtuns (including India's backing of the former and Pakistan's support for the latter). We so little understood the web of tribal and clan networks, we didn't realize that in helping one tribe we often antagonized its rival neighbor. Our efforts to persuade or coerce such folks to work together more often than not resembled shotgun weddings rather than reconciliation. Our goodwill and lofty aspirations ran headlong into ancient and contemporary enmities.

The effective exercise of power requires a thorough understanding of both the physical and the human terrain. Our failure to adequately understand the latter in Afghanistan proved costly.

Corruption oozed from every pore in the country. From time immemorial, an appointment in government was seen as a license to secure financial advantage for one's self and one's entire family and tribe. This filtered all the way down to the district and village level, where Afghan government officials demanded bribes for any and every action, and warlords simply demanded payment. Awarding contracts to family and friends was business as usual. Positions in the security ministries provided opportunities to siphon weapons and to menace rivals, whether personal, political, or tribal. Corruption was part of the warp and woof of Afghan culture. And once we arrived, with tens of billions of dollars—much of it in cash—for contracts, construction, and services and to underwrite Afghan salaries, there was a frenzied rush to the trough.

In earlier times, before the Soviet invasion, Afghanistan was poor but its farmers raised enough wheat, corn, barley, rice, cotton, fruit, nuts, and grapes to feed themselves and market a small surplus. As the Soviets turned millions of Afghans into refugees in Pakistan and Iran, and tried to drive most of the remaining rural population into the cities, where they could be more easily controlled, traditional agriculture in Afghanistan collapsed. That opened the way for the opium trade. Cultivation of opium in Afghanistan in some quantity began in the 1950s but quickly expanded during the Soviet occupation from 225 metric tons in 1981 to 1,200 in 1989. The civil war in the 1990s saw an even larger increase, to 4,600 metric tons in 1999. While production dropped dramatically in 2001 due to ruthless Taliban suppression of the narcotics trade as "un-Islamic," with their expulsion, production skyrocketed under the new Afghan government, rising by 2007 to 8,200 metric tons, mainly in the southern provinces of Helmand and Kandahar. By that point, Afghanistan was the source of more than 90 percent of the world's illicit opium and one of the principal suppliers of hashish. Between 2 million and 3 million Afghans, or roughly 10 percent of the population, were involved in the narcotics trade. Opium farmers had protection provided by landlords, traffickers, warlords, and corrupt officials; they got a better price for opium than for traditional crops; they didn't have to worry about how to get the crop to market; and, if necessary, it was a crop that could be stored for prolonged periods.

Dirty money and corruption from the narcotics trade washed all through Afghanistan, with government officials, warlords, and insurgents, including the Taliban, profiting. Despite some limited successes, counter-narcotics programs, under first the British and then the Americans, were a failure overall. Eradicating the poppy crop without providing an alternative source of income for farmers created new recruiting opportunities for the Taliban. Alternative (or substitute) crop programs had some success in the northern part of the country, where opium production was limited, but had little impact in the main growing areas in the south. In no small part this was due to the lack of a sustainable government presence and to a lack of overall security.

A further Afghan obstacle to our aspirations was the historical absence of a strong central government and the deeply ingrained resistance to cultural and social change. The effort in Bonn to reimpose King Zahir's 1964 reform constitution, which had much in common with King Amanullah's reforms in the late 1920s, seemed to ignore the reality that both reform efforts failed because of the enduring power of warlords, tribal and religious leaders, and the culture. "We were building on the weak foundations of an economy dominated by corruption and the narcotics trade," Rice wrote.

Beyond internal Afghan obstacles to our nation-building hopes, there were several serious flaws in our own efforts. Foremost among these was a lack of civilian resources for police and military training, creation of rule-of-law institutions from courts to prisons, building of infrastructure, economic development, agricultural improvement, and all other aspects of an effort to modernize a nation and achieve the goals set by both Bush and Obama. And it wasn't just a U.S. deficiency.

At the Bonn conference, the UN assigned different elements of Afghan reconstruction to different nations: training police and border guards to Germany, rebuilding the judiciary to Italy, counter-narcotics to Britain, and disarming militias to Japan. As Rumsfeld later pointed out, this process took place "without any realistic assessment of their ability to deliver. Afghanistan's reconstruction proved largely to be a series of unfulfilled pledges by well-intentioned but poorly equipped coalition partners." Germany was typical, sending just forty police advisers, and they all went to Kabul, where they were able to train only a few hundred police. The German performance was so bad the U.S. State Department took over responsibility for police training, but it too lacked the resources to do the job. As Rumsfeld complained to Rice in February 2005, State's eight-week basic training course didn't include weapons training, and just 3,900 of the 34,000 "trained" officers went through the course. Later that year, responsibility for police training was transferred to the Defense Department. As so often happened, rather than strengthen the civilian agencies that have responsibility for civilian programs, such as police training, our presidents and Congress just handed the ball to the military, even when it was clear the military lacked the requisite expertise.

On the international front, in late January 2002 the Japanese hosted a pledging conference in Tokyo to raise funds for reconstruction efforts in Afghanistan. The money was for emergency humanitarian relief, road construction, women's programs, health, and education. More than sixty nations pledged $1.8 billion (the U.S. offered $300 million) for these purposes in 2002. That wasn't even a drop in the bucket.

The paucity of U.S. civilian government experts in-country was a continuing problem in both the Bush and Obama administrations. On May 26, 2006, Bush held an NSC meeting focused on getting more such experts in-country. In a scenario to be repeated throughout my years as secretary of defense, the number of people preparing to deploy reported by the State Department was well below the number promised—and needed. While I believe State could have provided more bodies, no one was willing to admit that the real problem was that State, USAID, and other civilian agencies simply did not have the personnel, much less people with necessary experience and expertise, to meet the need. Moreover, State and USAID officers were not particularly "expeditionary"—easy to deploy, especially on short notice. These instruments of national power, so needed in Afghanistan, had been allowed to atrophy.

A challenge to effective use of the civilian experts who were in Afghanistan was the dicey security situation in much of the country, especially in the south and east. An innovative approach to addressing this problem was the creation in late 2002 of Provincial Reconstruction Teams (PRTs), units with military combat forces providing protection for embedded civilian experts in development and reconstruction. Ultimately, there would be twenty-six PRTs in Afghanistan, twelve led by the United States, and fourteen by other coalition countries. Each U.S. PRT reported to the commander of a brigade combat team. PRT projects included building schools, health clinics, and roads; strengthening provincial governments' capacity by helping local officials develop basic management skills; and facilitating communication between the provincial and central governments. The PRTs also served a monitoring and reporting function regarding local conditions.

The PRTs worked well and had real, if often temporary, impact wherever they were deployed. The problem was that there weren't nearly enough of them, there were too few civilian experts, and deterioration of the security environment could negate their impact at the local level. In 2007, for example, in the twelve U.S.-led PRTs, out of a total of 1,023 personnel, just twenty-nine were civilians. There were fewer than three civilians on average per PRT, while most PRTs had about eighty or so soldiers. (Just for perspective, the Obama NSC had nearly as many staff people in the White House working on Afghanistan and Iraq as there were civilians in all the U.S. PRTs in Afghanistan.) PRTs staffed by coalition partners such as Germany and Great Britain had on average twenty to thirty civilians. How does one explain that the United States, with all its assets, fielded far fewer civilian experts in each of its PRTs?

In the fall of 2008, a Bush administration review of Afghan policy called for a stronger counterinsurgency effort, including both more troops and more civilian resources. An Obama administration review in March–April 2009 called for a "dramatic increase" in the U.S. civilian effort. In May 2009, Ambassador Richard Holbrooke thought the more than 400 civilians the embassy requested still greatly underestimated the need. While there was an increase, it fell far short of the requirement. The months-long review of strategy in the fall of 2009 led to the same conclusion as always in the past: the need for more civilian expertise.

I was concerned that most of the additional people would end up, like too many civilian experts already in Afghanistan, working within the embassy compound in Kabul and not out in the provinces and districts where the need was greater. Of course, an important reason for that was the lack of security in the countryside. Commanders in the field pleaded for more civilian expertise, citing example after example where even a small number of diplomats or development experts would make a dramatic difference in provincial capitals, villages, and rural areas—but to no avail. Most of the new arrivals, as I feared, stayed in Kabul. By the end of 2010, two-thirds of the 1,100 U.S. government civilians in Afghanistan were stationed in Kabul.

A second flaw in our Afghan nation-building was the abject failure to share information about which strategies, projects, and programs were working and which were not, and the failure to coordinate projects undertaken by the U.S. government, international organizations, nongovernmental organizations, and different contributing nations. By 2007, there were probably more than one hundred different foreign entities trying to help the Afghans develop an effective government, improve the infrastructure, strengthen the economy, and carry

out humanitarian projects in Afghanistan. Each organization and government seemed loath to share information about its endeavors with
others. Many of the nongovernmental organizations were particularly
leery of sharing information with the military command or embassy,
seeking to avoid being "tainted" by the U.S. government. The opportunity to learn from one another was being lost; we were missing the
opportunity to apply lessons learned in one place elsewhere. Moreover, the opportunity to pursue complementary projects or to build on
another's success in the same place likewise was missed.

The lack of oversight and coordination of the civilian effort was
both an American and an international problem. I had expressed my
concern to Bush in my job interview for secretary that stronger coordination of the U.S. civilian and military efforts was needed and urged
the empowerment of someone in Washington to identify bureaucratic
obstacles to those efforts—someone who could call a cabinet secretary
in the name of the president if his or her department was not delivering what had been promised and force action. Hadley had come to
the same conclusion and ultimately the president named Lieutenant
General Douglas Lute to be the "czar" in the White House for such
coordination. Alas, the czar's office tended to focus more on how the
military campaign was being waged rather than on getting the civilian departments to provide the necessary resources and coordinating
their efforts.

The same lack of coordination, information sharing, and resource
management was true of the international civilian effort in Afghanistan. There simply was no organization or government empowered
or able to collect and analyze information on projects and then try to
use it effectively. The Afghan government lacked the capacity, many of
the NGOs tried to stay as far from the military as possible, the senior
NATO civilian representative had no authority, and the U.S. embassy
was regarded with suspicion by NGOs and foreign governments alike.
In March 2008, Norwegian diplomat Kai Eide was named by the UN
secretary-general as senior civilian coordinator, with a mandate from
the United Nations. I strongly supported Eide in this role, offering
technical support and personnel to help him gather the information
he needed to do his job. But he was never able to get sufficient coop-

eration from all parties to create the kind of structured coordination of international assistance that was so necessary.

A third flaw was the failure of the United States and everyone else to intimately involve the Afghans in decision making and implementation of development projects. It was a source of continuing frustration to President Karzai that he and his government had almost no idea what projects were being carried out in their country. Local Afghans too often were not consulted as to need or priority. A significant proportion of the U.S.-sponsored projects were outsourced to for-profit contractors, and even the U.S. government had problems keeping track of those efforts.

There is no question the Afghan government was incapable of administering aid projects of almost any size. The central government was not particularly interested in empowering provincial and district authorities, and getting qualified Afghans to do the jobs was a huge challenge. In late 2009, U.S. ambassador Karl Eikenberry offered to have the United States pay Afghan civil servants willing to work in dangerous districts. The call went out, including a promise of salary bonuses. Not one Afghan official in either Kabul or Kandahar signed up for the program.

Such systemic weaknesses in governance notwithstanding, there was no excuse for our frequent failure to at least consult, seek approval from, and share information and progress with the national and provincial leaders. What the Afghans wanted mostly was pretty simple: a schoolhouse; an all-weather road to get crops to market; a health clinic nearby; agricultural assistance; someone to adjudicate local disputes, such as those concerning landownership, or even just to issue identification cards (and carry out these tasks without requiring a bribe). But too frequently even these services were not forthcoming, while white elephant projects drained our coffers.

The lack of effective management and oversight of the U.S. (and allied) development assistance and reconstruction effort, along with corruption, was terribly damaging. Both Western and Afghan contractors made scandalous profits, and all too many simply stole money, hired relatives and friends as subcontractors, bribed Afghan officials at every level, and too often were incompetent. Hundreds of millions of dollars were distributed through the Commander's Emergency Response Program (CERP), usually for short-term projects funded by military officers with no contracting or oversight experience and little accountability. Commanders loved this program, which often allowed them to pay young men for picking up a shovel instead of a Taliban gun, but not much attention was paid to whether the guy with the shovel did anything useful with it. All the problems taken together, according to the U.S. Special Inspector General for Afghanistan Reconstruction, resulted in the waste of billions of dollars. Almost every American at every level in Afghanistan knew that there were problems in his own bailiwick, and almost no one was able to fix even those.

A final failing, despite the courage and sacrifice of hundreds of thousands of troops and the expenditure of three-quarters of a trillion dollars, was our inability to establish sustainable security throughout Afghanistan, which is imperative for any effort to bring political and economic improvements. Our lack of success was due primarily to Taliban safe havens in Pakistan and to the lack of confidence on the part of most Afghans in their own government and their disdain for the corruption, incompetence, and arrogance of so many government officials at every level—thus the unwillingness of many to join the fight against the Taliban. Also important was the utter brutality of the Taliban, who both literally and figuratively took no prisoners. The presence of large foreign armies, which too often disregarded and disrespected the Afghans, was a problem in a country that mainly hated foreigners. Additionally, I believe the U.S. military's policy of regularly rotating commanders at every level often disrupted productive personal relationships that developed between those commanders and local military, police, civilian officials, and ordinary citizens. As secretary of defense, I should have tried to make that policy more flexible.

After eighteen years of nation-building and tens of billions of dollars in assistance, Afghanistan can hardly be considered a success story. The picture is not all bad, though. In 2001, there were a million students in Afghan schools, all of them male. In 2017, there were 8.4 million students, 40 percent of them female. In 2008, more than 57 percent of the population lived within a one-hour walk to a health facility, up from 9 percent in 2002, largely due to USAID efforts. The under-five mortality rate decreased from 87 per 1,000 live births in 2005 to 55 per 1,000 in 2015. Afghans have continued to hold elections pretty much on schedule since 2004, and although there are many allegations of fraud, generally at least half of eligible voters turn out despite security threats. The media remain largely free. A number of women are involved in business and politics. Finally, despite so many years of war, corruption among officers, and significant casualties, Afghan men continue to enlist in the army and police to fight against the Taliban.

Our efforts over nearly twenty years made some Afghans very rich, modestly improved the lives of others, expanded education for the young, created opportunities for women, and planted the seeds of elective government. The cost has been stunningly high in lives and treasure. How do you measure the consequences for a country and its people of twenty years of war (forty years if you go back to the Soviet invasion)? Have our efforts to help the Afghans been a blessing or a curse for them? As the Taliban continue to expand their presence and control, how much of what we've done will prove lasting?

The Taliban and al-Qaeda were ousted from Afghanistan by early 2002. The campaign through September 2002 had cost twenty-seven American lives and about $20 billion.

Then we began nation-building. Counting both military and civilian efforts, between 2002 and 2018, the United States spent roughly $126 billion on relief and reconstruction in Afghanistan, most of it on security. As of July 31, 2017, we had spent $715 billion on direct war costs in Afghanistan, and as of July 2018 over 2,300 Americans had been killed and more than 20,000 wounded. During the ten years after 2002, $503.5 billion was spent by the Defense Department and $28.6 billion by the State Department and USAID. We stayed in Afghanistan after 2002 to bring democracy and improve the quality of life there, and yet during that period only a little over 5 percent of the money spent was allocated to the nonmilitary instruments for achieving those goals.

For all our good intentions, the American experience in Afghanistan has not been markedly different from that of the foreigners who preceded us. Those who seek to impose social, cultural, and governance changes in that ancient land should think long and hard. To encourage reform, institutional development, rule of law, human and political rights, and freedom, I believe we—and the Afghans—would have been better served had our military departed in 2002 and had we thereafter relied on our nonmilitary instruments of national power, and patience. By early 2002, Afghanistan had an internationally recognized multiparty government, a commitment by a number of nations to provide help with both development and security, and, as the situation on the ground reflected, a three-year breathing spell before the Taliban reentered the fight. If there had been no foreign armies in the country and the Afghan political leaders had been left to their own devices, who is to say that the Afghan government would not have had a lot more popular support, even in the south and east, when the Taliban tried to come back? Or that the Afghan parties, including the Taliban, would not have worked out some accommodation? There is no way of knowing whether this approach would have led to a different outcome, but we know for certain the results of the alternative. One of the enduring lessons of the Cold War and the demise of the Soviet Union is that lasting change in a country will come only from within, though it can be encouraged and hastened through the use over time of nonmilitary instruments of power.

We should have kept that in mind in Afghanistan after our initial military victory.

CHAPTER 7

Iraq

A Curse

*J*ust sixteen months after driving the Taliban from Kabul, the United
States invaded Iraq. The story of America's invasion and what happened in the years after has been the subject of many books, and countless
more will be written. My focus here, as with Afghanistan, is on President
Bush's decision to build a better, democratic Iraq after overthrowing Saddam Hussein; the failure to recognize the magnitude of that challenge; the
overreliance on the U.S. military to carry out the task; and the failure to
recognize and then remedy the weakness of our nonmilitary instruments of
power that were so essential to even attempting such an effort.

*P*resent-day Iraq was the birthplace of human civilization. In the
late fourth millennium BC, writing and recorded history were
born there. It has been the center of at least four empires and part
of fourteen others. In other words, like Afghanistan, Iraq has been a
battleground, literally, for thousands of years, with the United States
being only the most recent in a very long line of invaders.

The Iraqis have been at war or under crippling sanctions since
invading Iran in September 1980. For its part, the United States has
been at war in Iraq for nearly thirty years. Twice we sent vast armies
to defeat Saddam Hussein, more than 500,000 troops in 1991 and
200,000 in 2003 (plus tens of thousands of allied troops in both

cases). U.S. aircraft have been in combat or enforcing no-fly zones in Iraq for twenty-nine years, and we have had troops on the ground there for seventeen years. Like Iran and Afghanistan, Iraq has bedeviled successive American presidents, and the cost has been dear.

After the 1980–88 Iran-Iraq War, particularly in light of the theocratic Iranian regime's continuing hostility toward the United States, Presidents Reagan and Bush 41 attempted to use nonmilitary means—e.g., credits, agricultural exports, diplomacy—to improve relations with Iraq, both to encourage Saddam to moderate his behavior and to create opportunities for American business to participate in postwar reconstruction. This was done, as George H. W. Bush's national security adviser Brent Scowcroft would later write, despite evidence of his horrible human rights record, harboring of terrorists, progress in building chemical and biological weapons, acquisition of intermediate-range ballistic missiles, and attempts to build nuclear weapons. Nonetheless, in October 1989, Bush reaffirmed Reagan's strategy of engaging with Iraq and attempting to moderate its behavior through economic and political incentives. By early 1990, though, it was clear this policy was failing. Saddam threatened to "incinerate" Israel, and there was even more disturbing evidence of his efforts to acquire weapons of mass destruction.

During the summer of 1990, relations between Iraq and Kuwait worsened as Saddam, desperately in need of money after the long war with Iran, grew bitter over the Gulf states' overproduction of oil and the consequent drop in price. He pursued a border dispute with Kuwait (especially over the Rumaila oil field) and demanded that Kuwait forgive $30 billion in war loans to Iraq. On August 2, he invaded with nearly 100,000 troops. All the Arab leaders had assured Bush 41 that Saddam was bluffing.

The same day, the UN Security Council unanimously approved Resolution 660 condemning the invasion, demanding the withdrawal of Iraqi troops, and requiring negotiations. On August 5, Bush told the press, "This will not stand, this aggression against Kuwait." In the weeks that followed, the president led an international effort to impose draconian economic sanctions on Iraq and to obtain approval of additional UN Security Council resolutions punishing the regime in a nonmilitary effort to pressure Saddam to withdraw from Kuwait.

Bush was sincere in this diplomatic effort, but he and most of us advising him were convinced Saddam would figure out a way to peel off key governments—most likely Russia, China, and France—and somehow keep his forces in Kuwait. The president wanted to punish Saddam for invading his neighbor and to demonstrate that such aggression was unacceptable in a post–Cold War world. I believe that Bush, the consummate diplomat, concluded soon after the invasion that military force would be necessary to reverse it.

In the days before the Gulf War began, Bush did something no other recent American president has done: he asked that a directive be prepared for his signature specifying our war aims. We would liberate Kuwait and we would destroy the Iraqi army's Republican Guard divisions. We debated whether to seek regime change in Baghdad, but Bush and all his advisers agreed that objective was beyond the scope of the authorizing UN resolutions and the expectations of our coalition partners. We also were convinced that trying to effect regime change would likely require us to occupy much of Iraq without any assurance we could capture Saddam, who, we thought, likely would lead an insurgent resistance. There would be no mission creep, no nation-building under Bush 41. We would accomplish our specific objectives and then come home.

The air war began on January 16, the ground war on February 24. The war was over less than 100 hours later. Far-reaching restrictions were placed on the regime, including arms embargoes, severe limits on where Iraqi military aircraft could operate (no-fly zones), an intrusive inspections regime to discover and destroy all stockpiles of weapons of mass destruction and the means to produce them, prohibition of all missiles with a range greater than ninety miles, and limits on oil production.

Saddam survived the humiliation of the Gulf War, solidified his power, and soon began defying the UN resolutions—including draconian economic sanctions—imposed upon Iraq. A week before Bush left office, on January 13, 1993, the United States, Britain, and France launched air attacks on Iraqi missile sites and aircraft command and control bases in retaliation for repeated Iraqi breaches of the no-fly zones and military raids into Kuwait.

There was criticism at the time, and more later, of Bush's decision not to pursue "regime change"—that is, to send our forces north to oust Saddam—in 1991. Bush definitely wanted Saddam gone. However, those of us involved, beginning with the president himself, would long argue that expanding the mission so dramatically would have violated the UN Security Council resolutions we relied upon to legitimize the war and would have shattered the huge coalition Bush had assembled. In Bush 41's view, if the United States broke its word—its commitment—to limit the operation to getting the Iraqis out of Kuwait, no country would again be willing to ally with us in resisting aggression. Those arguments had merit in 1991 and still do. But the reality is that the outcome of the first Gulf War bequeathed to the region and to Bush's successors a festering cancer named Saddam Hussein.

The argument for not going after Saddam always focused on the uncertain consequences and impact on the coalition of sending ground forces north to occupy Baghdad and oust Saddam. In retrospect, I believe there was another course of action that offered a reasonable chance of ridding ourselves of Saddam without sending troops to Baghdad. The fighting ended on March 3, 1991, when U.S. Army General Norman Schwarzkopf, the coalition commander, met with Saddam's representative, Lieutenant General Sultan Hashim Ahmad, at the Iraqi border town of Safwan and laid down the terms for a cease-fire. An alternative would have been to demand that Saddam come to the meeting personally to surrender, and to then arrest him for a variety of crimes. The forcing strategy would have been to tell the Iraqi generals that we would continue air attacks on their units, equipment, and headquarters until they either removed Saddam or forced him to surrender in person. In other words, the war would not end until the person responsible for starting it was held accountable. We would not have violated the terms of the Security Council resolutions and would not have sent ground forces farther into Iraq. We just would have continued the air attacks that had begun in January.

Bush and Scowcroft wrote in their joint memoir that "we discussed at length the idea of forcing Saddam personally to accept the terms of Iraqi defeat at Safwan." The tough question was what they would do if he refused. The only options, they concluded, were to "continue the conflict until he backed down, or retreat from our demands. The latter would have sent a disastrous signal. The former would have split our Arab colleagues from the coalition and, *de facto*, forced us to change our objectives." However, I believe Bush 41's prestige was so high in the spring of 1991 that he could have forced the issue through continuing air attacks, not necessarily targeted at Iraqi soldiers but at their facilities, equipment, and command and control. I think most of the coalition would have stood by him—there was no love lost among Arab leaders for Saddam and there was deep resentment that he had lied to them about his intentions regarding Kuwait. When the war ended, Bush was counting on the Iraqi military leaders to take out Saddam after such a humiliating defeat; the approach I suggest would have given them considerable additional incentive to do so. Indeed, continuing U.S. air attacks on Iraqi military targets (and denying the Iraqi military the use of their helicopters, a concession we made at Safwan) might also have given the Kurdish and Shia uprisings at the end of the war more of a chance of success. Instead, Saddam escaped our grasp, ruthlessly put down uprisings, killed a large number of his generals he thought might be a threat, and lived to plague his own people and the next two American presidents. If Saddam had fallen or been killed in the spring of 1991, it would be hard to imagine a need to invade Iraq in 2003.

The cycle of Iraqi defiance and limited American military retaliation continued with Bill Clinton in charge, but 1998 was the turning point. Early in the year, Saddam blocked a United States–led UN inspection team as the opening move to try forcing the UN to lift the sanctions on Iraq. Clinton prepared to launch air strikes in February in response to expulsion of the team, but UN secretary-general Kofi Annan managed to persuade Saddam to resume the inspections. In August, Saddam again stopped cooperating with the inspectors. Congress soon passed the Iraq Liberation Act, which proclaimed that U.S. policy was "to support efforts to remove the regime headed by Saddam Hussein from power in Iraq and to promote the emergence of a democratic government." The vote was 360–38 in the House, unanimous in the Senate. The president signed the act on October 31. That same day Saddam shut down all international inspections and monitoring. Faced with the prospect of another U.S. attack in November, Saddam relented and promised full compliance. He was lying.

On December 16, 1998, the United States and Britain launched a massive bombing and missile attack on suspected chemical, biological, and nuclear weapons sites and military forces capable of threatening Iraq's neighbors. The attack lasted four days and involved 650 air sorties and 400 cruise missile launches. In announcing the attack from the Oval Office, Clinton called for regime change in Iraq:

> The hard fact is that so long as Saddam remains in power, he threatens the well-being of his people, the peace of his region, the security of the world. The best way to end that threat once and for all is with a new Iraqi government. . . . Heavy as they are, the costs of action must be weighed against the price of inaction. If Saddam defies the world and we fail to respond, we will face a far greater threat in the future. Saddam will strike again at his neighbors. He will make war on his own people. And mark my words, he will develop weapons of mass destruction. He will deploy them, and he will use them.

Such regime-change rhetoric from both the president and Congress, however, was hollow. After the attack, Saddam did not readmit UN inspectors into Iraq and was not forced to do so. The international inspections regime imposed on Iraq after the Gulf War eight years earlier was over. Saddam defied the UN and the United States, rid Iraq of the inspectors for good, and got away with it. The president essentially had thrown in the towel.

Instead of a one-time-and-done punitive strike, Clinton could have undertaken a much larger and more protracted U.S. offensive against Iraqi military targets, essentially sending the message to Saddam's generals that until Iraq returned to full compliance with the Security Council resolutions—including intrusive inspections—and/or they got rid of Saddam, the attacks would continue and the Iraqi military would be destroyed. Attacks also could have targeted Saddam's palaces and command centers in an effort to kill him and his senior leaders. Even if other countries, eyeing potential investments and deals with Iraq, had lost their appetite for holding Saddam accountable and for strictly enforcing sanctions, the United States had all the authority it needed to act in the Security Council's earlier resolutions. If Iraq had been forced to return to an intrusive inspections regime late in 1998 and those inspections had been sustained, the U.S. invasion in 2003 might never have happened.

One reason Clinton may have been deterred from open-ended air attacks on Iraq in late 1998 was that he was fighting for his political life at home. The House of Representatives impeached him on December 19 and his Senate trial began on January 7. His Republican opponents, and more than a few commentators, contended that even the limited strike he ordered against Iraq was simply a ploy to distract attention from what was happening in the Congress. Explicit comparisons were made to the 1997 movie *Wag the Dog*, in which a fictional president mired in scandal manufactures a war abroad to escape his fate. The challenge Clinton faced from Saddam, though, was real, and one can only wonder if the president might have acted more forcefully had he not been in serious political trouble. It's tough for a president to exercise power internationally when his power at home is weak.

After the limited December air attacks, the Clinton administration adopted a strategy of "dual containment" aimed at both Iraq and Iran. The strategy meant relying on military force to prevent Iraq from attacking its neighbors, combined with stricter enforcement of the no-fly zones, additional economic sanctions, and support for Iraqi opposition groups—but no inspections for weapons of mass destruction.

The enthusiastic support for regime change in Iraq in late 1998 among both Democrats and Republicans in Congress and by a Democratic president and his senior advisers quickly faded from memory after President George W. Bush (Bush 43) invaded Iraq in March 2003.

Regime change was a great idea when all it involved was rhetorical chest-thumping; over time, as the reality—and costs—of making it happen sank in, too many sunshine soldiers on Capitol Hill and from the Clinton administration fled the political battlefield.

E ntering the Oval Office on January 20, 2001, newly elected Bush 43 and his team faced an increasingly defiant Saddam Hussein. Bush's first National Security Council meeting addressed the state of the sanctions regime—it was in tatters—and how to make the no-fly zones more effective. In her preparatory memorandum for the principals, National Security Adviser Condoleezza Rice summarized the situation in Iraq as "unsustainable." There were differences within the administration on how to sharpen the UN sanctions, but more important, other permanent members of the Security Council—notably Russia, France, China, and Germany—were profiting handsomely from holes in the sanctions and resisted all efforts to make them more robust.

There were also doomed efforts to strengthen Iraqi opposition figures in exile and the Kurds in the north. U.S. programs to use exile groups to overthrow governments we don't like hardly ever work. I had argued at the CIA in the 1980s that the only beneficiaries of American support for exile groups were the exiles themselves and the owners of the cafés in Paris where those exiles would spend their days fantasizing about taking power. (Indeed, the only exile in recent times to return home and successfully seize power was Ayatollah Khomeini in Iran.)

Bush initially considered Saddam a problem that probably could be managed. The attacks of 9/11 changed his mind. He later wrote, "The lesson of 9/11 was that if we waited for a danger to fully materialize, we would have waited too long."

By February 2002, Bush had adopted a strategy of "coercive diplomacy." "If we could convince him we were serious about removing his regime," Bush wrote, "there was a chance he would give up his WMD, end his support for terror, stop threatening his neighbors, and, over time, respect the human rights of his people. The odds of success were long."

Like Clinton before him, Bush could have issued a warning to the Iraqi military that it would be attacked from the air and destroyed piecemeal until Saddam or his successor readmitted inspectors without restrictions. After 9/11, Americans probably would have supported such measures even if they proved unpopular abroad. Bush had all the international authority he needed under multiple earlier Security Council resolutions. It was another opportunity missed to avoid an invasion.

I believe that Bush 43 hoped that the threat of invasion would get Saddam to comply with the UN resolutions. Steve Hadley, his deputy national security adviser at the time, told me he thinks Bush clung to that hope until February 2003, when French president Jacques Chirac, German chancellor Gerhard Schroeder, and Russian president Vladimir Putin made clear they would never support military intervention in Iraq. With any international threat to him thus removed, Saddam continued his defiance. As in 1991, he seriously miscalculated.

In fact, Bush had begun preparing for war with Iraq only weeks after the dust settled at Ground Zero. Two months after the attacks, the president asked Secretary of Defense Rumsfeld to review battle plans for Iraq. Rumsfeld ordered General Tommy Franks, the head of Central Command, to begin that work on December 1. Bush was briefed on those plans just after Christmas. Between December 2001 and August 2002, Bush later wrote, he met with or spoke to General Franks more than a dozen times to refine those plans.

On September 12, 2002, Bush spoke at the UN and called for a resolution demanding that Saddam come clean about his programs to build weapons of mass destruction. In Washington, U.S. intelligence agencies issued an assessment that concluded: "Baghdad has chemical and biological weapons as well as missiles with ranges in excess of UN restrictions; if left unchecked, it probably will have a nuclear weapon during this decade." Influenced by the intelligence estimate, on October 11, 2002, Congress easily passed a resolution authorizing the president to use force against Iraq.

On November 8, the Security Council unanimously approved Resolution 1441 declaring Iraq in "material breach" of the 1991 cease-fire relating to weapons of mass destruction and construction of prohibited types of missiles, and gave Iraq thirty days to submit a complete declaration of all WMD-related programs. Failure to do so would lead to "serious consequences." Russia, China, and even Syria supported the resolution. In the subsequent controversies surrounding Iraq's WMD, too many would forget that the UN resolution passed because virtually every intelligence service in the world had reached the same conclusions as the U.S. agencies: Iraq had WMD or was working to get them. Saddam himself reinforced this conclusion by his boasting and his behavior, intended to persuade his own people—and his neighbors—of his success in developing such weapons. Resolution 1441 failed to prompt any change of policy or rhetoric in Baghdad. The exercise of diplomatic power had failed.

The notion that Bush lied about the Iraqi WMD program in order to justify going to war is dead wrong. U.S. and foreign intelligence agencies simply were in error, with grave consequences.

Bush determined early in the war planning that once the threat to U.S. national security from Iraq was removed, he "would have an obligation to help the Iraqi people replace Saddam's tyranny with a democracy," as he would write. On the aircraft carrier *Abraham Lincoln* on May 1, 2003, Bush had said, "The transition from dictatorship to democracy will take time, but it is worth every effort. Our coalition will stay until our work is done."

Not all of his top advisers agreed. Just as Rumsfeld had opposed expanding our goals in Afghanistan beyond the military mission, so he did in Iraq. He felt strongly that the United States needed to be "clear-eyed about democracy's prospects in the country" and told the president and National Security Adviser Rice that the administration should tone down the democracy rhetoric. He was skeptical that Iraq could quickly transform a millennia-old culture and decades of dictatorial rule into a functioning democracy. "The art of compromise," he later wrote, "which is central to a successful democracy, is not something people learn overnight. If we hurried to create Iraqi democracy through quick elections, before key institutions—a free press, private property rights, political parties, an independent judiciary—began to develop organically, we could end up with a permanent mistake." According to Rice, Rumsfeld argued that we had no obligation to bring democracy to Iraq, and "if a strongman emerged, so be it." Had I been secretary of defense at that time, I believe I would have made those same points.

Many in the United States, including me, believed at the time that Bush's "democracy agenda" was put forward after the invasion as justification for the U.S. action when no weapons of mass destruction were found. The record is clear that was not the case. Bush did not go to war in order to democratize Iraq, but once he decided to remove Saddam for national security purposes, he intended to bring democracy to Iraq. Beyond the idealistic aspiration, Bush also believed that the only way to hold Iraq together as a unified state and avoid a dangerous fracturing along ethnic lines after Saddam was gone was through a democratic process that provided Shias, Kurds, and Sunnis a shared role in governance. Rice later wrote that Bush believed "if war occurred, we would try to build a democratic Iraq." She underscored Bush's belief that success against terrorism required both force and ideology—the vision of a better future: "And democracy in the Arab heartland would in turn help democratize the Middle East and address the freedom gap that was the source of hopelessness and terrorism." It was a breathtakingly ambitious vision.

The wisdom of Bush's decision to invade Iraq in March 2003 will forever remain in dispute. The absence of weapons of mass destruction did not change the reality accepted by both the Clinton and Bush administrations that Iraq would remain a serious national security challenge as long as Saddam remained in power and that, given the opportunity, he would reconstitute his WMD programs. But in early 2003, no one in a senior position imagined that U.S. forces would still be in Iraq more than seventeen years later, or that the invasion would dramatically empower Iran in the region. No one anticipated the huge cost. Rumsfeld's (and others') skepticism that Iraq could be transformed into a stable, working democracy in any kind of reasonable time frame proved amply justified.

In a speech on May 1, 2003, less than six weeks after the war began, I offered my perspective as someone who had been part of the decision-making circle for the first Gulf War but was now out of government:

> The situation we face now [in Iraq] reminds me a little of the dog catching the car. Now that we have it, what do we do with it? I believe the postwar challenge will be far greater than the war itself. Only in recent days has the American government begun to realize the extraordinary potential power of the Shia Muslim majority in Iraq, and the possibility that a democratic Iraq might well turn out to be a fundamentalist Shia Iraq. . . . The challenge of rebuilding Iraq, providing food and services, and rebuilding the economy after a dozen years of privation and decades of Baathist socialism will be no small task—though I believe a more easily achievable task than our political aspirations for the country. . . . For all these reasons, I believe the United States should agree to begin replacing our forces with a large multinational peacekeeping force . . . as quickly as the security situation allows. . . . We will be making a big mistake if we keep a hundred thousand or so American soldiers in Iraq for more than a few months.

Once the United States had invaded Iraq and overthrown Saddam, though, finding an exit ramp was damnably difficult. It was imperative to keep Iraq from disintegrating and becoming dangerously destabilizing for the entire region as Shias, Sunnis, and Kurds each sought to enlist foreign allies for protection; align with their ethnic and religious cohorts in neighboring countries; and establish a dominant position in Iraq or, in the case of the Kurds, to join with Kurds in Iran, Turkey, and Syria in an attempt to form an independent state. A fractured Iraq would have created fertile ground for the proliferation of terrorist groups, probably ignited large-scale refugee flows, and worse. These concerns, hypothetical at the time of the invasion, were more than validated by the civil war in, and fracturing of, Syria a decade later.

Unlike Afghanistan in early 2002, Iraq after the U.S. invasion had no government with broad international legitimacy, no formal truce among the competing factions, and no UN-mandated peacekeeping force. In an effort to assemble a substantial international peacekeeping force, Secretary Powell visited multiple Arab and Muslim states seeking troop contributions to stabilize Iraq post-invasion. He came up empty. At the end of 2003, we owned Iraq and all its problems. Once we had invaded, there realistically was no exit ramp at that time that did not lead to even bigger trouble.

Military power had quickly defeated Saddam's army and eliminated him. Replacing the regime with something better represented a wholly different and dramatically more difficult challenge—in no small part because the situation inside Iraq was far worse than we'd anticipated. As I wrote in *Duty*, we simply had no idea how broken Iraq was before the 2003 war—economically, socially, culturally, politically, and in its infrastructure and education system. Moreover, "decades of rule by Saddam, who didn't give a damn about the Iraqi people; the eight-year-long war with Iran; the destruction we wreaked during the Gulf War; twelve years of harsh sanctions—all these meant we had virtually no foundation to build upon in trying to restart the economy, much less create a democratic Iraqi government responsive to the needs of its people," I wrote.

Replacing Saddam's dictatorship with a working democracy—fundamentally dependent on the rule of law, a vibrant civil society, and strong institutions—posed an enormous challenge. For starters, we really had no idea how to do it. Perhaps our confidence came from a flawed historical analogy rooted in the evolution of Germany and Japan after World War II: if we could successfully implant democracy in those countries, surely we could do so in Iraq. Unlike Iraq, however, both Germany and Japan had a deep historical sense of nationhood; no serious ethnic or religious internal conflicts (in fact, both were quite homogeneous demographically); and a sophisticated infrastructure and diversified economy (however badly damaged by the war). Japan had a continuing, respected authority figure in the emperor, while those in the Allied sector of Germany feared the Soviet Union. Perhaps we thought of South Korea as a model of evolving from a dictatorship to democracy—except that it took nearly forty years, from 1948 to 1987, even with a significant American military presence.

Bush clearly understood that an enduring democracy required

strong institutions, but according to Steve Hadley, he thought that elections could be a catalyst for creating those institutions. However, in practical terms, what did bringing democracy entail? Rule of law? New institutions? Less corruption? A healthy economy benefiting all Iraqis? Improved governance? With no little hubris, the administration decided it involved all of the above. Indeed, as Bush would later write, the administration developed plans for long-term reconstruction in no fewer than ten areas: education, health, water and sanitation, electricity, shelter, transportation, governance and rule of law, agriculture, communications, and economic policy. This was stunningly ambitious and unrealistic.

Beyond the challenges in Iraq, any realistic prospect of achieving those objectives would have required a restructuring of the national security apparatus in Washington, facilitating a massive influx of thousands of civilian experts from non-Defense agencies and departments of the government and from the private sector. None of that happened. After the early 1990s, State was anorexic—the victim of constant budget cuts and a lack of personnel—and, importantly, it was by statute very limited in its authority to call on others in the government for help. Nation-building was doomed before it even got started.

The president had indicated the previous fall that he wanted the Pentagon to be the lead agency for postwar planning, and so the new Office of Reconstruction and Humanitarian Assistance (ORHA) was placed in the Department of Defense to ensure the civilian postwar effort would be under the same chain of command as military operations. Secretary of State Colin Powell agreed with this decision, acknowledging that State was too small and ill prepared to tackle such a complicated task even as he insisted that his department have a clear supporting role.

Despite placement of ORHA in Defense, the military was not assigned direct responsibility for postwar reconstruction and kept the office at arm's length. ORHA was led initially by retired general Jay Garner, who arrived in Iraq on the heels of the invasion force with plans to hold elections within ninety days. Garner was dismissed within weeks, perhaps because those in Washington thought he was moving too fast to turn governance back to the Iraqis, including some former Saddam officials. He was replaced as head of ORHA on May 6 by Ambassador L. Paul "Jerry" Bremer, a retired Foreign Service officer whose last job had been ambassador-at-large for counterterrorism in the late 1980s. In May ORHA was transformed into the Coalition Provisional Authority (CPA), under which Bremer was empowered to rule Iraq by decree, though subject to the "authority, direction and control" of Rumsfeld. Bremer's first two decrees, banning Saddam's Ba'ath Party and dismantling the Iraqi army, were both disastrous decisions.

Facing daunting challenges in Iraq, Bremer also had to confront three major problems at home. The first was the dearth of nation-building expertise in the national security departments of the government, a reality acknowledged in the key players' memoirs. As noted, Powell had concerns about how little State could do. Rumsfeld admitted that even the Defense Department "could not perform all or even most of the nonmilitary tasks that needed to be done," which may be clearer in hindsight than it was at the time. The last time the American military had responsibility for overseeing both civilian and military postwar reconstruction had been in Germany and Japan after World War II, and that experience and expertise had long since disappeared, as Rumsfeld acknowledged. He would later observe that the U.S. government simply was not organized for postwar planning, lacking a single office that could take charge of both civilian and military planning. President Bush later wrote: "By having our plans and personnel ready before the war, I felt we were well prepared. Yet we were aware of our limitations. Our nation building capabilities were limited, and no one knew for sure what needs would arise." The United States may or may not have been "well prepared" in terms of planning; it was totally unprepared in terms of capabilities. The non-military instruments of power vital to nation-building in Iraq were not just "limited"—they were hopelessly inadequate. And the needs would prove astounding.

The shortage of U.S. civilian expertise in Iraq and the failure to integrate military and civilian reconstruction efforts would be an enduring problem. For example, in 2009, USAID had roughly 1,400 assistance personnel in Iraq; it had more than 10,000 such experts in Vietnam at one point during the war there (notable for the level of commitment, not the success of the effort). Only in 2004 was an office created in the State Department to carry out this mission, but it lacked the size and mandate to do the job effectively.

Another big problem was the failure to get everyone in Washington (and Bremer in Baghdad) on the same page. Contrary to conventional wisdom, there was a lot of planning for the postwar period, and a lot of coordination of that planning. What ultimately was deeply flawed was coordination of the execution of those plans, the uncertainty over who was in charge, and the lack of understanding of the resources that would be required. These shortcomings serve as an object lesson that wielding the instruments of power successfully requires effective implementation—and based on a realistic assessment of the challenge at hand.

As early as spring 2002, the State Department began work on its Future of Iraq Project, assessing the kinds of problems and issues the United States would face post-Saddam. Various working groups addressed health, finance, water, agriculture, and other expected challenges. Beginning in the summer of 2002, the policy office in Defense began working on how to engage the Iraqi opposition in an interim government, and about the same time, Central Command in Tampa created Combined Task Force 4 to deal with post-combat Iraq. Meanwhile, Rice had directed the NSC staff to work on humanitarian relief planning and, in August, assigned a senior director to coordinate postwar planning across the government. A final cook in the crowded postwar planning kitchen was USAID.

The interagency sniping began pretty quickly. Rumsfeld dismissed State's Future of Iraq Project as conceptual in nature and "not postwar planning in any sense of the word." "There were no operational steps outlined in them," he later wrote, "nor any detailed suggestions about how to handle various problems." As Rice tried to better coordinate planning "with a light touch," as the president wanted, "almost immediately the under secretary of defense for policy, Douglas Feith, made clear that the Pentagon neither needed nor welcomed the opinions of others." Rumsfeld would later observe that "postwar planning for Iraq lacked effective interagency coordination, clear lines of responsibility, and the deadlines and accountability associated with a rigorous process." While there were clearly shortcomings in managing the process at the NSC, the Defense Department itself was an important obstacle to better interagency coordination.

Bremer, the CPA head appointed by Bush, exacerbated the problem in Washington. The Department of Defense was still in charge of post-combat operations in Iraq, and Bremer reported to Rumsfeld. However, as Bremer would later write, "I was neither Rumsfeld's nor Powell's man, I was the President's man." Rumsfeld was annoyed by Bremer's access at the White House and by his relationships at the State Department. Rice couldn't understand why Defense and Bremer didn't work together better, especially since Rumsfeld was supposed to be his boss. And everyone in Washington was angry at Bremer's failure to keep the principals informed about his decisions and actions, including an op-ed he wrote for *The Washington Post* in September 2003 laying out a road map to Iraqi sovereignty that had not been vetted in Washington and produced a storm of protest in Baghdad.

Rumsfeld wrote in his memoir, "The muddled lines of authority meant that there was no single individual in control of or responsible for Bremer's work." More broadly, with respect to the lack of a clear line of authority, "there were far too many hands on the steering wheel, which, in my view, was a formula for running the truck into a ditch."

In response to Rumsfeld's complaints that the White House–based interagency coordination process was "broken," Rice and Hadley decided the way to eliminate the disconnect between Washington and the field was to shut down the Washington end and for Bremer to carry out interagency coordination from Baghdad, inasmuch as all the relevant agencies were represented there. They thought this would work because Defense had the lead in Iraq and Bremer reported to Rumsfeld. They would subsequently learn that Bremer was not getting guidance from Rumsfeld, nor was he doing the interagency coordination in Iraq. In short, interagency coordination of U.S. post-invasion activities in Iraq had become a bureaucratic standoff—and a mess.

Bush had been clear that Rumsfeld had the lead in postwar matters in Iraq and that Bremer reported to the secretary. But it soon became clear that Rumsfeld was ignoring Bremer, who was acting on his own. It was pretty obvious at that point that the only hands on the steering wheel were his.

Rice thus stepped in, formed the Iraq Strategy Group to bring civilian-military coordination back to Washington, and sent Ambassador Robert Blackwill, an experienced diplomat and colleague of Rice's in the Bush 41 administration, to Baghdad to work with Bremer on the political handover to the Iraqis (and to keep her informed about what was going on in Baghdad). According to Rice, Rumsfeld was furious over these arrangements and told her and Powell that "Bremer now works for the White House." She took heat for this from the Pentagon, Vice President Cheney, and even, to a lesser extent, from Bush for "usurping Don's power."

As I see it, three people bear responsibility for the bureaucratic snarl during the post-invasion period. Rumsfeld wanted nothing to do with post-invasion Iraq, failed to assert his authority over Bremer, didn't translate post-invasion plans and decisions into operational orders for either Bremer or the soldiers in the field, and had washed his hands of the whole business well before Rice tried to reestablish bureaucratic order and lines of authority. He abdicated the responsibility the president had given him. Rice, as national security adviser, should have made sure in the starkest terms that the president not only knew about this collapse of the post-invasion civilian command structure, but understood that his defense secretary was not doing the job the president had assigned to him. Whether Rice provided such warnings or not, Bush presumably was aware of the problems. And, ultimately, of course, when it comes to cracking cabinet-level heads, ensuring close military and nonmilitary cooperation, and demanding accountability from all involved, especially Rumsfeld, responsibility rested in the Oval Office.

There was then, and still is, a lot of finger-pointing about all the problems after the initial military victory. There was plenty of blame to go around. However, placing a predominantly civilian interagency effort under Pentagon authority required the direct engagement of the secretary of defense and especially intrusive and effective coordination and direction by the White House. Neither happened.

The third major problem at home was a clear difference of opinion between Defense on the one hand and State and the NSC on the other about how fast to transition authority back to the Iraqis. Defense urged broad use of Iraqi opposition figures and expatriates in forming an interim Iraqi government as quickly as possible (as had happened in Afghanistan). State and the NSC were concerned about whether such figures would have legitimacy inside Iraq and, further, believed that more time was needed to prepare the ground and begin to build an institutional foundation for the new Iraqi government. Bremer clearly supported a more prolonged process of transition and continued CPA suzerainty in Iraq. Differences among the principals on the speed of transition to Iraqi sovereignty and self-government would persist. In the event, Bremer negotiated the Transitional Administrative Law, which went into effect on March 8, 2004. It provided a road map for return of sovereignty to Iraq and creation of an interim Iraqi government, which occurred on June 28, followed by national elections in January 2005.

All these developments were greatly overshadowed, however, by growing violence in Iraq. The sacking of Baghdad by rampaging Iraqi looters soon after the United States took control of the capital city—for whatever reason, U.S. troops lacked orders to intervene—was a harbinger of worse to come. A Sunni insurgency developed soon after the fall of Baghdad and by the spring of 2004 was centered on the city of Fallujah in Anbar province. Nearly simultaneously, there was an uprising of Shia militias in the holy city of Najaf and in the area of Baghdad called Sadr City. Over time, a lot of lives—Iraqi and American—would be lost in Fallujah and Sadr City. Across Iraq, the Americans were increasingly seen as occupiers, not liberators. The fight against Shia militias and the Sunni insurgents, especially in the cities, resulted in considerable "collateral damage," further antagonizing Iraqis. Rising violence and the resulting lack of security largely put a stop to major reconstruction efforts despite recognition of their importance. The deteriorating security situation was not brought under control until the 2007 surge of U.S. forces.

In many respects, however, one of the most serious setbacks for the American effort in Iraq was self-inflicted: the revelation in April 2004 of serious abuse of Iraqi prisoners by U.S. military guards at Abu Ghraib. While there was disgust at home and around the world, it was minimal compared to the impact on the Iraqis and their increasingly hostile attitude toward Americans.

With the creation of an interim Iraqi government in June 2004, the U.S. "occupation" of Iraq nominally came to an end, the CPA was terminated, and dealing with the Iraqis became the responsibility of the Department of State and the new U.S. ambassador, John Negroponte. Just the same, the security situation continued to deteriorate.

Overcoming the growing hostility of ordinary Iraqis required providing them with improved security and figuring out how to improve their daily lives. The electrical grid, water, sewers, schools—everything was a mess because of Saddam's neglect, our bombing, years of sanctions, and the post-invasion looting. Local U.S. commanders did what they could to jerry-build fixes, especially for water and sewers, but that was not their primary mission, nor did they have the requisite expertise. Criticism by commanders of the lack of civilian support from the State Department grew steadily. There were just too few American civilian experts on the ground to seriously tackle the basic needs of the people. The complaint, however justified, obscured the reality that because of the lack of security, the military would need to provide protection for such civilians to do their work—and to protect whatever improvements they made from being destroyed by insurgents, terrorists, or militias.

Soon after becoming secretary of state in early 2005, Rice focused on how to not only improve State's support of the military but also make progress in winning over the Iraqis by improving their living conditions. The result was to borrow an innovation from U.S. efforts in Afghanistan by creating Provincial Reconstruction Teams (PRTs), a hybrid force (as she described it) including military officers, diplomats, and reconstruction workers from various U.S. civilian agencies such as Agriculture, Justice, and USAID. Rumsfeld, who had praised the work of the PRTs in Afghanistan, resisted their use in Iraq and delayed their deployment by as much as six months. Rice inaugurated the first Iraqi PRT in Mosul in November 2005.

The PRTs had a very broad mandate. As described in various documents, they were to assist "Iraq's provincial governments with developing a transparent and sustained capacity to govern, promoting increased security and rule of law, promoting political and economic development, and providing provincial administration necessary to meet the basic needs of the population." They also were supposed to focus on repairing or replacing infrastructure, such as roads and schools, and provide key municipal needs, such as water, electricity, and sewage treatment. In their spare time, they also were to provide technical expertise to Iraqis in banking and finance, public health, agriculture, police training, and preparation of provincial budgets. Such an expansive mission was an illusion. There was a yawning chasm between the drafters of such plans in Washington and the reality on the ground in Iraq.

In Iraq, PRTs were led by a senior State Department officer and were larger than in Afghanistan and almost entirely civilian. PRTs not located at the U.S. embassy or a regional embassy office relied heavily on the U.S. military for security, transportation, food, housing, and other support. At the high point, there were thirty-one PRTs in Iraq, all but three staffed by Americans. Brigade commanders of units with embedded PRTs sang their praises and complained only that more such civilians were needed, though there were practical problems created by different bureaucratic cultures. In November 2007, at the peak of the surge, the United States had just over 170,000 troops in Iraq. The highest number of non-Defense civilians assigned to the PRTs, in July 2008, was 360, a massive insufficiency and a reflection of the extraordinary imbalance of resources for a nation-building mission.

Bureaucratic mind-sets were an obstacle to providing adequate civilian expertise. Both Rumsfeld and then I offered to send—and pay for—Defense Department civilians with expertise to temporarily augment the capabilities from State and elsewhere. We sent lists of these volunteers to State, but somehow few, if any, were selected to go to Iraq. State would often say they weren't fully qualified, to which my response was that if each volunteer was 50 percent as capable as a full-time State professional, he or she would still be making a significant contribution. It fell on deaf ears.

As a former president of Texas A&M University, I knew that A&M and other land-grant schools had many experts in agriculture, water resources, and veterinary medicine who often traveled to inhospitable places—including Iraq and Afghanistan—to work and do research. They seemed to me to be an untapped reservoir of talent we could use. Moreover, the then head of the association of land-grant colleges and universities in Washington, D.C., was M. Peter McPherson, former president of Michigan State University and, more significantly, head of USAID under President Reagan. I knew Peter would be more than willing to try to get the universities involved, but again, I don't think either State or USAID ever reached out.

As happened so often after the Cold War, there was a lack of imagination in the White House and at State on how to access nongovernment civilian expertise in order to strengthen nonmilitary capabilities. They seemingly had no appreciation of the importance of the private sector, apart from contractors, as an instrument of power.

As secretary of defense, I thought it bizarre, and maddening, that Congress would give money for civil assistance to the Pentagon but not to the agencies primarily responsible for such help. There was a special program approved by Congress—it was always controversial—that allowed the Defense Department to transfer $100 million to $200 million annually to State for civilian projects in support of military operations and stabilization. At the same time, U.S. commanders in Iraq had access to the Commander's Emergency Response Program (CERP), which provided "tactical commanders a means to conduct multiple stability tasks that have traditionally been performed by U.S., foreign, or indigenous professional civilian personnel or agencies," such as reconstruction of infrastructure, support to governance, restoration of public services, and support to economic development. These funds, several hundred million dollars each year, were available to commanders down to the brigade level. The money (essentially a slush fund for unforeseen needs) was a huge asset for the commanders, but, again, it was a case of the Pentagon having ample funds while State and other civilian agencies were starved.

While virtually everyone agreed that each civilian in the field made a disproportionate contribution, the size of the civilian contingent beyond Baghdad and U.S. military bases was pitifully small (just as in Afghanistan). This was due to personnel policies and funding problems, a poor security environment that made civilian efforts outside of Baghdad quite risky without military protection, an inability to fully access American civilian expertise resident in (and out of) the government, and the lack of congressional support for State and USAID as well as hostility to "foreign assistance." But the most important reason is that the U.S. government is not structured or equipped to take on nation-building.

In a speech at Kansas State University in November 2007, I pointed out that during the 1990s America's ability to assist as well as engage and communicate with the rest of the world had been "gutted." State Department hiring had been frozen for a period of time, USAID's permanent staff dropped from a high of 15,000 during the Vietnam War to 3,000 in the 1990s, and the U.S. Information Agency had been abolished as an independent entity. "During the 1990s," I observed, "with the complicity of both the Congress and the White House, key instruments of America's national power once again were allowed to wither or were abandoned." The remedy? "The way to institutionalize these capabilities is probably not to re-create or repopulate institutions of the past such as AID or USIA. . . . We need to develop a permanent, sizable cadre of immediately deployable experts with disparate skills. . . . We also need new thinking about how to integrate our government's capabilities in these areas, and then how to integrate government capabilities with those in the private sector, in universities, in other nongovernmental organizations."

For all of my—and the Defense Department's—frustrations over those deficiencies, especially the lack of sufficient deployable civilian experts, the need to address them had been recognized since the Clinton administration's experiences in Haiti, Somalia, and the Balkans. Indeed, in May 1997, Clinton had signed a directive, Managing Complex Contingency Operations—Presidential Decision Directive (PDD) 56—that was intended to tackle planning and coordination problems relating to civilian contributions to peacekeeping. Its provisions were never formally implemented. In contrast, another Clinton directive (PDD 71) signed in February 2000 created a new office in the State Department to lead U.S. participation in the criminal justice components of peace operations and support for programs advancing the rule of law. Although too little time remained in the administration to implement the directive, elements of it were adopted by the new Bush administration.

But it was in the aftermath of the invasion of Iraq that the deficiencies in the civilian contribution to stabilization and reconstruction became blindingly clear. Absent such civilian capabilities, it fell to the military to rebuild government institutions and revitalize both the economy and civil society. In recognition of the problem, in mid-2004 Secretary of State Colin Powell created the Office of the Coordinator for Reconstruction and Stabilization to design and implement new structures within State and elsewhere that would enable civilian agencies of the government to develop the policies, processes, and personnel necessary for nation-building. The new office was also charged with creating a civilian "surge" capability to provide a rapid response to emergency situations overseas. President Bush put his weight behind the effort in December 2005, when he signed a directive focused on the execution of interagency reconstruction and stabilization operations. Secretary of State Rice elaborated on the president's intent in a January 2006 speech that focused on the "intersections of diplomacy, democracy promotion, economic reconstruction and military security" and the necessary organizational changes to carry out a strategy of nation-building.

Central to the success of these initiatives was the idea of a cadre of readily deployable civilians who could be dispatched on short notice in crisis situations, as well as a larger number of experts—also civilian—who could follow shortly thereafter. The concept was endorsed by Bush in his January 2007 State of the Union speech. During 2006 and 2007, the Bush administration began to build such a capability, but only in February 2008, with the Civilian Stabilization Initiative, was a full-scale reserve corps proposed. The original Bush/ Rice plan was for a three-tiered reserve corps: an active component of 250 that could deploy within two days, a standby component of 2,000 experts capable of being deployed within thirty days, and a reserve component of another 2,000 mostly nongovernment experts ready to go within forty-five to sixty days and for extended periods. The Obama administration and Secretary Clinton embraced the program, but it would remain a pale shadow of what was needed in the field. The corps was a great idea, but as with most innovations on the civilian side of foreign policy, it had little institutional support in the executive branch or in Congress. It was never fully funded nor staffed and, beginning in 2012, essentially just withered away.

Over the entire period of our military involvement in Iraq, the shortage of civilians was never solved. And with Congress's unwillingness to fund the "reserve" component of the corps, consisting mainly of experts from outside the government, we still haven't determined how to tap the wealth of experience and knowledge in the private sector or in higher education. This represents a significant instrument of American power that we haven't figured out how to bring on stage.

The Bush administration was reminded of the inherent unpredictability of war during 2006. Early that year, the U.S. command in Baghdad was planning to draw down American forces in Iraq by December from fifteen to ten combat brigades (each of which averaged about 3,500 soldiers), convinced that the large U.S. presence was stoking the insurgency and that it was time to begin transitioning responsibility for security to the Iraqis. In February, however, Sunni terrorists—probably al-Qaeda—blew up the golden dome of the al-Askari Mosque in Samarra, one of the holiest sites in Shia Islam. The attack ignited horrific sectarian violence that escalated all over the country. By October, three thousand Iraqi civilians were being killed every month. Under the circumstances, drawing down our troops would have led to even greater violence. It was also clear by the latter part of the year that we were losing in Iraq. As one of my briefing papers said, "We are on the strategic defensive and the enemy [Sunni insurgents and Shia militias] has the initiative." Facing such a dire situation, Bush courageously decided to change course, altering the primary military mission from transitioning security to the Iraqi

forces to protecting the Iraqis. We could not make any headway politically or economically in Iraq without providing security for the people,
especially in and around Baghdad. Accordingly, in January 2007 Bush
named General David Petraeus to take command in Iraq and ordered
a surge of 30,000 troops. Many in Congress and in the media were
outraged that the president was doubling down on what they regarded
as a lost cause.

Bush stuck to his guns through several difficult months in 2007,
and by fall the situation in Iraq had begun to stabilize. By the time
we began withdrawing the surge forces in early 2008, a semblance of
normal life had been restored to Baghdad for the first time in years,
and we could begin the transition of security responsibility to the
Iraqis without fear of serious reversals. The surge worked. As we had
hoped, it not only stabilized and then dramatically improved the security environment, especially around Baghdad; it bought time for Iraqi
politics to settle down and for making at least modest improvements
in the quality of life. Thanks to a tough president, a different strategy,
and the sacrifice of American soldiers and Marines, the Iraqis would
have a chance to move their country forward.

The UN Security Council resolution authorizing our military presence in Iraq was due to expire at the end of 2008, and the Iraqis
were not interested in extending, or "rolling over," the resolution. That
meant we needed to negotiate a new agreement with Baghdad providing for any continued U.S. or other foreign troop presence in Iraq
after December 31, 2008. The obstacles to a successful negotiation
were daunting because of the Iraqi political environment and strong
opposition to any continuing U.S. presence, especially among the
Iranian-backed Shias. Nonetheless, after months of difficult negotiations conducted by Secretary Rice, Ambassador Ryan Crocker, Brett
McGurk and Meghan O'Sullivan of the NSC staff, and David Satter-
field from State, on December 14 President Bush and Iraqi prime minister Nouri al-Maliki signed the Strategic Framework Agreement and
a Status of Forces Agreement in Baghdad. According to the terms, the
United States would withdraw all of its combat forces from Iraqi cit-

ies and villages by June 30, 2009, and remove all its forces from Iraq by December 31, 2011. To get Iraqi agreement, we had to agree to the one thing the president, Rice, and I had repeatedly warned against for two years: a firm, specific timetable for complete American military withdrawal. We consoled ourselves with the hope that, as the political situation in Iraq cooled, we could negotiate an extension of the U.S. troop presence sometime before that December 31, 2011, deadline.

On October 2, 2002, Illinois state senator Barack Obama, in reference to a possible war with Iraq, declared in a speech he was opposed to "dumb wars." He didn't change his views between then and winning election as president, and promised in his campaign to get U.S. combat forces out of Iraq in sixteen months and all U.S. forces out by December 2011. Just as Iraq had been on the agenda of Bush's first NSC meeting as president in 2001, so, too, was it the subject of Obama's first NSC meeting on January 21, 2009. While saying that he wanted to withdraw troops in a way that "preserves the positive security trends and protects U.S. personnel," he asked for at least three options, including his sixteen-month timetable. Ultimately, he accepted my recommendation for a nineteen-month drawdown of combat forces, leaving nearly 50,000 troops in Iraq until the latter part of 2011. Our combat role ended on August 31, 2010. As agreed by Bush and Maliki, all U.S. forces would be out by the end of December 2011.

Eleven months before that deadline, on February 2, 2011, the NSC principals met in the Situation Room to discuss the recommendation from James Jeffrey, our ambassador in Baghdad, and General Lloyd Austin, our military commander, that the United States try to get Iraqi agreement to allow a post-December U.S. presence of 20,000 people at the embassy (the majority providing security) and 20,000 troops. They reported that all Iraqi leaders wanted a continuing U.S. presence but none wanted to take the political risk of saying so publicly. I believed we would need a long-term residual military presence of some size in Iraq to sustain improved security, but said I thought neither the Iraqis nor Congress would support the numbers Jeffrey and Austin were proposing. Nor, I thought, would Obama, who just wanted out. In mid-April, the president asked Austin to explore the feasibility and risks of having 8,000 to 10,000 troops remain in Iraq. I believed we could make that work, and told the president so.

As I prepared to retire as secretary of defense in June, nothing had been agreed to with the Iraqis. I remembered vividly how difficult the negotiation had been in 2008 and how much time President Bush had spent on the phone cajoling Maliki and other Iraqis to get the agreements approved. I knew the negotiation of a post-2011 military presence would be even more challenging and would require substantial effort on the part of the president to get the Iraqis to agree. I don't know how hard President Obama tried (I suspect not very hard at all), and the Iraqi leaders, for their part, made no effort to get an extension approved by their parliament. Lacking any new agreement, the last 500 American troops crossed the border from Iraq into Kuwait on December 18, 2011. We thought our military involvement in Iraq was over.

We were wrong. A combination of spillover into Iraq of the Syrian civil war beginning in the fall of 2011, the incompetence of the Maliki government in Baghdad and its anti-Sunni policies, and the degradation of the Iraqi army due to corruption and political influence created the opportunity for the terrorist group Islamic State of Iraq and the Levant (ISIL) to move easily into Iraq. On January 3, 2014, ISIL seized control of both Fallujah and Ramadi, promising to protect the Sunnis there from the Shia-dominated government in Baghdad. Some six months later, ISIL occupied Mosul, Iraq's second-largest city, as the Iraqi army essentially disintegrated, leaving behind huge quantities of American military equipment. Shortly thereafter, on June 19, President Obama sent hundreds of American military advisers back into Iraq, mainly to help plan air strikes. Many more U.S. troops would follow in subsequent months, their presence augmented by steadily intensifying U.S. air strikes against ISIL. By the time Obama left office in January 2017, the American military presence in Iraq had grown to more than 5,000. The Americans were back in combat in Iraq, with no prospect of an early end. President Trump modestly increased U.S. troop numbers in Iraq during the spring of 2017 and, more important, greatly enhanced the authority of commanders in the field to attack ISIL more aggressively from the air and support the Iraqis on the ground. By the end of 2017, ISIL strongholds in Iraq had all been "liberated," although the cities ISIL had occupied were in ruins from the fighting.

As of this writing, it is still an open question whether Iraq will survive as an integrated single state or devolve formally or informally into Shia, Sunni, and Kurdish enclaves. The May 2018 elections ultimately resulted in the election of a Kurd, Barham Salih, as president and an independent Shiite, Adel Abdul Mahdi, as prime minister. As secretary, I knew and had worked with both and, along with most observers, thought that was about as positive and pragmatic an outcome as could be hoped for. Even so, disgust and frustration with unending corruption, economic hardship, and Iranian influence led to widespread and violent demonstrations in the fall of 2019, especially in the Shia-dominated south, and ultimately to the resignation of the prime minister. These events underscored that Iraq's future will depend on whether the national government can demonstrate any success in winning the support of Sunnis and Kurds, begin to rebuild ravaged cities and towns, create economic growth and jobs, tackle corruption, and fairly distribute oil revenues and political power.

Amid so much uncertainty, one thing seems clear: the United States will have little influence over the direction of future events in Iraq. There are many criticisms that can be directed at the Bush administration regarding Iraq, among them, that our nonmilitary instruments of power and the way in which they were wielded were unequal to the circumstances. But, above all, the president's nation-building aspirations for a country that had suffered Saddam Hussein and war for so long proved unrealistic. It is no small thing, however, that the country has held together, sectarian violence has not resumed, and Iraq has the only Arab working democracy in the region, however deeply flawed. To that extent, Bush's original vision has been at least partially vindicated.

But the cost was very high.

CHAPTER 8

Africa

A Success Story

O n January 28, 2003, less than two months before the United States invaded Iraq, President George W. Bush proposed in his State of the Union speech an American humanitarian assistance program for Africa unprecedented in scope and ambition "to turn the tide against AIDS in the most afflicted nations of Africa and the Caribbean." He asked Congress to commit $15 billion over five years with the goal of preventing 7 million new AIDS infections, treating at least 2 million people with life-extending drugs, and providing care for millions suffering from AIDS and children orphaned by AIDS. The extraordinary success of this program, the President's Emergency Plan for AIDS Relief (PEPFAR), offers multiple lessons in the effective use of nonmilitary instruments of power to take on a monumental challenge, sustain the efforts through multiple presidencies with bipartisan support, and actually exceed the original goals set for the program.

Nearly a year earlier, Bush had announced another initiative that would reshape how the executive branch and Congress approach foreign development assistance, traditionally the least popular endeavor in all of American foreign policy. The Millennium Challenge Corporation (MCC), established in law in 2004 (two years after Bush proposed it) as an independent government entity separate from the State Department, the Treasury, and USAID, would provide economic assistance to developing nations. It would rely on a competitive selection process that evaluated applications on *the basis of each government's effectiveness in ruling justly, investing in its people, and fostering economic freedom. While the dollars involved never exceeded 5 percent of the overall assistance budget, the MCC's focus on transparency, buy-in on the part of the applicant government, participation of indigenous civil society in determining proposed projects, focus on effective results, and accountability won broad support for the MCC and also established more broadly a model U.S. government approach to economic and development assistance.*

During a period of partisan polarization, involvement in two unending wars, and diminishing confidence at home and abroad in the direction of American foreign policy, these two initiatives, PEPFAR and the MCC, are examples of how bold leadership, creative thinking, smart politics, and the effective integration of the instruments of power can result in successful programs that effectively help others. These programs can also foster favorable attitudes toward the United States and advance our interests by contributing to the health, economic growth, and stability of poor countries that are often fertile ground for extremism.

Throughout the Cold War, U.S. involvement in Africa was shaped primarily by the determination to counter or preempt Soviet efforts to exploit for its own advantage widespread anti-Western sentiment there among newly independent former colonies. While the Cold War in Africa had roots in the independence movements of the 1950s and 1960s, it intensified in the 1970s. In September 1974, a communist faction in the Ethiopian army overthrew Emperor Haile Selassie. The new government turned to the Soviets for help. In July 1977, with massive Soviet assistance, Cuban troops—ultimately, nearly 40,000—were deployed to support the government.

In July 1975, again at Soviet behest, the Cubans deployed troops to Angola to support the leftist faction in a civil war there. Ultimately, more than 30,000 Cuban troops were sent. Soviet military advisers were sent to both countries and elsewhere. Throughout the continent, the Soviets' anticolonialist/national liberation credentials were an important asset. (The first assessment I wrote as a junior analyst at the CIA in the late 1960s was about Soviet infiltration of the labor movement in Africa. It deservedly garnered virtually no policy maker attention.)

While Soviet and Cuban activities in Angola and Ethiopia in the late 1970s drew the most attention, the Soviets supported black nationalist organizations in Rhodesia and the African National Congress, Nelson Mandela's party, in South Africa. During this period, Moscow became the largest arms supplier to Colonel Muammar Qaddafi in Libya. Meanwhile, Washington's concern with the Soviet "threat" in Africa in the 1960s and 1970s led the United States to embrace some sordid leaders, ranging from Mobutu Sese Seko in the Congo (later Zaire) to white supremacists in both Rhodesia and South Africa.

Presidents Gerald Ford and Jimmy Carter saw Soviet and Cuban involvement in Angola and Ethiopia, and other less visible Soviet efforts, as a major effort by Moscow to establish a strong foothold in Africa, but the U.S. response was tepid. Ford approved a significant covert program to help anti-leftist factions in Angola, but Congress, reacting to the failed attempt in Vietnam and in an effort to curb presidential war-making powers, passed legislation in January 1976—over Ford's objections—forbidding U.S. support for anybody in Angola. The Carter administration was divided internally over what to do about the Soviet-Cuban effort in Ethiopia and, as a result, did virtually nothing. Only in mid-1979 did Carter begin, very cautiously, to counter Soviet initiatives in the Third World.

This all changed with the arrival of Ronald Reagan in Washington. He denounced Soviet support for "wars of national liberation" and their efforts to undermine noncommunist governments in developing countries. He made clear that the United States would no longer watch these efforts from the sidelines. From the outset, the Reagan administration used covert action, foreign assistance, diplomacy, and even direct military intervention in Third World battlegrounds to oppose the Soviets and the Cubans. In August 1985, Congress repealed the legislation blocking assistance to the Angolan opposition, and in November Reagan authorized a major program of lethal aid to them and to anticommunist groups in other countries as well. By the mid-1980s, regimes that the Soviets had brought to power or helped keep in power during the 1970s were themselves facing serious insurgencies sponsored by the United States. The change marked the successful application of multiple instruments of power—diplomacy, covert operations, the supply of weapons, and development assistance. But as the Cold War wound down in the late 1980s and early 1990s, Africa quickly became a low priority for American policy makers once again.

President Clinton would later acknowledge that Africa was "too often ignored," and Albright conceded that "Africa played only a marginal role in U.S. foreign policy." Indeed, Clinton largely ignored Africa until the last two years of his presidency. Chastened by the loss of American soldiers in Somalia in October 1993, the administration took no military action six months later during and after the genocide in Rwanda (though by the time the magnitude of the slaughter was known, it was already too late to act). As the civil war in Sudan raged through the 1990s, Clinton, like Bush 41 and Reagan before him, stood aside, though he did impose some economic sanctions on the Khartoum government.

Even as Africa remained below Washington's policy radar, the continent, including Egypt, consistently received more American development assistance than any other region; Africa received a total of $14 billion in American assistance in 2001. The United States was by far the largest foreign donor to programs promoting education, health, population programs, water supply and sanitation, and government and civil society.

This largesse received little attention at home and earned little credit in Africa—USAID apparently was content to do "good works" for their own sake—and no one seemed interested in publicizing these activities throughout Africa for political or strategic gain. Effective development assistance is an instrument of national power; failure to recognize that reality and inform African, American, and other audiences about the good things we do is an opportunity lost.

Africa's low visibility in U.S. post–Cold War foreign policy changed in the late 1990s. This was due primarily to continuing and new conflicts across the continent. The worst were the Congo wars, which began in 1996—when Laurent Kabila, with the help of Rwanda and

Uganda, began a campaign to oust Mobutu—and continued until 2003 and, in many areas, until 2008. Kabila succeeded in ousting Mobutu in May 1997, but when he subsequently refused to help the Rwandans kill Hutu militias operating in eastern Congo, the Rwandans sent forces into the Congo in August 1998. This provoked Kabila into seeking outside help. Ultimately nine nations and some two dozen armed groups were engaged in a war that raged across central Africa. The several-years-long Congo civil war is estimated to have caused nearly 6 million deaths, mostly from disease and starvation.

Another, even longer-lasting, civil war between northern and southern Sudan began soon after Sudanese independence in 1956 and intensified in 1994–95 when Eritrea, Ethiopia, and Uganda began sending substantial military assistance to the rebels in the south and then sent troops into Sudan. Despite a peace agreement in 1997 between the government and the major rebel factions and a "comprehensive" peace agreement in 2005, fighting continued at a reduced level. The Sudanese civil war cost an estimated 2 million lives.

Because the Ugandan government was helping Sudanese rebels in the south, the radical Islamist government in Khartoum in 1994 began supporting an especially bloodthirsty Ugandan opposition group called the Lord's Resistance Army (LRA). Led by a self-declared prophet, Joseph Kony, the LRA proclaimed it wanted to rule Uganda by the Ten Commandments, but in practice, Kony's military strategy was murder, mutilation, and forcing children to fight in his ranks. Meanwhile, another years-long civil conflict in Sierra Leone flared up again in May 1997, war broke out between Ethiopia and Eritrea in May 1998, and a second civil war broke out in Liberia in April 1999 (the first had lasted from 1989 to 1997, with more than 200,000 killed).

American diplomats during the Clinton administration were deeply engaged in trying to stop all these conflicts. Assistant Secretary of State for Africa Susan Rice worked with both European and African counterparts to negotiate diplomatic solutions, but these efforts were like nailing Jell-O to a wall. The United States worked with the Organization for African Unity (OAU) to persuade Ethiopia and Eritrea to stop fighting, and cooperated with other African states, the UN, and the EU to negotiate at least a partial agreement in the Congo. In Sierra Leone, the Economic Community of West African States negotiated a cease-fire agreement. Similarly, American diplomats worked with others to bring an end to the Sudanese conflict. Unfortunately, in every case, the conflicts sooner or later relapsed into fighting. However, in no case was the use of the U.S. military seriously considered, mainly, I suppose, because of the huge scale of the effort that would have been required to make a difference in any of these places. As Albright later wrote, "The solution to these conflicts had . . . to be found through diplomacy, with outside force introduced rarely and selectively." The administration deserves credit for its continuing diplomatic efforts to address these conflicts. It was the principal nonmilitary instrument we had, and Albright, Rice, and others used it as well as possible despite the challenges.

Two events in 1998 brought Africa to the fore in American foreign policy. The first was Clinton's trip there in March, when he visited Ghana, Uganda, Rwanda, and Senegal and became the first president to visit South Africa. The second event, far more dramatic, was the aforementioned al-Qaeda-sponsored terrorist attack on the U.S. embassies in Nairobi and Dar es Salaam on August 7, killing 257 people, including twelve Americans, and injuring 5,000. Thirteen days later, as I said earlier, the United States launched seventy-nine cruise missiles from the Arabian and Red Seas, hitting al-Qaeda training camps in Afghanistan and a suspected chemical weapons facility in Sudan. The attacks were both in retaliation for the embassy bombings and in the hope of killing the al-Qaeda leadership that U.S. intelligence sources had reported would be meeting at one of the training camps. A number of them were killed, but not Bin Laden.

During Clinton's remaining time in office, he creatively employed a nonmilitary instrument of power by pursuing two economic initiatives in Africa with long-term beneficial consequences. One was large-scale debt relief. In March 1999, at a U.S.-African summit attended by forty-six countries, Clinton called for developed countries to forgive $90 billion in African debt. Many governments were so burdened by debt and repayment that little money was left for education, health care, and basic services. Clinton's proposed debt relief, however, was conditioned on reforms. The president told the assemblage that the United States would forgive $3 billion if others also stepped forward. Substantial relief followed, with salutary effects in a number of countries. The Clinton debt relief initiative was as clever as it was bold. In the case of the United States, most of the $3 billion we were owed had already been written off as uncollectable, and so the actual cost to the Treasury was only about $200 million.

The second initiative was the African Growth and Opportunity Act (AGOA), signed into law in May 2000, which lowered trade barriers on a broad array of African exports to the United States and continues to benefit African economies.

I n the spring of 1987, when I was serving as acting director of central intelligence, analysts prepared a special National Intelligence Estimate on the implications of the AIDS "pandemic" on sub-Saharan Africa. I sent it to the White House. The estimate reported that approximately 50,000 Africans had already died from AIDS, another 2 million to 5 million were infected, and "annual African deaths from AIDS after 1992 are likely to continue to climb into the millions." The report warned that the disease was spreading rapidly and was "out of control," hitting hardest at the healthy, productive fifteen-to-fifty age group. "Leaders are helpless to prevent AIDS or treat the victims" and the "long-range impact of AIDS will be devastating," with "irreplaceable population losses in those groups most essential to . . . future development: midlevel economic and political managers, agrarian and urban workers, and military personnel." The number of HIV-infected people could grow, the estimate forecast, to several tens of millions by the year 2000. It seemed that every day the CIA was learning of more senior military and civilian leaders in sub-Saharan Africa being infected, and members of their families as well. We were looking at the potential decimation of the political and economic elites in a number of countries.

The growing AIDS crisis in Africa, which the CIA first warned about in 1987, did not capture the attention of the Clinton administration until nearly the end of his presidency. In January 2000, Vice

President Al Gore chaired a UN Security Council special session on HIV/AIDS, the first time a disease was recognized as a danger not only to public health but also to international security. At the UN General Assembly the following September, Secretary Albright and the twelve other women foreign ministers called for all countries to join in the fight against AIDS and especially to recognize the need to protect women and girls. By the end of the Clinton administration, the United States was spending about half a billion dollars a year globally to fight AIDS. Then, as later, America was the largest single donor to programs for prevention and treatment of the disease, but the size of the contribution was dwarfed by the scale of the disaster.

As usual in the exercise of nonmilitary instruments of power, the problem for the United States in addressing HIV/AIDS internationally, as Albright later wrote, was the lack of money: "In all my efforts to exercise constructive American leadership, there was one recurring frustration, and that was money. Whether the specific need was debt relief for Nigeria or peacekeepers for Sierra Leone or judicial training for Rwanda, we were always left scraping for nickels and dimes." The USAID budget fell to its lowest level in agency history in 2000.

U.S. intelligence agencies continued to monitor the progress of HIV/AIDS, reporting increasingly dire findings to decision makers. However grim the forecasts, the reality turned out to be worse. An intelligence estimate released in December 1999 reported that to date there had been 11.5 million AIDS deaths in sub-Saharan Africa and that in eastern and southern Africa 10 to 26 percent of adults were infected. The infection rate among the military in these countries ranged from 10 percent to 60 percent. The assessment noted that worldwide nearly 35 million children in twenty-seven countries had lost one or both parents to AIDS; nineteen of those countries were in sub-Saharan Africa. The number of children thus affected globally was predicted to grow to 41.6 million by 2010.

The intelligence estimate issued in September 2002 was bleakest of all, predicting 30 million to 35 million AIDS cases in sub-Saharan Africa by the end of the decade. A major problem in all those countries was weak to nonexistent nationwide public health care infrastructure. According to the estimate, the only bright spot was Uganda, where, over a ten-year period, President Yoweri Museveni had dramatically reduced the infection rate through a campaign he succinctly summarized as "urging people not to have sex with multiple partners, publicly acknowledging the threat posed by AIDS, destigmatizing the disease and decentralizing HIV education programs down to the village level."

By early 2003, the pandemic had killed at least 20 million of the more than 60 million people infected worldwide. In Africa, nearly 30 million people were infected with the AIDS virus, including 3 million children under the age of fifteen; in some countries the infection rate was above a third of the adult population; and more than 4 million people required immediate drug treatment. Yet, across the continent, only 50,000 AIDS victims were receiving the medicine they needed. A catastrophe wasn't looming. It had already arrived.

George W. Bush intended an ambitious American outreach to Africa from the outset of his administration. Secretary Rice recounts that at one of her first meetings with then Texas governor Bush in 1999 they discussed Africa, especially the need to address the "scourge" of AIDS. At the same time, Bush believed that past assistance to Africa had mostly been a waste of money: "Our foreign assistance programs in Africa had a lousy track record. . . . While our aid helped keep friendly regimes in power, it didn't do much to improve the lives of ordinary people." He thought the traditional model of U.S. aid was "paternalistic," especially since donor nations often simply told the receiving government how to spend the money, thus enabling corruption and too often resulting in useless projects of no benefit to ordinary people.

For Bush, though, the highest priority was to address the humanitarian crisis of HIV/AIDS. In early May 2001, Bush met with Secretary-General Kofi Annan, who was proposing to create the Global Fund to Fight AIDS, Tuberculosis and Malaria. Despite Bush's lack of enthusiasm for the UN, Secretary of State Colin Powell and Secretary of Health and Human Services Tommy Thompson nevertheless persuaded the president to pledge $200 million to the fund. They thought it important for the United States to be the first contributor, so on May 11, 2001, Bush announced the contribution. He later wrote, "I had plans to do more."

Bush's leadership in the fight against HIV/AIDS in sub-Saharan Africa is a saga of presidential vision, moral conviction, good politics, and the effective deployment of nonmilitary instruments of power in ways that advanced American interests and influence in a previously neglected but huge part of the world. At the same time, it saved millions of lives and helped millions of other people survive. It was an exceptionally bold move, and his approach won strong bipartisan support in the Congress.

After 9/11, Bush quickly came to believe that any long-term success in battling extremism also had to address the underlying causes and conditions, reinforcing his resolve to vastly expand the American fight against AIDS. "Societies mired in poverty and disease foster hopelessness. And hopelessness leaves people ripe for recruitment by terrorists and extremists," he would write. By early 2002, Bush had increased the U.S. contribution to the Global Fund to $500 million. Additionally, on June 19, 2002, Bush announced the International Mother and Child HIV Prevention Initiative, focusing on the 17.6 million women and 2.7 million children infected with HIV/AIDS. A central feature of the new program was the distribution of newly developed antiretroviral medicines that promised to reduce mother-to-child transmission by 50 percent. The cost of such drugs had plunged from $12,000 per person per year to under $300, making their widespread use financially feasible. The proposal including spending another $500 million over five years to buy these medicines and to train local health care workers in the most heavily affected African and Caribbean countries.

The same day Bush announced the mother and child initiative, he told White House deputy chief of staff for policy Josh Bolten to "go back to the drawing board and think even bigger." A few months later, Bolten gave the president a recommendation for a huge program focused on HIV/AIDS treatment, prevention, and care. The proof of concept for the effort was Uganda, where the AIDS Support Organization (TASO) was distributing antiretroviral drugs door to door within the framework of an aggressive Ugandan government prevention program pushed by President Museveni. The "ABC" program called for abstinence (refraining from sex until marriage), being faithful (avoiding multiple sexual partners), and using condoms. The results were indisputable. The infection rate in Uganda had dropped from 15 percent of the population in 1991 to 5 percent ten years later.

In the State of the Union address on January 28, 2003, President Bush set a goal of preventing 7 million new HIV/AIDS infections, treating at least 2 million people with life-extending drugs, and providing humane care for 10 million more people suffering from the disease and for children orphaned by AIDS. Bush asked Congress to commit $15 billion over a five-year period, including $10 billion in additional funds. The key to success was getting local leaders to develop strategies to meet specific goals, at which point the United States would support them. The President's Emergency Plan for AIDS Relief (PEPFAR) would focus on the poorest and the sickest—twelve countries in sub-Saharan Africa and two in the Caribbean. As Bush told Congress that night, "Seldom has history offered a greater opportunity to do so much for so many."

In a rare display of bipartisan support for an assistance project—and a massive one at that—PEPFAR was enacted into law in near-record time, and with broad congressional support. It passed the Senate by a voice vote, the House approved it by a vote of 375–41, and it was signed into law on May 27, 2003. The quick passage of PEPFAR was a reminder that a bold, well-conceived nonmilitary exercise of national power was possible. It was a rare—and historic—achievement. Bush visited several African countries that summer, including a TASO clinic in Uganda. Not surprisingly, he received a very warm welcome wherever he went.

Key to PEPFAR's success was Bush's recognition that he had to change the usual way assistance programs were run in Washington. He had no intention of placing PEPFAR in the hands of multiple agencies stepping all over each other and lacking a single strategy, as had been the case with previous anti–HIV/AIDS programs. He created the position of global AIDS coordinator, reporting directly to the secretary of state, with the authority to coordinate U.S. international

HIV/AIDS programs in all agencies and departments and with over-sight of all resources of the program. As we will see, Bush was willing to break even more bureaucratic crockery to make other assistance programs more effective.

While the United States continued to contribute to the Global Fund, the president announced in June 2005 a five-year $1.2 billion program to fund malaria eradication in fifteen countries. Malaria accounted for more than a million deaths each year in Africa, most of the victims under the age of five. The President's Malaria Initiative (PMI), like PEPFAR, was designed to empower Africans to develop strategies appropriate to their needs. In the first two years, the pro-gram reached 11 million Africans. In 2007, at a G8 meeting in Ger-many, Bush persuaded the other leaders to match the U.S. pledges on HIV/AIDS and malaria.

PEPFAR originally was approved for five years and so was up for congressional renewal in 2008. On May 30, 2007, Bush asked Con-gress to renew the program and to commit an additional $30 billion over the following five years. His request was approved, and he signed legislation renewing PEPFAR on July 30, 2008.

By the time Bush left office six months later, PEPFAR had sup-ported treatment for 2.1 million people and care for more than 10 million. More than 57 million had benefited from HIV/AIDS testing and counseling. PEPFAR had partnered with more than 2,200 local organizations, distributed nearly 2 billion condoms, and supported prevention of mother-to-child transmission during more than 10 mil-lion pregnancies. The PMI had helped protect 25 million from that disease.

Bush also continued to support the two major Clinton administra-tion initiatives to help Africans. He worked with the G8 to cancel an additional $34 billion in debt incurred by poor countries. Bush also worked with Congress to expand the Africa Growth and Opportu-nity Act, signed by Clinton, which eliminated tariffs on most African exports to the United States.

PEPFAR was reauthorized again in 2013 under President Obama, and its funding continued under President Trump, although, over time, its priorities and approach would change. From 2003 to 2008,

PEPFAR was focused on an emergency response to the epidemic, reversing the climbing death rates and dramatically expanding access to HIV/AIDS prevention, treatment, and care. Under President Obama, PEPFAR continued to expand access to prevention and treatment but focused also on each country's government committing to support and sustain the effort to ensure that the health delivery systems to support previous gains would endure in the long term. During this period, new scientific breakthroughs—including the importance of voluntary medical male circumcision and more effective and less costly treatment regimens—were translated into program implementation.

At the same time, there were changes in emphasis in PEPFAR under President Obama, such as downplaying abstinence, the effectiveness of which the administration argued was not scientifically based. The role of faith-based groups was not a focal point, as had been the case under Bush, even though they remained critical to the success of the program. In the later Obama years, PEPFAR concentrated on controlling the HIV/AIDS epidemic as a public health threat and improving accountability and cost-effectiveness. This included embracing the DREAMS (Determined, Resilient, Empowered, AIDS-free, Mentored, Safe) program, an effort to reach adolescent girls and young women ages fifteen to twenty-four and address the factors increasing their HIV risk—poverty, gender inequality, sexual violence, and lack of access to education.

An important contribution of PEPFAR was the development of in-country laboratories in virtually all partner countries to accurately "detect, confirm, treat and monitor" disease in developing countries. The program enabled preventive screening for tuberculosis, with 42 percent of new PEPFAR enrollees in 2016 receiving preventive therapy. When there was an outbreak of Ebola in West Africa in 2014, PEPFAR-recipient countries, including Nigeria, Uganda, and Congo, were able to contain the crisis because their PEPFAR-funded labs quickly identified the disease and trained and provided health-care workers with the capacity to intervene. Liberia, Sierra Leone, Guinea, and other countries that had not been part of PEPFAR because of their low rates of HIV/AIDS infection lacked the labs and health systems necessary to detect the Ebola outbreak and thus initially were unable to contain it.

Although the Trump administration wanted to cut PEPFAR funding substantially in 2017, bipartisan support in Congress for the program prevailed. Thus, since 2008 funding has been sustained each year between $6.6 billion and $6.8 billion.

From 2003 forward, during a decade and a half when attitudes toward the United States soured worldwide, PEPFAR made America more popular than ever in Africa. Indeed, a 2007 Pew Global Attitudes Project report found that of the eleven countries with the most positive views of the United States, nine were in sub-Saharan Africa and six of those were PEPFAR countries. Between 2007 and 2011, PEPFAR countries had an average approval rating for the United States of 68 percent compared to a world average of 46 percent.

A study by the Bipartisan Policy Center published in November 2015 summarized the lessons learned from the success of PEPFAR: Bipartisan support and generous funding were crucially important. PEPFAR had a specific mission and benchmarks available to those responsible for oversight and monitoring progress. The need for the program was obvious. The program was tailored to each recipient country and, through data-driven processes, adapted at the local level to local conditions. The government of each country had to take responsibility (and this, in turn, had the unexpected benefit of strengthening the role of U.S. embassies and ambassadors). Sustaining PEPFAR over such a prolonged period was critical to its success and allowed countries to build stronger institutions and capacity. Finally, strong accountability and transparency won support for the program.

PEPFAR also succeeded because Bush consolidated authority and budget for the program under one entity, the AIDS coordinator; therefore, different bureaucracies within the government would not be allowed to compete for dollars or authority, nor to step all over each other.

American taxpayers and aid recipients both deserve better results. PEPFAR provides a road map for achieving them and should be the template against which all development assistance programs are measured.

Consistent with the president's deep belief that violence and poverty are the breeding ground for extremism, the Bush administration (like Clinton's before him) was aggressively engaged in trying to resolve Africa's many conflicts through the exercise of diplomatic power. Sudan continued to be riven by conflict, and Secretary of State Colin Powell and Special Envoy John Danforth helped negotiate a provisional cease-fire in January 2002. Assisted by professionals from the NSC staff and the State Department, they were successful in working out the Comprehensive Peace Agreement for Sudan addressing power-sharing and territorial arrangements. The agreement was signed on January 9, 2005. The administration also actively worked to reduce the violence in Darfur, which broke out in 2003, and played a major role in brokering the Darfur Peace Agreement in May 2006. They also were instrumental in getting an agreement to send a joint African Union–United Nations peacekeeping force of 26,000 troops to Darfur. As with the Clinton administration's efforts, a permanent end to the violence was elusive, but there is no doubt the U.S. role in Sudan under Bush significantly ameliorated the situation and saved many lives.

Our experience in Liberia was an example of the successful integration of diplomatic and military power. Charles Taylor led a rebel group there and in 1989 overthrew the government of Samuel Doe, igniting a years-long civil war. In a peace deal, Taylor became president in 1997. He governed ruthlessly at home and became involved in a civil war next door in Sierra Leone. He was later accused of war crimes and crimes against humanity. Internal opposition to him led to yet another civil war beginning in 1999. International pressure on him to resign increased, but it was President Bush who clinched his ouster in 2003 by sending a naval amphibious force with 2,300 Marines offshore of the country's capital, Monrovia. Taylor resigned on August 11. As important as his removal, though, was the election of Ellen Johnson Sirleaf as the new president, taking office on January 16, 2006. She was an extraordinary leader who brought peace and democracy, if not prosperity, to Liberia.

Other major U.S. diplomatic interventions during the Bush presidency involving him personally included interceding with Nigerian president Olusegun Obasanjo not to change the constitution and run for a third term, and working with South African president Thabo Mbeki to moderate the Congo war. Secretary Rice also made a special trip to Kenya in 2008 to help Kofi Annan broker a power-sharing arrangement after a disputed presidential election had led to violence.

More than a few Americans question the benefit to the United States of humanitarian assistance, such as PEPFAR, and diplomatic interventions to quell conflict in Africa. The idealist would argue that, for fellow human beings, these are the right and moral things to do. The realist would say that such actions help attack pandemics and extremism at the point of origin and keep both from our shores, foster relationships that open markets and opportunities for investment, and create potential allies for those times when U.S. interests require mobilizing international support. Friends and allies are an asset in a dangerous and unpredictable world. That asset is in itself an instrument of power, and most likely to be acquired and sustained through nonmilitary instruments of national power.

From the outset of his presidency, as noted earlier, Bush believed that traditional foreign assistance programs were wasteful, ineffective, and administered paternalistically by diverse bureaucracies in Washington. He announced a new approach on March 14, 2002, in remarks on global development at the Inter-American Development Bank in Washington, and then further elaborated on his plans eight days later at a development summit in Monterrey, Mexico. In the two speeches, Bush announced his support for the Millennium Declaration, signed at the UN-sponsored Millennium Summit in 2000, which called not only for greater assistance to developing countries but also for setting concrete targets and tailoring programs to each country's needs. He said a new level of accountability was necessary and that "greater contributions from developed nations must be linked to greater responsibility from developing nations."

Bush called for an increase in U.S. development assistance by

$5 billion over the following three budget years. The funds would go into the new Millennium Challenge Account (MCA), which would "reward nations that root out corruption, respect human rights, and adhere to the rule of law." Nations that invested in better health care, better schools, and broader immunization would also be rewarded. Nations with "more open markets and sustainable budget policies, nations where people can start and operate a small business without running the gauntlets of bureaucracy and bribery" would receive help. In short, countries that were "ruling justly, investing in their people, and encouraging economic freedom" would get more from America.

The new approach was embedded in Bush's National Security Strategy, issued on September 20, 2002. The strategy was as succinct a statement of the need to integrate all the elements of national power and a nonmilitary approach to the exercise of power as had been articulated since the end of the Cold War. It "committed the United States to make use of every tool in our arsenal—not exclusively military force—in countering the threat that terrorists and rogue regimes pose to our nation and our ideals . . . working with our allies to share intelligence and disrupt terrorist finances . . . opening societies to free commerce and access to markets . . . linking development assistance with good-governance reforms and shifts toward democratic governance." The United States would "reward countries that have demonstrated real policy change and challenge those that have not."

As noted earlier, the overall foreign assistance budget nearly doubled under Bush between 2001 and 2009. One ancillary benefit of those increases was that it reduced resistance within the traditional bureaucracy and within Congress to the MCA. The new initiative would not take money away from existing programs, which independently would see their budgets grow.

Getting congressional approval for the MCA proved much tougher than for PEPFAR. Proposed in 2002, the MCA was not approved until 2004. To the chagrin of some USAID old hands and others, the MCA was implemented and funded as an independent U.S. agency, the Millennium Challenge Corporation (MCC). It would not be part of the State Department or USAID. According to Rice, Bush did not believe the new organization could truly be held accountable for results and its funding protected from other needs if it were subordinated to the traditional bureaucracy. As with PEPFAR, Bush recognized that the existing structures for foreign assistance were deficient, and he was willing to create new ones.

The administration put in place a rigorous process for selecting recipients of MCA grants. Those countries selected to participate had to identify their priorities for achieving sustainable economic growth and poverty reduction, and their programs were required to be developed in broad consultation with civil society and the private sector. Rigorous and transparent monitoring of funds was required. The grants, called "compacts," were for five years.

As of 2018, the MCC board had approved thirty-three compacts in twenty-seven countries worth more than $11.7 billion. Projects have been weighted toward improving infrastructure such as roads, agriculture, energy (mainly electric power), health and education, water supply, governance, and financial services. Between 2004 and 2017, MCC claims to have trained 330,814 farmers, built 772 educational facilities, completed 2,500 miles of roads, and constructed 2,683 miles of electricity lines worldwide.

The Obama administration continued to support MCC and especially its emphasis on sustainable economic growth, good governance, the recipient's acceptance of responsibility, transparency, targeted U.S. operations, and rigorous standards for monitoring and evaluating results. As Secretary Clinton wrote in the 2010 MCC annual report, "MCC's experience is invaluable in shaping the future of U.S. development assistance." At the same time, the Obama administration expanded MCC's activities into new sectors and worked to strengthen its operations, transparency, monitoring, and evaluation.

While President Trump tried to cut the MCC budget in 2017 and 2018—Congress restored the funding to earlier levels—the administration continued to support the organization's mission. On April 23, 2018, Trump signed the Africa Growth and Opportunity Act and MCC Modernization Act, after it passed Congress with bipartisan support. The act continued the Clinton-initiated tariff breaks for African imports and authorized MCC for the first time to support regional compacts. This permitted the funding of projects involving two or

more countries sharing borders, especially important for infrastructure improvements related to roads, electric power, and water. As with
PEPFAR, bipartisan support in Congress was crucial for MCC.

Despite its flaws and occasional failures, and the fact that it never
accounted for more than 5 percent of the U.S. development assistance
budget, MCC has been assessed by outside experts as a success and a
model for providing U.S. aid. Indeed, some conservative members of
Congress wanted MCC to replace USAID altogether. A 2008 report
by the Brookings Institution described MCC as "one of the outstand-
ing innovations" of the Bush presidency and noted that "no other aid
agency—foreign or domestic—can match its purposeful mandate, its
operational flexibility and its potential muscle." After making a number of recommendations for improving MCC, the authors concluded
that "MCC has the potential to become the world's leading 'venture
capitalist' focused on promoting growth in low-income countries."

On several occasions when I was serving as secretary of defense in
the Obama administration, senior officials expressed to me their
envy because they had been unable to develop any initiative in the
realm of foreign assistance that could compare with the imagination,
boldness, and success of PEPFAR and MCC. In light of the perennial
unpopularity of development assistance in Congress, broad and sustained bipartisan support for these two nonmilitary initiatives through
three presidencies has been incredibly rare, if not unprecedented.

The reasons are clear. The humanitarian catastrophe and threat to
stability in Africa from the HIV/AIDS epidemic was broadly understood as a real crisis. Bush's proposal to deal with it, PEPFAR, was
both bold and practical, and with progress, its focus evolved from
emergency action to prevention. Its success was evident, which was
vital. MCC's requirement that applicants meet stringent criteria focused on governance and investment in the health and education of
ordinary people; stress on local buy-in; requirement that projects demonstrate a clear contribution to economic development; and, especially
important, emphasis on data-driven decision making, accountability,

and transparency had great appeal to otherwise skeptical members of Congress.

PEPFAR and MCC were both creative and remarkable examples of policy initiatives that improved the lives of tens of millions in Africa, won America friends and admirers among ordinary people as well as elites and governments, and were responsive to Bush's basic belief that countries with better governance, healthier people, and growing economies were likely to be more stable and more inhospitable to extremism.

Development assistance is an important instrument of American power. Properly structured and effectively administered, it protects and advances our own interests even as it helps others. High-mindedness, though, is no substitute for a rigorous business and operational model. The latter is what the Congress found in MCC. There were serious efforts during the Obama administration to reform USAID with MCC as the model. But established bureaucracies are notoriously difficult to change, which is why Bush created an independent agency.

The Trump administration shared Bush's early criticisms of previous foreign assistance programs. Its new Africa strategy, announced by National Security Adviser John Bolton in December 2018, was in many respects built on the principles of MCC (though Bolton's statement mentioned neither MCC nor PEPFAR). Motivated significantly by Russian and especially Chinese economic and political inroads in Africa, the administration's Prosper Africa initiative was meant to support U.S. private sector investment across Africa, grow the middle class, and improve the overall business climate. According to Bolton, "We will encourage African leaders to choose high-quality, transparent, inclusive, and sustainable foreign investment projects, including those from the United States. We will leverage our expanded and modernized development tools to support access to financing and provide strong alternatives to external state-directed initiatives." He added that the focus would be on African governments that act as strategic partners and are striving toward improved governance and transparent business practices—and that recipients of assistance must invest in "health and education, encourage accountable and transparent gover-

nance, and support fiscal transparency, and promote the rule of law."
In other words, pretty much the underlying criteria for MCC.

For a long time now, the United States has not been getting the
return it should on the $20 billion or so it spends each year on
development assistance. Relationships and projects need to be structured, administered, and evaluated using the MCC model. And there
clearly is need for bureaucratic reform and restructuring in Washington. PEPFAR is a powerful example of the president's empowering
a single organization and individual to coordinate and allocate funding to multiple departments and agencies engaged in addressing the
same problem. Without such empowerment of a single entity, agencies step on each other, compete for funds, pursue different priorities,
and generally waste money and time.

If the United States is to capitalize on the potential of nonmilitary
instruments of power and reap the potential advantages to our own
interests of helping others, a good start would be to apply the lessons
PEPFAR and MCC can teach us. That includes a willingness to take
credit for and publicize our efforts. The satisfaction of quietly doing
good works may be sufficient for religious orders; it is not for governments engaged in the exercise of power.

CHAPTER 9

Russia

Opportunity Missed?

W hat the hell was that all about?" the German chancellor asked me. It was February 12, 2007, and Angela Merkel and I were meeting immediately after Russian president Vladimir Putin had delivered an hour-long diatribe against the United States at the Munich Security Conference. I was the new U.S. secretary of defense, seated in the front row, across the aisle from Merkel, as Putin lambasted the United States for its "almost uncontained hyper use of force—military force—in international relations," "disdain for the basic principles of international law," and its participation in "military operations that are difficult to consider legitimate." He accused us of seeking a unipolar world in which "there is one master, one sovereign" and "one center of authority, one center of force, one center of decision making." He went through a long litany of complaints against the United States and the West, including the expansion of NATO, plans to deploy missile defenses in Eastern Europe, decisions by NATO and the EU to use military force against other countries without UN approval, and the deployment of frontline NATO troops to Russia's borders. The audience—including Senators John McCain, Lindsey Graham, and Joe Lieberman, seated immediately to my left—was stunned by the vehemence of Putin's jeremiad.

During his remarks, Putin had mostly stared directly (and darkly) at McCain and me, but when he concluded, he stepped off the stage, walked directly to me, smiled, extended his hand, and invited me to visit Russia.

Most of the attendees afterward buzzed about what had provoked Putin to vent his anger before a mainly European audience well disposed toward cooperation with Russia. The general view was that it had been a one-off tirade, especially in light of his seemingly friendly approach to me immediately after. Neither I, nor most in the audience, understood that Putin had driven a stake into the ground in Munich, in essence declaring his belief that the United States and the West more broadly would never treat Russia as an equal and that Russian efforts to partner with the West had not been reciprocated. Henceforth, Russia would assert its rightful role in the world on its own terms. The harangue had been a harbinger.

To understand Putin and how he arrived at that moment in Munich and whether a different American approach to Russia after the Cold War might have led to a different outcome, it is necessary to rewind the clock to when crisis preceded the collapse of the Soviet Union. The far-reaching reforms of Mikhail Gorbachev during the late 1980s dramatically weakened the economic structures that had met minimal individual and industrial needs. This, together with other disruptions, virtually guaranteed that the long Soviet economic slide would become a catastrophic avalanche. By the end of 1989, economic problems had reached crisis proportions, with severe consumer shortages, inflation, and violence. Widespread breakdowns in transportation and distribution systems interfered with the delivery of all kinds of goods from producers to consumers. The number of reported workers' strikes grew from a couple of dozen involving a few thousand workers in 1987–88 to more than five hundred strikes involving hundreds of thousands of workers during the first half of 1989. One of the key demands by Siberian coal miners on strike was for soap; just imagine, the Soviet superpower was unable to deliver soap to miners. Changes in the political system and the abandonment of coercive measures traditionally used to direct the economy produced an economic freefall nationwide.

Still, it was the multinational political structure that collapsed first. Gorbachev never understood that the non-Russian nationalities of the Soviet Union had long considered themselves "captive nations" and that the USSR was held together only by terror and force. Once his reforms removed the terror and he demonstrated he had no stomach for the level of violence required to suppress nationalistic feelings (despite short-lived military actions to suppress demonstrators in Lithuania and Azerbaijan), disintegration of the "Union" was inevitable. On March 11, 1990, Lithuania declared its independence. In the days following the failed coup attempt against Gorbachev on August 19, 1991, Russia, Uzbekistan, Ukraine, Moldova, and Belarus declared their independence. On October 8, eight republics agreed to establish an economic union, and in November, Russian president Boris Yeltsin began to assume authority from the Soviet Union over economic, financial, and political matters. On December 8, Yeltsin called President Bush to advise him of the creation of the Commonwealth of Independent States and that he and the presidents of Ukraine and Belarus had decided to dissolve the Soviet Union. On the 13th, Yeltsin called Bush again, informing him that the parliaments of the three countries had ratified the commonwealth arrangement, five central Asian republics had decided to join, and, as of the end of December, "the structures of the center will cease to exist." Gorbachev resigned as president on Christmas Day and on December 31 the Soviet Union ceased to exist.

At the time, and for years afterward, there was much criticism of the American government for failing to foresee the coming collapse and then failing to provide enough economic assistance and political outreach to help the Soviet Union and then Russia in the late 1980s and early 1990s.

Contrary to what became conventional wisdom, the CIA saw the collapse coming. I was present in an Oval Office meeting just before President Reagan's first meeting with Gorbachev in the fall of 1985 when CIA analysts told the president that the Soviet system could not survive. By the beginning of 1989, the agency's reporting on conditions inside the Soviet Union had become so dire that, in my role as deputy national security adviser, I asked for and received Bush 41's approval to establish a top-secret working group to begin contingency planning for the collapse of the country. The work began in early summer, nearly two and a half years before the actual collapse, led by NSC senior staff member Condoleezza Rice. In the months preceding the collapse, the CIA told Bush 41 that the centrally planned economy had broken down irretrievably and was in a downward spiral with no end in sight amid growing chaos.

I became director of central intelligence in early November 1991, just six weeks before the end of the USSR. At my request, U.S. intelligence agencies that fall prepared a number of assessments addressing key questions on senior U.S. officials' minds: What would happen to the 40,000 nuclear warheads the Soviets possessed? Might impoverished scientists and/or military officers try to sell nuclear weapons, material, or technology? Would the Soviet military splinter and spark a civil war? How likely was a famine? Would there be conflict among the republics or widespread disorder? One important result of Rice's working group and these estimates was Bush's decision to do all the United States and the West could to preserve a strong central government in Russia.

Just as there was no precedent for a huge empire collapsing without a major war, there was no precedent—and no handbook—for how other countries might provide effective outside help to mitigate the internal consequences of systemic failure of a vast empire. The challenge was comparable to trying to stop an avalanche with a snow shovel. The United States did try to help, and it is worth spending a little time looking at how we used nonmilitary instruments of power with Russia in the years just before and after the Soviet collapse. There we find the reasons why even more assistance would have been useless, and the roots of Vladimir Putin's bitterness.

During Gorbachev's visit to the United States at the end of May 1990, he asked Bush 41 for a trade agreement, including Most-Favored-Nation (MFN) status, with its benefits regarding tariffs. As a gesture of support for Gorbachev, Bush agreed to a public signing ceremony of such an agreement at the summit but privately told Gorbachev he would not submit the agreement to Congress for approval until the USSR had fulfilled all the requirements for MFN status and, further, until Gorbachev lifted his energy embargo on Lithuania (imposed after its declaration of independence that spring) and began negotiations with the Lithuanians. The agreement gave Gorbachev a political win but no near-term economic help.

A year later, Gorbachev again asked Bush for economic assistance, this time $1.5 billion in credits to buy grain. However, Soviet behavior in the Baltic states and obstinacy in arms control negotiations created political obstacles in the United States to granting such aid. Moreover, Bush himself was "pessimistic about the Soviet economy and the commitment to the reforms needed to foster a market economy. I had seen no evidence that even basic economic changes were being implemented."

The final discussion of Western economic help for the Soviet Union occurred in connection with the G7 meeting in London in July 1991. Gorbachev wanted to attend in person not only to ask for help but also to make the case for Soviet membership in the International Monetary Fund and the World Bank, a means to access financial assistance. Bush had the same negative reaction to these requests for membership (and aid) as on earlier occasions because of the lack of evidence of economic reform or willingness to cut military spending. As Scowcroft wrote, "In our own view, if we put no conditions on aid, we would all waste resources and do nothing to encourage the Soviets to transition to a market economy." Although Gorbachev was invited to London for meetings outside the G7 context, he didn't get much help. By the time Bush arrived in Moscow following the London meeting, Gorbachev had apparently reconciled himself to the reality that there would be no "windfall" of Western money to help bail out the Soviet economy.

In retrospect, the skepticism of Western leaders toward Gorbachev's requests seems fully justified. The Soviet Union by mid-1991 was splintering, there was no real commitment to economic reform, the banks were failing, and the country had no credit. No one knew how the prospectively independent republics would interact economically with each other or with foreign countries, and Gorbachev, having destroyed the Stalinist bureaucratic structures that minimally sustained the socialist economy, had no idea how (and perhaps no desire) to move to a market economy. As Bush later observed, "We had to see what relationships survived between the republics and the center before we offered any major financial support." The notion that Western legislatures would vote to throw untold billions of dollars at the Soviet economy under these conditions is preposterous.

Many in the West failed at the time—and still fail—to understand the magnitude of the social, political, and psychological effect inside Russia of the Soviet collapse, especially against a backdrop of economic disaster. Not only had the Soviet Union collapsed, so had the four-hundred-year-old Russian Empire. The borders of Russia on January 1, 1992, were essentially those that had existed in the eighteenth century before the reign of Empress Catherine the Great. Whereas Moscow once ruled more than 300 million people, it now had 140 million. In 1992, some 25 million ethnic Russians suddenly found themselves living in independent foreign countries, such as the Baltic states and Ukraine. Perhaps 90 percent or more of Soviet workers were employed by the state; when the state collapsed, they found themselves essentially jobless. Many continued to show up at their factories or other workplaces, but there was little or no pay and little to do. Older people, especially those on state-paid pensions, were especially hard hit. As the economy continued to implode in the early 1990s, the elderly and even soldiers could be seen on the streets selling what few possessions they had in order to survive. Profound humiliation in Russia was both national and personal.

Russian advocates of dramatic economic reform before and after the Soviet collapse understood the need to transition quickly from the Soviet "command" economy to a market economy. This involved lifting price controls (especially on consumer goods), legalizing private economic activity, eliminating subsidies to state-owned enterprises, and financial reforms—just for starters. But in the early 1990s, the Russian government was divided and the Duma (parliament) was generally opposed to most economic reforms. As private economic activity began to grow, the lack of legal protections and the levying of heavy taxes led to businesses concealing income, widespread corruption, and the rapid spread of criminal activity. With price controls removed, the cost of consumer goods skyrocketed, and this, added to growing budget deficits as subsidies to state-owned enterprises continued and tax receipts plummeted, contributed to massive inflation and budget deficits.

Although there was much talk about a "grand bargain" in which the United States and the West would provide significant sums of money to Russia in exchange for evidence of far-reaching economic reforms, realistically such a deal was never in the cards. In Russia, the political struggle over reforms offered little confidence that Western funds would be used effectively. Even those Western political leaders who wanted to help found little support in their legislatures or among international financial institutions. At a G7 meeting in the spring of 1992, the leaders agreed to provide $24 billion to Russia to support democracy and economic reform, but the financial institutions refused to release the money until Russia restructured its economy. Ultimately, though, the International Monetary Fund would disburse $22.1 billion to Russia between 1992 and 1999.

Both Presidents Bush (41) and Clinton wanted to help Yeltsin and Russia: Yeltsin because of his strong support for reform and democracy, and Russia because instability in a nuclear superpower is dangerous. They also sincerely desired to help Russia become a prosperous and freedom-loving country. On April 3–4, 1993, Clinton and Yeltsin met in Vancouver, British Columbia, where Clinton promised $1.6 billion in direct American assistance. The money was to help stabilize the economy by providing housing for decommissioned military officers; work programs for underemployed and often unpaid nuclear scientists; more assistance in dismantling nuclear weapons; food and medicine; aid to support small business, independent media outlets, NGOs, political parties, and labor unions; and an exchange program to bring tens of thousands of students and young professionals to the United States. The two leaders also agreed to establish a bilateral commission, cochaired by Vice President Al Gore and Prime Minister Viktor Chernomyrdin, to work through problems in the relationship. Upon returning to Washington, Clinton upped the aid package to $2.5 billion for all the former Soviet states, with two-thirds going to Russia. It was an important gesture of support for Yeltsin and the reform process, but the amount was a drop in the bucket compared to Russia's need.

Another form of well-intentioned help, originally proposed by Bush 41, was to provide technical expertise to assess disparate elements of the Russian economy and then provide recommendations for reform. It had negative consequences. Countless Western government experts and private consultants descended on Moscow in the early 1990s—a significant number disparaging what they found, and condescending in their approach. Many of their recommendations were technically appropriate but often oblivious to the political obstacles to implementation, particularly as Yeltsin and the parliament warred over the path forward. (The warring became quite literal in October 1993, when, at Yeltsin's order, the military shelled the parliament building and arrested the leaders.) The result was widespread resentment toward the Western experts.

Extreme nationalists and communists in the Duma openly claimed the West was trying to wreck Russia and consign it to permanent weakness. As former U.S. ambassador to the Soviet Union Jack Matlock wrote of the Russian critics, "Their argument was that the current economic and political disorder in what had been the Soviet Union had been caused by a Western plot to buy or hoodwink Russian leaders to break up the Soviet Union and then keep a remnant Russia weak. Their prescription was to reject the link with the West." The perception that the West was up to no good in Russia was no doubt reinforced by forty-five years of propaganda demonizing the United States and Western Europe. Yeltsin told Clinton in Vancouver that "he had to walk a fine line between receiving U.S. assistance to help Russia's transition to democracy and looking as if he was under America's thumb."

As we have seen elsewhere, economic assistance can be an important instrument of national power. U.S. efforts to use it in Russia were largely ineffective because of the magnitude of the economic transition being attempted and the limited resources Western governments were willing (and able) to allocate in light of Russia's internal chaos. Some critics argued, in retrospect, that we should have thought in bigger terms, such as a Marshall Plan for Russia, or pressed harder for shock therapy. They neglected to take into account a long history in Western Europe (and in Central and Eastern Europe as well) of market economies, private and public institutions, and laws that allowed the Marshall Plan to work and that decades later contributed to some success in places like Poland. Moreover, the critics often forgot that a key component of the Marshall Plan was that recipient countries were required to develop their own plans for economic recovery to qualify for the aid, and those plans had to be grounded in greater interstate economic cooperation, deregulation, and adoption of modern business practices. In Russia, by contrast, the state had played the central role in the economy not only under communism but for hundreds of years under the tsars, so it is not surprising that the process of transitioning to a market economy went awry. Sadly, for many Russians, the economic privation, corruption, powerful criminal organizations, assassinations, disorder, and chaos that began in the last days of the Soviet Union and continued into the 1990s became synonymous with democracy and market economics.

Presidents Bush (41) and then Clinton tried to reassure the Russians that German reunification and the continued existence of NATO did not pose a threat to the USSR and subsequently Russia. This was key to Gorbachev's acquiescence to the reunification of Germany in NATO. In May 1990, Secretary of State Jim Baker met with Gorbachev in Moscow to present him with "nine assurances," steps the West was willing to take to alleviate Soviet security concerns. These included pledges that Germany would not develop weapons of mass destruction, NATO forces would be kept out of the territory of the old East Germany, and NATO would be adapted politically and militarily to a post–Cold War environment. Senior members of the Bush 41 administration invested a lot of time and energy in developing ideas and proposals for how to repurpose the alliance for a post–Cold War, post-Soviet world.

On December 20, 1991, just eleven days before the USSR went into history's dustbin, the first session of the North Atlantic Cooperation Council (NACC) was held in Brussels. Created at the initiative of Baker and German foreign minister Hans-Dietrich Genscher, the NACC included all the former members of the Warsaw Pact. This was followed by creation of the Russia-NATO Permanent Joint Council in 1997 and, in 2002, the establishment of the NATO-Russia

Council—each an effort to reinforce the notion that NATO was not a threat to Russia but instead sought ever-closer collaboration. While none of these councils allowed Russia a vote in NATO, they provided a very real opportunity for Moscow to influence NATO debates and decision making. The Russians never took the opportunity seriously.

There were other U.S. diplomatic efforts to demonstrate respect for Russia and establish close relations with its leaders. Clinton formed a close personal relationship with Yeltsin, openly supporting him in 1993 in his conflict with the parliament. He tried to show respect for Russia by establishing the Gore-Chernomyrdin commission, persuading the G7 in Tokyo to approve an aid package for Russia, getting agreement to include Russia in meetings of the G7 when political matters were discussed, and trying to take into account Yeltsin's (and Russia's) political sensitivities as the United States shaped post–Cold War security arrangements in Europe. These gestures meant little to most Russians. The steady drumbeat of triumphalism in the West—especially in America—over the "defeat" and collapse of the Soviet Union and "victory" in the Cold War was far more impactful.

Sandwiched between the positive Clinton-Yeltsin meeting in Vancouver in early April 1993 and the aid package for Russia approved at the G7 meeting in Tokyo in July was the approval of a new Clinton administration policy toward Central and Eastern Europe designed "to bolster democracy, reduce trade barriers, and reward nations undertaking economic reform." The policy included opening the door to NATO membership for the new democracies. The administration believed that an "open and deliberate" process of enlarging NATO would help reassure Russia that its expansion toward the east would be a "step toward Russia, not against it."

Moscow wasn't buying any of it. They questioned the need for NATO to exist in light of the dissolution of the Warsaw Pact and the end of the Cold War. They perceived NATO as still using the threat from Russia to justify its continued existence, despite Clinton's reassurances that there were other threats, such as terrorism, proliferation of weapons of mass destruction, and ethnic cleansing. Such claims were belied by open declarations from the governments of Central and

Eastern Europe that the main reason they wanted into NATO was for protection against Russia in the future.

The Russians claimed that NATO enlargement was a violation of Western promises during the negotiations on German reunification that the alliance would not expand to the east. But the facts are clear. In their joint memoir, Bush and Brent Scowcroft wrote that in a meeting with Soviet foreign minister Eduard Shevardnadze on February 7, 1990, Secretary of State Baker had affirmed that "if Germany stayed in NATO there would be no movement of NATO's jurisdiction or forces eastward." Three months later, NATO secretary general Manfred Wörner publicly reiterated that position. These assurances were limited to not deploying NATO forces on the territory of East Germany. Because the Warsaw Pact had not yet dissolved at that point, NATO deployments beyond Germany weren't even on the table. Those realities did not deter the Russians from later arguing that the United States had promised there would be no NATO deployments in Eastern Europe and therefore they had been double-crossed.

In mid-1993, the Clinton administration developed a proposal, first put forward by the chairman of the Joint Chiefs of Staff, General John Shalikashvili, to invite the emerging democracies of Europe and the former Soviet Union to join a new entity, the Partnership for Peace (PfP). The members would participate in military training with NATO members, and those that did the most to improve their militaries, improve relations with their neighbors, and strengthen their democracy would become eligible for membership in the alliance. Clinton hoped the process for enlargement wouldn't cause Yeltsin "too many problems." He later wrote, "I had to make sure NATO expansion didn't simply lead to a new division of Europe farther to the east." Albright observed, "We had to walk a tightrope to keep faith with Europe's new democracies while not recreating our old enemy. Our critics didn't think we would be able to keep our balance. I thought we could."

Clinton and Albright both proved wrong. Yeltsin repeatedly pushed back on Clinton during the 1990s. At a summit meeting in Budapest in December 1994, Yeltsin publicly criticized Clinton for trading in the Cold War for a "Cold Peace" by moving so quickly to enlarge NATO by extending membership to Central European nations. In February 1997, Russian foreign minister Yevgeny Primakov told Madeleine Albright that Russia could not agree to NATO enlargement and that Russia needed guarantees that there would be no nuclear weapons on the territory of new allies and no increase in military infrastructure. Albright made no such commitments. On March 21, at a summit in Helsinki, Yeltsin asked Clinton to agree that enlargement would be limited to former Warsaw Pact nations and not include states of the former Soviet Union such as the Baltics and Ukraine. Publicly, Yeltsin again declared: "We believe that the eastward expansion of NATO is a mistake and a serious one at that." In private, Clinton told Yeltsin that "if he would agree to NATO expansion and the NATO-Russia partnership, I would make a commitment not to station troops or missiles in the new member countries *prematurely* [emphasis added], and to support Russian membership in the new G-8, the World Trade Organization and other international organizations. We had a deal." At the NATO summit in Madrid in July 1997, the Czech Republic, Hungary, and Poland were invited to join the alliance.

Differences between the United States and Russia over NATO expansion took place against a backdrop of events inside Russia that only underscored the country's weakness. Regional governors increasingly ignored Moscow, and the "oligarchs," usually former Soviet officials who through various nefarious schemes after the collapse gained control of the largest financial, industrial, and oil and gas assets in Russia, amassed great fortunes and political power. In December 1994, open rebellion broke out in Chechnya, a republic within Russia that had been agitating for independence long before the collapse of the Soviet Union. The fighting was vicious, including large-scale destruction of the capital, Grozny. Despite overwhelming military superiority in numbers and firepower, the Russians were unable to subdue the Chechens and declared a cease-fire in 1996. The war in Chechnya was hugely unpopular in Russia, and Yeltsin was bitterly criticized for his handling of the conflict. By February 1995, his popularity in Russia stood at 9 percent.

The Communist Party was successful in the 1995 Duma elections and thus able to block many of Yeltsin's initiatives. As the presidential election got under way in early 1996, Yeltsin was far behind in the polls. Through his own political skill, strong support from the media (which feared a Communist victory and depended on the government for licenses), the support of key oligarchs who bankrolled his campaign and further assured media support, and supportive measures by Clinton (including soft-pedaling NATO expansion during the Russian election campaign and a personal endorsement), Yeltsin ultimately won a runoff election against the leader of the Communist Party. But he had mortgaged himself to the oligarchs.

On July 10, Yeltsin had a heart attack. On November 5, he had heart bypass surgery. Health issues would trouble him during the remainder of his time in office.

The economy continued its downward spiral, aggravated by the 1997–98 Asian financial crisis, which in turn drove down the price of oil, Russia's main source of income. All this culminated in a Russian financial crisis in August 1998, when Moscow devalued the ruble, defaulted on its domestic debt, and declared a moratorium on repayment of foreign debt. Contrary to the subsequent Russian narrative of unremitting Western hostility, the Clinton administration organized an international financial assistance effort to stabilize the Russian economy after the ruble crisis. Without this constructive U.S. use of its economic and financial power, the Russian economy may well have collapsed altogether. Even so, Russia's economic output had shrunk during the 1990s by more than half, and more than two-thirds of the population was living at subsistence level.

Nineteen ninety-nine was an especially bad year for Russia—and for Yeltsin. On March 12, Poland, Hungary, and the Czech Republic joined NATO. Twelve days later, over strong Russian objections and without UN sanction, NATO began bombing Serbia, an air campaign designed to force Serbia to withdraw its military forces from Kosovo. On August 9, Islamist fighters reignited the war in Chechnya.

"The Russians were frustrated by the weak hand they had to play," wrote Madeleine Albright, accurately. By the summer of 1999, Russia was helpless to stop the NATO bombing of Serbia, its longtime ally and client; the economy was staggering; the central government was weak, with the regional governments ignoring its edicts; tax collections were negligible; the oligarchs held sway both politically and economically; and the country's president was in ill health and exhausted. Moscow also proved incapable of stopping NATO's expansion eastward; the alliance added states that once had been members of the Warsaw Pact and seemed likely to add some that had actually been part of the Soviet Union.

On August 9, the same day conflict resumed in Chechnya, Yeltsin appointed Vladimir Putin as acting prime minister. Yeltsin resigned the presidency on December 31, appointing Putin acting president. Putin's first act was to issue a decree ensuring that neither Yeltsin nor his relatives could be prosecuted for corruption. Putin was elected president on March 26, 2000, his victory due in no small part to his ruthless prosecution of the war in Chechnya and to his response to a series of bombings in three Russian cities, including Moscow, between September 4 and 16, 1999, in which 293 were killed and more than a thousand injured. The government blamed Islamist terrorists for the bombings, although there was substantial evidence they had been carried out by the Russian security services to enhance Putin's reputation for decisive toughness and to advance his political prospects.

Could a different and more skillful application of U.S. instruments of power by the Clinton administration have laid the foundation for a better, more collaborative, and positive future relationship with Russia? Could the United States have wielded its power differently in the 1990s to help Russia deal with its economic distress and avoid its growing sense of isolation and weakness?

Addressing the what-might-have-beens in history is always risky, but I believe larger-scale financial assistance to Russia in the 1990s would have been money wasted given the absence of structural reforms and stable institutions, the irresponsibility of the central bank, runaway inflation, opposition in the Duma to economic reform, and the extraordinary level of corruption. In July 1998, the IMF made its first disbursement, $5 billion, of the $22 billion loan package to Russia, a third of which had been contributed by the United States. The money disappeared virtually overnight as the ruble was devalued and Russians began to move large sums of money out of the country. Russia's default came the next month. Seventy-five percent of Americans polled opposed any help to Russia at all.

What limited U.S. messaging there was to Russia, while appropriately emphasizing the need for economic reform and democratic institutions, too often implied that all things Russian had to change and the only path forward was for Russia to fully embrace Western political and economic practices. Western experts and NGOs, moreover, too often conveyed to Russians an aura of superiority, not to mention triumphalism and hubris in victory. "Shock therapy" sounded sensible to Western economists; to most Russians it meant not having enough to eat.

The steps actually taken by Clinton and his team—targeted economic and technical assistance, support for Yeltsin and reform, encouragement of political and press freedom, establishment of the Gore-Chernomyrdin commission, continued efforts on arms control, help to secure Russia's nuclear weapons and materials, and initiatives to include Russia in the G7 and build a link between NATO and Russia—were well intended and hard to fault. I believe the Clinton administration used the instruments of power available to them as effectively as possible to help Russia, but the magnitude of the challenge was far beyond our capacity to help. The United States did a great deal, especially during the 1998 Russian financial meltdown, but we did too little to let the Russian people know what we and others were doing to try to help them.

That said, two developments made a longer-term, close relationship between Russia and the United States hugely problematic. The first was that the chaos and impoverishment of the 1990s rekindled Russians' deep cultural desire for order and for strong leadership. That, in turn, created the opportunity for an authoritarian like Putin to fill that need—and go beyond it. His actions internally would evoke strong, increasingly hostile reactions in the West, which had hoped for the emergence of a democratic Russia. His moves to consolidate power, curtail the opposition, and shut down the free media that had sprung up ensured continuing contention with the West.

When Putin became president of Russia, his highest priority was to restore a strong central government (along with enriching himself and his cronies). An early piece of business was to subdue Chechnya. After four months of combat, the Russians seized Grozny in February 2000. Moscow assumed direct rule of Chechnya in late May. Putin declared victory and increasingly relied on pro-Russian Chechen forces to fight the separatists. Fighting dragged on for several years more, with anti-Russian Chechens inflicting continuing casualties on Russian troops and launching periodic terrorist attacks elsewhere in Russia. Persistent U.S. criticism of Russian brutality in the conflict annoyed Putin no end.

Early on, Putin turned his attention to the rich and powerful oligarchs. They had played a big role in Yeltsin's reelection in 1996, supported Putin's selection as acting president, and assumed he would be their man. They misjudged badly. On July 28, 2000, Putin met with eighteen of the most powerful oligarchs in Stalin's old house, the symbolism unmistakable. Putin told them, in so many words, that he knew the many illegal ways in which virtually all of them had amassed their wealth. The president informed them that they could keep their wealth only as long as they stayed out of politics and out of his way.

At the end of his first year in office, Putin had already shut down or taken control of two of the three major independent television networks in Russia. Initially, he focused on controlling the electronic media, knowing that was where most Russians got their news. Only later would he turn to other journalists and the print media.

Restoring Moscow's control of the regions was just as important as putting the oligarchs in their place. Early in his presidency, he sent representatives to the regions to observe and report on, among other things, whether the local authorities were ignoring central government directives and carrying out tax collections. In 2001, the Duma changed the law to allow for "federal intervention" if regional governments were found to be violating the Russian constitution or federal laws. The most dramatic change, though, came in 2004 in the wake of a terrorist attack by Chechen and other Islamist extremists on a school in the northern Caucasus town of Beslan, an attack in which 334 people were killed, 186 of them children. Putin used the attack as a pretext to vastly increase the powers of the central government and especially the president. Seven federal jurisdictional districts were created, run by "super governors" appointed by the president. Five of the seven new regional governors were from the old KGB or the military, reflecting the rise of former security services personnel to positions of power under Putin. Later, Putin would abolish the election of regional governors altogether, replacing them with Kremlin appointees. Tax reforms further increased the dependence of the regions on the center. As Rice subsequently observed, these moves during Putin's first term as president snuffed out whatever chance a nascent federalism might have had in Russia.

The second development ensuring a difficult relationship between the United States and Russia was the decision to enlarge NATO. The expansion of NATO despite strong Russian objections inevitably led to resentment and the belief in Russia that the West would never accept it as a full and equal partner—that NATO existed solely to keep Russia in its place. George Kennan, architect of the "containment" strategy against the Soviet Union, declared NATO expansion as "the most fateful error of American policy in the entire post–Cold War era." He was far from alone in his criticism. Both Bush 41 and Clinton senior officials believed NATO could be repurposed in ways that would convince Russia it no longer was considered an adversary, but despite the rhetoric and reassurances from Western governments that NATO enlargement should not be a problem for Russia, an episode in the summer of 1999 validated Moscow's concerns.

After the Serbs agreed to withdraw from Kosovo in June, the Russians quickly dispatched a contingent of peacekeepers to the airport at Pristina, the capital of Kosovo, where they were greeted with great relief by the Serbs. The Russian military had prepared air transports to carry thousands more Russian troops to reinforce the contingent at the airport. The flights were unable to take off because, as Madeleine Albright described, "the Russians were denied permission to cross the airspace of Hungary, Romania and Bulgaria. Each of these countries had been a charter member of the Warsaw Pact. Now one was a

NATO ally and the other two were leading candidates for admission." While the Russians had been stopped from carrying out an end run that would have immensely complicated the peacekeeping mission in Kosovo, the actions of their erstwhile "allies" and subject nations had to rankle greatly and demonstrate beyond question the negative consequences for them of NATO enlargement.

As Putin was consolidating his and the government's power in Moscow, Clinton and then George W. Bush worked to establish a positive relationship with him. Secretary Albright was the first senior American official to meet with Putin in his role as acting president, in January 2000. They discussed Russia's economic problems, and Putin said he was committed to working with the IMF, trying to attract foreign investors to Russia, and reforming the tax code. Putin defended his actions in Chechnya. He told Albright that "Russia has to be firmly part of the West." But, Albright observed, "beneath Putin's nationalism and pragmatism, democratic instincts were hard to detect."

Six months later, Clinton held his first and only meeting with Putin. A few weeks earlier, Putin had put weight behind his calls to reduce nuclear weapons by securing Duma ratification of the START II Treaty and the Comprehensive Test Ban Treaty. He and Clinton agreed on plans to dispose of excess plutonium and to create a joint military operation to provide early warning of space and missile launches. They also discussed further reductions in strategic arms. Clinton pursued with Putin his ideas on a limited national missile defense and the potential threat presented by both the North Korean and Iranian missile programs. Putin didn't disagree with the threat analysis, but he was unmoved on changing the Anti-Ballistic Missile (ABM) Treaty.

As George W. Bush took office, there was still a strong desire in both Moscow and Washington to work together wherever possible (despite the U.S. expulsion of fifty Russian spies in March 2001 and reciprocal action by Russia). Bush first met Putin on June 16, 2001, in Slovenia, just prior to a G8 meeting. High on Bush's agenda was a dramatic reduction in strategic offensive weapons and his intention to get out of the 1972 ABM Treaty. He told Putin he wanted to cut the number of U.S. nuclear warheads by two-thirds and hoped Russia would simply follow suit. He hoped they could reach a mutual agreement to revise the ABM Treaty (or agree mutually to end it) to allow for limited defenses against small-scale missile attacks such as those that might be launched by Iran or North Korea. Unlike his predecessor, Bush was prepared to unilaterally abrogate the treaty.

Putin agreed on the spot to match the reduction in nuclear weapons. He could not have been surprised by Bush's position on the ABM Treaty, partly because the president had openly discussed his intentions during the campaign and partly because Clinton already had tried to persuade Putin to revise the treaty to permit limited defenses. Bush actually gave Putin three choices on ABM: the United States and Russia could both withdraw and cooperate on missile defense (Bush's preference), the United States could withdraw unilaterally with Putin's acquiescence, or the United States could withdraw from the treaty and Putin could criticize the action if necessary politically. In the event, Putin mildly criticized the U.S. decision to withdraw while saying it did not represent a strategic threat to Russia. Interestingly, formal U.S. withdrawal from the ABM Treaty a few months later came just before the two countries signed a far-reaching agreement reducing nuclear arms on both sides. Clearly, the withdrawal had not derailed the new offensive weapons deal.

In the same meeting in Slovenia, Putin also warned Bush that the Pakistani military and intelligence services were supporting Saudi-funded extremists like the Taliban and al-Qaeda. He said "it was only a matter of time until it resulted in a major catastrophe." After the attacks on September 11, Putin never let Bush forget his warning.

At a press conference following the meeting, a reporter asked Bush if he trusted Putin. The president replied, "Yes. I looked the man in the eye. . . . I was able to get a sense of his soul." While some later would say that the answer made Bush look naive, saying no would not exactly have been diplomatic. In reality, the relationship between the two leaders had gotten off to a strong start, both men plainspoken and direct but eager to find areas of potential cooperation.

Without yielding on either missile defense or NATO enlargement, Bush developed a good working relationship with Putin. During his presidency, Bush visited Russia seven times and Putin came to the United States five times. Putin was the first head of state to call Bush after the 9/11 attacks and to offer assistance. The day of the attacks, Rumsfeld called the Russian defense minister, Sergei Ivanov, to express concern that Russian combat aircraft were holding an exercise near Alaska and asked that the Russians stand down to avoid potential problems. Ivanov agreed to halt the exercise and offered Russia's cooperation. On September 22, Bush had a long telephone conversation with Putin during which the Russian president agreed to open Russian airspace to American airplanes and said he would encourage the leaders of Uzbekistan and Tajikistan to help get American troops into Afghanistan. This Russian help paved the way for continuing cooperation against terrorism. To my astonishment, even after relations soured in the years to come, we were allowed to ship military equipment by rail across Russia to Afghanistan.

An important instrument of power is the willingness of the American president to engage in personal diplomacy and to foster diplomatic relations. In the course of his presidency, Bush met with Putin forty times, including inviting him to the president's ranch in Texas and to the Bush family home in Kennebunkport, Maine. On May 24, 2002, the two presidents signed the Moscow Treaty, slashing the number of strategic nuclear weapons held by each side from 6,600 to between 1,700 and 2,200 by 2012. Four days later, in Brussels, NATO leaders and Putin established the NATO-Russia Council, intended to pursue "opportunities for consultation, joint decisions and joint action on a wide range of issues," such as terrorism, nonproliferation, crisis management, arms control, theater missile defense, military-military cooperation, defense reform, and new threats. The council, as noted previously, was the latest and most expansive organizational initiative to improve cooperation between the alliance and Russia—without actually inviting the Russians into the tent. Bush continued his outreach to Putin during the next several years, and the two countries sustained cooperation against terrorism and the proliferation of nuclear weapons, with the Russians supporting UN

Security Council resolutions sanctioning both North Korea (2006) and Iran (2007) because of their nuclear programs.

Subsequent events led Putin to strengthen his authoritarian rule at home and to become far more concerned about developments on Russia's periphery, especially in the republics of the former Soviet Union. Significant increases in the price of oil during the early 2000s (from $26 per barrel in 2001 to $71 in 2007) led to strong economic growth in Russia and fueled Putin's growing assertiveness at home and abroad. The aforementioned 2004 terrorist attack at Beslan provided a pretext to restructure the government and vastly increase the power of the central government and Putin.

It was the "color" revolutions in Georgia, Ukraine, and Kyrgyzstan, however, that contributed most to setting Putin on a path of cracking down on any opposition inside Russia. He became more assertive toward states on the periphery, concluding that Western efforts to promote democracy on the periphery and in Russia, by both governmental and nongovernmental organizations, represented a threat not just to governments of the "near abroad" but to his own government in Russia.

The trouble began in November 2003 in Georgia, where a disputed election led to the overthrow of the government of Eduard Shevardnadze and to his replacement after new elections the following March by Mihkeil Saakashvili, who became virulently anti-Russian. This was called the Rose Revolution. Even more ominously from Putin's point of view, in November 2004 a disputed second round of elections in Ukraine led to the annulment of the outcome and a repeat election in December 2004, in which pro-Western politicians Viktor Yushchenko and Yulia Tymoshenko defeated the pro-Russian candidate Viktor Yanukovych—the Orange Revolution. Then, in Kyrgyzstan, widespread demonstrations across the country after disputed elections in February 2005—the Tulip Revolution—ultimately led to the resignation of President Askar Akayev, whom Putin offered exile in Russia.

In each country, as in Russia and many of the other former Soviet republics, Western governments and NGOs had worked to help develop civil society and encourage the development of democratic institutions. Promoting democracy and freedom around the world has been at the core of American foreign policy and strategic messaging since the first days of the republic. These endeavors have been a vital instrument of national power, and they continued after the collapse of the Soviet Union. Accordingly, after 1991, USAID and the State Department worked in the former Soviet Union to encourage the emergence of civil society and of politicians seeking to build more democratic governments—as well as to strengthen their relationships with the West. NGOs in the United States and in Europe complemented and greatly extended the reach of government programs to this end.

The pro-democracy color revolutions in 2003–5, however, alarmed Putin and led him to take a much harder stand against his critics in Russia, the free press that had blossomed during the 1990s, and the Western-sponsored NGOs in Russia. Putin openly claimed that Western governments had used the NGOs to interfere in the elections, especially in Ukraine, and that these efforts were led and coordinated by the CIA.

With a very modest budget, USAID openly supported Russia's oldest human rights organizations, civic watchdog groups that provided oversight over electoral processes, and civil society organizations, whose number exploded from forty in the early 1990s to hundreds of thousands fifteen years later. Other organizations active in Russia fully or partially funded by the U.S. government included the National Endowment for Democracy, the National Democratic Institute, and the International Republican Institute. Privately funded NGOs included Freedom House and George Soros's Open Society Institute.

In 2005, Putin began to establish state control over NGOs, especially those dependent upon foreign funding. He repeatedly stressed his opposition to foreign funding of the "political activities" of NGOs and the need for strict controls over financial flows to them. In January 2006, the Duma passed legislation requiring all foreign NGOs to notify the Justice Ministry of their office locations, provide detailed reporting on foreign funding and how such funds were being spent, and inform the government registration office about their projects for the next year and the money allotted for specific projects. NGOs had to submit to annual audits as well as provide on demand unlimited information documenting the organization's daily management.

The crackdown on NGOs paralleled actions intended to suppress criticism of the government (Putin) and undermine the independence of other government institutions. After effecting government control of or influence over television, Putin moved against the print media, with increasing harassment of journalists, threats, and, in October 2006, the murder of journalist Anna Politkovskaya. A number of other journalists would be killed or badly beaten. Critics abroad weren't beyond Putin's reach. A former Federal Security Service (FSB, successor to the KGB) officer living in Britain, Alexander Litvinenko, was poisoned with polonium-210 and died on November 23, 2006. He had accused the FSB of planting the apartment building bombs in Moscow and other cities in September 1999 in order to ensure Putin's election as president and subsequently accused the Russian president of ordering the killing of Politkovskaya. A British official inquiry concluded in 2016 that the FSB had murdered Litvinenko, probably on the direct order of Putin. The Russian president also suborned the judicial system by using it to bring charges against oligarchs he wanted to punish, the most notable case being the arrest, conviction, and imprisonment of Mikhail Khodorkovsky, the richest man in Russia.

Authoritarianism came naturally to Putin, who didn't have it in him to become a democratic politician. Suppression of his enemies and critics began early but accelerated after the color revolutions. By his third election as president in 2012, he had eliminated the autonomy of the regions, subordinated the judiciary, exerted control of the mass media, and shown he would eliminate any stubborn adversary—literally.

Growing repression in Russia contributed to a steady worsening of relations with Washington. When Bush raised concerns about the arrests of Russian businessmen and journalists with Putin at a meeting in Slovakia on February 24, 2005, Putin fired back, "Don't lecture me about the free press, not after you fired that reporter." Putin was referring to reporter Dan Rather, who had been fired by CBS News over false allegations about Bush's military service. He deflected all criticism of developments in Russia as meddling in its internal affairs and none of anyone else's business.

There was still considerably more freedom in Russia than there had been in the Soviet Union. As long as Russians stayed out of politics, they were free to travel abroad, go to church (as long as they were Russian Orthodox), create businesses, and, if they could afford it, access all manner of luxury goods, food, cars, and newspapers and magazines. Still, if one broke the Putin bargain—order and economic freedom in exchange for staying out of politics—a person was far less likely to end up in the gulag than to be shot to death on a snowy bridge outside the Kremlin (like opposition leader Boris Nemtsov).

Events on the periphery of Russia and elsewhere continued to worsen relations with the United States. Most important, at the NATO summit in Istanbul in June 2004, the alliance formally admitted Romania, Bulgaria, Slovenia, Slovakia, Latvia, Estonia, and Lithuania. Then I recommended to the president on December 19, 2006 (my second day as secretary of defense), that the United States locate ten long-range missile interceptors in Poland and an associated radar installation in the Czech Republic to counter the Iranian missile threat to Europe. The Russians saw the proposed deployments as putting their nuclear deterrent at risk and as a further step in the "encirclement" of their country. That issue would dominate every meeting I had with Putin and my Russian counterpart for the next four and a half years. Our side unequivocally said that the deployment would not have any effect on their deterrent capability and technically would be incapable of targeting their missiles. I think they understood that. Still, they feared the capabilities of future generations of missile defenses so close to their territory and saw the deployments as a further violation of their understanding that there would be no permanent U.S. or NATO military installations east of Germany. Bush approved my recommendation, and short of war, there was nothing the Russians could do to stop us.

Soon after I became secretary, I heard that the Russians were pursuing a tough anti-American policy in the former Soviet republics in Central Asia, urging those governments to minimize the U.S. presence and limit American activities. The Russians leaned particularly heavily on the government of Uzbekistan, which had provided us with use of its airfields when we first entered Afghanistan in 2001. In 2005, the Uzbeks said we could no longer use their air bases. We were able to arrange the use of the Kyrgyz air base at Manas, though the Russians were trying to cause trouble for us there as well. In mid-2006, Rumsfeld had written to National Security Adviser Steve Hadley that "we are getting run out of Central Asia by the Russians. They are doing a considerably better job at bullying those countries [than] the U.S. is doing to counter their bullying." This was a problem I thought we should confront with a strategic communications effort not only highlighting our own friendly intentions but also exposing the Russian propaganda campaign. There was not the stomach for it in Washington. An opportunity missed, I thought, and another failure to harness this important instrument of power.

Two thousand eight was, I think, an important turning point in the U.S.-Russian relationship. In February, after months of diplomatic efforts to satisfy the Russians, the United States and several dozen other countries recognized the independence of Kosovo over the strong objections of the Russians. The latter objected on numerous grounds but were especially unhappy over the precedent set by recognition of a breakaway part of a sovereign state—and without UN sanction. The possibility of parts of their own country, such as Chechnya, following Kosovo's path was never out of mind for them. They were outraged as well that, in their view, Russian interests and long historical ties to Serbia had been ignored, even if their Serbian client was a bloodthirsty thug.

More significantly, the issue of NATO membership for Ukraine and Georgia came to the fore in the months leading up to the NATO summit in Bucharest in April. Yeltsin had told Bush 41 that "Ukraine must not leave the Soviet Union," and Gorbachev warned the president that if Ukraine left the Soviet Union, Crimea had threatened to "review its status" as part of Ukraine. Now both Yushchenko in Ukraine and Saakashvili in Georgia were pleading to be granted a Membership Action Plan (MAP), a preliminary step on the path to full NATO membership. The Germans and French opposed this while the Central and Eastern Europeans were supportive. I thought trying to bring the two states into NATO was overreaching. The roots of the Russian Empire traced back to Kyiv in the ninth century, and so I thought NATO membership for Ukraine was a huge provocation. Further, were Europeans, much less Americans, willing to send their sons and daughters to defend Ukraine or Georgia? I thought not. Secretary Rice laid out the pros and cons for Bush, and he came down on the side of Ukraine and Georgia: "If these two democratic states want MAP, I can't say no." Even so, the summit concluded with a compromise that did not grant MAP status but declared the good prospects for the two countries' future membership. Putin made clear his views on Ukraine when, speaking at the summit, he called it a "made up" country and spoke ominously about the fate of the 25 million ethnic Russians "orphaned" in the newly independent republics and Russia's historic duty to protect them.

Bush flew from Bucharest to a meeting with Putin at Sochi, on the Black Sea. There the two signed a declaration that covered the multiple areas where the two countries had worked productively together. While the personal relationship between Bush and Putin remained positive, the Russian invasion of Georgia in August 2008 sent the relationship into a deep freeze. Putin had baited the hotheaded Saakashvili into making the first move militarily, to which the Russians responded with overwhelming force.

"Moscow believed that it still had special privileges on the territory of the former Soviet Union and Warsaw Pact," wrote Condi Rice. "We believed that the newly independent states had the right to choose their friends and their alliances. That had turned out to be an irreconcilable difference."

Should the Clinton and Bush administrations have made different decisions with regard to Russia? Certainly not in terms of trying to promote the growth of democracy and civic society. Our advocacy on behalf of those struggling for liberty, for a more just and free society, is, as I've said, as old as the republic and a source of our global influence and power. There is little question, however, that Putin believed these efforts played a big part in the color revolutions and were intended to bring regime change in Russia as well.

I believe admitting the Baltic states into NATO was consistent with our decades-long refusal to recognize their incorporation into the Soviet Union. However, as I've indicated, I think the U.S. effort to bring Ukraine and Georgia into the alliance was a step too far. Given their geography and history, both countries need good relations with Russia and the West. Supporting their admission had far-reaching negative consequences for the U.S. relationship with Russia and, ultimately, for Ukraine and Georgia. Supporting Ukraine's independence, however, is critically important for the United States and for the West strategically. Zbigniew Brzezinski once told me that Russia could not be an imperial power without possessing Ukraine; a government in Kyiv subservient to Moscow would enable and fuel Russian expansionist and hegemonistic tendencies, and thus would be a destabilizing influence. I believe Russia's revanchism stems mainly from nostalgia for its imperial past but also from the presence of those 25 million ethnic Russians now living in independent countries and separated from Mother Russia. Putin speaks about them all the time. The largest single percentage of them live in eastern Ukraine. NATO expansion did not create Russian revanchism but probably is the surest defense against it, especially in the Baltic states.

Given the fundamental impact of NATO enlargement on the future of Russia's relationship with the United States and the West, was there a failure of imagination in Washington in the early 1990s to devise an alternative, post–Cold War security structure in Europe that could simultaneously provide reassurance to the liberated states of Central and Eastern Europe and, at the same time, avoid isolating Russia and begin to integrate it into the West? Could there have been brought to bear the kind of diplomatic imagination and new thinking that led to the peaceful liberation of Eastern Europe and the reunification of Germany? Should more serious consideration have been given to offering MAP to Russia as encouragement for political and economic reform, and to signal a willingness to eventually include Russia in European security arrangements? The obstacles would have been great, perhaps insurmountable both conceptually and politically, but I think we should have tried.

As he was subject to a two-term limit for Russian presidents, Putin switched jobs with Prime Minister Dimitri Medvedev in 2008. Medvedev's four years as president (2008–2012) were something of a respite in the growing tension between Russia and the West. His public statements reflected a clear understanding of what was wrong with Russia and what needed to change. He recognized the need for foreign investment and that, to encourage it, Russia needed stronger rule of law and transparent governance. He lamented Russia's excessive economic dependence on extractive industries such as oil and mining, and spoke often of Russia's need to devote more resources to technology. He visited technology centers in the West, including Silicon Valley, and vowed to build a Russian equivalent. Medvedev also clearly believed Russia's future lay with the West.

U.S.-Russian cooperation was relatively productive during Medvedev's time as president. He conceded that the United States had been correct in assessing Iran's nuclear and missile intentions, and Russia did not block American efforts to get new sanctions on Tehran at the UN, though it did work to water them down. Medvedev also refused to deliver the sophisticated S-300 air defense system to Iran and eventually even broke the contract. Under Bush, there was also agreement to impose sanctions on North Korea in response to its nuclear weapons programs. There was good cooperation on counterterrorism, nonproliferation, and the Middle East. Under Obama, another agreement on strategic weapons (the New START Treaty) was signed in 2010. The two countries agreed to additional sanctions on Iran and North Korea and expanded collaboration against terrorism. The United States helped Russia get admitted to the World Trade Organization, and Medvedev agreed not to block imposition of the no-fly zone over Libya in 2011.

Medvedev certainly brought a new tone to the U.S.-Russia relationship, but it was pretty clear that, behind the scenes, Putin was still dominant. In late 2010, I told French defense minister Alain Juppé that democracy did not exist under Putin, the Russian government was little more than an oligarchy under the control of the Russian security services, and although Medvedev was president, Putin was calling the shots. What I said was leaked by the French, and Putin responded that I was trying to "defame" either him or Medvedev, and described me as "deeply confused."

Events didn't help Medvedev. The United States had recognized Kosovo's independence a month before he was elected, and the invasion of Georgia took place five months later. In early January 2009, as a means of intimidation, Moscow cut off gas supplies to Ukraine and raised the price. The bilateral relationship was frozen when Obama became president the same month.

Every new president and his team like to blame the problems they face on the mistakes and ill-considered policies of their predecessors. The Obama administration was no different. In particular, the new president wanted to change the relationship with Iran and with Russia. On January 29, 2009, the new secretary of state, Hillary Clinton, handwrote a letter to Russian foreign minister Lavrov setting forth areas where she thought the United States and Russia could cooperate: a follow-on strategic arms agreement, global economic challenges, Middle East peace, Iran, North Korea, and Afghanistan. A few days later, Obama wrote to Medvedev setting out a similar agenda. He wrote that he and Medvedev were "both young presidents with a different mindset" than the Cold War generation and that if they could solve the Iran nuclear problem, the issue of missile defense in Europe would go away. On March 6, Clinton met with Lavrov in Geneva and presented him with the infamous "reset" button symbolizing the Obama administration's desire to reset the relationship.

It made little difference. At Obama's first meeting with then prime minister Putin in July 2009, the president led off by saying he understood Putin had some grievances. Fifty-five minutes later, Putin wrapped up his soliloquy. When Clinton made her first visit to Russia in October 2009, the Kremlin deeply resented her meetings with journalists, lawyers, and other civil society leaders and a radio interview she gave in which she supported respect for human rights and democracy in Russia, an independent judiciary, and a free press. She pledged that the United States would "continue to support those who also stand for those values," and openly discussed the imprisonment, beatings, and killings of journalists. One can only imagine Putin's reaction to her comments.

As with the Bush administration, there were areas of cooperation. A new strategic arms control agreement was signed. The Russians supported additional sanctions on both North Korea and Iran in an effort to curb their nuclear weapons programs. However, the Russians continued to strongly oppose the installation of U.S. missile defenses in Poland, seeing the new Obama approach as even more threatening than Bush's—truly ironic, since many hawks in the United States thought the new approach was a major concession to Putin.

In 2011, Medvedev announced he would not run for reelection and Putin announced he would run for a third term. That fall Putin wrote in a Russian newspaper about his plans to regain lost influence among the former republics and create "a powerful supra-national union capable of becoming a pole in the modern world." He was elected in March 2012 and took office in May.

Putin was convinced the United States had a role in fomenting large anti-Putin demonstrations in Moscow and elsewhere in Russia surrounding the parliamentary elections in December 2011 and his own election, a conviction only strengthened by Clinton's public comments in support of the demonstrators. External observers noted widespread reports of irregularities in the parliamentary elections of 2011 and the presidential election in 2012. For example, opponents of Medvedev, Putin, and their party found it especially difficult to get broadcast time on television.

Widespread protests in Moscow and Saint Petersburg surrounding the 2011 parliamentary elections led Putin back to his theme of Western interference. On one occasion he said that Secretary Clinton "set the tone for some opposition activists." He added that "it is unacceptable when foreign money is pumped into election processes" and that Russia's sovereignty should be defended from foreign interference. Clinton had told an international conference in Lithuania after the Russian election that "the Russian people, like people everywhere, deserve the right to have their voices heard and their votes counted, and that means they deserve fair, free, transparent elections and leaders who are accountable to them." Her remarks infuriated Putin, who never forgot Clinton's "interference" in Russia's elections. One indication of just how hostile Putin had become to the United States was his turndown of Obama's invitation to the May 18–19, 2012, G8 meeting at Camp David.

While Medvedev had eased the rules on NGOs somewhat before a visit by President Obama in August 2009, once Putin returned as president in 2012, the hammer came down again, with new restrictions requiring that organizations engaging in political activity and receiving foreign funding had to register as "foreign agents" and label all materials provided to the media and on the internet as products of foreign agents. To underscore the resumed hard line, the Russians threw USAID out of the country on October 1, accusing the agency of trying to influence the electoral process through its grants to NGOs.

Putin returned to office determined to crack down even harder on the opposition and critics domestically. He also brought renewed fervor to reasserting Russia's role as a great power whose interests and views must be taken into account, creating a buffer of friendly or intimidated states or frozen conflicts on Russia's periphery, and retaliating for perceived Western interference or "meddling" in the politics of Russia and of other former republics of the USSR. The techniques he employed to pursue those objectives bear close scrutiny because they offer lessons in the sophisticated use of both military and nonmilitary instruments of power, lessons the United States was slow to grasp.

In his first two terms Putin took advantage of the windfall revenues produced by the rising price of oil to invest heavily in the Russian military. He dramatically reduced the size of the conventional forces and focused on creating smaller, far more capable units—particularly special forces—that were highly trained and deployable. He also invested heavily in modernizing Russia's strategic forces and in new technologies that might allow Russia to leap ahead of the United States militarily in selected areas.

An opportunity for Putin to demonstrate Russia's return to the global stage came in Syria, where protests broke out in March 2011 as part of the Arab Spring. Medvedev had agreed to the UN Security Council resolution authorizing the no-fly zone in Libya that spring for humanitarian purposes—in Putin's view, a bait and switch by the United States designed to force regime change. He was therefore determined to support the Assad family—longtime Soviet and then Russian clients—in Syria when protests began there. As the disruption grew, Assad responded with increasing violence. In October 2011, Russia vetoed a proposed UN Security Council resolution condemning the Syrian regime's bloody suppression of the opposition and would continue to veto any effort at the UN to rein in Assad.

The situation evolved into a full-scale civil war in 2012–13, and the Russians moved to supply the regime with a steady flow of weapons and other supplies (as did Iran). The Russian hand was further strengthened when Obama laid down a "red line," warning Assad that any use of chemical weapons would bring a U.S. military response—and then failed to follow through when Assad did just that. The Russians subsequently brokered a deal in which the Syrians purportedly would place all their chemical weapons under international control, an agreement without effective means to verify implementation—and, indeed, Assad would use chemical weapons again and again in the future. Then, in 2015, the Russians intervened directly with their own military forces to help a hard-pressed Assad. In exchange, they received forty-nine-year-long leases (with the option to renew for another twenty-five years) for a naval base near Tartus and an airfield. Taking advantage of Obama's refusal to get involved in the Syrian civil war, Moscow assumed the lead role.

The Obama administration crowed early on that Russia was making a strategic mistake by getting so deeply involved in Syria and that it would find itself in a military quagmire. The administration was mistaken. As of this writing, the Russians have kept their military involvement modest. Thanks to Russian and Iranian help, Assad was able to reestablish control over much of Syria.

With Russian engagement and success in Syria and the perception that the United States was drawing back internationally, between 2011 and 2019 Moscow found many new opportunities to extend its influence globally for the first time since the Soviet collapse, using a

wide array of nonmilitary instruments of power. This was most evident in the Middle East, where authoritarian leaders who faced only
criticism from the United States were embraced by Russia, notably
the crown prince and king of Saudi Arabia. King Salman's state visit
in October 2017 was the first ever by a Saudi king to Moscow. On the
crown prince's third visit to Moscow, just weeks after the murder of
Saudi journalist Jamal Khashoggi, he received a warm public hand-
shake from Putin. During these visits, the Saudi Public Investment
Fund announced its intention to invest $10 billion in Russia and deals
worth another $3 billion were signed, including a Russian commit-
ment to build a billion-dollar petrochemical plant in Saudi Arabia.
The Saudis also see Moscow as an alternative source of sophisticated
weapons, a potential constraint on Iran, and a player once again in the
Middle East. For its part, Russia saw an opportunity to make inroads
with a longtime U.S. ally while attracting sizable investment. For reasons similar to Saudi Arabia's, the United Arab Emirates (UAE) and
Qatar reached out to the Russians, including a visit to Moscow by the
crown prince of Abu Dhabi, Mohammed bin Zayed, in June 2018. In
December, Russia played peacemaker among the disputing members
of the Organization of Petroleum Exporting Countries (OPEC), further underscoring its growing influence.

Russia made progress in Egypt too. For the first time since being
expelled in 1972, the Russians returned in 2017. The Egyptians soon
afterward agreed to a $3.5 billion arms deal, Russian military aircraft
using Egyptian airspace and bases, and the purchase of $2 billion
worth of Russian SU-35 combat jets. Moscow also established a position in Libya, supporting Khalifa Haftar, a Qaddafi general trained
in the Soviet Union. The Russians wanted a role in shaping Libya's
future, as well as construction contracts and a piece of the Libyan oil
industry.

In a remarkable turn of events, the leaders of two longtime U.S.
allies, Israel and Turkey, made the pilgrimage to Moscow, opening
channels of communication relating to military operations in Syria.
Israeli prime minister Benjamin Netanyahu visited Putin in Moscow
multiple times and was the only major Western leader to attend Victory Day ceremonies in Moscow, where he stood next to Putin, in

May 2018. Turkey's president Recep Tayyip Erdoğan was willing to place the long-standing military relationship with the United States at risk in order to buy the Russian S-400 air defense system. By 2019, Russia was the only major player in the Middle East in regular contact with all the key governments and groups: Iran, Saudi Arabia and the other Sunni Arab states, Israel, Turkey, the Kurds, the Palestinian Authority, Hamas, Hezbollah, and Syria.

The Russians also pursued active engagement with the Hugo Chávez/Nicolás Maduro government in Venezuela, signing contracts between oil companies, loaning the Venezuelans billions of dollars, and selling them arms—$4 billion worth. In December 2018, Maduro visited Moscow, where, he said, the Russians agreed to invest an additional $5 billion in Venezuela's oil industry and $1 billion in gold mining. Venezuela agreed to buy 600,000 tons of Russian wheat, and Putin signed up to modernize and maintain Russian-made weapons in the Venezuelan arsenal. During a period when China was abjuring further investment and just trying to figure out how Venezuela would repay Chinese loans, the Russians doubled down on new investment. By early 2019, the Russian oil company Rosneft had become Venezuela's biggest oil partner. Just as important, politically Putin had established a Russian position in South America and the chance to distract the United States in its own backyard.

In Africa, the Russians have become the largest source of weapons and are seeking to expand their political and economic influence. They involved themselves in the civil war in the Central African Republic beginning in 2013, "donating" weapons and training to the military. They created opportunities in neighboring countries, such as the Democratic Republic of the Congo, Sudan, South Sudan, and elsewhere. In the spring of 2018, Russia signed military cooperation agreements with Tunisia (which also by then had close intelligence, counterterrorism, and energy ties to Moscow), Burkina Faso, Burundi, and Madagascar. At about the same time, Mali, Chad, Niger, and Mauritania asked the Russians to help their militaries and security services contend with ISIL and al-Qaeda. Moscow also had signed oil and gas arrangements with Algeria, Angola, Egypt, Libya, Senegal, South Africa, Uganda, and Nigeria. In October 2019, Putin hosted a Russia-Africa summit in Sochi attended by representatives of forty-three of the continent's fifty-four countries. Russia's engagement on the continent lags well behind that of the United States, China, and the EU, but it is reasserting its old anticolonialist credentials and expanding its efforts to recapture its influence there through arms sales, military assistance, oil investments, and propaganda.

Putin has steadily increased Russia's outreach in Central and Eastern Europe to create opportunities and cultivate relationships with key players, as in Hungary, but also to disrupt and discredit democratic politics and institutions in targeted countries. The Russians were involved in a clumsy coup attempt against the prime minister of Montenegro in 2016 in an effort to derail the country's move toward NATO membership. More significantly, Russia is proceeding with the $11 billion Nord Stream 2 gas pipeline from western Russia through the Baltic Sea to Germany, a move that is largely political. Because virtually all Russian gas exports to Europe have flowed through Ukraine, Nord Stream 2 will bypass that country, allowing Russia to deny Kyiv transit fees but also giving the Russians the option of cutting off gas to Ukraine without impacting Germany. As *The Economist* observed, "Nord Stream 2 could make Ukraine, Poland and the Baltic states less secure, undermine the EU's energy strategy, give Russia a bigger stick for threatening western Europe and sow discord among NATO allies. To Mr. Putin, causing so much trouble for a mere $11 billion must seem like a bargain."

Finally, Putin has worked to strengthen collaboration with China at U.S. expense. The Russians have sold the Chinese sophisticated weapons systems, and China has become Russia's second-largest customer for energy (after Germany). The two governments consistently vote together at the UN. As U.S. director of national intelligence Dan Coats testified before Congress early in 2019, the relationship between Russia and China has become closer than at any time since the mid-1950s. China, though, is now in the economic driver's seat, providing Russia with technology and markets. A certain personal chemistry developed between Chinese president Xi and Putin, rooted no doubt in their mutual loathing of domestic dissent, quest for personal power, paranoia about Western interference, and belief that the United States is determined to hold them back. There are multiple areas in which cooperation between Beijing and Moscow is mutually advantageous but, I suspect, none so appealing as making common cause to disadvantage the United States whenever and wherever they can.

In all of Putin's global initiatives, his purpose is clear: to make money through arms and energy sales and economic deals, secure foreign investment in Russia, expand Russian influence, and create problems for the United States by undermining American influence and pulling nations like Saudi Arabia, Turkey, and Egypt away from the United States and the Western-led international system. While Russia cannot compete with the United States (or China) in terms of economic and development assistance or investment, Putin has employed an impressive array of other instruments of power to accomplish these purposes. Where the overt presence of the Russian military is awkward, Moscow has made use of military retirees and contractors. Putin has effectively used the leverage offered by Russian oil and gas resources to develop cooperative arrangements with a number of countries, and insinuated Russia into the politics of oil production in ways giving it influence it lacked even in Soviet days. The Russians have developed a broad and sophisticated arsenal of cyber tools for punishing its adversaries, fomenting internal discord, and weakening both national and international democratic institutions with a range of old KGB dirty tricks employing new technologies such as social media. The Russians have at their disposal a range of strategic communications channels to support governments they favor, stifle opponents, and discredit American actions and intentions. Even as Putin develops an ever more sophisticated Russian military, he has relied primarily on nonmilitary methods to achieve his goals.

The seizure of Crimea and invasion of eastern Ukraine in 2014 demonstrated a remarkable integration of old and new instruments of power.

In 2010, Viktor Yanukovych, whom Russia had supported in the 2004 Ukrainian presidential election, won the presidency. He tried to turn back the clock on reforms enacted after the 2004 Orange

Revolution, significantly strengthening the presidency and moving against the opposition. He tried to position Ukraine as a neutral state, cultivating economic and political relations with both the West and Russia. While he obtained a parliamentary vote to end Ukraine's effort to become a member of NATO, in the fall of 2013 he was prepared to sign an Association Agreement with the EU. However, under pressure from Putin, and with a Russian offer of a $15 billion bailout/economic assistance package in hand, on November 21 Yanukovych announced Ukraine would not sign the EU agreement and would seek stronger economic relations with Russia.

There was a small protest at Maidan (Independence) Square in Kyiv that same day in support of integration with the EU. The protests continued, and on November 30 the police cracked down and a number of student protesters were hurt. By December 8, there were perhaps a million protesters at Maidan Square. They demanded the government release arrested protesters and sign the EU agreement, and that Yanukovych resign. The violence increased, and on February 20, nearly a hundred protesters were killed. Two days later the government was ousted. Yanukovych fled, eventually to Russia. Putin told Obama on March 1 that those who had seized power in Kyiv had "made a coup d état."

Not surprisingly, Putin saw the U.S. and European hand behind Yanukovych's ouster, removing a pro-Russian leader from Ukraine and trying to move the country into both the EU and NATO. Such a shift had momentous strategic implications, potentially imperiling Russian use of Sevastopol in Crimea, Russia's largest naval base on the Black Sea since 1784. Almost immediately, Russian troops in military uniforms without insignia—the "little green men"—established checkpoints in the Crimean capital, Simferopol, and in Sevastopol, and soon controlled all of Crimea. Not wasting any time, the Crimean leadership held a referendum on rejoining Russia on March 16 and the parliament of the Russian Federation voted to annex Crimea on March 18. The speed with which the Russians acted strongly suggests that, at a minimum, contingency plans for seizing Crimea had been prepared well before the event, perhaps as early as the Orange Revolution.

Virtually simultaneously with the annexation of Crimea, there were large-scale anti-Ukrainian government demonstrations in eastern and southern Ukraine—where the population is predominantly ethnic Russian—over the ouster of Yanukovych and the strategic direction of the government in Kyiv. The demonstrations quickly escalated into armed conflict between Russian-backed separatist forces in the Donetsk and Luhansk regions (the Donbass) and the Ukrainian government. The evidence is overwhelming that Russian officers and specialists played a prominent role in supporting and even leading the separatists, again wearing no insignia identifying them as Russians. Meanwhile, that spring, the Russians began a major troop buildup on the eastern border of Ukraine—perhaps 30,000 to 40,000 troops. In August, multiple Russian columns of men and equipment were identified crossing into separatist-controlled territory. Russian media claimed that the Russian soldiers were in Ukraine "vacationing" or were retirees.

In 2017, the Russians dropped the charade of noninvolvement when Foreign Minister Sergei Lavrov said, "Would it be acceptable for Russia, considering its international standing, to keep mum and recognize the coup in Ukraine, and to leave Russians and Russian speakers in Ukraine in the lurch?"

Putin will keep pushing in Ukraine. In 2018, Russian warships seized three Ukrainian patrol boats operating in the Kerch Strait in international waters. A number of captured Ukrainian sailors were put on trial. Neither the U.S. nor European governments took any adverse actions in response to this blatant disregard of international law.

Beginning with the color revolutions in 2003 through 2005, I believe Putin has been convinced the United States seeks to foment regime change not just on Russia's periphery but in Russia itself. American support for human rights, democracy, and reform, he believes, is a facade behind which the United States seeks to bring to power friendly governments responsive to its interests. The 2014 "coup" in Kyiv was the last straw and set Putin on a course to do everything in his power to create turmoil, division, and chaos in the West, weakening governments and multilateral institutions such as

NATO and the EU. The more problems he could create in the West, the more the governments would be forced to turn inward and be less inclined to counter Russia's authoritarianism at home and its militant posture on the periphery.

Throughout the Cold War, both the Soviet Union and the United States attempted to influence opinion and domestic affairs in the other—as well as the outcome of elections and leadership struggles in other countries. In those days, however, the instruments for doing so were far less sophisticated. Covert actions included clandestine financial and other support for sympathetic parties and leaders, smuggling in propaganda, co-opting or recruiting thought leaders, and operating broadcast networks aimed at target populations. There were some successes on both sides, but overall, the efforts of each to influence the domestic political affairs of the other—and those of the other's clients and allies—played a marginal role in the outcome of the Cold War.

The twenty-first century, however, brought new tools with dramatically greater potential to disrupt societies and influence politics, above all the internet, social media, and cyber weapons. There are many reports of American use of cyber tools to weaken and attack ISIS and other terrorist groups, but the United States has been very reluctant to use cyber tools to attack or exploit internal problems in other major states, such as Russia.

Russia has had no such qualms and for years has been aggressive in its use of cyber capabilities to hurt its adversaries and advance its interests. Russia launched significant cyber attacks against both Ukraine and Georgia before and after physical assaults. Ukraine, in particular, has been subject to ongoing cyber attacks on its electrical grid, government sites, weapons systems, and other targets, but other independent former republics of the Soviet Union have been targeted as well. In April and May of 2007, Russia directed a major cyber attack against Estonia in retaliation for the decision to move a Soviet World War II memorial from downtown Tallinn. Financial, media, and government websites were taken down. In January 2009, Kyrgyzstan's main internet providers were shut down by an attack during a period when the government was being pressured by the Russians to shut down the U.S. air base at Manas.

Russia has been the most aggressive (so far) in its willingness to use cyber tools as an instrument of national power. Russian use of cyber attacks and social media to interfere in the 2016 U.S. presidential election has been well documented. Putin's loathing of Hillary Clinton, particularly subsequent to her criticisms of Russia's parliamentary and presidential elections in 2011 and 2012, makes it no surprise that he would do all he could to contribute to her defeat. But his anti-U.S. agenda—to exacerbate America's internal political and racial divisions—was even more ambitious, and he has the resources to launch and sustain these campaigns. The magnitude of the effort was described by Ben Rhodes, President Obama's adviser overseeing national security communications and public diplomacy, who wrote: "Whoever did my job in Russia was sitting on top of billion-dollar investments in television stations, marshaled an army of internet trolls who populated social media, and was empowered to lie with impunity. I had five people working in the NSC press office and my own official Twitter feed. U.S. government broadcasting has a legal firewall against editorial direction from the White House." In a 2014 meeting with Obama on how to make American international broadcasting more relevant and more responsive in competing with the Russians, the president was told that to replicate just the television component of their effort would take "hundreds of millions of dollars, hundreds of people, and greater White House supervision."

The United States wasn't Putin's only target. The Russians worked to help the election campaign of French right-wing nationalist Marine Le Pen through hacking and spies, and even loaned her millions of euros during the election. They engaged in aggressive cyber espionage of German politicians, meddled in the December 2016 referendum on the fate of the Italian government, and even tried to influence the 2016 Brexit vote in the United Kingdom. Putin has shown a willingness to do anything to weaken the EU, European cooperation, and multinational democratic institutions.

It is hard to make the case that the Russians' use of its cyber capabilities and social media was decisive or even significant in any of these elections, but there is little doubt that their efforts had an impact, if only to cast doubt on what was fact and what was fiction online.

The Russians will continue to use these instruments of power in the United States and elsewhere. Our ability to defend against such interference in our domestic affairs and elections has been greatly hampered by President Trump's steadfast denial of the Russian effort, much less its scope and effectiveness. While individual states and departments of the federal government, such as Homeland Security, have taken some measures on their own to improve our defenses, without an integrated effort by the federal government led by the president, we will continue to be at a great disadvantage in thwarting Russian interference. Trump's skepticism of U.S. intelligence information about Russian activities in the United States and his continuing willingness to believe what Putin tells him leave us dangerously vulnerable.

The techniques Russia has exploited are part of a new hybrid approach to conflict that it employed in Georgia and Ukraine. In February 2013, the chief of the Russian general staff, General Valery Gerasimov, wrote an article emphasizing the importance of nonmilitary means of achieving strategic goals. He wrote:

> The very "rules of war" have changed. The role of nonmilitary means of achieving political and strategic goals has grown, and, in many cases, they have exceeded the power of force of weapons in their effectiveness. . . . The focus of applied methods of conflict has altered in the direction of the broad use of political, economic, informational, humanitarian and other nonmilitary measures—applied in coordination with the protest potential of the population. . . . All this is supplemented by military means of a concealed character, including carrying out actions of informational conflict and the actions of special operations forces.

There are few more succinct descriptions of the use of nonmilitary instruments of power and how they can be integrated with covert military operations than Gerasimov's.

The U.S. military has long studied and implemented techniques of information warfare and psychological operations to be exploited in the conduct of military operations, as per Gerasimov's article. What we have lacked is the civilian capacity to use those techniques in non-military environments and contexts. Through their control of television channels, intelligence organizations, and a broad network of outsourced hackers, the Russians are well ahead of us in this arena. Moreover, the Russians are taking steps to exert control over the internet in Russia, allowing it to filter incoming information and even cut itself off from global online traffic.

The United States arrived late to the use of this new instrument of power for political or economic purposes against other nation-states. Washington has the offensive and defensive technical capability but has lacked an integrated government strategy and structure for creating and executing such campaigns. Part of the problem is institutional and legal. Outside of the White House, there is no entity in the American government that can orchestrate a propaganda or cyber campaign on behalf of the entire government on anything like the Russian scale. Further, as Rhodes pointed out, for many years there have been strictures against the executive branch dictating programming on government broadcast channels such as Voice of America. Finally, I suspect there is concern that use of these tools might expose capabilities we prefer to keep hidden for intelligence purposes or to preserve their viability in the event of a major conflict. Even so, there is no reason the United States should not develop the capability to defend ourselves against cyber attacks intended to aggravate our internal divisions and influence our politics, *and* to take the offensive when desirable and necessary. The capabilities will be found only in the National Security Agency, but development and direction of both strategy and tactics must be outside the Defense Department. Authoritarian governments like Russia that use these methods to undermine democratic governments and processes not only must be stopped, they must get a taste of their own medicine.

L ooking at the U.S.-Russian relationship since the collapse of the Soviet Union, one can see where different decisions and more effective use of our array of instruments of national power might have led to different outcomes. It is difficult, though, to imagine what the United States might have done to prevent or even significantly mitigate the economic and political disasters of the 1990s in Russia. Those disasters paved the way for the emergence of a strong leader, one ruthless enough to bring the regions and the oligarchs back under control. Forgoing NATO expansion might have avoided antagonizing Russia, but had we done that and even kept silent about the need for reform and democratization, those choices would not have prevented the color revolutions or Putin's drive for internal control. In retrospect, failure to expand NATO would have left us without an important political and military instrument of power for deterring and containing a resurgent, revanchist Russia.

The one opportunity for a different course for Russia had nothing to do with the United States but rather with the accession to the presidency of Dimitri Medvedev, who at least understood his country's weaknesses and believed Russia needed to be integrated into the West. But Medvedev was not strong enough, nor willing, to thwart Putin's thirst for power.

So, once again, the United States and Russia are adversaries, and we face a confrontation at least for as long as Putin remains in power. As was the case with the Soviet Union, there will be instances in which both powers cooperate because their interests coincide. But in this confrontation, as in the Cold War, nonmilitary instruments of power will play a critical role. Russia is far from the power the USSR once was, but its military strength and its ability to marshal the nonmilitary instruments of power make it a formidable competitor, mainly in Europe, but also in the Middle East, Africa, and Latin America—a disrupter in some places and a nuisance elsewhere. Everywhere possible the Russians will be capitalizing on the perception, and reality, of the United States pulling back from global leadership.

Russia had the opportunity to take a different path that would have been far better for its people and the world, but Vladimir Putin chose otherwise.

CHAPTER 10

Georgia, Libya, Syria, and Ukraine

To Intervene or Not to Intervene

*In Iraq, the U.S. intervened and occupied, and the result was
a costly disaster. In Libya, the U.S. intervened and did not
occupy, and the result was a costly disaster. In Syria, the U.S.
neither intervened nor occupied, and the result was a costly
disaster.*

—PHILIP GORDON, SPECIAL ASSISTANT TO THE
PRESIDENT AND WHITE HOUSE COORDINATOR FOR THE
MIDDLE EAST, NORTH AFRICA, AND THE GULF REGION,
2013–15

I ntervention in other countries is a risky business. Between 2008
and 2014, Presidents Bush and Obama faced four very different
crises, each of which required a decision as to whether the United
States should intervene and, if so, how. Two, Georgia and Ukraine,
were provoked by Russia. Two, Libya and Syria, were sparked by local
anti-regime protests growing out of the Arab Spring movement, and
resulted in brutal repression. Russia moved to take advantage of both,
reasserting its role in the Middle East for the first time in more than
forty years. As secretary of defense, I participated in the decisions on
intervention in both Georgia and Libya.

By 2008, the long, grinding wars in Iraq and Afghanistan had
raised the bar very high for American military intervention in distant

conflicts, especially when neither our vital interests nor our security were at risk. Further, there was no appetite for military engagement in conflicts where there was the possibility of a confrontation with Russia in places where it had overwhelming strategic military advantage. Nor was there much support for sending American forces to stop the internal depredations of yet another in the multitude of nasty dictators. The United States decided not to confront Russia directly in Georgia and Ukraine, nor to oppose Assad in Syria. The question is whether we should have done less in Libya and more in the other three—and, in each case, what?

A review of these four countries' crises makes plain the complexities facing an American president when savage civil wars and aggression abroad bring pressure for the United States to do something. The events involving these countries between 2008 and 2014, and subsequently, strike chords familiar from the U.S. interventions in Somalia, Haiti, and the Balkans twenty years earlier. There will always be internal repression and aggression against neighbors by predator governments. If military intervention is not an option for whatever reasons, what alternative instruments of power are available and how should they be used? What are the lessons from Georgia, Libya, Syria, and Ukraine that might help guide future presidential decisions?

GEORGIA

As the Soviet Union was collapsing and Georgia (an ancient country in the Caucasus annexed by Russia in the early nineteenth century) declared its independence, two pro-Russian Georgian provinces, South Ossetia and Abkhazia, declared their own independence. A bloody conflict ensued between the breakaway provinces and the Georgian government, lasting until 1994, when Russia negotiated a cease-fire and stationed peacekeeping forces in both provinces. In January 2004, an aggressive and impetuous Georgian nationalist, Mikheil Saakashvili, was elected president and the following summer sent troops into South Ossetia to reestablish Georgian control. The Georgians were forced to withdraw, but the Georgian initiative infuriated the Russians. Their hatred of Saakashvili intensified when, in 2007, he went to the border of Abkhazia and promised pro-Georgian loyalists they would be "home" within a year.

Responding to the West's recognition of Kosovo's unilateral declaration of independence in February 2008, Putin asserted that precedent ought to apply to South Ossetia and Abkhazia and threatened to recognize the independence of the two breakaway provinces. Throughout the spring, the Russians added more troops in South Ossetia and even announced plans to issue Russian passports to Ossetians living in what was still formally Georgian territory. After a bitter telephone conversation between Putin and Saakashvili in April over the Russians' recognition plans, Georgia mobilized its troops and Russia sent paratroopers and artillery to the cease-fire line. On August 7, South Ossetian forces began shelling Georgian villages near Tskhinvali, the capital of South Ossetia, and Georgia launched a major attack to retake the capital itself. The next day, the Russians sent the Georgians reeling, destroying their military infrastructure and equipment. Bush had personally warned Saakashvili in the Oval Office, "Don't bait the Russians. You can't handle them—and I can't bail you out." Putin had set a trap, and Bush's warning notwithstanding, the Georgian president had fallen right into it.

The Bush administration didn't have a lot of cards to play. Immediately after Russian troops had occupied large parts of Georgia beyond Abkhazia and South Ossetia, the president, Secretary Rice, National Security Adviser Steve Hadley, Chairman of the Joint Chiefs of Staff Admiral Mike Mullen, and I were all on the phone with our counterparts in both Russia and Georgia, urging the Russians to withdraw and telling the Georgians not to do anything else stupid. Hoping to avert a Russian occupation of even more territory, I told the Georgian minister of defense, "Georgia must not get into a conflict with Russia you cannot win."

The Georgians had 1,800 troops in Iraq helping us, and they now wanted those troops home. We agreed to provide the transport. We worried that the Russians would interfere with this airlift and our subsequent military flights bringing in humanitarian assistance, and so Admiral Mullen spent a lot of time on the telephone with his Russian counterpart. Our embassy staff were also in touch with Russians on the ground in Tblisi, Georgia's capital, both providing information when each of our planes would enter Georgian airspace and saying we expected them to be left alone. We were clear with the Russians that we were not providing the Georgians with additional military capability to take on their forces.

The first U.S. military aircraft with humanitarian assistance began landing at Tblisi on August 13, and many more would follow over the ensuing days. Several American warships entered the Black Sea and headed toward Georgia in a demonstration of support, and a U.S. Coast Guard ship put 76,000 pounds of supplies ashore in Georgia. While not confronting the Russians militarily, these moves did signal our resolve, injected some uncertainty into Russian calculations, and may well have played a role in deterring Russian military forces from going farther into Georgia—and, ultimately, in their decision to withdraw to the positions they held before the invasion.

As I wrote in *Duty*, from President Bush on down, the administration wanted to take strong political and economic action against Russia for its aggression. At an NSC meeting on August 12, as Condi Rice later wrote, there was a good bit of "chest beating" about the Russians and Hadley intervened to ask, "Are we prepared to go to war with Russia over Georgia?" That led to a more thoughtful discussion about real options.

We focused primarily on nonmilitary tools available to us to stop the fighting and get the Russians to withdraw from Georgia, to underscore our support for Georgia's territorial integrity and independence, and to provide financial and humanitarian assistance to the Georgians. During a visit to Georgia on September 4, Vice President Cheney announced that the United States would provide $1 billion in economic and humanitarian assistance aimed at helping those displaced by the war, assisting with economic and infrastructure recovery, and working to develop regional and international trade opportunities. International agencies and other governments pledged $4.5 billion to help Georgia. Diplomatically, our internal debate about how to respond notwithstanding, the United States had been supporting the efforts of French president Nicolas Sarkozy to negotiate a cease-fire beginning on August 12 (although the Russians didn't start withdrawing until August 18, and did not fully withdraw until mid-October).

While most of our European allies were supportive of the Georgians, it was clear that a number thought the temperamental Saakashvili was partly responsible for the conflict, and there was little appetite for strong economic sanctions against Russia. We considered more far-reaching unilateral economic measures but backed off when we realized such an action would leave us, not the Russians, as the isolated party. Nonetheless, the NATO-Russia Council was suspended indefinitely, and NATO issued a statement of support for Georgia, calling upon the Russians to remove their troops. The alliance also declared its intention to "support the territorial integrity, independence and sovereignty of Georgia and to support its democratically elected government and to deny Russia the strategic objective of undermining that democracy." The United States ended its support for Russian membership in the World Trade Organization and pulled from congressional consideration a bilateral agreement with Russia on civilian nuclear cooperation.

There was another reason for some caution on sanctions that August and September: the global economic meltdown. It began, of course, with the sharp decline in the housing market in 2007. Bear Stearns collapsed the following March, and the crisis worsened over the summer. Then, five weeks after the Russians invaded Georgia, Lehman Brothers went under, as did AIG the very next day. Suddenly the world was facing the worst economic downturn since the Great Depression. Few modern presidents have the luxury of one crisis at a time.

Altogether, the response to Russia's aggression in Georgia may seem like pretty thin gruel. Still, the overall U.S.-Russian relationship went into a deep freeze through the rest of Bush's presidential term and until Obama's "reset" the following spring. The administration had used an array of mostly nonmilitary tools in its kit to respond to Putin's aggressiveness in Georgia, but could we have done more? The Russian leader's action against Georgia was popular at home, so any effort to communicate broadly to the Russian people his violation of international norms would have had no effect or even backfired.

In terms of international audiences, actions on both sides leading up to the Russian invasion complicated the story line. Looking back, I believe that the Bush team (including me), while wanting to take stronger action, bowed to the reality that there was little more we could have done to prevent the conflict or to punish the Russians.

In terms of lessons learned, there has been debate whether the Russians would have been deterred from invading if Georgia had been a member of NATO or even had been granted a Membership Action Plan at the NATO summit the previous April. Had Georgia been admitted into full NATO membership and invoked Article 5 (committing all the members of the alliance to assist if another member is attacked), would the United States and the other allies actually have been willing to send forces to assist in a doomed effort? (It would have been doomed because the Russians would have overrun all of Georgia long before NATO could act, leaving the alliance with no viable military options short of a large-scale war to expel the Russian forces.) NATO membership does have deterrent value, but only if it is backed up over time by alliance military deployments demonstrating intent to fight, as has happened in Estonia, Latvia, and Lithuania, all of which, like Georgia, share a border with Russia.

Leaving the hypotheticals about Georgia and NATO aside, a U.S. president must take into account strategic military realities and recognize that nonmilitary measures may be all he or she has available in the event of either civil war or aggression. Those measures, however, can be effective. Skillful use of those tools, in cooperation with allies such as France, was sufficient to get Russian forces out of the additional Georgian territory they had seized in August, protect Georgia's territorial integrity and sovereignty, preserve its democracy (among other things, by refusing to accede to Russian demands that Saakashvili be ousted), and get the country back on its feet—essentially, a return to the status quo ante. A satisfactory outcome, given the circumstances.

LIBYA

On February 15, 2011, a group of lawyers in Benghazi, in eastern Libya, demonstrated against the jailing of a colleague. Perhaps motivated by the democracy movements of the Arab Spring in Tunisia and Egypt, which they had followed on social media, other Libyans joined the continuing protests. Two days later, Muammar Qaddafi's security forces killed more than a dozen protesters, and armed resistance to the government broke out in Benghazi. Unlike in Tunisia and Egypt, the protests in Libya quickly turned into a widespread armed conflict between the government and rebels, the latter within days gaining control of important areas in eastern Libya and launching attacks elsewhere.

The international response was unusually prompt. The UN Security Council issued a statement on February 22 condemning the use of force against civilians and calling for an immediate end to the violence. The council also urged Qaddafi to allow the safe passage of international humanitarian assistance to the people of Libya. The same day, the Arab League suspended Libya's membership. On February 23, President Obama condemned the use of violence and announced he had asked his national security team for a full range of options to respond. He sent Secretary Clinton to Europe and the Middle East to consult about the Libya situation. The Security Council acted again on February 26, demanding an end to the violence and imposing an arms embargo, travel ban, and asset freeze on Qaddafi, his family, and government officials. Politicians in Europe and the United States talked about imposing a no-fly zone over Libya to keep Qaddafi from using his aircraft to attack the rebels, and also discussed removing him from power. The French and British were especially vocal in urging this action. The United States imposed sanctions on the Libyan regime and undertook to provide humanitarian assistance.

As Obama faced decisions on what to do, his national security team was divided. Vice President Biden, National Security Adviser Tom Donilon, Chief of Staff Bill Daley, Admiral Mullen, and I all urged caution about using military force. In one meeting, I said, "We are already engaged in two wars. Do we have to go looking for a third?" UN Ambassador Susan Rice and NSC staffers Ben Rhodes and Samantha Power urged aggressive U.S. action to prevent a massacre of the rebels. Secretary Clinton initially withheld judgment but finally came down in support of military action.

The most immediate challenge was the exodus of tens of thousands of foreign workers from Libya, mostly Egyptians fleeing to Tunisia, which created a significant humanitarian problem for the new (and weak) government in Tunis. The solution ultimately was an "air bridge," in which a number of nations, including the United States, provided aircraft to evacuate the refugees.

Focused on extricating the United States from Iraq and impatient with developments in Afghanistan, Obama was unenthusiastic about getting involved militarily in Libya. Even though he said in a press conference on March 3 that Qaddafi "has lost the legitimacy to lead and he must leave," it was clear Obama would consider military action only if we were joined by other countries and the operation had international sanction. I continued to oppose military action but urged that, if we did authorize it, we limit both the scale of our effort and the duration given that we were already fighting two wars that were consuming all available military resources.

By March 14, Qaddafi's military was beginning to move eastward to crush the rebel stronghold in Benghazi. Two days earlier, the Arab League had voted to ask the UN Security Council to impose a no-fly zone in Libya and to protect civilians there. In a meeting with the president on March 15, Admiral Mullen and I observed that a no-fly zone would not stop Qaddafi's ground operation. It was clear that to protect civilians, any Security Council resolution would need to authorize not only a no-fly-zone but the use of "all necessary means"—i.e., authorization to attack Qaddafi's ground forces. On March 17, Obama decided to intervene, acknowledging that it was a close call but that we couldn't stand by idly in the face of a potential humanitarian disaster. He was clear that no U.S. ground forces would be involved (except to rescue downed pilots), and that while we would take the lead in destroying Qaddafi's air defenses, we would then scale back our involvement. His decision to act was reinforced by Qaddafi himself the same day when he publicly warned the citizens of Benghazi, "We are coming tonight, and there will be no mercy."

At the end of March, Obama directed us to transfer leadership of the military operation to NATO and to reduce our involvement—what one of his aides infelicitously described as "leading from behind," a phrase that would haunt Obama. He also stated publicly that using the U.S. military to remove Qaddafi would be a mistake. The military campaign, as so often happens, lasted longer than its proponents had predicted, and the list of targets grew far beyond air defenses, aircraft and helicopters, and ground force units to include any government installation. It soon became evident that Qaddafi himself was a target. The mission of the NATO air attacks had morphed from protecting civilians to forcing regime change. The rebels captured Tripoli in late August, and Qaddafi was captured and killed on October 20.

The power vacuum in Libya post-Qaddafi, the absence of any stable government institutions, the flood of weapons from Qaddafi's arsenals into the cities and countryside, and the weakness of the National Transitional Council (a temporary government) all foreshadowed future problems. A relatively free and fair parliamentary election was held in July 2012, and a new entity, the General National Congress, assumed power in Tripoli the next month. The weak government that emerged was badly divided internally and never able to control the plethora of militias and armed groups. A civil war broke out in 2014, and despite numerous cease-fires and accords, the factional fighting has continued, a situation further complicated in early 2015 by military operations and terrorist acts carried out in the country by ISIL. The internationally recognized but weak government in Tripoli increasingly was challenged by opposition forces led by former Qaddafi general Khalifa Haftar, who claimed he was fighting "terrorism" and seeking to defeat all Islamist groups in Libya, including ISIL, al-Qaeda, and the Muslim Brotherhood. Although Haftar had once been supported by the United States (before the civil war), by 2015 the Obama administration was supporting the UN-backed Government of National Accord in Tripoli. By early 2019, Haftar's forces controlled Benghazi, much of the east, and key oil fields. In early April he launched an offensive against Tripoli, and on April 19, President Trump endorsed him.

Once Obama decided to intervene in Libya, I believe two strategic mistakes were made. The first was agreeing to expand the original NATO humanitarian mission from protecting the people of eastern Libya against Qaddafi's forces to regime change. A proverbial line in the sand could have been drawn by NATO somewhere between Tripoli and Benghazi, where a no-fly zone and attacks on Qaddafi's ground forces could have protected the rebels in the east (and the main oil fields) without destroying his government. Under those circumstances, perhaps some kind of political accommodation could have been worked out. As I said at the time, Qaddafi had given up his nuclear program and posed no threat to U.S. interests. There is no question he was a loathsome and vicious dictator, but the total collapse of his government opened the way for more than 20,000 shoulder-fired surface-to-air missiles and countless other weapons from his arsenals to find their way across both Africa and the Middle East, sparked a civil war, opened the door to the rise of ISIL in Libya, and created the opportunity for Russia to claim a role in determining Libya's future. The country remains a dangerous shambles. As in Somalia, Haiti, Iraq, and Afghanistan, expanding our military mission in Libya beyond the original military objective created nothing but trouble.

The second strategic mistake was the Obama administration's failure to plan in any way for an international role in reestablishing order and a working government post-Qaddafi. (This is ironic in light of Obama's, Biden's, and Clinton's earlier criticisms of Bush's alleged failure to plan properly for a post-Saddam Iraq). There were a number of steps that could have been taken, again drawing on nonmilitary tools. In a paper for the Brookings Institution in April 2016, Shadi Hamid wrote that such measures might have included a U.S. training mission to help the Libyan army restructure itself, sending in a multinational peacekeeping force, expanding the UN Support Mission's advisory role, helping design a better electoral system that would not have "exacerbated tribal and regional divisions," and restraining the Gulf states and Egypt from their meddling in the lead-up to and after the outbreak of the 2014 civil war.

The United States did provide limited assistance to Libya after Qaddafi fell, much of it for treating victims of the fighting and locating weapons stockpiles. A Wilson Center paper issued on September 10, 2012, summarized thirty different nonmilitary U.S. programs to help the Libyans, focusing on areas such as constitutional development, building a transparent judicial system, improving financial governance, promoting economic growth, and improving chemical weapons security and destruction. The funding for implementation, however, between the intervention in 2011 and the outbreak of the civil war in 2014, was $230 million. If ever there was a mismatch between the importance of the nonmilitary mission and the funding available, this was it. By comparison, the cost of U.S. military operations between March and October 2011 was about $1 billion.

There were a number of nonmilitary ways in which we—and our allies—might have been able to stop the fighting and help stabilize Libya in the summer and fall of 2011. But there was no plan, no funding, and no desire. The nonmilitary instruments of power, as so often after the Cold War, were weak, and so were the will and imagination to use them. The NATO-Arab coalition bombed the hell out of the place and then just went home, leaving Libyans to fight over the remains, creating another source of instability in the region and a new base for terrorists. The harshest judgment about U.S. policy was from Obama himself. He had said in March it would be a mistake to use the military to remove Qaddafi, but that is what happened, and he would characterize the failure to plan for a post-Qaddafi Libya as the worst mistake of his presidency.

SYRIA

A revolution or a war can be ignited with a single spark if there is ample kindling. The Syrian civil war was triggered on March 6, 2011, by the arrest of several teenage boys for painting graffiti saying, "The people want the fall of the regime." Tribal leaders of their town asked the regime for the release of the boys, but President Bashar al-Assad's response was to send in Syrian security forces. During the following weeks, the demonstrations demanding government reform became massive and provoked a brutally violent crackdown. In early April, the focus of the protesters gradually shifted from calling for reform to calls for the overthrow of Assad. By the end of the third week in April, protests had expanded to more than twenty cities. On April 25, the Syrian army launched large-scale attacks using tanks and artillery, leaving hundreds of civilians dead. By the end of May, more than a thousand civilians had been killed and thousands more arrested. Armed opposition militias appeared across the country by midsummer—a civil uprising had become a civil war. On July 29, a group of Syrian army officers who had defected announced formation of the Free Syrian Army and a serious rebellion was under way.

The spark in Syria landed in a highly combustible country, afflicted with a years-long drought resulting in high food prices, mass migration of farmers to cities unprepared to take care of them, deep corruption, political repression, and more than a million refugees from the war in Iraq. A Sunni-majority country harshly ruled for decades by the Assad family and their Alawite Muslim minority, making up just 15 percent of the population, Syria was ripe for an explosion.

For Obama, the use of force in Libya had been a very close call even though he had UN Security Council and Arab League sanction, a number of allies prepared to participate with their own military forces, a dire humanitarian crisis, and an identifiable opposition holding a significant swath of the eastern part of the country. None of those conditions existed in Syria during the last half of 2011 or subsequently, except for a growing humanitarian crisis, so the chances of Obama agreeing to use the U.S. military in support of the revolt against Assad were zero.

Obama would use only nonmilitary measures—once again, economic sanctions and rhetorical condemnation. Between the end of April 2011, right after the Syrian army began its broad offensive against protests in multiple cities, and mid-August, Obama signed three executive orders adding more sanctions to those imposed by President Bush in 2004 and 2006 for Syria's support of terrorism. The sanctions froze the assets of the Syrian government and those of multiple companies and individuals; banned exports by Americans to, and investments in, Syria; and prohibited any dealings in or import of Syrian oil.

On August 18, Obama issued a statement condemning Syrian government actions and said, "For the sake of the Syrian people, the time has come for President Assad to step aside." According to Obama's deputy national security adviser and close associate Ben Rhodes, the administration was relying on building pressure from inside Syria and growing isolation externally to "cause the regime to crumble." Meetings were held to plan for a post-Assad Syria and opportunities were pursued to see if he would leave peacefully. By the end of the summer, many in the administration were anticipating Assad's ouster. Obama himself was skeptical, saying, "Syria could be a longer slog than we think." He was right.

If the intervention in Libya influenced Obama on Syria, as I believe it did, it certainly also influenced the actions of both the Russians and the Chinese. In October 2011, both vetoed a UN Security Council resolution condemning Assad's human rights abuses and demanding that peaceful protests be allowed. Feeling suckered by the United States into supporting the Libya "humanitarian" UN Security Council resolution the previous spring that led to regime change, Moscow and Beijing would not permit any UN action creating problems for Assad.

There were two international efforts at a diplomatic solution to the Syrian civil war during its first eighteen months, with the United States playing only a behind-the-scenes role. The first began with an Arab League peace proposal on November 1 calling for a dialogue between the government and the opposition, and for the Syrian government to cease violence against protesters and release political prisoners. Eleven days later, the league suspended Syria for failing to implement the peace agreement and two weeks after that imposed sanctions on Syria. Under pressure, on December 19 Syria agreed to allow Arab League monitors into the country to observe implementation of the November 1 peace plan. Ongoing violence, however, prompted the league to withdraw its monitors at the end of January.

The second peace effort began in February 2012 with the appointment of former UN secretary-general Kofi Annan as a joint UN and Arab League peace envoy for Syria. On March 16, Annan submitted to the Security Council his peace plan proposing that the Syrian government cease its attacks on the opposition and accept a UN-monitored cease-fire. After the Security Council unanimously agreed to a (nonbinding) statement threatening Syria with further action if it failed to end the violence, on March 27 Annan was able to announce Syrian agreement to his peace plan with a deadline of April 12 for implementation of a cease-fire and withdrawal of tanks and artillery from the cities as required by the plan. A lull in the fighting followed, and on April 15 the first UN monitors arrived in Syria. Only days passed before fighting resumed, and in mid-June the UN monitoring mission was suspended.

At a UN-sponsored conference in Geneva on June 30, Annan laid out his transition plan for Syria, a unity government that would exclude Assad. The participants, including the five permanent members of the Security Council, Turkey, Iraq, Kuwait, Qatar, and the EU, agreed that the transitional body would "include members of both the government and the opposition chosen 'on the basis of mutual consent.'" The Russians said that under the terms of the Geneva Communiqué Assad could stay in power, but the Americans and others contended he had to go. The United States wanted to authorize tough sanctions for noncompliance, but the Russians refused to go along. Two days later, on August 2, Annan resigned in disgust over the failure to adopt his plan.

The Obama administration was supportive of Annan's and other efforts but pursued parallel diplomatic initiatives. Secretary Clinton helped convene more than sixty nations in Tunisia at the end of February 2012 to figure out ways to increase both pressure on the Syrian government and humanitarian assistance. They agreed to cut off Syrian sources of funding, send emergency supplies to refugees, and increase training of Syrian opposition leaders. The question of supplying the opposition with weapons came up in Tunis. The United States remained opposed. As Clinton later wrote, "There were also reasons to be wary of further militarizing the situation and accelerating the spiral to full-blown civil war. Once guns went into the country, they would be hard to control and could easily fall into the hands of extremists." As though there was a shortage of weapons already in Syria.

Even as the Russians, Iranians, and the Lebanon-based, Iranian-sponsored terrorist group Hezbollah provided large-scale military supplies, advisers, and even troops to the Syrian government, the debate over whether to provide armed support to the opposition went on within the Obama team all year. Various Republican members of Congress, including John McCain, excoriated their unwillingness to do so. But as then secretary of defense Leon Panetta later pointed out, "there was little coordination between the opposition groups, and some had unsavory ties to terrorist groups."

In July 2012 Clinton met with CIA director David Petraeus to ask whether it was possible for the CIA to train, vet, and equip moderate opposition fighters. Petraeus said he was prepared to present a plan to that end and did so to the president in late August. As was his wont, Obama asked many questions. He was skeptical that arming the rebels would be sufficient to oust Assad, wondering how a modest U.S. effort could be decisive given all the other weapons flowing to the opposition from the Saudis and others, and he was worried about unintended consequences. Clinton countered that the goal was not to create a force that could defeat Assad but rather to create a partner on the ground strong enough to convince Assad that a military victory was not possible. She acknowledged the risks and shortcomings of the plan but characterized it as "the least bad option." As I had seen firsthand on several occasions as Obama's secretary of defense, there was a deep rift between virtually all of the senior national security officials of the government—at State, Defense, and the CIA, plus the Joint Chiefs of Staff and the director of national intelligence—and the president's advisers at the White House and the NSC. The former urged going forward with the Petraeus plan, the latter were opposed. Obama decided against any change in policy.

A threat by the president of the United States is a potent deterrent only if it is credible and the president is prepared to act upon it. For this reason, I always urged that we avoid "red lines" and ultimatums, telling more than one president, "If you cock that pistol, you had better be ready to fire it." During the first half of 2012, the United States had received a number of unsubstantiated reports of the Syrian army using chemical weapons against the opposition—and civilians. On July 23, Obama warned the Syrians that "they will be held accountable by the international community and the United States should they make the tragic mistake of using those [chemical] weapons." Less than a month later, on August 20, Obama was asked what might lead him to use military force in Syria. He replied, "We have been very clear to the Assad regime that . . . a red line for us is we start seeing a whole bunch of chemical weapons moving around or being utilized. That would change my calculus."

Reports of Syrian army use of chemical weapons continued to arrive. By early summer 2013 a cautious intelligence community finally confirmed with confidence their use. On June 13, the White House issued a low-key statement (under Ben Rhodes's name, of all things) confirming that the Syrian government had used chemical weapons on multiple occasions. At the same time, the president allowed his subordinates to quietly publicize that he had decided, as a result, to begin supplying arms to the Free Syrian Army.

On August 21, the Syrian government launched a massive chemical attack near Damascus, killing more than a thousand men, women, and children. It was a blatant crossing of the president's red line, and there was a general expectation that a U.S. military strike—as well as action by the British and French—was imminent. At an NSC meeting, the chemical attack had changed the minds of many in favor of some limited military action, no doubt mindful of the president's red line. Obama had a number of questions, but at the end of the meeting he ordered the preparation of military options. Although some members of Congress, mainly hawkish Republicans, had been urging military action against Syria, it quickly became clear during the last week in August that many in Congress were, in fact, skeptical of military action and, even more important, that there was strong opposition to Obama's acting without specific congressional authorization. Even within the White House, the lawyers were warning the president that there was no international legal basis for bombing Syria.

British prime minister David Cameron put the use of military force against Syria to an "advisory" vote in Parliament the night of August 29 and lost, 285–272. He said that although the vote was not binding, he would not proceed with military action. The next day, Obama held another NSC meeting in which White House Chief of Staff Denis McDonough was the only one to oppose military action. Obama decided that night to go to Congress for authorization and announced that decision the next day.

As the administration worked to drum up congressional support, during a press conference on September 9, when Secretary of State John Kerry was asked how Assad might avoid American military action, he responded that the only way would be by turning over "every single bit of his chemical weapons to the international community in the next week." Kerry said he thought that highly unlikely to happen. The Russians, however, picked up on Kerry's point and proposed negotiating an agreement that would result in Assad's giving up his stockpile of chemical weapons. Obama withdrew his request for congressional authorization to use military force to give diplomacy "a chance." The two sides reached agreement on September 14, with the first international inspection to take place in November and destruction to begin in 2015. In the event, Assad gave up more than a thousand metric tons of chemical weapons. The agreement was touted by the administration as a significant achievement that avoided a military attack on Syria.

The fly in the ointment was that the agreement provided no sanctions or consequences for the Syrians for noncompliance, no enforcement mechanism, no ongoing unrestricted inspections, and no assurance that all the chemical stocks had been given up and that more would not be made. The last of the "declared" chemical weapons were taken out of Syria in June 2014, but even the head of the international watchdog group cautioned that "we cannot say for sure [Syria] has no more chemical weapons." We now know the Syrians hid a stockpile of sarin and also turned to other chemicals, such as chlorine, to make new weapons—which would be used regularly against the opposition in 2015–16.

The president had allowed his red line to be crossed without any consequences for the Syrian regime. The deterrent power of a warning from a U.S. president had been significantly diminished.

Critics of the administration continued to urge Obama to provide lethal defensive weapons and other equipment to the opposition in Syria. He had finally authorized providing support to the Free Syrian Army in June 2013 after Assad's chemical attack, and light weapons, vehicles, communications equipment, and other gear began arriving in Syria in early September. The underlying challenge for the United States was identifying armed groups that had real fighting capability, would not hand over the weapons to extremist groups, and were relatively "moderate" in the kind of successor government they sought. With between one and two dozen major armed groups and more than a thousand smaller bands, the "opposition" was hopelessly fragmented. The approved effort to create an opposition force from scratch that met American strategic and behavioral objectives cost hundreds of millions of dollars and produced a laughably small number of fighters. U.S. assistance to the Syrian opposition seeking to overthrow the regime remained limited in the years to come, and there would be no U.S. strikes on the regime until early in 2017, when President Donald Trump in April ordered the launch of dozens of cruise missiles against regime targets in retaliation for another chemical weapons attack.

In a twist of fate, so common in international affairs, the emergence of a new threat in Syria resulted not only in major and sustained U.S. air strikes but also the involvement of American troops on the ground in military operations there.

In October 2006, a successor organization to al-Qaeda in Iraq was established, the Islamic State of Iraq (ISI). Its goal was to seize power in the central and western parts of Iraq and establish a Sunni caliphate. It enjoyed considerable success until the U.S. troop surge in 2007. By 2009, ISI had lost its bases in Baghdad and Anbar province, and in April 2010 its top two leaders were killed. Abu Bakr al-Baghdadi became the new leader. With the anticipated departure of all U.S. forces at the end of 2011, ISI began new offensive operations in Iraq. In August 2011, Baghdadi began sending jihadists into Syria to establish an organization and take advantage of the civil war there. Taking the name al-Nusra Front, within a year the organization had become one of the most militarily effective elements of the opposition to Assad, establishing a significant presence in the Sunni-majority city of Raqqa and in several provinces. Even though the United States declared the

Nusra Front a terrorist organization in December 2012, the group often fought against Assad in cooperation with the Free Syrian Army (which Washington was supporting) and other opposition groups.

In April 2013, Baghdadi announced that ISI and the Nusra Front were merging and would henceforth be known as the Islamic State of Iraq and the Levant (ISIL). But the aims of the two groups had diverged significantly, with the Nusra Front focused on overthrowing the Assad regime and taking power for itself and ISIL determined to create a caliphate encompassing both Iraq and major parts of Syria. In January 2014, ISIL seized Raqqa in Syria and Fallujah in Iraq and overran Mosul in June. With the collapse of the Iraqi army in Mosul and ISIL's momentum, Iraq itself was at risk. Alarmed by the success of Sunni-dominated ISIL, Iran deployed forces to help stabilize the situation in Iraq in June 2014, and on August 7, at the request of the Iraqi government, President Obama announced the United States would undertake air strikes against ISIL in Iraq. In September, the United States and several Arab countries expanded the air strikes to attack ISIL targets in Syria. On September 30, 2015, the Russians intervened in Syria militarily, deploying naval and air forces as well as some troops. They maintained that their air and missile strikes targeted ISIL, but somehow most of the munitions fell on opponents of the Assad regime.

By the fall of 2015, one needed a scorecard to keep track of the players in Syria. The United States, Russia, Iran, the Syrian government, other Arab governments, Kurdish forces, and the Nusra Front (among other opposition groups) were all attacking ISIL while those same Arab governments, the Nusra Front, and other opposition groups supported by the United States were attacking the Syrian government, which was being defended by the Russians, Iranians, and Hezbollah.

The tide began to turn against ISIL and the caliphate in 2016 and against the rebels in Syria in 2017–18. ISIL faced three powerful enemies: Kurdish forces supported by the United States with constant air strikes and U.S. Special Forces troops on the ground, pro-Assad forces led by Russia and Iran, and a Turkish-backed coalition of rebel groups. Assad benefited from a steady flow of weapons and materiel from the

Russians as well as their direct military intervention, supplies and fighters from Iran, and significant support from Hezbollah fighters.

While estimates vary, by the end of 2018, at least 450,000 to 500,000 Syrians are believed to have died during the civil war, with 6 million internally displaced persons and 5 million Syrian refugees outside the country. The United States was the largest provider of humanitarian assistance to the Syrian victims of the civil war—$9.1 billion between 2012 and the end of 2018. About half this sum went to people in Syria for emergency food assistance, medical care, shelters, safe drinking water, and other critical relief supplies. The remainder was allocated to support Syrian refugees and host communities in Lebanon, Jordan, and Turkey. Through the inadequacy and ineptitude of American strategic communications, the magnitude of this assistance has been unknown to virtually the entire world.

Should the United States have intervened earlier and more aggressively to overthrow Assad, as it did Qaddafi? Could we have done more to stop the fighting and the killing? Were there tools we might have used short of military action? Early in the civil war, there were major diplomatic initiatives to end the fighting. A major sticking point in each was the determination by the United States and others that President Assad had to step aside and could not be a part of any transitional government. One lesson from Syria is that American presidents should not call for another leader, however odious, to relinquish power without a plan for, or some prospect of, making that happen. It severely limits political and diplomatic options.

In this vein, Assad had learned the lessons from the Arab Spring only too well. Hosni Mubarak stepped aside and soon found himself under arrest and on trial (after he was pressured by the United States to leave office). Assad undoubtedly saw the photographs of Mubarak in a hospital bed in a courtroom cage. Qaddafi's fate was well known and had to strike fear into the heart of every authoritarian in the region, especially Assad's. Did the United States and its allies' insistence that Assad had to go foreclose alternative transition arrangements in which he might have agreed to constraints on his power; the beginning of a succession process, perhaps at some point including luxurious exile; and/or the participation of some officials of his regime in a new government or at least a transition? Additionally, might large-scale U.S. covert weapons assistance to relatively moderate groups such as the Free Syrian Army early on, as proposed by Clinton and Petraeus in late summer 2012, have created the opportunity for enough pressure on Assad to force him to negotiate with the opposition? Were there other covert operations, from propaganda to sabotage, that might have evened the playing field between Assad and the rebels?

There is little assurance these options, and others, would have made a significant difference. But the U.S. failure to act at all, especially in the first year or two of the civil war, had strategic consequences. If the invasion of Iraq and its aftermath showed the risks and dangers of taking military action, Syria demonstrated the risks and dangers of failing to do so. From 2011 to 2013, both Republican and Democratic foreign policy experts warned publicly that the longer the Syrian civil war continued, the more people would die, the more extreme the opposition would become, the more the situation would destabilize the region (through the spread of both terrorists and refugees), and the more it would open the door to ISIL and al-Qaeda. Of course, all that came to pass. Moreover, the massive flow of refugees to Europe destabilized critical American allies and contributed to the rise of domestic political disaffection.

There were further consequences. Russia reemerged as a key player in the Middle East more than four decades after it had been expelled from Egypt thanks to U.S. diplomacy; Russia now has permanent naval and air bases in Syria. Iran has a strong presence in Syria, as does its foster child, Hezbollah. Assad is politically deep in their debt. And the perception in the region that the United States is pulling back has been reinforced. Had I been secretary of defense, I would have opposed outright military intervention in Syria, as I did with respect to Libya. In this, I believe Obama's wariness was justified. There were just too many potential unintended consequences. But I would have counseled against a presidential "red line" and against telling Assad he had to leave when the declaration was purely for effect. I would have joined the rest of the senior national security team in late summer 2012 in supporting a significant program of covert support for the opposition. By 2013 it was too late, as the "moderates" were increasingly outgunned by Islamist forces opposing Assad.

To portray the American options in Syria during this period as either intervening militarily or not is too simplistic. There were other instruments of power available to us that may or may not have had an impact on the outcome but should have been tried.

UKRAINE

All four post–Cold War presidents understood that sustaining Ukrainian independence was critical to the future of Eastern and Central Europe and to the West's relationship with Russia. The success of democratic governance and economic growth in Ukraine likewise was of strategic importance. Between Ukrainian independence in 1991 and 2018, the United States invested more than $7 billion trying to help the country's struggling economy, promote good governance and the rule of law, address pervasive and persistent corruption, and help deal with the aftermath of the 1986 Chernobyl nuclear catastrophe. A high priority for President Clinton was getting Kyiv to give up its inherited Soviet arsenal of 176 intercontinental ballistic missiles and 1,500 nuclear weapons and turn them over to Russia, a goal achieved in 1994 in exchange for Russian, U.S., and British guarantees of Ukraine's territorial integrity. A ten-year treaty was signed by Russia and Ukraine in 1997, including arrangements under which the latter ceded 90 percent control of the former Soviet naval base at Sevastopol to Moscow, and there was a joint declaration that Ukraine's borders were "inviolable." Under Bush, in 2006 Ukraine was selected to participate in the Millennium Challenge Corporation's Threshold Program to help it address two core MCC policy areas, control of corruption and rule of law. And, as mentioned earlier, Bush pressed in 2008 for eventual Ukrainian membership in NATO. Overall U.S. assistance to Ukraine increased under Obama, but with regard to NATO membership, his views were much more akin to those of the Europeans—i.e., it was premature (and strategically unwise).

During the Ukrainian political crisis between late November 2013

and the Russian invasion of Crimea in March 2014, the Obama administration relied on diplomacy, political pressure, and strategic
communications. Obama, Vice President Biden, and others in the
administration reached out repeatedly to both the Ukrainian and Russian leaders, condemning the use of violence against protesters and
calling for a political solution. On December 9, the day after nearly
a million protesters in Maidan Square were met with riot police and
bulldozers, Biden called President Yanukovych to remind him that the
United States had for weeks been urging him to listen to the protesters and those wanting justice and a future in Europe. The next day,
Secretary of State Kerry issued a statement demanding the protection
of human life and warning that "Ukrainian authorities bear full responsibility for the security of the Ukrainian people." The statement
concluded, "As church bells ring tonight amidst the smoke in the
streets of Kyiv, the United States stands with the people of Ukraine.
They deserve better." After a number of calls to Yanukovych during
the ensuing weeks, on February 21 Biden told the Ukrainian president
that he had lost the confidence of the Ukrainian people and should
"call off his gunmen and walk away"—resign. Yanukovych fled Kyiv
the next day, first to eastern Ukraine and then to Russia.

However strong the rhetoric from Biden and Kerry, throughout the
months of political crisis, Obama and his team were quite cautious,
undoubtedly influenced by the disappointments of the Arab Spring
and ongoing challenges in Libya and Syria. According to Ben Rhodes,
the president did not see the protests in Kyiv "as a chance to transform
Ukraine because he was skeptical such a transformation could take
place." With regard to negotiations, the administration let the Germans, French, and Poles take the lead with both Ukraine and Russia
so as to keep the Europeans united on developments in Ukraine but
also to manage "the risk of Putin seeing Ukraine even more conspira-
torially through the lens of a U.S.-Russian proxy fight." By ceding the
diplomatic lead to others, Obama and his advisers weakened their
position and subsequently were frustrated when they tried to insert
the United States into the negotiations and were shut out.

It is odd that the administration didn't seem to understand that
Putin from the start saw what was happening in Kyiv as clearly a

U.S.-Russian proxy fight. Since the previous fall he had been openly blaming developments in Ukraine on U.S. scheming to force another regime change (as in 2004), get rid of Moscow's man Yanukovych, and replace him with a pro-Western figure willing and eager to tie Ukraine to both the EU and NATO. Putin was so convinced of U.S. involvement in events in Kyiv and so concerned about a strategic shift toward the West by Ukraine that, as we've seen, within days of Yanukovych's departure, he moved to reassert Russian control over Crimea and, specifically, the entire Sevastopol naval base. On February 26, 2014, Russia placed 150,000 troops on high alert; the next day, Russian troops in unmarked uniforms seized the Crimean parliament; and the day after that, similarly uniformed forces took control of two airports in Crimea. On March 1, Putin asked for and received the Duma's (rubber-stamp) approval to invade Crimea, and completed the takeover within two days. On March 16, a referendum in Crimea overwhelmingly voted in favor of Russian annexation. It is hard to overstate the strategic consequences: for just the second time since the beginning of the Cold War, the borders of a European country had been changed by force. (The first had been NATO's military intervention against Serbia leading to the independence of Kosovo, although that had taken place under very different circumstances and only after months of intense diplomacy, which included the Russians.)

How would the United States respond? Military intervention to reverse the Russian conquest of Crimea was out of the question, and not even the most hawkish members of Congress suggested such a course of action. Nonmilitary measures were available, and the issue was how far to go. The American rhetoric was tough but vague. On February 28, with reports of Russian troops in the streets of Crimea, Obama warned that "there will be costs for any military intervention in Ukraine." He did not elaborate. The next day, Kerry assured the acting president of Ukraine of U.S. support and commended Ukrainian "restraint" even as the secretary proclaimed publicly that "unless immediate and concrete steps are taken by Russia to deescalate tensions, the effect on U.S.-Russian relations and on Russia's international standing will be profound." In a television interview on March 2, Kerry called Russia's invasion of Crimea an "incredible act of aggression." In a series of lengthy telephone conversations during this period, Putin told Obama that the protests in Ukraine had been initiated by the United States and cited the American democracy-promotion programs. On March 6, he referred to the "coup d'état" the previous month that ousted Yanukovych. Obama told Putin we had no interest in controlling Ukraine and respected Russia's historic bonds with that country. He said the United States sought only to uphold the basic principle that "sovereign states should be able to make their own decisions about their politics internally and externally."

Obama's strategy was to "thread a needle: hold together a Europe wary of conflict with Russia; pursue coordinated economic pressure through sanctions; and stabilize the Ukrainian government." Working with Angela Merkel, Obama did manage to keep the Europeans on board with sanctions and to arrange a significant assistance package for Ukraine from the International Monetary Fund. The sanctions included those on specific individuals responsible for undermining Ukraine's territorial integrity and sovereignty, and on "entities operating in the arms sector in Russia and individuals who provide material support to senior officials of the Russian government." He arranged the ouster of Russia from the G8, cut off a number of civilian and military cooperation programs, and imposed more travel and economic sanctions. Obama announced he would travel to Europe to reaffirm the U.S. commitment to NATO and to make clear to Russia that further provocations would only further isolate that country. He asserted there was still time to resolve the situation diplomatically, called upon Russia to withdraw its forces to their bases in Crimea, and reaffirmed "unwavering" support for Ukraine.

The tough rhetoric out of Washington, at the UN, and from European governments notwithstanding, Putin had confronted the world with a fait accompli. Crimea henceforth would be a part of Russia, because for Putin the return of historically Russian territory, the boost to Russian nationalism, and, even more so, the strategic benefits (especially permanent control of the huge naval base there) far outweighed the potential political and economic costs, which he accurately presumed would be manageable.

Crimea was only the beginning. Even as the Russian takeover proceeded in March, pro-Russian, anti-government groups began protests in the predominantly ethnic Russian regions of Donetsk and Luhansk in eastern and southern Ukraine, demanding a referendum like Crimea's on independence from Ukraine. Separatists in Donetsk in April voted in favor of independence from Ukraine and proclaimed the Donetsk People's Republic. In little over a week, the pro-Russian separatists took control of government buildings in a number of cities in the region. Several of these takeovers were led by a "retired" Russian intelligence officer, Igor Girkin. Many other Russian operatives were involved. The Luhansk People's Republic was proclaimed on April 27. (Putin told Obama that, in occupying government buildings in the east and south, the separatists were only doing the same thing anti-Yanukovych protesters had done in Kyiv the previous November. Putin loves using such moral equivalency arguments to brush back Western leaders.)

Fighting between pro-Russian separatists and Ukrainian security forces escalated throughout the Donbass in May and June 2014. A significant number of Russian citizens and military personnel participated in separatist operations, often in leadership positions. Moscow also provided large supplies of arms, armored vehicles, tanks, and other equipment to the insurgents. Government counteroffensives during June and July recaptured a number of cities taken by the insurgents. By early August, Ukrainian forces had surrounded the cities of Donetsk and Luhansk. With pressure increasing on the insurgents, in late August a sizable Russian military force crossed into the Donbass and helped reverse many of the government's gains.

On September 5 the Russians, Ukrainians, and separatist officials from both Donetsk and Luhansk under the auspices of the Organization for Security and Cooperation in Europe (OSCE) agreed to a cease-fire, the Minsk Protocol. The president of Ukraine, Petro Poroshenko, pledged that the Donetsk and Luhansk regions would be granted "special status" and guaranteed the use of the Russian language there. Violations of the cease-fire occurred almost immediately. In early November, OSCE observers reported—and NATO Supreme Commander General Philip Breedlove later confirmed—large movements in eastern and southern Ukraine of unmarked armored personnel carriers, trucks, and tanks with men in dark-green uniforms without insignia: the Russians were back. The cease-fire collapsed completely in January 2015. Poroshenko claimed at that time that more than 9,000 Russian soldiers along with 500 tanks and other equipment were in the Donbass.

On February 7, French president François Hollande and German chancellor Angela Merkel proposed another cease-fire plan after talks with Putin and Poroshenko. The plan, Minsk II, was signed on February 12. Since that time, there have been many cease-fires in the conflict between the Ukrainian government and the pro-Russian forces in the Donbass, and although every one was broken, there have been no major territorial gains by either side. It is truly a "frozen conflict," with ongoing violence. Putin's willingness to inject significant Russian forces and armor into the struggle left Ukraine divided, with little prospect for reconciliation or resolution—just as Putin wants it.

Russia's seizure and annexation of Crimea and poorly disguised takeover of eastern and southern Ukraine in the spring of 2014 ignited a fierce debate in the United States about how to respond to the Russian aggression. The options were limited. As with the Russian invasion of Georgia in 2008, no one in the White House or in Congress seriously contemplated any kind of direct involvement of U.S. military forces. The Russians held all the high cards militarily in terms of proximity, ability to escalate, and logistical advantage. Even nonmilitary U.S. options were constrained because of the weakness of the Ukrainian military, pervasive corruption, political dysfunction, and economic weakness.

The U.S. response focused on three instruments of power: economic sanctions, diplomacy, and security assistance. New sanctions were imposed on Russia eleven times between 2014 and 2018. The initial sanctions in March and April 2014 focused on two dozen individuals, including Igor Sergun, the head of Russian military intelligence (GRU), and Sergei Ivanov, former minister of defense and first deputy prime minister and, in 2014, chief of staff of the Presidential Executive Office. Others sanctioned included oligarchs close to Putin, government officials, parliamentary leaders, and separatists, as well as entities in the Russian energy and other key economic sectors. For those who had no assets in the West and rarely traveled there, the sanctions had little or no impact. Cumulatively, the sanctions on banks and other institutions did have economic effect. Although they were far from being serious enough to cause Putin to reconsider his actions, they may have deterred him from going farther into eastern Ukraine or taking action elsewhere. Even if the Obama team had proposed additional, even-more-punitive sanctions, the Europeans likely would have balked. However offended they might be by Russia's aggressions, they consistently did not want to do too much damage to their political and economic relationship with Moscow.

Although President Obama, Vice President Biden, and Secretary Kerry were visibly involved in diplomacy in the early stages of the Crimean-Ukrainian crisis, with multiple visits to Europe and Ukraine, what is surprising is the limited diplomatic and political role played during 2014–15 by the leader of the free world. The United States remained in the background diplomatically throughout the tensest parts of the crisis, neither a participant in nor a signatory to the Minsk cease-fire negotiations and two agreements.

The nature and quantity of security assistance to the Ukrainian armed forces was, by far, the most controversial of Obama's decisions. From the outset, the president opted for only nonlethal and defensive forms of military assistance—training, counter-artillery and counter-mortar radars, secure communications, logistics infrastructure and IT, tactical drones, night-vision goggles, and rations. The administration's position was influenced by recognition of the Russians' ability to overmatch any assistance we might provide with even more sophisticated weaponry for the separatists, as well as the risk of escalating the fighting at greater human cost and to the ultimate advantage of the pro-Russian forces. The Obama team was also mindful that allies such as France and Germany strongly opposed arming the Ukrainians, and so they worried about fracturing Western unity.

I believe the United States, as a signatory to the 1994 Budapest Memorandum on Security Assurances guaranteeing Ukraine's territorial integrity (in exchange for giving up its nuclear weapons), had an obligation to do more than it did, if only to demonstrate that we take our commitments seriously. There were other tools the administration could have used, not to reverse Russia's military actions but to increase their political and economic costs. Congress passed legislation in 2014 requiring Radio Free Europe–Radio Liberty and Voice of America to increase their broadcasting in eastern Ukraine and Crimea. Such broadcasting may or may not have had an impact among the heavily Russian and pro-Russian populations in those areas, but by late 2015, there were signs of war-weariness in eastern Ukraine, and communicating the devastation wreaked on their cities might have affected the morale and will of the local population. Stepped-up overt and covert communications into Russia itself may have at least heightened awareness of the costs of Russian intervention in lives and treasure, as well as the impact at home of Western sanctions. More could have been done in Western Europe to publicize the role of the Russians in Ukraine and the humanitarian crisis and physical damage their intervention was causing in an effort to strengthen European governments' willingness to take tougher economic and political measures against Russia.

While the economic sanctions imposed on Russia were aimed at Putin's cronies and certain sectors of the economy, the United States pulled its punches on sanctions, forgoing some of the most potent tools that had been developed in both the Bush and Obama administrations for use against Iran and North Korea. Perhaps the administration placed too high a value on maintaining unity with our European allies. One is also left to wonder whether, in its obsession with getting a nuclear deal with Iran and the need for Russian help to achieve that deal during 2014–15, the administration held back in responding to Putin's Crimean and Ukrainian aggressions.

There is no public evidence that the Obama administration seriously considered covert operations or the use of cyber attacks or sabotage to increase the costs to Russian forces of their intervention in Ukraine. The limited nature of economic sanctions and our backseat role in diplomacy constituted "intervention-lite."

Every president faces the question of whether or not to intervene in a foreign country when our national security or interests are not directly at risk. The U.S. interventions in Georgia, Libya, Syria, and Ukraine offer very different lessons for future presidents.

Foremost, a president must decide whether intervention is truly in our national interest. Just because we have the ability to intervene doesn't mean it is wise to do so. Bush knew that using force to stop the Russian military in Georgia was not an option, but believed we needed to use all nonmilitary means at our disposal—as well as military measures that signaled resolve without risking war—in the hope of deterring Putin from overrunning the entire country and forcibly removing Saakashvili. He believed that imposing costs on Russia for its aggression was important to our interests as a means of deterring further military action elsewhere on its borders, and also to send the message to a wider audience that America would stand up for a democratically elected government of a sovereign state. Obama intervened in Libya despite believing that doing so was not in our national interest. But it was important to our British and French allies, and he thought preserving those relationships, and preventing a humanitarian disaster, was in our national interest. I thought that was a mistake. Similarly, Obama concluded that getting involved in the Syrian civil war was not in our interest, a view shared by Trump, although destroying ISIL clearly was important to both. As with Georgia, Obama knew that U.S. military intervention in Ukraine was not an option, but he could have done much more short of that to support the democratically elected government in Kyiv and impose higher costs on Putin for both Crimea and his actions in the Donbass, recognizing that doing so was important to stability in Eastern Europe, and thus to our interests.

Absent a threat to American vital interests, we should avoid intervening with U.S. military forces in places where another power has overwhelming advantages in proximity, numbers, and logistics, and cares a lot more about prevailing than we do. This was clearly the case with Russia in Georgia and Ukraine. A corollary is to avoid providing weapons in numbers and sophistication that might well prompt a hotheaded ally to provoke a wider conflict that is not in America's interest. This clearly guided Bush's policy in dealing with Saakashvili in Georgia (and with Israeli prime ministers vis-à-vis Iran) and contributed to a diplomatic outcome there that stabilized the situation on the battlefield and preserved a sovereign and democratic government in Tblisi. Obama's caution in providing Ukraine with even sophisticated defensive weapons probably was the right approach during the takeover of Crimea and the early stages of the insurgency in the Donbass, but providing more-lethal defensive weapons, such as antitank missiles, should have been reevaluated after the open Russian military intervention in eastern Ukraine in the latter part of 2014. That said, Putin was determined to split Ukraine and extend an umbrella of protection and autonomy over the ethnic Russians in the Donbass, and he probably was prepared to use whatever force was necessary to accomplish that objective. Thus, any lethal assistance needed to be carefully calibrated.

Presidents should avoid ultimatums and red lines unless they are fully prepared to intervene militarily to enforce them. Obama's red line in Syria and his failure to follow through had significant repercussions, and not just in Syria. A limited U.S. strike after Assad's use of chemical weapons, as was initially expected, might have provided the opportunity for the United States, not Russia, to propose negotiating the removal of the Syrian chemical stockpile or for us to accept a Russian proposal to that end—but from a position of strength, not as a concession to avoid humiliation.

As appealing as tough rhetoric is, presidents should avoid calling for a foreign leader, no matter how despicable, to leave office without considerable confidence that this might actually happen or be arranged. Obama's doing so in the case of Syria's Assad looked feckless; doing so with respect to Qaddafi was more realistic. Perhaps more important, presidents should remember that there may be occasions when a despotic leader, or those close to him, might have a transitional role as part of a diplomatic or political process, as could have been the case early on in Syria. Calling for Assad's removal or departure potentially foreclosed options for compromise outcomes that might have ended the violence and led to a peaceful transition.

Since the end of the Cold War, American presidents have become overly fond of calling for regime change abroad, with an approving chorus of foreign policy hawks in and out of government, as well as certain media commentators and members of Congress and liberals passionate about the Responsibility to Protect. Such rhetoric is usually hollow and leads to no useful end. On the other hand, if a president is serious about intervention to bring regime change, he or she had better have a plan for how to make it happen *and* a plan for what happens next if the effort is successful, or not.

When military intervention is not an option or is deemed unwise but nonmilitary intervention is chosen, presidents should use the full array of instruments available for bringing pressure on the parties involved. Economic sanctions or inducements are usually the first choice, but other tools are available and underappreciated: overt and covert messaging (information operations), covert operations such as neutralizing (not killing) individual leaders or sabotage, the use of cyber attacks and manipulation, security assistance and training, and expelling relatives of major players from the United States (when legally possible), to name just a few. Some of these measures were used in Syria and against Russia in connection with Crimea and the Donbass, but too often too sparingly and too late to affect outcomes.

As I said at the outset of this discussion, military interventions are a risky business. Nearly every time, they end up lasting longer and being bloodier, more costly, messier, and more controversial than anticipated. To repeat: they should be avoided unless important American interests are at stake. Presidents should eschew threats and tough rhetoric they are unprepared to back up.

When using nonmilitary means to take a stand, help a friend or ally, deter an adversary, or impose costs for aggression or brutality, presidents should apply the full array of available instruments of power ruthlessly. When a president decides that nonmilitary intervention is in America's interest, he or she must use all the tools in a manner that demonstrates seriousness of purpose and impresses upon others the risks of challenging the United States. That means devoting the resources to ensure that all those nonmilitary tools are well funded, robust, supple, powerful—and effective. Since the end of the Cold War, we have allowed too many to wither, limiting the effectiveness of those tools the country and its presidents need, and thus requiring overreliance on our military.

CHAPTER 11

North Korea

Crazy Like a Fox

*N*orth Korea's relentless pursuit of nuclear weapons and the ballistic missile capability to deliver them has frustrated all four post–Cold War American presidents. Each has offered the North (the Democratic People's Republic of North Korea, or DPRK) a cornucopia of economic benefits if it would abandon its nuclear ambitions; each president thought he had made progress toward that goal and offered concessions to achieve it, only to have the North renege on its promises and return to truculence and its nuclear and missile programs. Each president promised not to make the mistakes of his predecessors, only to find himself caught up in the cycle of the North escalating tensions, offering to come to the bargaining table in exchange for concessions, negotiating in bad faith, and then starting the cycle all over again. Each cycle saw the North's nuclear and missile capabilities advance, to the point where today it likely has several dozen nuclear weapons and growing assurance of the ability to deliver one or more to targets in the United States. As I told Chinese president Hu Jintao in Beijing in January 2011 at the direction of President Obama, "North Korea is now considered a direct threat to the United States."

Every post–Cold War president has used a wide array of instruments of power—except direct military attack—to stop North Korea, to no avail, and now we face a real threat. How did we come to such a pass and what can we do?

"Dear Leader" Kim Jong-il died on December 17, 2011, after seventeen years of despotic rule and a long period of ill health. In the bizarre world that is the DPRK, his eldest child, Kim Jong-nam, seems to have lost his heir-apparent status in 2001 after being arrested for attempting to enter Japan on a fake passport to visit Tokyo Disneyland (a stunt rather more innocent than his father's kidnapping in 1978 of a South Korean actress to help create a North Korean film industry). By 2009, the leader's number two son, Kim Jong-un, already had assumed the role of successor. I was secretary of defense at the time, and many of us believed the unprovoked North Korean sinking of the South Korean warship *Cheonan* in March 2010 and the artillery barrage aimed at the South Korean island of Yeonpyeong the following November were attempts by Kim Jong-un to prove his mettle—that he was tough enough and ruthless enough to succeed his father—to the North's military leadership. Subsequently, Kim brutally executed several of those generals, including his own uncle.

With his accession to power at the end of 2011, Kim Jong-un significantly accelerated the nuclear and missile programs begun by his grandfather, Kim Il-sung. In 1955, Pyongyang established an Atomic Energy Research Institute, and four years later signed an agreement with the Soviet Union to train North Koreans in nuclear disciplines. With Soviet help, the North established a nuclear research center and in 1969 began operating a research reactor at Yongbyon. The North continued to build its nuclear research capabilities throughout the 1970s and 1980s. Available evidence suggests the North began pursuing the ability to enrich uranium in the mid-1990s, its efforts receiving a considerable boost from A. Q. Khan, architect of Pakistan's nuclear program. Although the DPRK signed the Nuclear Non-Proliferation Treaty (NPT) in 1985, by the time Bush 41 announced in September 1991 that the United States would withdraw its land- and sea-based nuclear weapons from South Korea (and other overseas sites), Kim Il-sung had a robust nuclear establishment.

On January 20, 1992, North and South Korea signed a Joint Declaration on the Denuclearization of the Korean Peninsula, both agreeing not to "test, manufacture, produce, receive, possess, store, deploy or use nuclear weapons" or to "possess nuclear reprocessing and uranium enrichment facilities." Kim Il-sung adhered to the agreement only until the North acquired the technical capability to violate it.

President Clinton made the first American attempt through diplomacy and economic sanctions to stop the North's nuclear program. Faced with demands from the International Atomic Energy Agency (IAEA) for special inspections in early 1993, the DPRK soon dramatically ratcheted up tensions by announcing its intention to withdraw from the NPT. After discussions with the United States, the North suspended its decision to pull out of the NPT and agreed to IAEA safeguards in exchange for assurances from Washington against the threat and use of force and noninterference in North Korean internal affairs. After a second round of talks with the United States, in July 1993, the North agreed to "begin consultations" with the IAEA on safeguards and to negotiate IAEA inspections of its nuclear facilities—safeguards and inspections it had previously agreed to in January 1992. In short, the pattern was established early of North Korea engaging in threatening behavior, agreeing to terms, stalling on implementation, and then later agreeing to negotiate once again on the same issues.

At the end of 1993, the CIA estimated that North Korea had separated about twelve kilograms of plutonium from spent fuel rods from its reactor—enough to make one or two nuclear weapons.

On March 1, 1994, IAEA inspectors arrived in North Korea and in mid-March were refused access to a plutonium reprocessing plant at Yongbyon. Within a week, President Clinton ordered the deployment of Patriot missiles to South Korea and asked the UN to impose economic sanctions. At the end of March, at Clinton's behest, Secretary of Defense William Perry publicly talked tough about the North Koreans' actions, on March 30 telling editors and reporters that the president was determined to prevent North Korea from developing a nuclear arsenal "even at the risk of war." Perry also said publicly that the United States would not "rule out a preemptive military strike." To balance the message, Clinton had the State Department say that the United States preferred a peaceful solution. As Clinton later wrote, "I believed that if North Korea really understood our position, as well as the economic and political benefits it could realize by abandoning its nuclear program in favor of cooperation with its neighbors and the United States, we could work it out." Not having learned the lesson from Lyndon Johnson's spurned offers of vast economic assistance if only North Vietnam would leave the South alone, Clinton and his successors just never could grasp why the North Korean leadership would forgo the economic benefits the United States was offering in exchange for giving up their aspiration for nuclear weapons. What they did not seem to understand, or accept, was that the regime considered nuclear weapons essential for its survival.

By May 1994, the IAEA had confirmed that North Korea was removing spent fuel from its nuclear research reactor in the absence of inspectors, creating the opportunity to obtain even more plutonium. As tensions built, former president Jimmy Carter called Clinton on June 1 and said he'd like to go to North Korea and see if he could work something out. Ultimately, Clinton gave Carter the go-ahead, as long as Kim Il-sung understood that economic sanctions would not be suspended unless the North let the inspectors do their jobs, agreed to freeze their nuclear program, and committed to a new round of talks with the United States on building a non-nuclear future. On June 16, Carter reported success in his talks, progress formalized a week later in a letter from Kim to Clinton confirming that he would not expel the IAEA inspectors as long as good-faith efforts were made to resolve differences over inspections, and accepting other U.S. preconditions for talks. The sides agreed to start talks in Romania on July 8, 1994, and Clinton agreed to suspend U.S. sanctions while the talks were under way.

Kim Il-sung died the day the talks were to begin, and the talks in Romania were postponed for a month. Kim was succeeded by his son, Kim Jong-il. After intense negotiations, led on the U.S. side by Ambassador Robert Gallucci, on October 21 the Agreed Framework was signed. The agreement required that North Korea freeze all activity at existing nuclear reactors and allow them to be monitored, ship 8,000 unloaded fuel rods out of the country, eventually eliminate its existing nuclear facilities, and account for spent fuel produced in the past. The United States agreed to organize an international consortium to build two light-water reactors for electric power (that could not produce usable amounts of weapons-grade material); guarantee delivery of 500,000 tons of heavy fuel oil per year; reduce trade, investment, and diplomatic barriers; and provide formal assurances against the use of nuclear weapons against the North.

Considered at the time a substantial diplomatic achievement, the Agreed Framework underpinned the U.S.-DPRK relationship from 1994 until 2002, when, among other developments, the United States received credible intelligence that North Korea had begun secretly producing highly enriched uranium as early as 1998—a second path to weapons-grade nuclear material and a clear violation of the Agreed Framework.

During the interval, there were ongoing U.S.–North Korean contacts and negotiations dealing primarily with the DPRK's missile development programs and their sale of missiles and missile technology to a range of international clients. In April 1996, the United States suggested that the North should adhere to the Missile Technology Control Regime, a voluntary international agreement aimed at controlling the sale of ballistic missile systems, components, and technology. The North Korean negotiators responded by saying that if they did so, the United States should compensate them for lost missile sales and find other countries to launch DPRK satellites. A month later, the United States imposed sanctions on the North (and Iran) for missile technology–related transfers. Additional missile-related sanctions were imposed in both 1997 and 1998. On August 31, 1998, the North launched a three-stage Taepodong-1 missile over Japan, demonstrating a range and technology more advanced than intelligence experts expected.

Even while imposing additional sanctions on the North, the Clinton administration kept the diplomatic channel open. There were four rounds of U.S.-DPRK missile talks between 1996 and 1999, and other bilateral diplomatic contacts throughout the late 1990s. On November 12, 1998, Clinton asked former Defense Secretary Perry to lead a review of U.S. Korea policy and recommend a new approach to try to get the North to give up its weapons and missile programs and reconcile with the South "while minimizing the risks of failing to do so." Perry visited Pyongyang on May 25–28, 1999, and met with senior North Korean political, diplomatic, and military officials to discuss expanding the bilateral relationship. Perry delivered a letter from Clinton to Kim Jong-il providing a "road map" by which the United States would provide North Korea with a broad range of economic assistance if they gave up their attempts to develop nuclear weapons and long-range ballistic missiles.

The following September, the North responded positively, declaring a moratorium on missile tests as long as talks with the United States about improved relations continued. In return, Clinton announced his intention to suspend sanctions that had been imposed during and after the Korean War relating to commercial and consumer goods, financial transactions, travel, and official contacts. The president had lifted decades-old punitive sanctions on the DPRK in exchange for a temporary cessation of missile testing. There were no further North Korean ballistic missile tests for nearly six years, until 2005—no small thing, but no long-term solution either. And the North had won a significant easing of U.S. sanctions even as it continued its nuclear enrichment program in secret.

Meanwhile, the relationship between South and North Korea seemed to warm. In December 1997, Kim Dae-jung was elected president of South Korea. He was determined to pursue reconciliation with the North, what he called his "Sunshine" policy. The first North-South Korean summit meeting took place June 13–15, 2000, in Pyongyang, between Kim Dae-jung and Kim Jong-il. At the conclusion, the two leaders signed a declaration saying they had agreed to resolve the question of reunification of the Korean Peninsula. There were promises to reunite families and to develop economic and cultural exchanges. In response, Washington further eased sanctions on the North relating to commercial and consumer goods, investment, and direct personal or commercial financial transactions without, in turn, the North rolling back any aspect of its nuclear or missile programs. Sanctions relating to terrorism and missile proliferation remained unchanged.

Talks between the United States and the North on missile testing and proliferation continued through the summer and fall, including a meeting between secretary of state Madeleine Albright and her North Korean counterpart at a meeting of the Association of Southeast Asian Nations (ASEAN) in Bangkok at the end of July 2000. They discussed whether Kim Jong-il might send a high-level emissary to Washington, apropos of Bill Perry's visit to Pyongyang fourteen months earlier. The North Korean leader decided to do so, and Vice Marshal Jo Myong-rok visited Washington on October 9–12, meeting with both the secretaries of state and defense and personally delivering to Clinton an invitation from Kim to visit Pyongyang—along with "unexpectedly constructive" suggestions regarding their missile programs. Clinton and Albright concluded that a summit might result in an agreement in principle that, "if fleshed out," could have positive consequences for East Asia. At the end of the vice marshal's visit, a joint communiqué was issued in which both sides pledged "no hostile intent" toward each other. The North Korean envoy also agreed to a preparatory meeting prior to a summit and invited Albright to Pyongyang.

The American secretary of state showed up on Kim's doorstep on October 22, 2000, making clear to him that she could not recommend a summit without a satisfactory agreement on missiles. Kim told her the missile program was intended to give the North the capability to launch "peaceful communications" satellites and that if some other nation agreed to launch the North's satellites, there would be no need for missiles. When Albright raised missile exports as a major problem, Kim responded, "If you guarantee compensation, it will be suspended." He said that the missiles had also been developed for self-reliance, and "if there is an assurance that South Korea will not develop five-hundred-kilometer-range missiles, we won't either." Kim made clear he wasn't about to dismantle missiles already deployed, but that it would be possible to stop production. At a meeting the next day, Albright said a list of questions had been provided to his advisers and Kim promptly answered them himself: "Yes, the proposed ban on missile exports would apply to existing as well as new contracts, provided there was compensation. Yes, the ban would be comprehensive and apply to all missile-related materials, training, and technology. Yes, North Korea intended to accede to the multinational Missile Technology Control regime, provided South Korea did as well." With regard to verification of these commitments, Kim demurred—those issues "would require further discussion."

In terms of a possible presidential visit to North Korea, time was running out on the Clinton administration and so there was some urgency in trying to reach an agreement. At Albright's suggestion, experts from both sides met in Malaysia November 1–3, 2000. The U.S. demands were extensive: North Korea had to agree to refrain from production, testing, deployment, and export of whole classes of missiles, including those threatening Japan, in exchange for which the United States would arrange for North Korean satellite launches outside the country; missiles already deployed had to be phased out; an agreement on verification principles was necessary, coupled with a commitment to work out the means of implementation; the North had to publicly accept the presence of U.S. troops on the Korean Peninsula; and the North was expected to adhere fully to the Agreed Framework and refrain from unauthorized nuclear activities. The United States would not agree to full normalization of relations until "all our conditions were met." Albright thought the toughest issues would be the already deployed missiles and verification.

Albright and National Security Adviser Sandy Berger thought Clinton should make the trip to Pyongyang if it would lead to an acceptable deal on missiles. South Korea's Kim Dae-jung thought he should go, but there was significant opposition in the U.S. Congress, with some members concerned that a summit would legitimize Kim Jong-il. Clinton, immersed in a last-ditch effort to get a Middle East peace agreement, told Yasir Arafat that he had a chance to get an agreement with North Korea to end long-range missile production, "but I would have to go there to do it." Despite Albright's confidence that if he went an agreement could be reached, Clinton decided he was so close to sealing a Middle East deal that he could not take the chance of being gone a week halfway around the world. Even though Clinton didn't make the trip, when he met with President-elect George W. Bush on December 19, he told his successor that he had almost "tied up a deal with North Korea to end its missile program, but that he [Bush] probably would have to go there to close the deal."

I t is hard to avoid connecting the unprecedented intensity of North Korean diplomatic engagement with the United States from 1994 through 2000 to the severe famine in the North. Beginning in the early 1990s, both China and Russia (in the aftermath of the Soviet collapse) withdrew their food subsidies to the DPRK. This, together with the failures of collectivized agriculture and then flooding and drought between 1995 and 1997, dramatically reduced the availability of food in the North. Between 1992 and 1994, food distribution by the government in the northeast of the country became "intermittent" and then in 1994 was shut down altogether. According to most estimates, 2 million to 3 million people died of starvation and hunger-related diseases between 1994 and 1998.

Widespread flooding in August 1995 led the North Korean leadership to appeal to the World Food Program (WFP) for food aid. Despite decades of hostility with North Korea, the United States, according to WFP reporting, gave substantially more food aid to the North for four straight years, 1997–2000, than did China; in 1999, it donated more than the rest of the world combined and three times China's offering. As so often, the U.S. government failed to publicize this large-scale humanitarian assistance throughout Asia and made virtually no effort to figure out how to let the North Korean people know who was feeding them, another significant failure of strategic communications.

The Agreed Framework on the nuclear program signed in October 1994, the overall easing of tensions between North and South, and U.S. actions to relax sanctions relating to consumer goods in the late 1990s all contributed to increased international assistance to a regime under extraordinary pressure. According to a United States Institute of Peace report in 1999, "North Korea has sustained more destabilizing change over the past five years than it has over the previous forty years combined." Indeed, there were reports of a coup plot against Kim by the Sixth Corps of the North Korean army in 1995. Presumably because of plotting against him, during the worst of the famine in late 1996 and early 1997, Kim Jong-il purged general officers who had led the military for decades. No wonder Kim was willing to engage with the United States during this period: his back was to the wall.

Critics, including former secretary of state James Baker, accused the Clinton administration of "appeasement," arguing that the Agreed Framework did not result in dismantlement of the DPRK's nuclear facilities and only delayed the North's nuclear program, even as Pyongyang cheated by starting its uranium enrichment program in 1998. And despite many rounds of negotiations, no agreement was ever reached on its missile program. In exchange, the North received substantial sanctions relief, 500,000 tons of oil annually for several years, and the pledge to build two light-water reactors at a cost of $4 billion. The fact that the North between 1994 and 2000 repeatedly would invite the IAEA to visit for safeguards inspections and then refuse to comply with inspection requirements ought to have raised suspicion about their nuclear activities. Clinton's defenders point out that the Agreed Framework stopped the North's production of plutonium for a number of years, and the missile talks resulted in a moratorium on missile testing from 1999 to 2005.

Both the Agreed Framework and missile talks bought time, but neither contributed to dealing with the North Korean nuclear or missile threat long-term. Further, they bought time for the North to continue its research and start the covert nuclear enrichment program. By significantly easing sanctions on consumer and commercial goods, not to mention the delivery of food aid, they also bought time for Kim Jong-il to survive the famine politically. In retrospect, it seems to me the United States had leverage and instruments of power from 1994 through 2000 that we did not use, whether because of moral qualms or skepticism or lack of imagination. Covert operations, strategic communications, holding the DPRK accountable for its failure to allow IAEA inspections, manipulating existing sanctions, vastly expanding (or shrinking) humanitarian assistance, going after North Korean financial assets abroad—all could have been employed more aggressively. Whether these measures might have created sufficient pressure on Kim to abide by the Agreed Framework; dismantle some of his nuclear facilities, as promised "eventually"; allow more intrusive IAEA inspections; or forgo enrichment is anybody's guess. But I believe we left chips on the table.

George W. Bush entered the presidency believing his predecessor had erred on two counts in dealing with North Korea: first, by relying on bilateral negotiations and thus ignoring the role played by China in Pyongyang, and second, in making concessions—easing sanctions—prior to the North delivering fully on its promises. His attitude toward the North could not have been improved by a DPRK threat in February 2001 to restart long-range missile tests if the United States did not continue negotiations on normalizing relations. On March 6, 2001, Bush met with his national security team and told them the previous administration's policy had not worked and that he intended to change it. Henceforth, North Korea "would have to change its behavior *before* America made concessions." The next day, Bush met with South Korean president Kim Dae-jung and informed him that the new administration would not pick up negotiations with the North where Clinton had left off and would take time to review the entire U.S. approach. Although the meeting was cordial, there was a yawning chasm of disagreement between the presidents. Bush 43 considered the North Korean nuclear program a global, not just regional, issue and felt strongly about the dictatorship's treatment of its people. Kim Dae-jung, as Condi Rice wrote, wanted to accommodate the regime in the North to maintain peace and stability and would "never challenge North Korea in any way."

Three months later, the administration completed its North Korea policy review, and the statement Bush made on June 6, 2001, about his new policy could have been made by his predecessor. He said he had directed his team to undertake serious discussions with the North on a broad agenda, including improved implementation of the Agreed Framework, verifiable constraints on the North's missile programs and a ban on missile exports, and a less threatening conventional military posture. Bush said he would also pursue the discussions in the context of a comprehensive approach seeking to encourage progress toward North-South reconciliation, peace on the Korean Peninsula, a constructive relationship with the United States, and greater stability in the region. The statement concluded, "Our approach will offer North Korea the opportunity to demonstrate the seriousness of its desire for improved relations. If North Korea responds affirmatively and takes appropriate action, we will expand our efforts to help the North Korean people, ease sanctions, and take other political steps." There was no mention of a multilateral approach in dealing with Pyongyang. Indeed, a week later, Bush's special envoy for Korea met with the North Korean representative to the UN to make arrangements for bilateral talks. At the same time, Bush made clear to his team that he would not use food aid as leverage—he didn't want to punish the victims of Kim's dictatorship in order to pressure him.

Almost from the beginning, the Bush 43 administration was deeply split on how to deal with North Korea. Vice President Cheney and Defense Secretary Rumsfeld wanted to toughen the sanctions and increase the North's isolation in order to lay the groundwork for regime change. According to Rice, the president was "squarely" on their side. Secretary of State Powell was more in favor of engagement and diplomacy. Rice, then the national security adviser, also believed in pressure but felt that no amount of economic pressure and privation would spark overthrow of the regime, and that a policy of complete isolation over the long term would not have the support of either China or South Korea, and pursuit of such a policy would create constant tension with both.

Both the United States and North Korea made positive noises about the relationship over the next eighteen months, with Kim Jong-il reaffirming his pledge to maintain the moratorium on missile testing and Secretary Powell reiterating the American willingness to resume the dialogue with the North at "any time, any place, or anywhere without preconditions." But the relationship headed sharply downhill in 2002, beginning with the president's inclusion of the North in his "axis of evil" during the State of the Union speech in January, followed on April 1 by his announcement that he would not certify the North's compliance with the Agreed Framework because of its failure to provide a complete and accurate declaration of its nuclear activities and refusal to allow IAEA inspections.

During the summer, U.S. intelligence agencies began receiving reports about linkages between the North and the A. Q. Khan network and of DPRK efforts worldwide to acquire components for uranium enrichment. In early September 2002, the CIA informed the president and his team of its assessment that the North had built a production-scale facility for uranium enrichment. According to Rice, there was an "unbridgeable disagreement within the administration about how acute the threat was," although everyone agreed that the North was "seriously cheating" on the Agreed Framework. Pyongyang earlier had sent word it would welcome an American envoy, and after much debate, Bush allowed the assistant secretary of state for East Asian and Pacific Affairs, John Kelly, to go in early October. Kelly informed the North Koreans that the United States had discovered their secret enrichment facility and that no progress was possible in the bilateral relationship until that was undone. The North Koreans subsequently acknowledged the existence of the enrichment program.

Bush was finished negotiating bilaterally with the North and told his team that he needed to "rally" China, South Korea, Russia, and Japan to present a united front against the regime in the North. The president invited Chinese leader Jiang Zemin to his ranch in Texas on October 25, where he made the case that the North was a threat not only to the United States but also to China and that they should work together to confront Kim Jong-il diplomatically. Jiang responded that the North was Bush's problem and that "exercising influence over North Korea is very complicated."

At this point in late 2002, Bush reaffirmed his strong tilt toward the hawks in the administration, deciding at an NSC meeting on November 13 that the U.S. goal would be to change the North's behavior through pressure, a policy described as "tailored containment." Bush compared dealing with Kim to dealing with his two daughters when they were little. When they wanted attention, they would throw their food on the floor. He and Laura would quickly pick it up. When they wanted attention again, they'd throw the food again. Regarding Kim, Bush said, "The United States is through picking up his food."

After briefing allies, the administration announced it would cut off the supply of heavy fuel oil to the North and secured the agreement of

South Korea, Japan, and the EU to follow suit. The last delivery of fuel was on November 18. Three days later, the North issued a statement blaming the United States for the collapse of the Agreed Framework. In December, North Korea informed the IAEA that it was restarting its reactor and reopening other facilities that had been frozen under the Agreed Framework. Within days, the North cut all the IAEA seals on its nuclear facilities and disrupted the monitoring equipment, then ordered all IAEA inspectors out of the country. In January 2003, the DPRK announced its withdrawal from the Nuclear Non-Proliferation Treaty.

Despite Jiang's earlier rebuff, Bush remained convinced that China, and Chinese pressure, was the key to getting the North to abandon its nuclear aspirations. In a January 2003 phone call, Bush told Jiang that if the North's nuclear program continued, he would be unable to stop Japan from developing its own nuclear weapons. He warned Jiang in February that if the problem couldn't be solved diplomatically, he "would have to consider a military strike against North Korea."

Then Bush invaded Iraq. The president's warnings, and the invasion, appear to have gotten the attention of the Chinese. In late April, the United States, China, and North Korea met in Beijing (where the North Koreans for the first time told the Americans they had nuclear weapons).

The Six-Party Talks the United States had sought to tackle the North Korean nuclear problem finally opened in Beijing on August 27, 2003. The participants were China, the United States, North and South Korea, Russia, and Japan. Four rounds of talks took place over the ensuing two years with not much to show for it. In June 2005, the DPRK refueled its reactor at Yongbyon and began reprocessing the 8,000 spent fuel rods removed earlier. In mid-September, the United States froze $24 million of North Korean funds in a Macau bank, funds rumored to be Kim Jong-il's personal piggy bank.

With the Six-Party Talks stalled, Secretary Rice visited Beijing on July 9–10. She was able to work out a compromise statement with Chinese foreign minister Li Zhaoxing that allowed for the possibility of the North keeping the nonthreatening parts of its nuclear infrastructure—those relating to peaceful nuclear energy—and even receiving a light-water nuclear reactor, but only after it had abandoned its nuclear weapons program. Probably due to Chinese pressure, the North announced two weeks later that it would return to the negotiating table.

The talks resumed in September and the participants agreed upon a set of principles to guide future negotiations, with the North concurring that it was "committed to abandoning all nuclear weapons and existing nuclear programs and returning, at an early date, to the Treaty on the Nonproliferation of Nuclear Weapons and to IAEA safeguards." North Korea asserted its right to peaceful nuclear energy, and the other parties "expressed their respect" and agreed to discuss "at an appropriate time" the subject of providing a light-water reactor to the DPRK. The Six also agreed to promote economic cooperation, including energy assistance to the North, and to negotiate a permanent peace regime on the Korean Peninsula "in an appropriate separate forum." With renewed hope of progress, the Six-Party Talks resumed in November only to stall out yet again for a variety of reasons, including the North's fixation with getting their $24 million unfrozen and their announcement that they would resume construction of two new reactors that had been suspended under the Agreed Framework. Same song, second verse.

Two actions by North Korea during the latter half of 2006 further iced diplomacy. On July 4, the North test-fired seven ballistic missiles, including its longest-range missile, the Taepodong-2. The latter failed less than a minute after launch, but the other tests appeared to be successful. The UN Security Council quickly passed a resolution condemning the launches and demanded that the DPRK suspend its missile activities and return to the Six-Party talks. The Security Council also imposed additional sanctions on the North, but without an enforcement mechanism. Three months later, on October 9, the North conducted an underground nuclear test. This time, its actions both angered and insulted the Chinese. Hu Jintao issued a statement saying: "The Chinese government strongly opposes this. We engaged in conversations to appeal to the North Koreans for restraint. However, our neighbor turned a deaf ear to our advice." In less than a week,

the Security Council unanimously passed another resolution imposing sanctions targeting military equipment and luxury goods, this
time with enforcement authority. Independently, the United States
targeted sanctions on North Korea's banking system.

Rice visited China again just eleven days after the nuclear test
and was asked if the United States would consider a resumption of
the Six-Party Talks. She told Hu Jintao that "China had to stop acting
like the meeting planner and take real responsibility for making the
Six-Party Talks work." She added that Bush might be willing to restart
the talks if there was a clear understanding with China on how to
proceed. The North agreed within two weeks to return to the talks.

The ups and downs of negotiating with North Korea over the last
two years of the Bush administration represented the triumph of hope
over experience—and continuation of the split within the administration. Rumsfeld had been skeptical of negotiations, later writing that in
Bush's second term "unambiguous records of deception, provocative
behavior, and broken promises stretching back decades were set aside
in the hope of obtaining reversals from countries such as . . . North
Korea through diplomatic engagement." He warned that "some problems cannot be solved through negotiations." Cheney was even more
skeptical than Rumsfeld and basically felt the administration was
being suckered. The dynamic in the administration changed when I
succeeded Rumsfeld at the end of 2006. I was deeply pessimistic the
North would ever give up its nuclear weapons, but I was prepared to
let the diplomacy play out, especially since we didn't exactly have a lot
of options. When it came to North Korea, apart from sanctions, there
weren't many nonmilitary instruments to play.

In January 2007, the U.S. negotiator, Ambassador Christopher
Hill, met with his North Korean counterpart in Berlin and reported
back to Rice that the North was prepared to shut down the reactor at
Yongbyon and readmit IAEA inspectors in exchange for their $24
million in frozen funds. Within a month, the Six-Party Talks had
resulted in agreement that the North would shut down its nuclear
facilities at Yongbyon in exchange for a shipment of 50,000 tons of
fuel oil. Then the North was to provide a complete declaration of all
its nuclear programs and disable all existing nuclear facilities, after

which it would receive an additional 950,000 tons of fuel oil. The
United States agreed to begin the process of removing Pyongyang
from the list of states supporting terrorism and to stop applying the
Trading with the Enemy Act to North Korea. The North got its $24 mil-
lion in late June, and the IAEA confirmed the shutdown of the Yongbyon nuclear facilities three weeks later.

The seeming breakthrough palled as new evidence emerged during the year of North Korea's continued cheating and intransigence.
In April, we were shown evidence by the Israelis of a nuclear reactor
under construction in Syria. The North Koreans were building it in
violation of all the promises about not proliferating their nuclear technology. Every senior official in the Bush administration agreed that we
could not allow the reactor to become operational even if we had to
destroy it ourselves, but Rice and I (and others) first wanted to expose
the reactor as an example of North Korean (and Syrian) perfidy. The
Israelis simply wanted to destroy it and did so on September 6, 2007.
Toward the end of the year, North Korea failed to meet the deadlines
for its declaration and for fully disabling the three nuclear facilities
at Yongbyon.

The last year of the Bush administration pitted the "glass half-
empty" Rice against the "empty glass" Cheney. Rice pointed out that
the North had taken significant steps toward disabling its known
nuclear capability, sealing and breaking down much of the infrastructure associated with Yongbyon, and readmitting IAEA inspectors.
The DPRK's plutonium production capability was inoperable. She
acknowledged that the North's uranium enrichment capability providing a second path to nuclear weapons was a serious concern that
had to be acknowledged by the North in its declaration and included
in the inspection regime. Cheney felt that the North was not living
up to its part of the bargain by refusing to admit the existence of its
enrichment program and denying its proliferation activities in Syria.
He argued that the Six-Party Talks simply provided the North a way to
hide what they were doing and that the United States was rewarding it
with "benefits and concessions in exchange for missed deadlines and
false declarations." It didn't help that the U.S. negotiator, Chris Hill,
was deeply mistrusted by almost everyone in the government, and

skeptics like Cheney were convinced they weren't being kept abreast of the negotiations or being told the full story.

On June 26, 2008, North Korea presented its long-awaited declaration, which failed to mention either its enrichment activities or its proliferation efforts. While the declaration reported the amount of plutonium North Korea had produced, it fell short by not providing the number of nuclear devices the North had made. A few days later, North Korea blew up the cooling tower at Yongbyon. Delivery of the declaration, as I said, was supposed to trigger removal of restrictions on the North imposed by the Trading with the Enemy Act as well as lifting the designation of the DPRK as a state sponsor of terrorism. (In a case of "you can't make this stuff up," the actual copy of the North Korean declaration handed over was covered with dust that contained particles of enriched uranium—which the North still denied having.) The inadequacies of the declaration sparked an intense debate inside the administration. Cheney was adamantly against rewarding "bad behavior." Nonetheless, the same day the declaration was delivered, Bush sent Congress the required notice that in forty-five days he would lift the terrorism designation.

To get at the enrichment program, Rice proposed coming at the problem indirectly by demanding that the North agree to a verification protocol that would ensure on-site inspections of all aspects of the North's nuclear program at sites both declared and undeclared. The proposal also would require the North to acknowledge its proliferation of nuclear technology and know-how to others (Syria). The forty-five-day waiting period passed, and on August 26, the North announced it was suspending its disablement work at Yongbyon because the United States had not lifted the terrorism designation and agreement on a verification protocol had not been a condition of the U.S. commitment. A month later, the IAEA announced that, at the North's request, it had completed removing the seals from the reprocessing facility and had been informed by Pyongyang that it would begin introducing nuclear material there in a week's time, and that inspectors would no longer have access to the plant.

In early October, Hill reported he had reached an oral agreement with the North on verification that would grant the inspectors access to all declared sites relating to plutonium production and access as well to undeclared sites based on "mutual consent." Inspectors would also be allowed to carry out "scientific procedures," such as soil sampling, at the declared sites. The agreement would consist of a written joint document and oral assurances that would need to be approved by the other four parties to the talks. The verification arrangements left a lot to be desired, and there was an intense debate in the Oval Office on October 9 over whether to take the DPRK off the state sponsors of terrorism list. The next day, the president authorized Rice to sign the de-listing document.

Then it all fell apart—again. On November 13, the North Korean Foreign Ministry issued a statement denying that the North had agreed to allow inspectors to take soil or nuclear waste samples from Yongbyon. The Six-Party Talks in Beijing on December 11 failed to reach agreement on verification, with the North taking the position that verification would be limited only to the plutonium reactor site at Yongbyon and that it would not be bound by any oral agreement Hill had with them.

Like Clinton before him, Bush had pushed the negotiating track hard. He authorized forward-leaning diplomacy, applied new economic sanctions and eased or lifted others, pressured Chinese leaders Jiang Zemin and Hu Jintao to lean on Kim Jong-il, and raised the specter of Japan acquiring its own nuclear weapons and the United States striking militarily, all to no avail. After years of negotiations, North Korea had taken no significant long-term steps to curtail its nuclear or missile programs.

Despite Clinton's and Bush's efforts, both bilaterally and in concert with other major powers, no progress was made over a sixteen-year span to limit the North's ambition to possess nuclear weapons and the missiles to deliver them. It took the United States too long to wise up to the North's tactics of creating a crisis, the United States and others making concessions to get them back to the table, and then Pyongyang routinely making and breaking promises and commitments. Yongbyon, for example, was opened and closed so many times it needed a revolving door. When Bush left office, diplomacy with the North was at a standstill.

The story of President Obama's interactions with North Korea is a short one. While in his inaugural address he told leaders seeking to sow conflict that "we will extend a hand if you are willing to unclench your fist," there were no letters of outreach to Kim Jong-il such as he wrote to the ayatollah nor any offer to "reset" as with Russia. The only overture was from Secretary of State Clinton, who, on a visit to South Korea in February 2009, in public remarks told the North Koreans that if they would completely and verifiably eliminate their nuclear weapons program, the Obama administration would be willing "to normalize relations, replace the peninsula's long-standing armistice with a permanent peace treaty, and assist in meeting the energy and other economic and humanitarian needs of the North Korean people." Kim Jong-il wasn't buying this any more than his father had.

During the first year of the Obama administration, the North dramatically accelerated the pace of both its nuclear and its missile programs. The North Koreans launched a long-range three-stage Unha-2 rocket on April 5 (a failed test). In response to a statement by the UN Security Council president calling for strengthening punitive measures as a consequence, on April 14 Pyongyang formally withdrew from the Six-Party Talks and announced it would reverse steps taken to disable its nuclear facilities under earlier agreements. It said it would fully reprocess the 8,000 spent fuel rods from Yongbyon to extract plutonium for nuclear weapons. Two days later, all IAEA and U.S. monitors were kicked out of Yongbyon. On May 25, the North conducted its second underground nuclear test. In the now familiar dance, the UN Security Council responded with a new round of financial and other sanctions, including a ban on further DPRK missile tests.

Diplomacy showed a faint pulse in August 2009, when former president Clinton visited Pyongyang to secure the release of two women journalists the regime had seized the previous March. The official North Korean news agency stated that the visit would help build bilateral confidence. In September, a State Department spokesman said Washington was prepared to enter into a bilateral discussion with the North as a first step toward reconvening the Six-Party Talks. The new U.S. special representative for Korea policy, Stephen Bosworth, subsequently led a delegation to Pyongyang in December.

On March 26, 2010, the North Koreans torpedoed and sank the South Korean warship *Cheonan*. As the year wore on, tensions only grew as new sanctions were imposed on the North. To make matters worse, on November 12 the North announced it had constructed a 2,000-centrifuge uranium enrichment facility at Yongbyon, and even showed it off to a visiting American scientist. On the 23rd, North Korean artillery barraged the South Korean island of Yeonpyeong, killing two soldiers, wounding seventeen, and injuring three civilians. Both the military and the civilian leadership in the South wanted to react strongly with aircraft and artillery. It took considerable pressure from the president, Secretary Clinton, the chairman of the Joint Chiefs of Staff, and me to persuade Seoul to respond in kind, limiting its response to hitting the artillery batteries responsible for the attack.

Although over the remaining years of the Obama administration there were periodic talks between the United States and North Korea and occasional half-steps toward resuming the Six-Party Talks, the death of Kim Jong-il on December 17, 2011, and succession of his son Kim Jong-un rang the death knell for diplomacy on Obama's watch. The administration adopted a policy of "strategic patience," presumably in the hope that sanctions would lead Pyongyang to change its ways or that the North would come to its senses. It didn't work.

Kim Jong-un was determined to accelerate the North's nuclear and missile programs. From 2012 to 2016, North Korea conducted missile tests on at least twenty separate occasions, including the testing of a submarine-launched ballistic missile. It also carried out three more nuclear tests. Kim Jong-un clearly was obsessed with demonstrating as quickly as possible that North Korea was a nuclear-armed state that could launch missiles capable of reaching targets in the United States. Throughout, the UN Security Council repeatedly passed resolutions condemning the North's actions and imposing new sanctions, to no avail.

During President Trump's first year in office, North Korea carried out missile launches on sixteen occasions, including the successful launch of an intercontinental ballistic missile on two occasions and at least one launch from a submarine. It also conducted yet another underground nuclear test. In an act demonstrating to the world Kim Jong-un's ruthlessness, on February 13, 2017, his older half-brother (and potential rival) was assassinated in Malaysia in an attack using the nerve agent VX. Everyone assumed Kim had ordered the killing.

Although a State Department official in April described U.S. policy toward North Korea under Trump as "maximum pressure and engagement" and Secretary of State Rex Tillerson said the United States was open to direct talks with the North on "the right agenda" with the goal of denuclearization, the emphasis was much more on pressure than engagement. The U.S. rhetoric was tough, asserting that Trump would not repeat the mistakes of his predecessors and that no sanctions would be lifted until denuclearization had taken place. There would be no "step-by-step" process.

Three new UN Security Council resolutions in 2017 further tightened the screws on the DPRK with a complete ban on exports of coal, iron, and seafood (August); a ban on textile exports and a cap on imports of petroleum products (September); and a reduction in refined petroleum products by 90 percent as well as expulsion of all North Korean workers from other countries within two years (December).

Beginning in late summer, Trump dramatically ramped up his rhetorical attacks on the North, on August 8 telling reporters that "North Korea best not make any more threats to the United States. . . . They will be met with fire and fury like the world has never seen." Three days later, he warned that "military solutions are now fully in place, locked and loaded, should North Korea act unwisely." On September 19, at the UN, Trump threatened to "totally destroy North Korea." Two days after that, Kim Jong-un responded with a statement calling Trump "mentally deranged" and threatening to make Trump "pay dearly for his speech." On November 7, Trump warned Kim not to underestimate the United States but also said that in order to begin talks, the North would first need to take steps toward denuclearization. Two weeks later, the president re-designated North Korea as a state sponsor of terrorism.

Even as Trump's rhetoric heated tensions between the United States and the North, a very different dynamic was playing out between Seoul and Pyongyang. On May 9, 2017, Moon Jae-in was elected president of the Republic of Korea and committed to a policy of engagement with the North. He kept Seoul's policy closely tied to that of the United States throughout 2017, hosting Trump's visit to Seoul in November and signing on to a joint statement that the two countries would work together to counter the North Korean threat and to encourage China to pressure the North to seek a diplomatic solution. But Moon had a different agenda than Trump.

The atmosphere between the United States and Pyongyang changed dramatically during the first three months of 2018, with the two Koreas leading the way. On January 1, Kim Jong-un offered to send a delegation to South Korea for the Olympic Games, even expressing a willingness to have the North participate in the games. The next day, the South said it was willing to meet the North at Panmunjom, and a hotline between the two was reestablished. On January 4, Trump and Moon agreed to postpone a joint military exercise until after the Olympics, and on January 9, representatives of the North and South met at Panmunjom for the first time in three years. The North announced it would send a delegation to the Olympics. Kim sent his sister as his representative, and she met with Moon on February 10, bringing an invitation for Moon to visit Pyongyang.

Moon's national security adviser, Chung Eui-yong, met with Kim in Pyongyang on March 6 and reported that the North had indicated a willingness to begin negotiations with the United States to discuss denuclearization and pledged not to conduct nuclear or missile tests during those talks. Two days later, Chung briefed Trump in the Oval Office about his meetings in Pyongyang and emerged from the briefing to announce that Trump had accepted an invitation to meet with Kim Jong-un by May "to achieve permanent denuclearization." No U.S. president had ever met with the leader of North Korea, and the

announcement had a stunning effect, especially after the heated rhetoric of the previous year.

Encouraging events followed in quick succession. CIA director
Mike Pompeo visited Pyongyang in early April to begin working out
the details of the summit, and a few days later Kim announced he
would suspend nuclear and missile testing. Kim Jong-un and Moon
Jae-in met in Pyongyang soon thereafter. They agreed to cooperate to
"establish a permanent and solid peace regime on the Korean peninsula." Kim then met with Chinese leader Xi Jinping, after which
Kim said he hoped there could be step-by-step measures to eventually
achieve denuclearization and lasting peace on the peninsula. Trump
announced the same day that Pompeo, now secretary of state, would
again go to Pyongyang to meet with Kim to prepare for the summit.
After a series of hiccups, including at one point Trump's cancella-
tion of the summit, on June 1, North Korean general Kim Yong-chol
met with Trump and delivered a letter from Kim Jung-un. Afterward
Trump announced the summit would take place as originally scheduled, on June 12 in Singapore.

Many foreign policy experts cringed at Trump's agreement to meet
with Kim. Some felt that a meeting with the U.S. president would be
a big political victory for Kim, legitimizing him. There was also the
risk of the inexperienced Trump cutting a deal with Kim that would
be disadvantageous to the United States, South Korea, or Japan by, for
example, agreeing to a limit on missile tests for long-range missiles
that might hit the United States but leave our allies exposed. In light of
the many failed attempts over the preceding quarter century to make
any headway in stopping the North's nuclear and missile programs, I
thought the agreement to meet was a risky but bold move that might
actually lead to a meaningful result.

In the event, fears of a quick, unwise deal were unfounded. The
atmospherics of the meeting in Singapore were positive and the agreements aspirational. North Korea committed to "work toward complete
denuclearization of the Korean Peninsula," and both sides committed
to recovering POW/MIA remains from the Korean War. Kim said he
would destroy a missile engine test site, and Trump agreed to sus-

pend U.S.–South Korean military exercises, which the president complained were "tremendously expensive."

The ensuing eight months followed a familiar pattern. Pompeo, after visiting Pyongyang on July 5–7, 2018, called his talks "productive" and "good faith negotiations," while the North Korean foreign ministry's statement referred to U.S. proposals as "unilateral and robber-like denuclearization demands" that went "against the spirit of the North-U.S. summit meeting." In congressional testimony later in the month, Pompeo acknowledged that the North was continuing to produce fissile material. Two days later, the remains of fifty-five American servicemen from the Korean War were returned to the United States. In August, the IAEA expressed "grave concern" in its annual report over the further development of the DPRK's nuclear program, and on August 24, Trump called off another Pompeo trip to North Korea because of a lack of progress on denuclearization. However, the secretary of state did return to Pyongyang in early October, when arrangements for a second Trump-Kim meeting were discussed. In November, Vice President Pence conceded that the United States would not require a complete list of nuclear weapons and missile sites from the North prior to a second summit meeting, although "a verifiable plan" to disclose that information had to be agreed to at the summit.

Trump and Kim Jong-un met a second time, on February 27–28, 2019, in Hanoi. The summit ended without agreement. The United States claimed that the North had called for sanctions to be lifted entirely in exchange for partial denuclearization, while the North Korean foreign minister said that the North had asked for the partial removal of sanctions in exchange for a permanent halt to nuclear and ballistic missile testing as well as the verifiable dismantlement of the facilities at Yongbyon. Regardless, Trump walked away from the table and Kim returned home empty-handed and embarrassed.

In the weeks after the Hanoi meeting, the two sides remained far apart. The United States was firm in its unwillingness to make concessions on sanctions relief without first seeing at least some significant steps by the North toward denuclearization. Pyongyang, on the other hand, insisted on at least some significant sanctions relief before tak-

ing steps toward denuclearization. As the weeks passed, Kim manifested his growing impatience by resuming visits to military units
and weapons sites and witnessing the test of a short-range guided
missile. Trump, in an Oval Office meeting with South Korean president Moon Jae-in on April 11, indicated that a piecemeal, step-by-step
approach to negotiations might be possible, but basically ruled out
easing sanctions without a commitment by the North to complete
denuclearization. The next day, Kim gave a major speech, declaring
that "if the United States sticks to its current political calculations, it
will darken the prospects for solving the problem and will in fact be
very dangerous." Kim also made clear he wanted nothing further to
do with Secretary Pompeo. Putting both China and the United States
on notice that he had other options, at the end of April Kim met with
Putin in Vladivostok.

At Trump's initiative, the two leaders met again on June 30 at Panmunjom in the Demilitarized Zone separating the two Koreas. The
brief meeting, with Trump's steps across the line into North Korea,
was a colorful photo opportunity but the results were meaningless.

For all the rhetoric and photo opportunities of the three summit
meetings, by mid-2019, Trump had made no more progress toward
North Korean denuclearization than had his three predecessors. He
had made three major concessions: agreeing to meet with Kim in
the first place, a political boon for the North; a cessation of major
U.S.–South Korean military exercises; and placing the North's declaration of its nuclear facilities, weapons, and nuclear material well
down on the negotiating agenda. In return, the North had dismantled
a clapped-out missile launch facility, claimed (without any independent verification) to have destroyed major elements of a nuclear test
site that was reportedly collapsing due to the test of a small thermo-
nuclear device there, and returned the remains of dozens of American
servicemen.

Over a quarter of a century, four very different American presidents tried with three North Korean leaders to end the North's
nuclear weapons program. The United States employed a number of

instruments of power to achieve that goal: military demonstrations of power; a remarkable and wide-ranging array of economic sanctions, some unilateral and some imposed by the UN Security Council; humanitarian assistance, especially food aid; and repeated offers not only to lift sanctions but to assist in the economic development of the DPRK (which included showing a video Trump had made of development potential in the North—a real estate developer's ploy). Nothing worked. North Korea retains its entire nuclear and ballistic missile enterprise. While the number of its nuclear weapons remains uncertain, the arsenal may number in the dozens and is growing.

For years, the United States has seen China as the indispensable source of leverage on North Korea in negotiations. In the effort to get China to lean more heavily on Pyongyang to negotiate denuclearization, there have been countless trips to Beijing and countless conversations between presidents and other senior U.S. leaders with their Chinese counterparts. China will participate in sanctions, but never to the extent that they threaten to break the regime in Pyongyang. Beijing's highest priority is to avoid collapse in the North, which would send millions of refugees across the Chinese border and destabilize the Korean Peninsula. A related concern is that instability in the North could lead to reunification of the Peninsula, but on the South's terms and in alliance with the United States. U.S. policy makers, I believe, have often overestimated China's influence in Pyongyang, as Jiang Zemin, Hu Jintao, and Xi Jinping all have cautioned their U.S. counterparts. Indeed, there are reports that many of the senior North Korean military officers Kim has executed, including his uncle, were useful channels of information and influence for China.

One definition of insanity is doing the same thing over and over again and expecting different results. That perhaps characterizes the post–Cold War U.S. effort to negotiate an end to North Korea's nuclear program. One thing seems clear: North Korea has no intention of *ever* completely giving up its nuclear weapons capability and the means to deliver such weapons. Three generations of Kims have seen the capability as essential to the North's—and their own—survival. Events over the past fifteen or so years can only have hardened that conviction. They observed Qaddafi give up his nuclear program and soon be eliminated; Saddam Hussein, who had no nuclear weapons, is also dead, his regime gone; and Ukraine, which gave up some 1,500 nuclear weapons in 1994 in exchange for guarantees of its territorial integrity from Russia, the United States, and Britain, has lost Crimea and the eastern half of its territory.

At some point, we must come face-to-face with reality. The only way to eliminate North Korea's nuclear program is militarily—at the cost of a major war (potentially including China) with casualties at least in the hundreds of thousands on both sides of the DMZ and with the significant likelihood we will be unable to find and target all the hidden underground storage and deployment sites. With the instruments of power available, if neither force nor nonmilitary instruments will work, what option is left?

Obama's strategy of "strategic patience," Trump's de facto policy, will only see the North's arsenal of nuclear weapons grow. A goal of more than a few U.S. policy makers has been to solve the North's nuclear challenge through regime change. A number have believed that if we squeeze the North hard enough economically, a cabal of senior North Korean military officers—probably pro-Chinese—will kill Kim and create an alternative path forward for the DPRK. The longevity of the regime and the ruthlessness of all the Kims (especially Kim Jong-un) in executing anyone who might pose a threat make regime change a slender reed upon which to hang a policy. And, of course, there is no evidence to suggest one or another of those generals would retreat from the nuclear program. They may, in fact, believe just as strongly as Kim that survival of the DPRK depends upon those weapons.

As we look back over the repeated failures of diplomacy and sanctions, perhaps we need to acknowledge that North Korea provides an example where the exercise of a range of instruments of power has failed to achieve our strategic goal of comprehensive denuclearization and will do so for the foreseeable future. Perhaps, then, we should change the goal, lower our sights, and seek an agreement that limits the North's nuclear weapons arsenal to a very small number of weapons; dismantles their capability to make more such weapons through either reprocessing or enrichment; bans all future testing

of both nuclear devices and ballistic missiles; and establishes verification arrangements that provide reasonable assurance that these
serial cheaters and liars do not cheat again—or, at the least, provide
us with the capability to catch them before their cheating becomes
strategically meaningful. And perhaps, one day, after the Kim family
regime has passed into history, a new government will emerge more
committed to the well-being of its people and willing to give up its
nuclear arsenal to achieve that objective.

Failure of such an approach—and based on the record, I acknowledge it would be a long shot—would leave us no worse off than we
are now. I can hear hard-liners gasping in horror, but what alternative
do they have to offer apart from a growing North Korean threat (the
status quo) or a major war?

CHAPTER 12

China

Competition, Conflict, or Something New?

The future is hard to predict in China, although I'm still betting on the triumph there of the tidal wave of freedom that is sweeping across our world.

—Ronald Reagan

If people have commercial incentives, whether it's in China or in other totalitarian systems, the move to democracy becomes inexorable.

—George H. W. Bush

Greater trade and involvement would bring more prosperity to Chinese citizens . . . and, we hoped, the advance of personal freedom and human rights.

—Bill Clinton

I believed that, over time, the freedom inherent in the market would lead people to demand liberty in the public square.

—George W. Bush

I believe in a future where China is a strong, prosperous and successful member of the community of nations; a future when our nations are partners out of necessity, but also out of opportunity.

—Barack Obama

S uch high hopes.
    China will be the most complex, the most daunting, and, potentially, the most dangerous of the many foreign challenges the United States will face in the years ahead. A generation after America became the sole superpower, another has risen to challenge our political, economic, ideological, and institutional dominance. Contrary to the hopes of the early 1990s, the collapse of the Soviet Union did not mark the final victory of liberal democracy but rather the end of just another battle in the age-old conflict between those who believe the state exists to serve the people and those who believe the people serve the state and those who control it.

American political leaders across the spectrum, as well as businesspeople and the intelligentsia, believed that long contest would go our way in China, based not on evidence or observation but rather on the *assumption* that a richer China would be a freer, more open China. Maybe that will happen one day, but not anytime soon.

At the same time, I do not believe military conflict between the United States and China is inevitable, that a rising power and a declining or static power at some point must go to war—the so-called Thucydides trap based on the ancient conflict between a declining Athens and a rising Sparta. A long competition between China and America is already upon us. If leaders in both Beijing and Washington are wise, that competition will remain peaceful and include areas of cooperation. It will, hopefully, be waged primarily with nonmilitary instruments of power. For now, at least, China, with all of its very real problems, has the advantage in that arena, partly because it has a wide range of important assets and a strategic focus on how to use them, and partly because over the last thirty years we have weakened so many of our own capabilities, are so politically divided at home, and have no strategy for a decades-long competition with China.

T he U.S.-Chinese relationship between 1971 and 1991 was primarily geostrategic for both sides, a collaboration targeted against the Soviet Union, which in the 1970s had a million troops deployed along the border with China. Richard Nixon's epic visit to China in 1972 was all about Beijing becoming a strategic partner in containing the USSR. I was special assistant to National Security Adviser Zbigniew Brzezinski working in the West Wing of the Carter White House when U.S.-Chinese relations were normalized and Deng Xiaoping visited from January 29 to February 4, 1979. At that meeting, Carter and Deng reached a secret agreement to cooperate in building technical intelligence collection sites in western China to monitor Soviet missile tests, and I accompanied CIA director Stansfield Turner to China in late December 1980 to implement the agreement. There was little discussion of bilateral economic matters in those days, and Carter, for all his commitment to promoting human rights around the world, did not make much of China's lamentable record in that regard.

By the end of Carter's presidency in January 1981, even though geopolitics continued to dominate U.S.-Chinese relations, dramatic changes were under way inside China that would reshape the bilateral relationship for the next four decades, changes necessitated by staggeringly catastrophic internal decisions by Mao Zedong. China went seriously off the rails in 1958 when his Great Leap Forward, intended to transform China from an agrarian country to a socialist society through rapid industrialization and collectivization of agriculture, led to a famine that cost between 30 million and 55 million lives. In 1959–60, the damage to the country was so great that Mao, the "Great Helmsman," was forced to let go of the tiller and step down as president, yielding power to Deng Xiaoping, among others. Deng pursued economic reforms in the early 1960s aimed at restoring the economy after the Great Leap, and thus he and his closest allies were high on the target list when, in 1966, Mao rallied politically and launched the Cultural Revolution (the "Great Proletarian Cultural Revolution"), purging, as he put it, the remnants of capitalist and traditional China, which included all those who had opposed him, beginning with Deng. Purged of all offices in 1969, Deng spent the next four years working in a rural tractor factory. Along with him, millions of bureaucrats and university students were sent to the countryside to work, millions were persecuted, and between 400,000 and 3 million were killed or committed suicide. Most universities were closed from 1966 to 1972, setting Chinese education, science, and technology back a generation.

When Premier Zhou Enlai was diagnosed with cancer, he was able to persuade Mao in 1974 to rehabilitate Deng and make him first vice-premier and Zhou's likely successor. Deng once more focused his attention on rejuvenating the Chinese economy. After Zhou's death in early 1976, a radical leftist group led by Mao's wife—the Gang of Four—again came after Deng, who was purged once more. Fortunately for China, and for Deng, Mao died in September 1976 and the Gang of Four was itself purged the next month, paving the way for Deng's return to power. He was restored to his senior posts in mid-1977 and by 1981 was China's "paramount leader," although he never took the official position as head of the party or premier. In the late 1970s, he was finally able to initiate the economic reforms that set the stage for China's remarkable economic growth over the next forty years.

Determined to prevent another Chinese leader from becoming as singularly powerful, and dangerous, as Mao, and to prevent such a person from again doing such terrible damage to China, Deng took steps to ensure no one could again amass so much power. Above all, he enshrined in the constitution in 1982 that the president of China would be limited to two 5-year terms in an effort to institutionalize collective leadership.

Just a few years into China's economic boom, its leaders confronted two challenges of historic consequence: one, to their internal authority, was the massive protest at Tiananmen Square; and the other, internationally, was the collapse of communism in Eastern Europe and the Soviet Union. Both occurred between June 1989 and December 1991. These climactic events determined the Chinese leaders' internal strategy: there could be no political reform or loosening of the political control of the Communist Party, unlike in Gorbachev's USSR; and economic growth would be of paramount importance, especially as it had become the only source of legitimacy for the regime.

A too quickly forgotten aspect of the events surrounding Tiananmen Square was that the architect of China's economic reforms, Deng Xiaoping, personally had labeled the student demonstrators as counterrevolutionaries and sent a powerful message that political reform—greater democracy and political rights—was not part of his agenda. Too many in the West saw the smiling, elfin Deng and lost sight of the reality that he was a ruthless and cunning authoritarian determined to make China a world power again.

President George H. W. Bush tried to preserve the strategic relationship with China after the massacre at Tiananmen Square, but events at home and abroad conspired against him. The liberation of Eastern Europe in the latter half of 1989 and its sudden transition to democracy and freedom stood in stark contrast to the repression in China. Further, as the Soviet Union itself began to totter, the geostrategic importance of China to the United States for twenty years as a counterweight and strategic partner quickly faded, opening the way for members of Congress to demand linkage between China's desire for increased trade with improving its record in observing human rights. Bush resisted efforts by congressional Democrats to formally establish that link throughout 1990 and 1991, and the accusation that he was "coddling dictators" worked against him in the 1992 election.

Bush's opponent, Bill Clinton, embraced that linkage mainly because it was good politics and because it allowed him to be tougher on a key foreign policy issue than his Republican opponent. As one observer wrote, "For him, linking the protection of human rights to the extension of trading privileges to China followed the logic of partisan and electoral politics."

During the first few months of his presidency, Clinton firmly linked the future growth of U.S.-Chinese trade with performance on human rights, demanding political changes in China so far-reaching as to potentially change the very nature of the regime. Even as he asked Congress not to legislate the linkage between human rights and trade for a year, Clinton signed an executive order on May 28, 1993, conditioning renewal of Most-Favored-Nation status (MFN, granting concessions on tariffs and import quotas) in 1994. This came after the secretary of state's determination, among other things, that China had made "overall, significant" progress with respect to adherence to the Universal Declaration of Human Rights and had provided an acceptable accounting for Chinese citizens imprisoned or detained for the nonviolent expression of their political and religious beliefs, "including in such expression of beliefs in connection with the Democracy Wall and Tiananmen Square movements." Other conditions were that China ensure humane treatment of prisoners, including allowing access to prisons by international humanitarian and human rights organizations; protection of Tibet's distinctive religious and cultural heritage; and permission for international radio and television broadcasting into China.

In March 1994, three months ahead of Clinton's deadline, Secretary of State Warren Christopher flew to Beijing to persuade the Chinese to comply with Clinton's conditions. The visit, marked by bitter exchanges, was a complete failure. Premier Li Peng bluntly told Christopher that China "would never accept the United States's concept of human rights." Political reform was a price China would not pay for expanded economic ties. By May, the Chinese had made a couple of very modest gestures, such as agreeing to an "understanding" on the prison labor issue and saying it would adhere to the Universal Declaration on Human Rights, which gave Clinton cover to throw in the towel on linkage. As he later wrote, "Because our engagement had produced some positive results, I decided . . . to extend MFN and, for the future, to delink our human rights efforts from trade." His rationale? "The United States had a big stake in bringing China into the global community. Greater trade and involvement would bring more prosperity to Chinese citizens; more contacts with the outside world; more cooperation on problems like North Korea, where we needed it; greater adherence to the rules of international law; and, we hoped, the advance of personal freedom and human rights." He was right about greater prosperity for Chinese citizens; about the rest, not so much.

Henceforth, economics would dominate the U.S.-Chinese relationship—and almost entirely on Chinese terms. It was an instrument of power China wielded with great effectiveness under successive leaders. The playing field was never level. As China's manufacturing sector grew, so too did the trade imbalance with the United States as we imported ever-increasing quantities of goods of every kind, usually resulting in lower prices for American consumers but at the cost of jobs in the U.S. manufacturing sector. China embraced practices that structurally disadvantaged American and other foreign companies eager to participate in the world's largest market. In many cases, the Chinese required foreign firms to share their most sophisticated technologies in order to sell to or manufacture in China; in others, they simply stole technologies and intellectual property. According to a 2017 commission led by former U.S. ambassador to China Jon Huntsman and former director of national intelligence Admiral Dennis Blair, Chinese spying and cyber attacks stealing trade secrets cost the U.S. economy between $225 billion and $600 billion a year. American music and movies were bootlegged and sold in China. Restrictions were placed on joint ventures, often requiring Chinese-majority ownership. The Chinese bought American firms to acquire access to their technology. State-owned enterprises, with heavy subsidies, undercut foreign prices and gained trade advantages all over the world. Beijing manipulated regulations, licensing, and enforcement, including rigged customs inspections, and foreign participation in some areas of the economy was prohibited altogether. In order to access the Chinese market and to manufacture in China, U.S. companies acquiesced in these practices. Indeed, beginning in the early 1990s, American business became a powerful lobby in Washington for a cooperative U.S.-Chinese relationship. Successive U.S. presidents protested these unfair Chinese policies and practices but failed to use our own economic power as leverage to demand—and get—change.

During the years after the liberation of Eastern Europe and collapse of the Soviet Union, when American supremacy was at its apex, China needed to be cautious. It was therefore no coincidence that Deng's Twenty-Four-Character strategy was first articulated in 1990: "Observe calmly, secure our position, cope with affairs calmly, hide our capacities and bide our time, be good at maintaining a low profile, and never claim leadership." In short, don't panic, lie low, build strength. Deng's "hide and bide" strategy was very much in keeping with the wisdom of Sun Tzu's sixth-century BC treatise *The Art of War*, where he wrote that "to subdue the enemy without fighting is the supreme excellence." Avoiding conflict with the United States and any confrontation that might hinder Chinese economic growth were of paramount importance to China's rise. Deng was all about increasing Chinese power in ways that did not set off alarm bells in the United States, encouraged foreign investment and trade, and avoided both an arms race and economic retaliation. Still, there should have been no mistaking Deng's objective of unchallenged Chinese dominance in Asia and someday matching and then overtaking the United States in terms of global power.

Bill Clinton announced on January 10, 2000, that he planned to extend Permanent Normal Trade Relations Status to China. In March, he spoke at Johns Hopkins University's School of Advanced International Studies and stated his support for China's joining the World Trade Organization (WTO), again sounding an optimistic note: "By joining the WTO, China is not simply agreeing to import more of our products; it is agreeing to import one of democracy's most cherished values: economic freedom. . . . When individuals have the power not just to dream, but to realize their dreams, they will demand a greater say." Congress approved Clinton's proposals that spring, and China joined the WTO on December 11, 2001. Membership theoretically subjected China to a rules-based equitable global trading system—that is, if China chose to play by the rules, which it often did not. Meanwhile, WTO membership provided a steroidal boost to the Chinese economy. In 1980, U.S.-Chinese trade was $5 billion; in 2000, it was $16 billion. By 2017, it was over $600 billion.

The significant increase in Chinese assertiveness internationally began with Jiang Zemin and Hu Jintao. In 1999, during the latter years of Jiang's leadership, China adopted the Going Global strategy, an initiative designed not only to break with Mao's policy of self-reliance but also to take advantage of the dramatic growth of the global economy by investing abroad. Going Global hit its stride with membership in the WTO. Chinese investment abroad, especially by state-owned enterprises, soared from $3 billion in 1991 to $35 billion in 2003 and $92 billion in 2007. During Hu's presidency, China rose from the sixth- to the second-largest economy in the world and managed to glide through the 2008 economic crisis largely unscathed.

China's dramatic economic growth, and accompanying monumental internal infrastructure programs, demanded massive inputs of fuel, food, minerals, and other imports and thus propelled Beijing's deal making in Africa and elsewhere. Beginning in 2005, Chinese direct investment in Africa increased thirtyfold, and by 2009 China had supplanted the United States as Africa's largest trading partner.

In November that same year, Obama visited China, where he received a "lukewarm" reception, not to mention a number of lectures on America's economic and budgetary problems. China's leaders were feeling "ascendant and assertive," especially given the apparent discrediting of the American economic model because of the Great Recession of 2008–9. As Secretary Clinton wrote, "hide and bide" had been supplanted by "show and tell." There would be a number of instances of China flexing its military and economic muscle during the remainder of Hu's leadership. Beijing's growing assertiveness was not the whim of an aggressive individual but rather a broadly supported policy of a newly confident leadership.

Xi Jinping became general secretary of the Communist Party and chairman of the Central Military Commission on November 15, 2012, and was "elected" president on March 14, 2013. He quickly consolidated his power at home, within a year or so sidelining any notion of collective leadership and gathering more personal power than any leader since Deng—and perhaps since Mao. Within months of becoming leader, he created (and appointed himself to head) a number of "Central Leading Groups," essentially allowing him to bypass the bureaucracy in virtually every arena of governance. He undertook an anticorruption campaign aimed at both miscreant officials and his political enemies. Several hundred thousand lower-level officials and dozens of senior party members were soon caught up in the dragnet, with punishments ranging from fines and warnings to execution.

On the day of his selection as general secretary in November 2012, Xi observed that the Chinese people "expect better education, more stable jobs, better income, more reliable social security, medical care of a higher standard, more comfortable living conditions, and a more beautiful environment." The next month, Xi traveled to the countryside, calling for further economic reform—and for strengthening the military. On this trip he first proclaimed the importance of the "China Dream," never clearly articulated but widely understood to mean prosperity at home as well as recognition of China's return to the global stage as a major power. The China Dream was, in essence, an appeal to nationalism. Xi later called for more economic reform, and at a Party plenum in November 2013, he announced that market forces would begin to play a decisive role in the future and that China welcomed foreign and private investment.

THE CHINESE SYMPHONY

Over the course of a generation, led by Hu Jintao and Xi Jinping, the Chinese have developed and strengthened a number of the instruments of power necessary to achieve dominance in Asia and beyond. China has many internal problems, but no other modern nation—apart from the United States during the Cold War—has assembled such a broad and sophisticated set of tools to expand its power and influence around the world.

The Military. On February 20, 1995, the Philippine navy, in the shadow of two U.S. warships, challenged Chinese ships at Mischief Reef in the South China Sea and replaced Chinese flags with Philippine flags. The Chinese backed down that day. U.S. secretary of defense William Cohen publicly stated, "Mischief Reef is a territory of the Philippines hence that is why we sent our warships to support the Philippine Navy in reclaiming what belongs to them." Later in the year, though, the Chinese reclaimed the reef. The United States would never again so directly challenge China militarily over its claims to disputed reefs and islands in the region or its construction of military facilities on them. Acting strongly and consistently at the outset of Beijing's aggressive claims would have been the only way to have deterred them, an opportunity lost after that February day.

When, in March 1996, the Chinese carried out threatening missile tests and exercises aimed at influencing the Taiwanese presidential vote, President Clinton deployed two aircraft carrier strike groups to the region. The Chinese again stood down in the face of superior forces. The Chinese response was similar to that of the Soviet Union after the Cuban Missile Crisis, when the Soviets, forced to retreat in the face of American strategic superiority (while pocketing a secret agreement removing U.S. missiles from Turkey), resolved never to be in that position again and began a massive buildup of their strategic forces. In 1996, the Chinese almost immediately began a significant expansion of their military power, especially the navy. Over the next twenty years, China's declared military budget rose from $20 billion in 1998 to $170 billion in 2018, with a focus on military modernization and advanced weaponry development. And that was just the "official" budget.

Many of China's military modernization programs began under Jiang Zemin and Hu Jintao. During their tenures, the Chinese navy greatly expanded its submarine fleet, including ballistic missile–launching subs; commissioned its first aircraft carrier and began building a second; initiated a major shipbuilding program as well as anti-ship missile programs; and began developing stealth fighter aircraft. By 2019, China had built the region's largest navy, with over three hundred surface ships and submarines and, according to the Department of Defense, planned to deploy as many as seventy-eight submarines by 2020.

While there were vast increases in funding for modernization programs before Xi, especially under Hu, corruption in the People's Liberation Army (PLA) was rampant, with senior officers buying promotions and stealing money. Further, there were at least three occasions when it appeared that the military took action without first informing the civilian leadership, much less seeking its approval, suggesting that Hu was not fully in control of the PLA: an anti-satellite test in January 2007; the Chinese navy's harassment of the U.S. Navy ship *Impeccable* in March 2009; and the public rollout of the J-20 stealth fighter during my visit to China in January 2011.

The old ways of doing military business changed under Xi, who dramatically purged and restructured the military to rid it of corruption, improve its competence, and ensure its obedience and loyalty to the Party (and to Xi). More than a hundred officers were sacked, and the vice chairman of the Central Military Commission—my host during a 2011 visit—escaped likely execution only by dying of bladder cancer. In 2015, Xi cut the PLA by 300,000 soldiers. He separated the operational command structure from training and acquisition, and created five joint-service commands responsible for integrating air, land, naval, and other capabilities—all very similar to the way the U.S. military is organized and operates. The net effect was to make the Chinese military a much more combat-ready, capable force.

The military has become more aggressive under Xi, especially in the East and South China Seas. In November 2013, a year after Xi took over the leadership, China declared a vast "air defense identification zone" (ADIZ) over the East China Sea, requiring all foreign aircraft to report their flight plan to the Chinese government, maintain radio contact with Chinese authorities, and follow Chinese instructions. The Chinese ADIZ included the airspace over islands administered by Japan and significantly overlapped the Japanese ADIZ. The United States said it would ignore the new Chinese rules, but most civilian airlines complied. Also in 2013, unchallenged by the United States, the Chinese began dredging in the disputed Spratly Islands in the South China Sea, the beginning of a large-scale island-building effort establishing a permanent Chinese presence. In September 2015, Xi pledged to Obama during a visit to the White House that China would not militarize the islands. He lied. Several new islands created by China were fortified, with their airstrips often being used by military aircraft. Under Xi, Chinese naval and air forces exercised more aggressively near Taiwan and also around Japanese islands. In September 2015, several Chinese warships ventured as far north as the Bering Strait and entered U.S. territorial waters off Alaska. Two years later, a Chinese flotilla exercised in the Mediterranean on its way to the Baltic Sea for joint exercises with the Russians. Meanwhile, the Chinese established their first overseas navy base, in Djibouti, and others are likely to follow as China expands its area of naval operations into the Indian Ocean and Arabian Sea to protect its oil supply line and commercial interests, and to show the flag.

Military strength is the ultimate instrument of power. While on a global basis China lags behind the United States and Russia and is a distant third in nuclear capabilities, it seeks a global presence and aims eventually to supplant the United States as the dominant military power in Asia. That ambition is not a pipe dream.

Economic Power. Until fairly recently, the American economy dwarfed that of China. As an instrument of power to advance our geopolitical interests, we have used it far less adroitly. Since the 1960s or so, the United States has used its economic power principally through sanctions to punish countries and individuals or to pressure them to change behavior or policies. It has reached the point that if a government offends us in almost any way, we slap sanctions on them. We have weaponized sanctions and layered them so much that it is difficult for U.S. companies, not to mention the firms of our friends and allies, to keep track. We have ample economic sticks to inflict pain.

We are, however, really short on carrots. The U.S. government cannot mobilize our private sector, the locus of American economic power, to advance our interests. The government cannot direct American companies to invest in specific countries and has limited resources at its disposal for development assistance (or inducements). Additionally, our economic assistance comes with strings attached in terms of observance of human rights, anticorruption efforts, and restrictions on contracting. Recipient countries must also run a gauntlet of often embarrassing congressional and media attention airing any dirty laundry a government or leader may have. Once the assistance is granted, the U.S. government seems to work overtime to make sure no one—including in the receiving country—knows about it, with PEPFAR in Africa one of the few exceptions.

In contrast, over the years, China has become the foremost practitioner in the world of geo-economics—the use of economic instruments of power to achieve unrelated political and strategic objectives even as it pursues its economic interests. China's include development assistance, trade, investment, and economic coercion. It has an ample supply of both carrots and sticks. Because of the structure of Chinese authoritarian state capitalism, the government in Beijing can direct both its massive state-owned enterprises and its banks to allocate large sums of money and people to specific initiatives and leverage its economic power both to promise great benefits for working with China or to bring great pressure on governments that oppose or try to thwart its policies. The favored U.S. stick, sanctions, usually requires the cooperation of other countries to have much hope of success. The Chinese, on the other hand, have applied sanctions rarely, and then primarily as part of international efforts to induce countries, including North Korea and Iran, to go to the negotiating table. In the long competition for global power and influence that lies ahead between the United States and China, the latter has a strong advantage in the flexibility that its system provides to use the instruments of economic power—in being able to leverage its economy more effectively than the United States. Let's see how.

In recent years, Xi Jinping's 2013 Belt and Road infrastructure initiative has garnered global attention, but it builds on a long history of such Chinese projects. One of the earliest major projects, and for years the most well-known, was construction between 1970 and 1975 of the Tanzam Railway in Africa, a $500 million undertaking that linked landlocked Zambia with the Tanzanian port of Dar es Salaam. The project, funded with an interest-free thirty-year loan, was first embraced by Mao in 1965 as part of an effort to win influence in Africa at Soviet expense. From early on, Chinese development assistance and investment have consistently been intended to advance Beijing's political as well as its economic interests. Altruism has never been on the agenda. Witness the fact that Chinese humanitarian assistance after natural disasters in other countries has for years been ridiculously small given the size of its economy.

According to AidData at the College of William & Mary, between 2000 and 2014, predating the Belt and Road Initiative, China provided $355 billion globally in official financing of projects, more than 70 percent of them infrastructure. In Africa alone, from 2000 to 2013, there were 2,300 Chinese projects worth $94 billion, about half of them transport, storage, energy, mining, and construction infrastructure projects. The Chinese will extend assistance to anybody if it suits their strategic purposes. While they don't necessarily advantage authoritarian or corrupt governments (although the leaders of such governments seem to benefit significantly personally), internal policies are no obstacle to Chinese development assistance or investment. Authoritarian regimes need not worry about pesky questions from the Chinese regarding human rights, political freedom, or corruption—the kinds of questions so often associated with assistance from the United States or international financial institutions.

The Chinese do impose their own conditions on potential recipients. According to AidData, countries that consistently vote with China in the UN General Assembly are more likely to get higher levels of aid and investment. China also insists that recipients of its investment recognize the "One China" policy and cut all ties with Taiwan. In 2008, the Chinese induced Costa Rica to take such an action by tying it to the purchase of $300 million in Costa Rican bonds. Within five years of China's earliest investments in Africa, the number of African governments recognizing Taiwan "fell from thirteen (roughly half of all states to recognize Taipei globally) to four."

There are other examples of China using its aid and investment to strategic advantage. From the time of China's earliest investments abroad to the present, China has worked to lock up access to the natural resources needed to continue its economic growth, including oil, gas, and minerals. As Chinese companies acquired mines and other natural resources in Africa, the workforce at many locations was primarily Chinese, construction was carried out by Chinese, and there was little attention to environmental damage or the consequences for local communities. In a number of cases, there was growing local criticism but, until fairly recently, little consequence inasmuch as local politicians' palms had been heavily greased.

China's assistance programs in Africa have also included the construction of high-profile facilities, such as sports arenas, highways, and other infrastructure projects, prominently located in big cities and often a source of pride to locals who let visitors know who built those facilities. In contrast, whereas the United States may have done far more through its assistance programs to help the local population, its role is often unknown. As Secretary Clinton observed, "Few people could identify tangible symbols of American aid."

At the same time, China uses "coercive economic diplomacy" to punish countries whose policies—political, military, or economic—run counter to Chinese interests and to pressure them for change. In 2010, a Chinese fishing trawler collided with two Japanese coast guard boats near the disputed Senkaku/Diaoyu Islands. The Japanese arrested the Chinese trawler captain. In retaliation, the Chinese restricted the export of rare earth minerals to Japan, minerals critical to industry and especially Japanese production of electronic components. Also in 2010, after Chinese dissident Liu Xiaobo was awarded the Nobel Peace Prize, undeterred by the fact that the Norwegian government has no role in the selection of Nobel Prize recipients, Beijing imposed severe restrictions on the import of Norwegian salmon; salmon imports from Norway dropped 60 percent in 2011. In 2012, Philippine warships arrested Chinese fishermen near Scarborough Shoal, a contested area. In retaliation, the Chinese refused to allow the import of Philippine bananas, slowed the import of other Philippine agricultural products, and discouraged Chinese tourism to the Philippines. Beijing relented only after an agreement by both sides to withdraw their ships from around the shoal (in violation of the agreement, Chinese fishing boats remained). When South Korea agreed to deploy the U.S. Terminal High-Altitude Area Defense (THAAD) missile system in 2016, China imposed a number of coercive economic measures on Seoul, including cuts in tourism and restrictions on certain categories of imports, such as automobiles. Based on alleged fire code violations, China also shut down ninety Korean-owned Lotte Mart stores in China. (Lotte had provided the land for the THAAD deployment.)

China is the largest trading partner for more than eighty countries around the world (the Chinese claim 130). As Beijing's global economic reach continues to grow, its use of bilateral coercive economic measures will increase in importance as a unique instrument of political power. After the 1950s and 1960s, the United States had rarely used economic leverage for an unrelated political purpose. Then Trump came along and threatened to impose draconian tariffs unless Mexico addressed the immigration problem on the U.S. southern border, and used a similar threat against Turkey to secure the release of an imprisoned American pastor.

In this realm, nothing compares to the ambition and scale of Xi Jinping's Belt and Road Initiative (BRI), announced in the fall of 2013. ("Belt" refers to overland transportation routes that roughly track the medieval Silk Road connecting China with Central and South Asia, the Middle East, and Europe, although the Belt also extends to Southeast Asia. "Road" refers to sea routes linking China to Oceania, Southeast Asia, South Asia, East Africa, the Middle East, and Europe.) The focus of the BRI is construction of infrastructure—a huge network of railroads, highways, power grids, airports, industrial centers, ports, and other such projects. As of April 2019, according to the Chinese, 115 countries have signed up as partners. The total cost of the BRI is expected to be in excess of $1 trillion.

The BRI is far from a development assistance plan in the Western sense. Funding for most projects is in the form of loans from Chinese banks and state-owned enterprises. Chinese banks alone extended more than $50 billion in loans in 2016 for more than 400 BRI projects. In addition, in October 2013, in conjunction with his announcement of the BRI, Xi proposed creation of the Asian Infrastructure Investment Bank (AIIB). In June 2015, the articles of agreement establishing the bank were signed in Beijing by fifty founding countries, and the bank opened for business the following January. As I mentioned earlier, President Obama, in a major strategic mistake, declined to join the bank, even though many of our Asian and European allies did so.

The Chinese might not impose conditions on loans in terms of corruption and human rights abuses by recipient governments, but they do impose economic conditions. For instance, recipient countries usually are required to use Chinese firms to construct the projects; 70 percent of Chinese loans are tied to the involvement of a Chinese company. Between 2015 and 2017, China provided its companies with $670 billion in export financing. Compare that with the $590 billion in financing the American Export-Import Bank has given to American companies—*over its entire eighty-one-year history.*

A few examples convey the magnitude and reach of the BRI. To create the China-Pakistan Economic Corridor, China is financing and building an 1,800-mile-long highway, a high-speed railroad, and an oil pipeline between the Chinese city of Kashgar and the Pakistani port of Gwadar, which the Chinese will vastly expand (and from which they will receive more than 90 percent of port revenues over the next forty years). The total cost of projects in Pakistan is estimated to be around $62 billion. The China Ocean Shipping Company (COSCO) has invested in creating the Khorgos Gateway in Kazakhstan, a huge dry port or transshipment hub for cargo moving between China, Central Asia, and Europe. In Sri Lanka, China has built an airport and large port at Hambantota as well as a highway connecting both to the capital, Colombo. Chinese workers are modernizing major Iranian railways, one connecting Tehran to Turkmenistan and Afghanistan and another from the capital and Mashhad to ports in the south. They are also constructing railways in Kenya, Nigeria, Indonesia, Laos, and Malaysia. In September 2018, Xi promised more than forty African leaders gathered in Beijing that China would offer another $60 billion in new funding. China is also the financier and developer of a new Egyptian capital city being built in the desert east of Cairo. Under an agreement signed in October 2017, the Chinese are building the central business district of the new city, financing it through loans from Chinese banks that also obligate Egypt to hire the Chinese State Construction Engineering Corporation to do the work.

The Chinese have invested in and now operate dozens of ports and terminals in more than thirty countries. They have built manufacturing centers in Thailand and in Ethiopia, largely occupied by Chinese factories. By the end of 2018, fifteen Latin American governments had signed up for the BRI, including under that rubric infrastructure projects that had begun earlier but soon adding railroad projects in Argentina, Peru, and Brazil; a massive dam in Brazil; and a trans-Pacific fiber cable with Chile. Five Caribbean countries have signed up for BRI funding, an add-on to Xi's 2013 announcement that China would provide $3 billion in development loans for infrastructure projects in Caribbean countries. In Europe, Italy has signed up as a participant in the BRI, the Chinese are building a highway in Montenegro, and they are constructing bridges and railways in Serbia as well as modernizing its electrical and telephone systems.

There are a number of motives behind the BRI. In its scale and reach, it announced to the world that China had retaken a leading role on the global stage for the first time in nearly two centuries, a role all the more important after the 2008 economic crisis in the United

States and as Washington was increasingly perceived as seeking to draw down its global commitments. The BRI offers the opportunity to safeguard vital supply lines of needed imports, such as oil, by developing overland routes that avoid pinch points such as the Strait of Malacca. It provides China an economic path to political and economic influence in scores of countries, in many cases at U.S. expense. After a long period of building China's infrastructure, BRI projects offer state-owned enterprises a means to use excess supplies of materials such as concrete and steel, as well as provide jobs for workers who could be sent to construction projects abroad. A number of BRI projects include infrastructure development in western China, where one of Beijing's objectives is to use the projects to weaken Uighur Muslim resistance there, partly through more effective control and repression and partly through economic growth.

Central Asia is a particular focus of the BRI as China seeks overland routes for commerce and the flow of energy to and from Kazakhstan, Azerbaijan, Turkmenistan, Iran, the Middle East, and Europe. For all the professions of cooperation and alignment between China and Russia, Beijing's encroachment on the latter's historic relationship with former republics of the Soviet Union (and Imperial Russia before that) is bound to lead to friction. Putin's seizure of Crimea and occupation of eastern Ukraine had to send shivers down the spines of the region's leaders, especially in Kazakhstan, which, like Ukraine, gave up its nuclear weapons in 1994 in exchange for "guarantees" of its territorial integrity. There are 4 million ethnic Russians living in Kazakhstan, 21 percent of the population. So, while there are long ties between the states of Central Asia and Russia, they also fear the Russians, which explains their desire to cultivate close relations with the Chinese, not to mention the economic benefits of BRI projects.

While Xi calls Putin his "best friend and colleague," there is no doubt who is the junior partner. The Chinese economy is six times larger than Russia's (in purchasing power parity), and China is a huge market for Russian oil and gas. In an example of China's technological and business superiority, Huawei will build Russia's 5G network. China invests very little in Russia. The main thing that has brought the two countries together is their mutual hostility toward liberal democracy and the United States. This collaboration may be an alliance of convenience, but it will create more challenges for America and other democracies. In the triangular relationship among Russia, China, and the United States, for the first time since 1972, China seems to hold the upper hand—at least for now.

Some contend that the BRI gives Beijing a golden opportunity over time to establish control over dozens of ports that could support Chinese navy ships, as well as airports and electrical power and communications systems in scores of countries, giving the Chinese multiple levers to disadvantage the United States and the West economically, politically, and militarily. Others suggest that the Chinese expect to make money over the long term, and opening up more direct and more modern trade routes will improve the economies of its partner countries and contribute to sustaining healthy Chinese economic growth. The BRI also creates the opportunity for China to gain control of dispute settlement regarding claims arising out of BRI projects and resolution of other commercial issues through institutions such as the Chinese International Commercial Court, an all-Chinese court independent of broadly recognized Western institutions for dispute resolution (such as the World Bank) that was established in 2018. Functionally, there are two courts, one in Shenzhen and another in Xi'an.

One of the strongest criticisms of the BRI is that Chinese loans to fund projects impose too much debt on developing countries. This not only has economic consequences but also allows China to seize control of a country's infrastructure when it can't repay the debt—as happened with the Chinese-built port and airport in Sri Lanka. Pushback began in 2018, when newly elected leaders in Pakistan and Malaysia criticized their predecessors for taking on too much debt through BRI projects and for being exploited by China. BRI projects also routinely employ primarily Chinese workers rather than locals, and environmental and labor standards are often low. As I've said, the Chinese happily do business with some of the globe's worst authoritarians and ask no embarrassing questions. Finally, a criticism probably uttered quietly in private in Beijing but widespread outside China is that a number of big projects do not make sense economically or financially and may well end up as white elephants resented by the receiving country and unwanted by China itself, leaving Chinese banks and state-owned enterprises to deal with uncollectable debt.

President Xi has responded to many of these criticisms by adjusting the process of selecting BRI projects. In a speech in 2018, he announced that in the future the initiative would be more cautious and more consultative. The head of the AIIB, Jin Liqun, told Chinese contractors in April 2019 not to get involved in corruption. Projects in Pakistan and Malaysia have been scaled back and prices lowered in response to criticisms from new leaders in those countries. China has also asked major international financial institutions for help in developing best practices for infrastructure projects. In a speech that same month, Xi invited foreign and private-sector partners to play a bigger role in the BRI. He said, "We need to pursue open, green and clean cooperation" and promised to adopt "widely accepted rules and standards." Xi added, "We welcome the participation of multilateral and international financial institutions in Belt and Road investment and financing, and we encourage third market cooperation." Ahead of Xi's speech, the governor of the People's Bank of China, Yi Gang, addressed the "debt trap" issue, saying that "a country's total debt capacity should be taken into account" in making decisions.

In practice, China has been pretty flexible when it comes to repayment. A 2019 report counted forty Chinese debt renegotiations with twenty-four countries, which represented about $50 billion in write-offs, deferments, and renegotiations. China thus far has seized only one or two projects for nonpayment, including the aforementioned airport in Sri Lanka. Even as Xi and other Chinese leaders adjust the BRI to address problems and, they hope, minimize criticism, there is no doubt Xi sees the BRI as a major personal legacy and will continue full steam ahead. In fact, at the Nineteenth Party Congress in October 2017, Xi arranged for the BRI to be written into the Chinese constitution, underscoring both its importance and its anticipated long-term role.

Whatever the mix of motives and mistakes, one thing is certain: the BRI is an extraordinarily challenging instrument of power on a global scale, in no small part because the U.S. government does not have the authority or capacity to compete with so vast a program. The question is whether the United States can develop new tools in this arena that draw on our strength—the private sector. The establishment in 2018 of the U.S. International Development Finance Corporation to finance private development projects, with $60 billion to loan, was a good start, but more creativity is needed to leverage American private investment in developing countries. Moreover, continuing attempts by the Trump administration to slash the USAID budget sent a strong, wrong signal to many countries that the U.S. government is abandoning the development assistance arena, thus offering China open-field running in the competition for markets and influence.

Despite China's establishment and enforcement of the set of rules, regulations, and practices described earlier that govern—and systematically disadvantage—foreigners wanting to do business in China, many American companies have made a lot of money doing business there. For decades they were publicly supportive of broader economic ties and a closer bilateral relationship. Yet, even though there has been some mitigation of forced technology transfers and other such practices, in recent years the challenges of doing business day to day in China and continuing unfair policies have moved American business from cheerleader for the bilateral relationship to skeptic. Broadly speaking, business leaders are no longer a political safety net for U.S.-Chinese relations in Washington. The so-called tariff wars between the two countries that President Trump began in 2018–19 revolved around not just the yawning gap in the trade balance but, more importantly, the U.S. demand for structural changes in China to achieve reciprocity in opportunities for business. Needless to say, the Chinese resisted yielding up unilateral advantages that represent an effective instrument of power in the economic arena. The ensuing mutually harmful trade war between the United States and China was the result.

Cyber Capabilities. The Chinese have devoted substantial resources to developing a wide range of cyber capabilities, a third intimidating instrument of power. The PLA's primary cyber organization, Unit 61398, with over 100,000 personnel, and the Ministry of State Security have for years carried out countless attacks on U.S. (and other) companies and government entities. The unit has stolen software source code, trade secrets, personnel records, technology, weapons designs, and other military information. Indeed, the unit has stolen, or tried to steal, just about anything the Chinese government wants to know. In 2015, Presidents Obama and Xi agreed to stop hacking involving trade and businesses, but the ensuing lull in attacks was short-lived. China has developed sophisticated cyber weapons capable of crippling critical infrastructure, such as the electrical grid, and is devoting significant resources to developing a weapons system enabled by artificial intelligence. There is great concern among American defense planners that China is developing the capability to use cyber attacks militarily to disable advanced U.S. weapons as well as space-based communications and intelligence satellites.

The Chinese have also developed a Digital Silk Road component to the broader Belt and Road Initiative, seeking to provide digital infrastructure for countries all over the world. They had committed an estimated $79 billion to such projects as of early 2019. Central to this effort has been Huawei, China's principal telecommunications company, which has been able to sign contracts with dozens of countries in no small part because of its ability to offer significantly lower prices than its competitors in the West. The U.S. and other governments recognized the problem late and tried, largely unsuccessfully, to block Huawei's expansion out of concern that their equipment would be used by the Chinese government to establish cyber access to countries across the globe, not to mention enabling authoritarian governments to use the equipment to surveil and control their populations.

China is not alone in developing cyber capabilities. But the range of their targets—economic, social, political, and military—and scale of their endeavor places them in the top tier of those pursuing development and use of this awesome instrument of power.

Strategic Communications. No other country, including the United States, comes close to China's comprehensive and far-reaching communications strategy and apparatus for shaping perceptions about it and advancing its interests. The effort involves the media, educational institutions, civil society groups, entertainment, and business.

In the early 2000s, a period when the U.S. government's media efforts had been pared to the bone, Hu Jintao committed $7 billion to build "a modern media system and enhance the power of news media for domestic and world service so as to create a favorable social environment and atmosphere for public opinion." China then began to vastly expand its international media presence in multiple channels. According to a 2018 study cosponsored by AidData, the Center for Strategic and International Studies, and the Asia Society, in terms of news coverage the Xinhua News Agency grew to 180 bureaus delivering content in eight languages, and added to its reach through television and social media. China Central Television (CCTV) has over seventy foreign bureaus broadcasting to 171 countries, and China Radio International (CRI) is the world's second-largest radio network, broadcasting in sixty-four languages. Chinese companies often buy stakes—even majority ownership—in domestic media outlets in a number of countries, especially in Africa.

When it comes to the media, the playing field between China and the West is decidedly uneven. Whereas Chinese television, radio, websites, and publications are readily available in the United States, there is no reciprocity in China. No American company can operate a television network in China, American publications are limited to those dealing with fashion and business, and access to Facebook, Twitter, Google, YouTube, and other services is blocked. By the same token, China happily embraces outlets like Facebook outside of the country to spread propaganda. Its news pages in 2018 yielded 370 million "likes."

Confucius Institutes (CIs), usually set up in partnership with local universities ostensibly with the purpose of promoting the Chinese language and culture, spread China's message internationally. The Chinese government retains control of all CIs, and most of the instructors are sent by the Chinese government. Globally, between 2004 and 2018, more than 525 CIs were established, along with Confucius Classrooms in more than a thousand primary and secondary schools. As of mid-2019, there were Confucius Institutes at eighty-three university campuses in the United States and six more in public school districts. In the United States, Australia, and elsewhere, the CIs became increasingly controversial as they were viewed simply as instruments for Chinese propaganda and a means of keeping an eye on Chinese students at those universities, and as they exerted direct and indirect pressure on faculty members and the universities themselves to avoid—or take the Chinese line on—sensitive subjects such as Taiwan, Tibet, Falun Gong, repression of Uighurs, and Tiananmen Square. As a result of such controversies, more than a dozen CIs in the United States were closed. Nonetheless, the CIs remain an important element of Chinese strategic communications and outreach.

The United States tried to create counterparts to the CIs in China. By 2012, the State Department had made grants of $100,000 each to two dozen U.S. universities to establish American cultural centers on Chinese campuses. State left decisions about programming entirely up to the U.S. universities, which signed up jazz bands, dance groups, folk artists, and other representatives of American culture. By 2015, the centers had attracted Chinese government attention, and soon the Chinese universities were barring cultural groups and speakers from America. As Beijing increased its scrutiny, the American universities, lacking support from Washington, soon lost their appetite for cooperating. By the time State shuttered the program, it had spent $5 million on twenty-nine centers, ten of which were never opened. Meanwhile, most of the CIs in the United States remained open.

As with the media, Western NGOs face multiple obstacles in China. Civil society groups, religious organizations, and think tanks are restricted in their activities or blocked altogether, and all are heavily surveilled. In January 2017, a new law came into effect requiring NGOs in China to register with the Ministry of Public Security, obtain permission for their activities, and refrain from fund-raising in China. When the new law was enacted, there were some 7,000 foreign NGOs in China. By 2019, there were just 400.

Although the United States remains the premier destination for foreign university students—about a million each year—China sees providing an education as an opportunity to influence foreign students, especially those from developing countries and BRI partners. The number of foreign exchange students in China grew sharply from 85,000 in 2002 to 442,000 in 2016. About 40 percent come from the East Asia/Pacific region, with South Korea having the largest single contingent at just over 70,000. Beijing has even created a scholarship program to compete with Fulbright and Rhodes scholarships in attracting the most-promising students and future leaders. China's open-arms approach comes at a time when it is increasingly difficult for students from a number of foreign countries to get permission to enter the United States.

China's efforts to shape the attitudes and policies of leaders and governments in recent years have generated strong pushback by Western governments, including accusations of Chinese subversion and interference in the political process. The most notorious case was the revelation in Australia in 2017 of widespread Chinese meddling in politics and universities. Chinese businessmen apparently donated substantial funds—more than $5 million—over a period of years to both major political parties and to individual politicians. Moreover, government investigations revealed that informants were reporting back to Beijing on the activities, including participation in demonstrations, of Chinese university students in Australia. State-owned Chinese media companies and pro-Beijing businessmen had taken over Australia's Chinese-language media. In September 2017, the *Financial Times* reported that a New Zealand member of parliament had taught at a Chinese spy college for years and somehow neglected to mention it. In 2010, the Canadian intelligence services reported that certain provincial cabinet ministers and government employees were Chinese agents of influence. And in December 2017, German intelligence accused China of using social media to contact 10,000 German citizens, including government officials, trying to glean "information and recruiting sources." Other countries, including Britain, have also reported Chinese efforts to recruit politicians.

In a speech on October 4, 2018, Vice President Pence accused China of "meddling in America's democracy." He alleged that "China is targeting U.S. state and local governments and officials to exploit any divisions between federal and local levels on policy" like trade tariffs. Pence went on to say that China had mobilized covert actors, front groups, and propaganda outlets to shift American perceptions of Chinese policy. The vice president cataloged all the ways in which China was trying to exert influence in the United States, from pressure on Hollywood to portray China in a positive light to spending heavily on propaganda outlets in the United States, mobilizing the Chinese Students and Scholars Association on U.S. campuses to report to Beijing on Chinese students who stray from the party line, and funding universities and scholars who avoid ideas offensive to China.

Even if government leaders in key developed countries warn their publics about China's efforts to spread its message, influence foreign opinion, and meddle, the scale of the endeavor and the multiple mechanisms employed will blunt defensive efforts. The Chinese will continue to buy or otherwise exploit media outlets and use various cultural and educational programs it runs around the world to shape opinion. Increasingly most effective will be Beijing's ability to leverage its economic power in many countries to facilitate its political messaging. Ample funding and centralized direction make China's strategic communications program a pervasive instrument of power.

Science and Technology. China's universities and research centers were virtually destroyed during the 1966–76 Cultural Revolution, with predictably disastrous results for its scientific and technology community. Since the late 1970s, though, China's leaders have consistently pursued a strategy aimed at placing the country in the forefront of global scientific and technological research and development long-term. Deng initiated the recovery in the late 1970s by encouraging Chinese students to go abroad for their science and engineering degrees, and many of them came to the best American universities. Early on, the Chinese undertook a vast effort to steal technology from the West and Japan, including the use of researchers and graduate students in advanced research labs.

The companion Chinese strategy was to build the capacity at home to compete with and eventually surpass American science and technology capabilities. Between 2001 and 2014, China built more than

1,800 new universities and produced some 5 million science, tech-nology, engineering, and medicine graduates—"nearly ten times the equivalent American figure." Chinese investment in research and development grew by more than 20 percent annually between 2000 and 2010, and by nearly 14 percent between 2010 and 2015, while U.S. spending on research and development was about 4 percent dur-ing the same period. By 2015, China was spending over $400 billion each year for research and development. (The U.S. government spent $66.5 billion on basic and applied research in 2017, nearly half of it going to the National Institutes of Health. Most federal funding for research on computing, artificial intelligence, physics, and the like is through the National Science Foundation, which received just $5.6 billion in 2017. This, of course, does not count non–federally funded research in the private sector and universities.) Many of the students Deng encouraged to study abroad remained there and so, to recover some of that valuable resource, in 2008 the Chinese initiated the Thousand Talents program to lure them back (and attract foreign sci-entists and engineers) with promises of high salaries and well-funded labs. Thousands have returned.

Scientific and technological achievement is an effective instru-ment of power in terms of fueling economic growth and developing advanced military capabilities. It also confers prestige internationally and generates nationalistic pride at home. In that regard, China's investments have borne fruit. The country can boast of having more than 200 of the world's five hundred most powerful supercomputers (sixty more than in the United States), building the largest radio tele-scope, being the only country to land a space vehicle on the far side of the Moon, and cloning a monkey—and a human. China now files the largest number of new patents in the world and has surpassed the United States in the number of scientific papers published. In 2015, Premier Li Keqiang announced the Made in China 2025 plan, setting the goal of being self-sufficient in ten key industries, includ-ing semi-conductors, 5G mobile communications equipment, robots, biopharmaceuticals, electric cars, aerospace, and materials. Beijing has also set out to be the global leader in technologies such as artificial intelligence, quantum computing, and bioscience by 2035.

Beneath the gross numbers and impressive veneer of progress, Chinese performance has been somewhat less spectacular. Some of the new Chinese universities are nothing more than diploma mills. Many Chinese published scientific papers are of low quality, and a number of patents are for incremental improvements or changes, not major breakthroughs. As one expert wrote, "Interventionist government bureaucracy, stodgy state-owned enterprises, a rigid school system and—above all—harsh restrictions on individual freedoms continue to stifle independent thinking and creativity and constrain China from realizing its full innovation potential."

All that said, in many areas Chinese science and technology are excellent, and some experts predict the sector as a whole will be on a par with America's in ten to fifteen years. In the meantime, high-profile achievements like the Moon shot, success in dominating global 5G communications, and breakthroughs in artificial intelligence, weapons technologies such as hypersonics, and bioscience will all buttress China's claims that it is ahead of the United States in some areas and catching up in others, and intends to surpass America across the board in science and technology by 2050.

The Soviet Union gained significant international prestige when it launched the first space satellite in 1957. That served as a huge stimulus for American investment, resulting in a U.S. lead over the Soviets in science and technology that grew steadily over the following thirty-five years. In contrast, China's challenge in this arena will become ever more potent over time because of its continuing high level of investment as well as the continuing and concomitant decline in American government funding of basic and applied research. As the director of national intelligence reported in his worldwide threat assessment in January 2019, "During the past two decades, the U.S. lead in S&T fields has been significantly eroded, most predominantly by China, which is well ahead in several areas." In terms of the global competition with the United States, the economic and military consequences of China's sustained investment in research and development, as well as the growing perception of Chinese strength in that arena, represent a significant instrument of national power for Beijing.

Ideology. Communism as an appealing ideology for society and governance is dead, including in China. While the Chinese Communist Party is a convenient vehicle for maintaining dictatorial control, its only claim to legitimacy, as mentioned earlier, is a steadily improving quality of life for the Chinese people. Its success in lifting literally hundreds of millions out of poverty and dramatically expanding the middle class is real, despite growing income inequality. Likewise, the Chinese are justifiably proud of their extraordinary achievements in developing the country's infrastructure as well as its scientific and technological advances. The leadership in Beijing is also widely viewed as effectively defending the ancient civilization and dignity of China and the Chinese people. The Chinese see their country, after nearly two centuries of humiliation and foreign domination, as having been restored to its rightful place as one of the most powerful countries in the world, with aspirations to be *the* preeminent power.

Xi has gone beyond these successes to tout Chinese authoritarian state capitalism as a model for other countries, especially for leaders eager to develop their economies quickly and rely on the resulting prosperity to cement their own authority. At the Nineteenth Party Congress in October 2017, Xi boasted that China had "stood up, grown rich, and become strong." He claimed that China offered "a new option for other countries" involving "Chinese wisdom and a Chinese approach to solving the problems facing mankind." In another speech, he suggested that China offers a "new option for other countries who want to speed up their development while preserving their independence." As one scholar put it, "Not since Mao Zedong had a Chinese leader so directly suggested that others should emulate his country's model." The model Xi offers involves a mix of huge state-owned economic enterprises along with room for private companies and entrepreneurialism, all run according to rules set by the government; centralization of all authority in the hands of a "president for life"; reinsertion of the Party into every facet of society, the economy, and even individual companies. (By 2019, 70 percent of all private enterprises and joint ventures had Party committees.) Add to that a pervasive suppression of unauthorized political activity and expression, and an increasingly sophisticated surveillance state using the most modern technologies, such as artificial intelligence, to monitor individuals' every activity. Indeed, Chinese development of a "social credit score" for each of its citizens based on tracking their daily personal behavior through artificial intelligence is a totalitarian's dream come true.

Chinese communism, like its Soviet counterpart, failed. But authoritarianism—autocracy—has very deep historical roots and has been the dominant form of governance for most of human history. Xi's China faces many problems and challenges, but the country's economic success internally, and its growing web of investments and trade worldwide, taken together with its increasing military power, represents a formidable challenge to Western liberal democracies paralyzed at home and drawing back abroad. Xi's China does not have an ideology to sell, but it does offer a model of how to combine accelerated economic prosperity with political control and "efficiency."

Some in the West believe that Beijing intends to overturn the international structures created mainly by the United States after World War II and replace them with organizations in which China makes the rules. I think the Chinese strategy is more sophisticated than that. The Chinese have benefited greatly from the World Trade Organization and rules-based commerce, especially when the West abides by those rules and China picks and chooses when it complies. China is a strong supporter of the United Nations. It is the third-largest contributor to the UN regular budget (the United States is first, Japan second) and the second-largest contributor to the UN peacekeeping budget. Since 1986, the Asian Development Bank has committed more than $40 billion for 1,200 projects in China. It would not be in China's interest to upend any of these institutions. Further, Beijing has participated in international anti-piracy and counterterrorism efforts, and has worked with the United States and others to block the proliferation of nuclear weapons, most notably in North Korea and Iran. China is a signatory to the 2016 Paris climate agreement (voluntary compliance), and remarkably—and cynically—at Davos in January 2017, Xi criticized protectionism ("No one will emerge as a winner in a trade war").

What China seeks from these institutions and from others it creates, such as the AIIB and the Commercial Courts, is the ability to shape the international system in ways that elevate its status, increase its influence, and facilitate the achievement of its strategic objectives. The Chinese also clearly intend to fill the void created by America's withdrawal from agreements such as the Trans-Pacific Partnership and its diminishing participation in others.

For all China's strengths and instruments of power, Xi and his fellow leaders face many problems at home. China carries a heavy load of debt at every level, from state-owned enterprises to local municipalities. The environment, while improving, is still terrible in many places. The population is aging; the birth rate is the lowest since 1961, and there is a significant gender imbalance among the young because of the now-abandoned one-child policy and the female infanticide that accompanied it. There are tens of thousands of strikes and demonstrations every year against authorities at every level. Corruption is still widespread. The regime faces a separatist movement in Xinjiang Province, where nearly a million Uighurs are in "reeducation camps." Economic growth, the mainstay of Party rule, is slowing, and in the cities there are some 90 million young migrants from the countryside, poor workers often denied services such as education and health care, often unmarried, lacking savings, and "with little to lose and less to keep them loyal to the party." Xi's assumption of singular power, his anticorruption campaign, and other actions doubtless have created many enemies. There are constant rumors of coup plots and even assassination attempts. In charge of everything, he will be blamed for anything that goes seriously wrong.

It is clear, in fact, that China's leaders are scared to death of their own people. As noted earlier, at the very beginning of the economic reforms forty years ago, Deng declared there would be no political reform, no lessening of controls over the people. Tiananmen Square was a fire bell in the night. The massive and prolonged protests in Hong Kong in 2019 served as a new, vivid reminder that the greatest danger to communist rule in China is not from abroad but from within—the Chinese people.

In light of all these problems, for China's leaders, stability at home and standing abroad will depend more than ever on the economy. Fittingly for a bunch of self-proclaimed Marxists, everything going forward in China will be determined by economics.

The bet that a richer China would become a freer China has been lost. The model China offers the world is antithetical in every way to American liberal democracy. China began its long march toward matching U.S. power forty years ago; it has aspirations, and plans, to surpass us within two decades. I believe the U.S.-Chinese relationship can be a peaceful competition and include cooperation in areas of mutual interest. It will take wisdom and restraint in both Washington and Beijing to accomplish this, and both sides will need to make adjustments. China's rise does not require America's decline. Whether the United States descends depends far less on what happens in Beijing than on what happens in Washington.

The rivalry will have a military component as China seeks to establish dominance in Asia by placing U.S. forces there at risk. Barring an incident that spirals out of control or some rash provocation, such as Taiwan declaring independence, the two nuclear-armed militaries will work very hard to avoid a mutually disastrous confrontation.

Some in the United States hope for "regime change" in China as the solution. If by that they mean the collapse of the Party's dictatorship and its replacement by a non-communist alternative, I think they have a very long wait in store. Moreover, an unstable China, with 1.4 billion people and nuclear weapons, is not in our interest. The most likely future is one of long-term competition and rivalry, waged primarily through nonmilitary instruments of national power. At this point, China has important advantages: its ability to marshal huge economic resources, such as the BRI, and to establish economic, trade, and political linkages and dependencies; its multifaceted, well-funded strategic communications programs, which are centrally controlled and orchestrated, and reach into every country; its growing scientific and technological prowess; and its willingness to use its trade and investment clout—its geo-economic tools—to pressure governments and companies into decisions favorable to Chinese interests.

The Chinese accuse the United States of trying to contain or stop

China's rise. It is therefore a supreme irony that over the last forty years we have done so much to facilitate that rise. We have opened our economy to China; encouraged American companies to invest there; supported China's inclusion—on advantageous terms—in international bodies such as the WTO; soft-pedaled criticism of its dishonest and one-sided economic policies as well as its suppression of human rights; invited Chinese students into our best universities (with access to the most advanced scientific and technological developments); and promoted commerce and trade. What nonmilitary instruments of power we had we either used to help China or failed to use to stop its predatory practices and policies. We woke very late to the realization that our assumptions about a prosperous China becoming a freer China were wrong, and to the scope of the challenge China now poses to us.

As we look to the future, perhaps the most important nonmilitary instrument of power is a long-range strategy for waging this competition. The Chinese have one. The United States does not.

CHAPTER 13

Lessons Learned

America remains the most powerful country in the world economically and militarily. But nearly thirty years after our victory in the Cold War and the collapse of the Soviet empire, and after eighteen years of war in the Middle East and Southwest Asia, we live in a world that is more complicated and more unpredictable than at any time since the late 1940s. China and Russia are growing ever stronger militarily, and they are aggressively seeking to extend their influence and presence into new regions and countries. The United States is engaged in a decades-long political, economic, and military competition with China. North Korea poses an increasingly sophisticated nuclear threat in East Asia and to the United States, and Iran remains a determined adversary to America and our closest allies in the Middle East. We still have thousands of troops in Afghanistan and Iraq. Despite the loss of its "caliphate," ISIL continues to conduct terrorist attacks across Eurasia, the Middle East, and Africa and remains an enduring threat. Our strongest allies in Europe are beset by deep divisions—internally, among themselves, and with us. Long-standing international norms, from inviolate borders in Europe to freedom of navigation on the high seas and general adherence to multilateral agreements and treaties, are all under attack. Whether the world descends into a dog-eat-dog, might-makes-right environment or moves in the direction of peaceful resolution of differences, rules-based behavior by the major powers, and new opportunities for the growth of freedom depends almost entirely on long-term American strength, engagement, and leadership. Yet this need for U.S. leadership comes at a time when much of the world is rightly convinced we are pulling back from that kind of role.

At a time of deep political polarization in America, there is rare and broad bipartisan agreement that the United States should reduce its commitments and obligations abroad and focus on problems here at home. The farther right and farther left you go on the political spectrum, the more agreement you find on this point. President Trump's rhetoric rarely mentions the necessity of American global leadership, and both his words and his actions focused on abandoning most previous bilateral and international agreements we have signed and shunning obligations we have undertaken. This political reality is reinforced by the belief at home that America's friends and allies have taken advantage of us economically and failed to pull their weight in providing for our common defense, a view held by a much broader swath of the public than just Trump supporters.

What many commentators expressing concern over this political reality forget is that, historically, most Americans have not been particularly interested in U.S. engagement in the rest of the world, much less in spending money to help foreign countries or sending their sons and daughters to fight in places where the threat to the United States is unclear. Every war we have fought but two has been unpopular with a substantial proportion of the American people. (World War II had broad support after the attack on Pearl Harbor, but by late 1944, war-weariness had become a real problem for the country's leadership. The first Gulf War had strong support, in no small part because the ground campaign lasted just 100 hours.) The war against the Taliban in Afghanistan was initially popular because they had sheltered those who attacked us on September 11 and military victory was achieved in three months. But as the goals there changed and the war dragged on year after year, support declined significantly. Foreign assistance, especially development assistance—foreign aid—has long been one of the most unpopular government programs. When it comes to the world around us, most Americans have long wanted to just mind our own business and be left alone.

The challenge for presidents always has been to help Americans understand that ignoring the rest of the world simply is not possible and has not been so for a very long time. In the modern age, our economy, our security, and even our personal health are inextricably bound up with developments beyond our borders, a reality recent presidents have been relatively unsuccessful in bringing home to Americans (apart from George W. Bush in the immediate aftermath of 9/11). Franklin D. Roosevelt was explicit about the importance of presidents "persuading, leading, sacrificing, teaching always, because the greatest duty of a statesman is to educate." I wrote earlier that a critical nonmilitary instrument of power was "wise and courageous leadership." Following Roosevelt's dictum, the task before each president is to develop a foreign policy that he or she can persuade the public to support and then patiently, repeatedly, educating the citizenry as to why that policy is necessary and deserving of support.

STRATEGY

Baseball great Yogi Berra observed that "if you don't know where you're going, you'll wind up somewhere else." That applies to presidents. A president should identify a few key objectives for his or her foreign policy and develop a strategy or strategies for accomplishing those objectives—how the president can drive the international agenda rather than be driven by events elsewhere. Some presidents enter office already having settled on their objectives. Richard Nixon assumed office with three aims: to end the Vietnam War on terms that did not represent a strategic defeat for the United States, to turn down the heat in the Cold War through arms control negotiations and other agreements with the Soviet Union (and get its help in ending the war in Vietnam on acceptable terms), and to reach out to China with the aim of isolating the Soviets and dramatically shifting the balance of power. Ronald Reagan wanted to build up U.S. military strength post-Vietnam, force the Soviet Union to spend more on defense than it could afford, and counter their efforts in the developing world, all with a view to aggravating their internal problems and ultimately forcing collapse. George H. W. Bush did not become president with a set of specific objectives, but within months of his inauguration, he responded to developments with strategies to facilitate the liberation of the nations of Eastern Europe and the reunification of Germany in NATO and manage the collapse of the Soviet Union without military conflict. Similarly, responding to the attacks of September 11, 2001, shaped George W. Bush's foreign policy from the wars in Iraq and Afghanistan to his belief that the only way to deal with terrorism long term was to attack the root causes in authoritarian and corrupt countries—his "freedom agenda." Bill Clinton never really had broad foreign policy objectives, largely reacting to events tactically, with the exception of promoting trade relations globally. Barack Obama simply wanted to end the wars in Iraq and Afghanistan, as well as improve relations with Russia and, in his second term, conclude an agreement limiting Iran's nuclear program. Trump had no objectives other than opposition to what most of his predecessors had done and a determination to overturn any and all agreements he thought did not unilaterally advantage the United States, in the belief that he could get a better deal.

It is telling that of the eight presidents I worked for, beginning with Lyndon Johnson, only two, Nixon and Reagan, had strategically ambitious foreign policy objectives when they became president and were able to succeed in achieving those objectives. In doing so, both dominated the international scene.

Every president, sitting under that big funnel I described earlier, faces countless and endlessly diverse problems and crises, usually on a daily basis. Distractions are a constant. A president must deal with those but, at the same time, never lose sight of the big picture—keeping as top priority the development and implementation of long-term strategies for dealing with the most important challenges. Today that means China and Russia above all, but also North Korea and Iran. American leadership is also needed in dealing with global challenges, from the growing tens of millions of displaced refugees worldwide to the threats posed by terrorism, climate change and disease, and their geostrategic consequences.

In deciding upon strategies for the big issues—those involving the vital national interest of the nation—the president must take into account how to win the support of the American people for the long haul and how he or she will go about "persuading, leading, sacrificing, teaching always" to bring the people along, as Roosevelt counseled. While technologically it is easier than ever for presidents to reach the public, getting the public to tune in has been far more difficult for post–Cold War presidents than for their predecessors. The fact that during the Cold War we were dealing with the possibility of nuclear catastrophe tended to get people's attention. For much of the Cold War, there were just three major television networks, and an Oval Office speech by the president broadcast on all three would reach most Americans. The explosion of the means of communication has splintered the national audience. Moreover, many of the new outlets are highly partisan, which further complicates a president's challenge in getting a message through to the broader public. Deepening polarization leads a substantial portion of citizens simply to tune out a president they dislike. The challenge is not insurmountable—political campaigns are constantly devising new ways of reaching people, some of them more sophisticated than 140-character tweets.

Making it happen requires the time, attention, and priority of the president. A more manageable approach, even though more distasteful to presidents, is spending more time with members of Congress of both parties, helping them understand the environment abroad and what we should do. A sincere approach, in private, might pay higher dividends than recent presidents have thought possible as those members return home and perhaps pass along helpful messages to the public. A president's efforts must also be targeted to the media itself, for it is most often through their filter that the public will be informed and educated. Recent presidents have, in my view, underestimated or ignored the importance and value of such efforts.

Looking to the future, based upon the lessons to be learned from the examples described in the preceding chapters, how can a president develop a foreign policy that can protect America's security and its economic well-being and, at the same time, receive public support? How can presidents help Congress and the people understand the importance of American leadership in international affairs? As Churchill said, "The price of greatness is responsibility. . . . The people of the United States cannot escape world responsibility." The plain fact is that the president of the United States must assume that responsibility, because without presidential leadership, there is no global American leadership.

USING THE MILITARY

I have focused especially on the weakness of the nonmilitary American instruments of power and how essential it is for our future prospects that they be strengthened. But make no mistake about it: a strong military underpins every other instrument of power and is the ultimate protector of the nation. As President Washington put it so succinctly in his first inaugural address, "To be prepared for war is one of the most effectual means of preserving peace." While the gross numbers we spend on the military are huge, the unpredictability of the ups and downs of funding and the failure of Congress every year for a decade to complete its work in approving the defense budget before the beginning of the fiscal year has, over time, imposed significant costs in dollars. This has also led to delays in getting new capabilities into the field. There may be a dumber way to cut the federal budget than through the 2011 sequestration legislation, but if there is, I can't think of it. Most of the sequestration cuts in defense have been borne by operations, maintenance, and training—in short, the tip of the spear. Repeated "continuing" resolutions every year for the first weeks or months of the fiscal year paralyze planners and operators alike, who have no idea when they will get funding, how much it will be, or what programs will be affected.

There is, no doubt, waste and inefficiency in our military efforts. When I was secretary of defense, with just a few months' work we identified $180 billion in overhead costs that could be cut—and that was on top of our success a year earlier in cutting some three dozen programs that, had they been built to completion, would have cost taxpayers $330 billion. Tough leadership and management, and predictability from Congress, would save money and produce a more effective and lethal military.

It is the president's responsibility to ensure that the American military is the strongest, most technologically advanced in the world, capable of dealing with the full spectrum of conflict, from terrorists and insurgents to Russia and China. Stable, predictable budgets and holding Defense executives accountable for efficient management and spending are essential for maintaining our military superiority.

That said, there are lessons to be learned from the past quarter century about using our military. Foremost among them is to determine whether the U.S. military is the right, or optimal, solution to a problem. Are there other instruments of power that can achieve even partial success, even if they take longer? Does the use of the military entail collateral costs, and how well can the inevitable unintended consequences be identified and anticipated? Does the situation justify putting the lives of young Americans at risk? The answers to those questions might have led to different decisions in Somalia, Haiti, the Balkans, and Libya, and in both Iraq and Afghanistan after the initial military objectives had been achieved. Despite public war-weariness, there are those on the left convinced that the Responsibility to Protect compels the use of the American military to intervene in internal conflicts such as Libya, Sudan, and Syria to safeguard innocent civilians. Some on the right advocate the use of force against Iran, North Korea, and China in the South China Sea, or providing military assistance to the opposition in Syria and the government in Kyiv. A president who ignores one or the other camp is considered either morally bereft or a wimp. Accordingly, too often since 1993, presidents have regarded the use of the military as a first choice in dealing with a problem rather than as a last resort.

To be clear, there are times when the use of military power is inescapable: a president must respond forcefully to foreign attacks or threats affecting American vital interests; a show of force is often an effective deterrent to would-be aggressors. Ironically, using military capabilities is usually the only effective response to humanitarian and natural disasters, from an earthquake in Haiti to a tsunami in Southeast Asia to both in Japan. It is the gray areas—such as internal conflicts in the Balkans, Somalia, Syria, and Libya; attacks by Iranian surrogates; and the Chinese building islands in the South China Sea—that are the toughest for presidents and require great caution. This is especially true when the problem involves intervening militarily in another country.

In deciding whether a mission is appropriate for the military, presidents would do well to take note of this observation by military historian Max Hastings: "Soldiers observe wryly that the unique selling point of their profession is that they kill people. It is too much to ask of most that they should resolve political and social challenges beyond their . . . experience, conditioning and resources."

A particularly tough problem for presidents is discerning when the limited but sustained use of force today will prevent a much bigger problem or conflict tomorrow. After American warships helped the Philippines successfully challenge China's claims at Mischief Reef in the South China Sea early in 1995, had Clinton and his successors consistently continued to deploy warships to challenge China's claims and early moves to build bases on contested islands and other reefs (or protected comparable dredging and construction efforts by other claimants), the now expansive Chinese effort that has changed the military equation in the South China Sea might have been averted. Had Clinton in late 1998 sustained the military attacks on Iraqi forces until Saddam readmitted the international inspectors, the 2003 invasion of Iraq might never have happened. After signing the nuclear deal with Iran in 2015, Obama could have mitigated—perhaps significantly—criticism of the deal had he resolved to enforce the UN Security Council resolution calling upon Iran not to test ballistic missiles for eight years and more aggressively countered subsequent Iranian meddling in the region. The resolution had no enforcement provision, but he could have collaborated with other signatories (at least the Europeans) in taking action, which might have removed the grounds for Trump's abandonment of the deal.

The objective of any military deployment or mission must be clear and specific. What exactly are the troops expected to do? The resources authorized must be sufficient to accomplish the mission. I have witnessed presidents decide the number of troops to be sent and duration of a deployment based more on domestic politics than on a mission's requirements, as was the case with Obama in Afghanistan. When the mission changes, as it did in Somalia under Clinton (from famine relief to peacemaking and improved governance) or in Iraq under Bush (from toppling Saddam to occupation and fighting an insurgency), there must be a commensurate change in the resources applied. As in Afghanistan, is there a mismatch between our aspirations and our capabilities?

I cannot emphasize enough that the objective of military intervention must be clear, and the strategy and resources committed must be adequate to achieving the objective. Too often presidents, sensitive to domestic politics, are tempted to use just enough military force to avoid failure but not enough to achieve success. Such an approach is not only strategically unwise and imprudent, it is also immoral. The lives of American men and women in uniform must not simply be thrown at a problem and squandered in halfhearted or impulsive efforts. In the use of military force, the Yoda rule from *Star Wars* must be applied: "Do or do not; there is no try."

Presidents must beware of "mission creep," the gradual expansion of the effort to achieve new and more ambitious objectives not originally intended that may require additional or different resources or may, in fact, not be achievable or may have significant unintended consequences. The shifts from stopping the slaughter of innocents in Somalia, Haiti, Kosovo, and Libya to regime change and nation-building are examples of mission creep.

Presidents and commanders alike should be mindful of the perils of overreach, that is, achieving the original objectives but, with success, feeling emboldened to pursue more-ambitious goals (arguably, Bush in both Iraq and Afghanistan; Clinton in Haiti and Somalia). Know when to stop.

Presidents must differentiate between preemptive and preventive wars. Preemptive wars are launched when there is unambiguous information indicating that an attack on you is imminent and you move first. The Israeli attack on the Arabs on June 6, 1967, was a pre-

emptive war. Preventive wars, by contrast, are those launched to pre-
clude or interrupt a hostile government from eventually developing
the capability to attack. The war against Iraq in 2003 was a preventive
war undertaken in the belief that Saddam was developing weapons
of mass destruction, specifically, a nuclear weapons capability. A big
problem with preventive war is that the decision depends overmuch
on the reliability and accuracy of intelligence information, intelligence
that is, in my experience, all too often inaccurate or ambiguous.

Presidents should scrupulously avoid red lines and ultimatums
unless they are fully committed to enforcing them militarily. Once a
president cocks the pistol, he or she must be ready to fire it. Obama's
failure to enforce his own red line with respect to Assad's use of
chemical weapons against the Syrian opposition echoed around the
world—but especially in Moscow, Beijing, Tehran, and Pyongyang.
Trump's repeated threats of massive military attacks on North Korea
and Iran by the end of 2019 increasingly were viewed by adversaries
as hollow bluffs.

TO INTERVENE OR NOT

The U.S. intervened militarily or contemplated doing so in twelve
of the fifteen countries I have discussed. The most important military lessons to be drawn from that relate to how presidents should
think about the use of military power short of all-out war with a
nuclear-armed adversary.

There have been earlier attempts to establish criteria for the use of
combat forces. In a November 1994 speech, Defense Secretary Caspar
Weinberger offered six such criteria, drawing upon our experiences
in Vietnam and in 1983, the loss of 241 Marines in Beirut: (1) the
U.S. should not commit forces to combat unless the vital national
interest of the United States or its allies is involved; (2) U.S. troops
should be committed wholeheartedly and with the clear intention of
winning—otherwise, troops should not be committed; (3) U.S. combat troops should be committed only with clearly defined political and
military objectives and with the capacity to accomplish those objectives; (4) the relationship between the objectives and the size and

composition of the forces committed should be continually reassessed and adjusted if necessary; (5) U.S. troops should not be committed to battle without a "reasonable assurance" of the support of U.S. public opinion and Congress; and (6) the commitment of U.S. troops should be considered only as a last resort.

Another attempt to establish criteria for deciding on the use of force was put forward by former chairman of the Joint Chiefs of Staff, General Colin Powell. Known as the Powell Doctrine, its varied iterations posed several questions that needed to be answered affirmatively before the United States took military action: Is a vital national security interest threatened? Do we have a clear, attainable objective? Have the risks and costs been fully and frankly analyzed? Have all other nonviolent policy means been fully exhausted? Is there a plausible exit strategy to avoid endless entanglement? Have the consequences of our action been fully considered? Is the action supported by the American people? Do we have genuine broad international support?

Both Weinberger's and Powell's efforts were controversial. Powell's questions were labeled an attempt by the military to get politicians to avoid the mistakes and misjudgments of civilian leaders that led to tragedy and loss in Vietnam. Others complained that the Powell Doctrine was an effort by the military to tell political leaders what kinds of conflicts warranted the sacrifice of our troops. Yet others described both the Weinberger and Powell criteria as formulas for "all-or-nothing war" and "checklist" diplomacy. I believe that both were simply trying to force presidents and their senior advisers to think long and hard and tackle tough questions head-on before committing young Americans to battle.

I am confident that any similar effort I make along these lines will also be subject to criticism from both civilians and those in uniform. Still, I began participating in White House Situation Room meetings on the use of force almost forty years ago, and over the years, I took part in dozens of debates over whether to deploy our military. Along the way, I saw, and was party to, both good and bad decisions. All of them cost lives. And I learned a lot.

Specific criteria or checklists that must be satisfied or answered affirmatively before taking military action are, I think, too confining in a complicated and dangerous world. Sometimes action must be taken before public support can be rallied; there are instances when initial negative public opinion becomes overwhelmingly positive when there is quick success. Sometimes the mission and its objectives must be adjusted midstream to reflect reality on the ground. Sometimes, when all nonmilitary options have been exhausted, it's too late to have any impact except through military force. There are times when "winning" is not about an adversary surrendering but is simply about preventing something worse from happening. Finally, in the conflicts of today, our ally in one phase occasionally becomes our adversary in the next, or those we supported in a successful outcome squander that success through their own failings. These are real-world realities, and no president or presidential team can anticipate them all. There is no checklist for determining whether to use that most deadly instrument of national power, military force.

There are, however, questions that common sense and experience dictate must be addressed, even if not answered, before we lock and load. Too often I have seen groupthink in the Situation Room; too often I have seen those who raise tough, awkward questions derided or silenced by stern, disapproving looks from the fire-breathers; too often I have seen the fear of the consequences of not acting drive action; too often, I have seen outrage rather than careful consideration predominate in making decisions. I believe, therefore, that a president and his or her national security adviser, for the sake of the country and all those young men and women in uniform whose lives will be on the line, must ensure that hard questions get a thorough airing before any decision to intervene militarily.

First, there are the broadest questions applicable in every circumstance: Are core U.S. national interests or those of our allies threatened? What other countries are willing and able to help us? What is the legal basis for intervening? Are our objectives realistic? Is the intervention time-limited? What is the potential cost in lives and treasure? What is the level of support in Congress and among the public? What are possible unintended consequences? What can go wrong?

Have we thought out several moves in advance—if we do X and then Y happens, what do we do, and so on?

Second, in terms of specific situations: Does an international aggression threaten the United States or our allies? Has there been use of weapons of mass destruction—chemical, biological, or nuclear? Does internal disorder in one country threaten to spill over national borders and menace U.S. allies? Will our involvement make a difference or facilitate a negotiated outcome? What are the prospects internally for an enduring cessation of violence—is our intervention simply a time-out or a game changer? What are the resources necessary for achieving our objectives, and are we prepared to commit those resources? In terms of international peacekeeping, are there security guarantees from the internal factions, cooperation between parties, and readily achievable mandates?

Third, when intervening in a specific country: Do we have a strong local partner? Does the country's government want our help? Are there strong local government institutions or at least foundations on which to build them? Can and will the locals lead the fight, with us in a supporting role?

It is probably obvious at this point that I believe the bar for use of our military for purposes short of protecting our vital interests and those of our allies should be a high one. The patience of the American people for protracted, much less stalemated, military combat is finite, and we must not draw down that well of patience for purposes that are not clearly in our own interest. There are just too many uncertainties. As the military says, "Sergeant Murphy [of Murphy's law that whatever can go wrong, will go wrong] goes on every mission." I have seen too many American lives lost propping up corrupt, ineffective leaders who were unable to win their own people's commitment and willingness to sacrifice. I have seen too many lives lost to unintended consequences or because obvious questions were not asked before the first soldier set foot on a plane.

Finally, presidents should always bear in mind the advice given to Generals George Marshall and Dwight Eisenhower, who, as young officers, were taught three maxims of war by their mentor, Major

General Fox Connor: Never fight unless you have to, never fight alone, and never fight for long.

FIXING THE NONMILITARY INSTRUMENTS: CREATING A SYMPHONY

Effectively countering China and Russia, as well as other rivals, in the years ahead requires a dramatic restructuring of the government's national security apparatus. The current structure, created by the National Security Act of 1947, has outlived its usefulness and is a serious obstacle to success in the future. Successive presidents rhetorically summon a "whole-of-government" effort to tackle problems, creating the impression that all relevant agencies and departments will be yoked together in a common effort bringing vast resources to bear. Apart from the military, this is largely smoke and mirrors. I have previously described the shortcomings of the State Department, USAID, strategic communications, cyber capabilities, and covert operations, and the inability to harness the multiple aspects of American economic power. Our capacity to develop and implement integrated strategies bringing together all these instruments of power and operating them in concert is negligible. All of the noncoercive American instruments of power need revitalization and restructuring.

The State Department has just over 8,000 commissioned Foreign Service officers (FSOs)—diplomats—just a couple of thousand more people than are required to crew one aircraft carrier. USAID has approximately 10,000 employees, nearly 1,900 of them FSOs from State. The government's principal strategic communications arm is the Bureau of Global Public Affairs, one of nearly three dozen bureaus within the State Department (and it doesn't even report directly to the secretary of state). By contrast, the Defense Department has nearly 2 million men and women in uniform and another 800,000 civilian employees. The national security enterprise today reminds me of a nineteenth-century tricycle, with a giant front wheel (Defense) and tiny back wheels (everyone else).

As we engage with China, as well as face lesser challenges, the key is to sustain military superiority while strengthening the nonmilitary instruments of power, which, if we are both smart and lucky, is where the competition will play out. The latter requires far-reaching restructuring along with more resources.

Though the State Department and USAID are staffed by some of the most impressive and talented people in government, institutionally they are bureaucratic and political nightmares. State has a stultifying bureaucracy that frustrates its best people and hugely impedes its agility and speed in tackling problems. Its resources are misaligned overseas (e.g., too many people in posh places like London, Paris, Berlin, and Rome; not nearly enough in New Delhi, Beijing, the Middle East, and key developing countries). Even under pressure from both Bush 43 and Obama, the secretary of state had difficulty getting FSOs to "volunteer" to go to Baghdad and Kabul. The bureaucracy and culture stifle creativity and boldness, and more than a few secretaries of state have, for all practical purposes, walled themselves off from the professionals in the department.

State should be the most critical and central nonmilitary instrument of American foreign policy. To meet the challenges of the future, it needs a dramatic bureaucratic reorganization and cultural shake-up—and significantly more resources. The department needs to be reimagined for the twenty-first century, and that will involve breaking a lot of rice bowls. I won't pretend enough knowledge of the department to make specific recommendations for its future structure or for how to change its culture. But changing it, and getting it in the game, is critical to the future of American national security.

Ideally, a restructured State Department would be the hub for integrating and managing all the parts of the government involved in applying nonmilitary resources to foreign policy or national security problems. A good example of how this might work is Bush 43's PEPFAR project to combat HIV/AIDS in Africa, in which a number of agencies had a role to play but the president empowered a single coordinator at State to control the budget and bring them all together in a coordinated and effective campaign. Sadly, for most issues, the bureaucratic situation in the government right now resembles multiple people trying to play the same cello at the same time.

The U.S. strategic communications effort is a joke. Multiple entities are involved in this arena—the White House, State, Defense, Treasury, and the CIA, to name just a few. For the most part, each goes its own way, with its own issues and emphasis. There is some effort at the White House and the NSC to coordinate the messaging, but it is weak, inconsistent, and often highly political. Iran is an example of lost opportunities because of our lack of an aggressive strategic communications strategy. We have not done nearly enough to inform Iranians in detail about the corruption, power struggles, and repressive measures of their leaders; to create problems internally by helping opposition groups; or to find other ways to complicate the lives of the regime leaders. Similarly, through strategic communications, we can make another instrument of power—nationalism—work to our advantage by highlighting Russian and Chinese efforts to interfere surreptitiously in the internal affairs of other countries. We also have done a lousy job communicating to the world the scale and impact of our development assistance programs and the humanitarian assistance we have provided all over the world, including to our enemies in Iran and North Korea.

A new top-level organization is needed, a USIA-like organization on steroids, preferably located within State but empowered by the president—as the PEPFAR coordinator was—to enable consistent, ubiquitous strategic communications using all the venues and technologies available to the government. It would oversee all traditional and electronic messaging, including social media, and all foreign policy–related public statements and efforts by other departments. Such an entity, working with other appropriate agencies, would be charged with developing new tools to break through social media firewalls in places like Russia and China and find other means of getting information through to the subject peoples of authoritarian states, just as we did in the Soviet Union. It would be empowered to explore and recommend new technologies for communicating America's message around the world.

An important outlier in the strategic communications domain is the U.S. Agency for Global Media (probably the biggest agency you never heard of), an independent federal organization that operates all U.S. broadcasting abroad—Voice of America (VOA), Radio Liberty, Radio Free Europe, Radio Martí (to Cuba), Radio Free Asia, and Middle East broadcasting. Not only does the agency not report to the secretary of state, it has an independent board, the principal purpose of which is to ensure against political interference in the "journalistic product." In 2016, its budget was over $700 million and its broadcasts in sixty-one languages reached some 226 million people in a hundred countries. Even before USIA was dismantled, there were long, hard fights pitting the executives and staffs of the broadcasts against the White House and the State Department, which thought such U.S. government-funded organizations ought to be willing to take at least broad guidance from the secretary of state. Presidents were always sensitive about VOA broadcasting unvarnished, unbiased news about domestic developments in the United States—airing our dirty laundry around the world, if you will. But such honesty did add to its credibility. A great strength of both overt USIA/VOA and covert CIA messaging during the Cold War was that it told the truth about what was happening in the USSR and Eastern Europe. The president needs to find a way to reassure VOA and other agency journalists that they can continue to report globally about events in the United States without interference, but some means must be found to tie the Agency for Global Media into the broader U.S. strategic communications effort overseen by the State Department, still reporting factually but working in tandem in terms of themes and emphasis, e.g., repression and corruption in places like Russia, China, North Korea, and Iran.

Successive U.S. presidents have been frustrated with the inadequacies and failures of our foreign assistance programs. Frustration with and suspicion of USAID led Bush 43 to establish the Millennium Challenge Corporation as a separate entity. Afghanistan is an example of failure in this regard on several levels, from the lack of effective management oversight to pervasive corruption, unwillingness to involve the Afghans themselves in decision making on projects in their own country, and the lack of information sharing across districts and provinces about what was working and what was not—not to mention the near-total absence of such collaboration with other countries and numerous nongovernmental organizations.

Even if the entire U.S. assistance effort is not folded into MCC, as some conservatives have urged, its principles guiding the selection of countries and projects ought to be fully adopted. Greater accountability, both for recipients of aid and for the American administrators, is critical. Political support in Congress might be improved by the adoption of such reforms and by taking into consideration whether potential recipients are friendly or hostile toward the United States. Self-interest in apportioning scarce development dollars would not be a sin.

Greater creativity is needed in countering China's Belt and Road Initiative and its other investment programs in developing countries around the world. The new U.S. International Development Finance Corporation is a strong start to expanding U.S. efforts to encourage private investment in developing countries. If China's advantage is being able to loan hundreds of billions of dollars to countries for projects, America's advantage is in the vastly greater economic power of our private sector not only to invest but to do so in economically viable projects that truly serve the long-term economic interest of the recipients. If we take long-term competition with China seriously in this arena, we need to be smarter in figuring out incentives to make investment in developing countries more attractive for American companies. A reformed State Department and USAID also need to be imaginative about how to persuade American private foundations, other nongovernmental organizations, and universities to become more involved.

Our economic sticks with which to punish countries that cross us are highly developed. We need to work on carrots—positive economic tools—for those we wish to win over. Again, State should be the hub, empowered by the president, for convening the Treasury, Commerce, Agriculture, and Labor Departments, the Special Trade Representative, and others to develop new ideas for competing in this arena. Aggressive, bold leadership is needed. The old ways of doing business are not good enough.

If there is one further lesson, it is that the United States needs to be much smarter about publicizing the assistance projects and programs we undertake. We need to be less monastic order and more Madison Avenue.

Another instrument of power often neglected by policy makers is intelligence information. Everyone knows about the contributions made through covert action and espionage. But for decades the CIA has shared intelligence information—analyses—with not only our closest allies and NATO but many other countries as well. Photos taken by U.S. satellites have been used in presentations to the UN Security Council. Using intelligence analyses drawn from many sources, in the 1990s the United States was able to give the World Health Organization highly accurate estimates of HIV/AIDS infection rates in Africa when affected governments often refused to provide data or distorted it; indeed, it was the CIA's early reporting that alerted Presidents Clinton and Bush 43 to the AIDS pandemic. U.S. analysts have forecast crop yields globally, allowing governments to plan ahead for shortages, and identified vulnerabilities of oil and gas infrastructures to terrorist attacks or natural disasters. Policy makers need to be more attuned to the benefits of providing such information to governments as a way to help anticipate problems.

For decades, U.S. intelligence has developed detailed information on the infrastructure of many countries, including such things as the capacity of bridges and water and electrical systems. This information is easily declassified and could be provided by the Commerce Department or others to American companies considering investments. Such information could save the companies considerable money and could be another way to encourage them to invest.

Cyber capability is in a class by itself as an instrument of power because it can be used effectively not only against military targets but also in economic competition (as the Chinese have shown so vividly), influence operations (as the Russians have demonstrated) and in strategic communications. The United States has developed powerful cyber tools for offensive military use and for defending our networks. According to the press, we have disabled (at least temporarily) Russian hacking organizations involved in trying to influence our politics and elections. However, as far as I know, we have not—for policy, not technical, reasons—gotten very far in figuring out a strategy for using our cyber capabilities to break through firewalls in China, Russia, and elsewhere for strategic communications purposes. At a minimum, we need to show these countries that two can play this game and that, in this particular arena (getting information to the public), we have a very real advantage. We need to take seriously the opportunities it affords as an instrument of power beyond the military and economic spheres.

As noted earlier, higher education and the science and technology sector are both important instruments of power. We will shoot ourselves in the foot if we allow our partisan debates over immigration to curtail the flow of foreign students coming to U.S. universities and seeing firsthand what freedom looks like. Similarly, the government's failure to adequately fund basic research will have dire consequences down the road. As secretary, I increased Defense funding in this area, but those increases have long since disappeared.

RESTRUCTURING

Fundamental to any effort to centralize and focus various U.S. nonmilitary instruments of power is restructuring the national security apparatus. It is crucial that departments and agencies that to date have not been statutory members of the NSC or interagency processes—e.g., Treasury, Commerce, Agriculture, the Agency for Global Media, the

Special Trade Representative—be integrated into policy and decision making as well as operational activities.

Some may argue that oversight of the interagency efforts I have described should be in the White House, under the NSC. I disagree. The kind of integration and centralization of the nonmilitary instruments I believe are needed must involve day-to-day control. I served on the NSC staff under four presidents, and the kind of operational and budgetary integration and coordination I believe is necessary in each of those endeavors is beyond the capabilities and the writ of the NSC staff. To be used effectively, these nonmilitary instruments of power must rely on the professionals and specialists of the government departments to implement strategies and policies approved by the president. The role of the NSC should be to ensure, on behalf of the president, that the diverse instruments are indeed being strengthened and harmonized as directed, and that the instruments are being used in a coordinated, mutually reinforcing manner so that the entire symphony is a dramatic manifestation of American power. The NSC must ensure that both the military and nonmilitary instruments of power are being used effectively to achieve the president's strategy.

All that said, if the State Department and USAID simply cannot be restructured and reformed, an alternative might be to create small yet empowered agencies independent of the State Department but reporting to its secretary to oversee, fund, and coordinate specific tools such as strategic communications and development assistance. There may be other ways to restructure our symphony of power so it is far more effective. But Congress would never agree to hand the baton to the NSC, because that would place these nonmilitary instruments beyond the reach and oversight of Congress and would concentrate all the government's strategic communications apparatus in the hands of the White House, where there would be considerable potential for political abuse.

To up our game in the nonmilitary rivalry with China and Russia, we also need to look at how to reform the alliances and international organizations we helped create, to make them more effective.

In NATO, for example, it is imperative to keep the pressure on other members to spend more on defense. But we should work with the members to see where there are opportunities to pool the resources of smaller countries to create new military capabilities. For example, a little over a decade ago, half a dozen allies collaborated in buying three C-17 cargo aircraft, which would have been unaffordable for any one of those countries. Denmark decided some time ago to specialize in just two or three military areas. The United States should focus not just on getting allies to spend more money but also on how to help them spend it more wisely and in ways that enhance the military capabilities of NATO as a whole. While there have been improvements in NATO's decision-making processes, the alliance still is lumbering and slow. We need to determine how we can better work together with NATO and EU countries to coordinate our nonmilitary instruments, from development assistance and investment to countering Chinese and Russian political interference, theft of technology and intellectual property, and strategic messaging. The international economic institutions we created in the 1940s at Bretton Woods also merit a hard look. We should determine whether they are operating today as we intended seventy years ago, whether they need modernizing for today's world, and if so, what kinds of changes we should seek. Similarly, the WTO has value, but we need to examine whether all the members, especially China, are playing by the same rules. (They are not.) I do not advocate leaving any of these institutions; indeed, as I've said, I think it was a strategic mistake for President Obama not to join China's Asian Infrastructure Investment Bank and for President Trump to leave the Trans-Pacific Partnership. But, out of self-interest, we should be very tough-minded about how organizations we created or helped to create are operating.

CONGRESS

For too long, Congress has ceded its powers in foreign policy to the executive branch. That the president could undertake military operations throughout the Middle East in 2019 based on the Authorization for the Use of Military Force passed by Congress on September 18,

2001, is absurd and a genuine dereliction of duty to the Constitution. Congress's refusal to get out of the foxhole is partly due to deep partisanship and a determination by each party not to go against a president from that party. Also, Congress is loath to outright deny the president the authority to act, because that would mean accepting for itself responsibility if anything goes wrong. On the whole, members would rather micromanage through budgets than be held accountable on the tough issues.

This is unfortunate because Congress can play a very constructive role in foreign policy. As pointed out, congressional restrictions on the number of U.S. troops allowed to deploy to Colombia shaped and limited the American military role there, forcing the Colombians to do nearly all the fighting while we mainly advised and trained. From the use of military force abroad to approval of foreign arms sales and more, congressional oversight and actions can influence executive decision making and often make it better. As noted above, winning the support of Congress can also be a significant help to presidents in persuading the American people that their actions abroad make sense and are in our national interest. The views of members of Congress matter a lot back home on issues most voters don't understand or care about. Recent presidents have invested little time and energy in such cultivation (and education) of the people's elected representatives.

Congress bears heavy responsibility for the weakening of America's nonmilitary instruments of power over the past twenty-five years. It was Congress that exterminated USIA and authorized the dismantling of USAID, both in the 1990s. It is Congress that, with a couple of exceptions under Bush 43, has starved the State Department of resources. It is Congress that represents a huge obstacle to restructuring the State Department and USAID. The irony is that the more uncomfortable Congress has become with U.S. military engagement around the world, the more it has constrained our nonmilitary instruments of power. During the wars in Iraq and Afghanistan, Congress was always willing to give the Defense Department hundreds of millions of dollars for tasks that were properly the province of the State Department or other civilian agencies—even as they denied such funding to those same agencies. To give credit where credit is due, when President Trump wanted to slash State and USAID by some 30 percent in 2017, it was Congress that restored the money to those budgets. But that was simply a return to the status quo ante.

If Congress wants to play a constructive role in the long rivalry ahead with China, it should be prepared to act decisively in several areas. It should work with the executive branch in deciding how to restructure State, USAID, and the NSC to strengthen our nonmilitary instruments. In fact, State and USAID can only be fixed with the support of Congress. With restructuring and reform as the precondition, Congress should robustly increase funding for those agencies and the enhancement of the other nonmilitary tools.

In the aftermath of 9/11, Congress and the Bush administration made many sweeping structural changes in the executive branch to deal with a new international environment—including creation of the Department of Homeland Security, the director of national intelligence, and the National Counterterrorism Center—and wrote significant new legislation empowering the government to deal with a new threat. Now, as we look to a long-term rivalry with China, Congress and the president must work together to create new institutions for effectively strengthening and employing our nonmilitary instruments of power, just as our predecessors did at the outset of the Cold War and after the attacks in 2001 on our homeland.

Finally, Congress needs to fix itself (in many ways). The current committee structure in both houses ensures that members look at each component of the national security enterprise in isolation—the Armed Services Committees for Defense, the Foreign Affairs and Foreign Relations Committees for State, the Intelligence Committees for the CIA and other agencies. Even in the House and Senate Appropriations Committees, there are subcommittees for each of those components with hardly anyone looking at the big picture. There is, of course, some overlapping membership between the committees, but it hasn't counted for much. I am enough of a realist to know that changing the congressional committee structure is a Sisyphean task. There is an alternative, though: create in both the Senate and the House an overarching "National Security Committee" composed of a small number of members from the Armed Services, Foreign Affairs,

Foreign Relations, Intelligence, and Appropriations Committees who can understand and oversee the big picture of how the nonmilitary instruments are working together and are integrated with our military. Only thus can they have the same perspective as the president and his secretaries of defense and state, and be in a position to provide necessary resources, understand and then support or oppose presidential actions, and provide effective oversight.

AMERICA: REALIST, IDEALIST, AND TRANSACTIONAL

Labels in politics are a barrier to clear thinking. Pigeonholing leaders as realists or idealists or, in the case of Trump, as purely transactional, obscures the fact that nearly all leaders are, to one degree or another, all three. Each example I've discussed reflects that reality.

Bill Clinton was a realist when he recognized that bombing Serbia was the only way to get Milošević to negotiate, an idealist when he thought the United States could improve governance in Haiti and Somalia, and purely transactional when ending the fighting in Bosnia through the Dayton Accords. In trying to negotiate a deal between Israel and the Palestinians in late 2000, he was all three at once. Similarly, George Bush was being a realist when he ordered removal of the Taliban regime in Afghanistan, an idealist in believing America could bring democracy to Iraq and Afghanistan, and transactional in signing the nuclear arms accord with Moscow. He was both realistic and idealistic in his PEPFAR and MCC initiatives. Barack Obama was realistic in avoiding intervention in Syria, idealistic in believing we could just suddenly end our military involvement in Iraq and Afghanistan, and transactional in intervening in Libya.

In the real world, there is a close link between being realistic and being transactional, and the tension between both and idealism has deep roots in American history. From the very beginning, we have wrestled with the appropriate role this country should play in advancing freedom and democracy in the world and how to incorporate our democratic ideals and aspirations into our dealings with other countries. We have grappled with when and whether we should try to change the way other nations govern themselves. And so I return to the question I posed at the outset: Should America's mission be to make the world "safe for democracy," as Woodrow Wilson said, or, in the words of John Quincy Adams, should America be "the well-wisher to the freedom and independence of all" but "the vindicator and champion only of her own"?

Every president's primary responsibility, apart from defending the Constitution, is to protect the United States from harm and to advance its interests wherever and whenever possible. "America First" is a slogan tainted by history (its association with pre–World War II anti-Semitic, pro-fascist isolationism), but in truth, it is every president's charge, and has been since the founding. During the French Revolution, George Washington, understanding the great fragility of America's position at the time, adopted a policy of neutrality toward France and signed a peace treaty with Great Britain. Consider the historical irony: the United States had recently won its independence from Britain only with the help of an absolutist French king, yet when France turned in the direction of popular rule and was confronted by Europe's monarchs, the United States took a pass and made amends with our old British foe. To win and protect our freedom, America has made common cause with countries that were far from free, from the France of Louis XVI to the Soviet Union of Joseph Stalin, one of history's true monsters. Without the one, there is no American independence; without the other, no end to the Third Reich. It is neither hypocrisy nor cynicism to believe fervently in freedom while adopting different approaches to advancing freedom at different times along the way, including temporarily making common cause with despots to defeat greater or more urgent threats to our freedom or our interests. Thus do we work with autocrats in Saudi Arabia, Egypt, and elsewhere to counter the threat to the region and our interests posed by Iran.

It ought not be the role of the American military to try to shape the future of other countries. The power of our military's global reach has been an indispensable contributor to peace and stability in many regions and must remain so. But not every outrage, every act of aggression, every oppression, or every crisis can or should elicit an American military response. We must be realists about the limits of our military to bring about enduring reform and determine the political future of others.

That said, our ideology is fundamental to America's role in the world, keeping alive the belief among the oppressed and unfree that this country will use every nonmilitary instrument we have to advance the cause of freedom and democracy. We must not be silent when either our adversaries or our friends violate human rights and oppress their people. The promotion of freedom must be a core component of our diplomacy and our strategic communications. While we must do business with autocrats in the real world, we need not embrace them in the same way we embrace democratic governments. People around the world must know that America stands on the side of liberty and human dignity, despite whatever compromises we make to protect our interests. If we abandon that role, we will lose that which makes us historically unique. We will lose some piece of our national soul.

A FOREIGN POLICY AMERICANS CAN SUPPORT

I believe Americans want a military that is technologically superior to and stronger than that of any other country, but they want it used sparingly and only if necessary to protect us and our vital interests abroad. Few want to go abroad, to use John Quincy Adams's phrase, "in search of monsters to destroy." I think there is a view across the political spectrum that, after the Cold War, presidents have turned too readily and too often to the military to resolve challenges abroad. Too often we have acted as global policeman. The public's patience with overseas deployments has been exhausted by eighteen years of war in Afghanistan and Iraq. I suspect Obama's steadfast refusal to engage militarily in Syria and Trump's reluctance to use force (despite his bombast and threats) had the support of most Americans. We must always be prepared to defend our interests, but greater restraint in sending the world's finest military into combat is essential for popular support of America's global leadership role.

Strengthening our nonmilitary instruments of power would, I believe, have broad support under two conditions: that it diminish the need for military action, and that the money be spent on effective programs that actually advance our interests and win us friends abroad. In terms of development assistance, encouraging investment overseas by the private sector in partnership with government will be more readily supported than outright government grants. I think support in Congress would be enhanced by strict adherence to the Millennium Challenge criteria relating to effectiveness, reform, accountability, and regular evaluation—and by demonstrating that support for American policies by potential recipients, including international institutions like the UN, is a factor in the approval process for development assistance.

Public support for a president's foreign policies, as I've said, would be enhanced by evidence that Congress, by and large, is in broad agreement with those policies. In a time of extreme partisanship, this is a tough challenge and will have greater prospects for success if such engagement is informal and done in private. Behind the partisan rhetoric, I think there is broader agreement on a number of the big issues, such as the economic relationship with China, than is evident publicly. Public support will also hinge on a president's tenacity and consistency in explaining his policies in speeches and press conferences as well as through other media.

Americans, I think, understand the value of allies and how they are a unique asset for the United States, especially compared to both Russia and China, neither of which have any. At the same time, those allies are expected to pull their weight. Every president, secretary of state, and secretary of defense since the end of the Cold War has jawboned our NATO allies to spend more in their own defense. That pressure must be sustained, but we must also take into account individual allies' contributions to our mutual security beyond cash expenditures. Certain allies, including Turkey and Germany, must be made to understand that on matters important to the alliance, they cannot play both sides of the street by collaborating closely with Russia and China on security-related issues (such as Turkey's purchase of the Russian S-400 air defense system and Germany's support for the Nord Stream 2 pipeline, which will have a significant impact on both Ukraine and Poland).

Finally, I believe most Americans want our country to stand for something beyond just our military strength and economic success. A lot of people are uncomfortable with an American president cozying up to autocratic foreign leaders, full of praise for how "wonderful" they are and siding with them on issues while deriding American government institutions. We must work with these leaders, but we don't need to say we love them. More important, I am convinced most of the public wants the United States to be seen by others as the world's strongest advocate for liberty and democracy—a beacon of reassurance to the oppressed.

When we are formulating an American foreign policy the public will support, the Woodrow Wilson and John Quincy Adams approaches must coexist. We must protect our interests. We must not be the world's policeman, and we must be very cautious about deploying our military forces to resolve others' internal problems. But we must also use every nonmilitary instrument of power we possess to promote freedom and encourage reform, with friends as well as rivals, because these objectives serve our national interest. With reform, restructuring, and more resources, our nonmilitary instruments can be formed into a remarkable symphony of power.

The critical question, though, is whether, even with all the right military and nonmilitary tools, presidents, Congress, and the American people will recognize that our long-term self-interest demands that we continue to accept the burden of global leadership.

Acknowledgments

This is the first book I have written for which I could not rely throughout on my personal involvement, experiences, and notes. Along with a number of secondary sources, I have depended on the memoirs of key figures, fully aware that such writings, including my own, benefit from hindsight and also tend to describe things in the best possible light. Still, they provide insight into the motives and actions of those in the room. So I thank the post–Cold War presidents, vice presidents, secretaries of state and defense, and others who have written firsthand accounts of their service, even as I am confident they will take exception to some or all of what I have written.

I asked several people to review the manuscript, and I want to thank them for their time and effort: Eric Edelman, Richard Haass, Stephen J. Hadley, and Michele Flournoy. Their comments, suggestions, and criticisms were immensely helpful. Obviously, the views I express are my own, as is sole responsibility for any errors or mistakes. I am deeply grateful to my assistant, Charles Crimmins, for his help in preparing this book. Without his technical expertise and management of my time, I could not have completed it.

Both the CIA and the Department of Defense reviewed the manuscript to prevent the disclosure of classified information, and I thank them for their professional and expeditious responses. Needless to say, all statements of fact, opinion, and analysis are mine and do not reflect the official positions or views of the CIA, the Defense Department, or the

U.S. government. The public-release clearance of this publication does not imply CIA or Department of Defense endorsement or the factual accuracy of the material.

Special thanks to Wayne Kabak of WSK Management, who has represented me for more than twenty-five years and through four books. He has become a close friend, adviser, and counselor. I also want to express my heartfelt appreciation to Jonathan Segal of Alfred A. Knopf, a superb and patient editor through three very different books. I also want to thank the late Sonny Mehta and others at Knopf for their important contributions to the book.

Finally, this book and those that preceded it would not have been possible without my wife, Becky, whose patience and understanding while I was writing were surpassed only by her patience and understanding through fifty-three years of marriage. She has been my love, my companion, and my best friend through many trials and adventures.

Notes

Prologue

5 And yet, from the moment Eisenhower signed: Jean Edward Smith, *Eisenhower in War and Peace* (New York: Random House, 2002), xiii.

Chapter 1 THE SYMPHONY OF POWER

14 By early 1947: Halberstam, *Coldest Winter*, 177, 179.

15 In both conflicts the United States ignored Machiavelli's: Machiavelli, *Prince and Discourses*, 375–78.

19 There is therefore the need to carefully define the mission: Machiavelli, 299–300.

22 The list also included: Alan P. Dobson, quoted in Blackwill and Harris, *War by Other Means*, 163.

26 "Any gain for free trade anywhere": David Singh Grewal, quoted in Blackwill and Harris, 177.

27 For decades now, the application: Blackwill and Harris, 20.

31 In fact, the United States ranks twenty-first: Statistic Brain, "Countries That Give the Most."

32 However, during the Bush 43 years: Tarnoff, *U.S. Agency for International Development*, 15.

33 In 2013, the EU and its member states: European Commission's Directorate-General for European Civil Protection and Humanitarian Aid Operations, "EU Development Aid."

34 In 2016 alone, the United States provided: UN Office for the Coordination of Humanitarian Affairs Financial Tracking Service, "Donor Profile: United States in 2016."

34 Between 1975 and 2013, the U.S. military: U.S. Department of Defense, Office of the Under Secretary for Personnel and Readiness, "Humanitarian Service Medal," table 9.

34 We have been doing this for a long time: McMeekin, *Russian Revolution*, 323–24.

43 Counting all categories: Dillinger, "Nobel Prize Winners by Country."

48 Chinese (and Russian) leaders: Brands, "Democracy vs Authoritarianism," 66.

48 Liberal democracy "rests on a commitment": Tony Smith, quoted in Brands, 66.

Chapter 3 IRAN: GREAT SATAN'S BANE

83 For the second time in eight years: Risen and McManus, "U.S. OKd Iranian Arms."

84 Albright, seizing on these signals: Albright, *Madam Secretary*, 322.

85 As she later acknowledged: Albright, 322.

85 Indeed, at the end of 1998: Albright, 326.

86 She was trying to straddle: Albright, 326.

89 Vice President Cheney and Secretary of Defense Donald Rumsfeld were not sold: Rice, *No Higher Honor*, 158.

90 "While we were talking with the Europeans": Gerami, "Nuclear Breakthrough Unlikely."

90 Rice saw it all as a first step: Rice, *No Higher Honor*, 336–37.

91 They reached an agreement that the Iranians: Rice, 422–24.

91 His third option was a military strike: Bush, *Decision Points*, 417.

91 In April, Secretary of Defense Don Rumsfeld wrote a memo: Rumsfeld, *Known and Unknown*, 639.

93 As Rice later wrote, "Forced to choose": Rice, *No Higher Honor*, 522.

95 According to Rice, Putin delivered: Rice, 627.

102 On September 21, the Iranian government: Clinton, *Hard Choices*, 424.

104 As Secretary Clinton later wrote, powerful forces: Clinton, 442.

106 According to Peter Baker in his book: Baker, *Obama*, 325.

116 Forty percent of the population is under twenty-five: Robin Wright, cited by Seib, "A Regime Still Fighting Great Satan," C2.

Chapter 4 SOMALIA, HAITI, AND THE YUGOSLAV WARS: GOOD INTENTIONS AND THE ROAD TO HELL

119 Similarly, he was concerned about: Meacham, *Destiny and Power*, 529.

120 At the end of March 1993: Albright, *Madam Secretary*, 142.

121 According to then U.S. ambassador to the UN: Albright, 143.

121 They believed that arresting Aidid: Clinton, *My Life*, 550.

121 Clinton would later pose the question: Clinton, 551–52.

122 "The original humanitarian mission: Albright, *Madam Secretary*, 146.

122 As Secretary Albright admitted in her memoir: Albright, 141.

126 Clinton himself underscored that disparity: Clinton, *My Life*, 649.

127 Madeleine Albright wrote of Haiti in her memoir: Albright, *Madam Secretary*, 161.

130 Peter Galbraith, the first U.S. ambassador to Croatia, later pointed out: Galbraith, "Washington, Erdut and Dayton," 644.

130 As then Secretary of State Jim Baker would write in his memoir: Baker, *The Politics of Diplomacy*, 636.

133 Baker summarized the outgoing national security team's: Baker, 651.

133 He recalled that he didn't want to unilaterally lift: Clinton, *My Life*, 513.

133 As his UN Ambassador, Madeleine Albright, wrote: Albright, *Madam Secretary*, 182.

134 When Colin Powell objected: Albright, 183.

135 National Security Adviser Anthony Lake: Albright, 190.

136 She also advocated: Albright, 390.

137 The U.S. government, Condoleezza Rice wrote, was convinced: Rice, *No Higher Honor*, 682.

137 Rice later acknowledged: Rice, 684.

138 As one scholar put it, "The humanitarian interventions": Mandelbaum, *Mission Failure*, 76.

141 She later wrote, "The experts had concluded": Albright, *Madam Secretary*, 152.

Chapter 5 COLOMBIA: THE PLAN THAT WORKED (MOSTLY)

143 Because of the challenges of travel and communication: Rochlin, "Plan Colombia," 718.

143 The limited reach and power of the central government: Rochlin, 719.

144 The FARC subsequently suffered: Rochlin, 720.

148 During the visit, Clinton pledged: Clinton, *My Life*, 822.

150 As Condi Rice would later write: Rice, *Democracy*, 242.

152 Condi Rice would later write that Bush: Rice, 242.

152 Rumsfeld recommended that: Rumsfeld, *Known and Unknown*, 629.

153 Rice would later write that "everyone generally": Rice, *Democracy*, 245.

153 As Rumsfeld wrote, "stopping the flow": Rumsfeld, *Known and Unknown*, 628.

154 And Uribe said he intended to do just that: Rice, *No Higher Honor*, 257.

157 The number of kidnappings had dropped: Boot and Bennet, "Colombian Miracle."

158 There were few alternative development programs: USGAO, *Plan Colombia*, 48.

159 The Justice Department provided $115 million: USGAO, 47–59.

161 The FARC representatives responded: Kerry, *Every Day Is Extra*, 432.

Chapter 6 AFGHANISTAN: WAR WITHOUT END

169 In late February 1987, Foreign Minister Andrei Gromyko said: Taubman, *Gorbachev*, 376.

169 Gorbachev's principal foreign policy aide: Taubman, 377.

173 Omar agreed to talk: Albright, *Madam Secretary*, 371.

174 As Albright recounted, "We offered rewards": Albright, 372.

174 The director of central intelligence, George Tenet: Tenet, *At the Center of the Storm*, 125.

174 Clinton told Sharif plainly: Clinton, *My Life*, 866.

175 According to Tenet, after January 1, 2000: Tenet, *At the Center of the Storm*, 126–27.

175 "Bin Laden's network is global however": Tenet, *At the Center of the Storm*, 129.

175 Rice later wrote that Bush: Rice, *No Higher Honor*, 65.

176 "In terms of seriously damaging al-Qaeda itself": Rice, 66.

177 "The effort would combine the use of satellite": Rumsfeld, *Known and Unknown*, 376.

177 Bush spoke to Musharraf shortly afterward: Bush, *Decision Points*, 188.

179 In Afghanistan, Dobbins met: Fields and Ahmed, "A Review of the 2001 Bonn Conference," 14.

180 "A democratic Afghanistan would be a hopeful alternative": Bush, *Decision Points*, 205.

181 "Thus freeing Afghan women emerged early": Rice, *No Higher Honor*, 91.

182 "We ought not to make a career out of transforming": Rumsfeld, *Known and Unknown*, 398.

182 "It struck me," Rumsfeld added, "that sending U.S.": Rumsfeld, 682–83.

186 Bush's goal was to "stabilize the country": Bush, *Decision Points*, 194, 205.

187 Bush and Obama, their advisers, and the international community: Machiavelli, *Prince and Discourses*, 378.

190 While production dropped dramatically in 2001: Blanchard, *Afghanistan*, 4.

190 "We were building": Rice, *No Higher Honor*, 109.

191 As Rumsfeld complained to Rice in February 2005: Rumsfeld, *Known and Unknown*, 685.

192 In 2007, for example, in the twelve U.S.-led PRTs: USGAO, *Provincial Reconstruction Teams*, 9.

193 PRTs staffed by coalition partners: Abbaszadeh et al., *Provincial Reconstruction Teams*, 5.

193 Most of the new arrivals, as I feared: Chandrasekaran, *Little America*, 179.

195 Not one Afghan official in either Kabul or Kandahar: Chandrasekaran, 166–67.

197 The campaign through September 2002 had cost: Cordesman, *U.S. Cost of Afghan War*, 4.

197 Counting both military and civilian efforts, between 2002 and 2018: Wellman, "Afghan Forces Struggling."

197 During the ten years after 2002: Cordesman, *U.S. Cost of Afghan War*, 4.

Chapter 7 IRAQ: A CURSE

200 This was done, as George H. W. Bush's national security adviser Brent Scowcroft would: Bush and Scowcroft, *World Transformed*, 305.

203 The former would have split: Bush and Scowcroft, 489.

206 Bush's first National Security Council Meeting addressed: Rice, *No Higher Honor*, 31.

206 He later wrote, "The lesson of 9/11": Bush, *Decision Points*, 229.

206 "If we could convince him we were serious": Bush, 230.

208 Bush determined early in the war planning: Bush, 232.

208 "The art of compromise," he later wrote: Rumsfeld, *Known and Unknown*, 498–99.

208 According to Rice, Rumsfeld argued: Rice, *No Higher Honor*, 187.

209 She underscored Bush's belief: Rice, 187.

212 Indeed, as Bush would later write, the administration: Bush, *Decision Points*, 248–49.

213 Rumsfeld admitted that even the Defense Department: Rumsfeld, *Known and Unknown*, 505.

213 "Our nation building capabilities were limited": Bush, *Decision Points*, 249–50.

214 Rumsfeld dismissed State's Future of Iraq Project: Rumsfeld, *Known and Unknown*, 486.

214 As Rice tried to better coordinate planning: Rice, *No Higher Honor*, 192.

214 Rumsfeld would later observe: Rumsfeld, *Known and Unknown*, 487.

215 However, as Bremer would later write: Rumsfeld, 506.

215 Rumsfeld wrote in his memoir, "The muddled lines of authority": Rumsfeld, 507.

219 The highest number of non-Defense civilians: USGAO, *Provincial Reconstruction Teams*, 13.

Chapter 8 AFRICA: A SUCCESS STORY

231 President Clinton would later acknowledge that Africa: Clinton, *My Life*, 780.

231 Albright conceded that "Africa": Albright, *Madam Secretary*, 450.

233 In Sierra Leone, the Economic Community: Albright, 454.

233 As Albright later wrote, "The solution to these conflicts": Albright, 454.

235 At the UN General Assembly the following September: Albright, 456.

235 "Whether the specific need was debt relief": Albright, 455.

236 Secretary Rice recounts that at one of her: Rice, *No Higher Honor*, 228.

236 At the same time, Bush believed: Bush, *Decision Points*, 335.

236 For Bush, though, the highest priority: Bush, 335.

236 They thought it important for the United States: Bush, 336.

237 "And hopelessness leaves people ripe": Bush, 336.

237 The same day Bush announced: Bush, 338.

238 The infection rate in Uganda: Bush, 338.

240 Liberia, Sierra Leone, Guinea: Daschle and Frist, *Building Prosperity*, 27.

241 Between 2007 and 2011, PEPFAR countries: Daschle and Frist, *Case for Strategic Health Diplomacy*, 13.

241 Finally, strong accountability and transparency: Daschle and Frist, 22–23.

244 In short, countries that were "ruling justly": Bush, *Decision Points*, 348.

244 It "committed the United States": Rice, *No Higher Honor*, 155.

245 Between 2004 and 2017, MCC claims to have trained: Curt Tarnoff, *Millennium Challenge Corporation*, 22–23.

246 A 2008 report by the Brookings Institution: Fox and Rieffel, "Strengthen Millennium Challenge Corporation," 1–2.

246 After making a number of recommendations for improving MCC: Fox and Rieffel, 6.

Chapter 9 RUSSIA: OPPORTUNITY MISSED?

251 On the 13th, Yeltsin called Bush again: Bush and Scowcroft, *World Transformed*, 555–57.

253 Moreover, Bush himself was "pessimistic": Bush and Scowcroft, 503.

253 As Scowcroft wrote, "In our own view": Bush and Scowcroft, 506.

253 As Bush later observed, "We had to see what relationships": Bush and Scowcroft, 540.

255 Ultimately, though, the International Monetary Fund: Odling-Smee, "IMF and Russia," 169.

255 The money was to help stabilize: Clinton, *My Life*, 506.

256 "Their prescription was to reject the link": Matlock, *Autopsy on an Empire*, 735.

256 Yeltsin told Clinton in Vancouver: Clinton, *My Life*, 507.

258 The administration believed that an "open and deliberate": Albright, *Madam Secretary*, 167.

259 In their joint memoir, Bush and Scowcroft wrote: Bush and Scowcroft, *World Transformed*, 239.

259 The members would participate in military training: Albright, *Madam Secretary*, 168.

259 Clinton hoped the process for enlargement: Clinton, *My Life*, 569.

259 Albright observed, "We had to walk": Albright, *Madam Secretary*, 254.

260 Albright made no such commitments: Albright, 255.

260 In private, Clinton told Yeltsin: Clinton, *My Life*, 750.

261 "The Russians were frustrated by the weak hand": Albright, *Madam Secretary*, 417.

263 Seventy-five percent of Americans: Clinton, *My Life*, 506.

265 As Rice subsequently observed: Rice, *Democracy*, 104–105.

265 The flights were unable to take off: Albright, *Madam Secretary*, 426–27.

266 But, Albright observed, "beneath Putin's nationalism": Albright, 442–43.

267 After the attacks on September 11, Putin never: Rice, *No Higher Honor*, 62–63.

271 Putin was referring to reporter Dan Rather: Bush, *Decision Points*, 432.

273 In mid-2006, Rumsfeld: Rumsfeld, *Known and Unknown*, 636.

273 Yeltsin had told Bush: Bush and Scowcroft, *World Transformed*, 512, 552.

274 Secretary Rice laid out the pros and cons: Rice, *No Higher Honor*, 671–72.

274 "We believed that the newly independent": Rice, 693.

277 She pledged that the United States would "continue to support": Clinton, *Hard Choices*, 229–30.

278 That fall Putin wrote in a Russian newspaper: Clinton, 239.

278 Clinton had told an international conference: Clinton, 235.

282 By 2019, Russia was the only major player: Stent, "Putin's Big Move," C4.

282 In December 2018, Maduro visited Moscow, where: Faiola and DeYoung, "Russia Sees Opportunity," A1.

282 Moscow also had signed oil and gas arrangements: Schmitt, "Russia's Military Mission Creep," A1.

283 "To Mr. Putin, causing so much trouble": *Economist*, "Putin's Pipeline," 12.

285 Putin told Obama on March 1: Rhodes, *World as It Is*, 271.

288 In a 2014 meeting with Obama on how to make: Rhodes, 382.

289 In February 2013, the chief: General Valery Gerasimov, "The Value of Science Is in the Foresight," trans. Robert Coalson, *Military-Industrial Kurier*, February 27, 2013.

Chapter 10 GEORGIA, LIBYA, SYRIA, AND UKRAINE: TO INTERVENE OR NOT TO INTERVENE

295 At an NSC meeting on August 12: Rice, *No Higher Honor*, 688–89.

296 The alliance also declared its intention: Rice, 692.

301 In a paper for the Brookings Institution in April 2016: Hamid, "Everyone Says Libya Intervention Was a Failure."

301 A Wilson Center paper issued on September 10, 2012: Wilson Center, "U.S. Assistance."

304 Obama himself was skeptical: Rhodes, *World as It Is*, 158.

305 The participants, including the five permanent members: Clinton, *Hard Choices*, 458.

305 "Once guns went into the country": Clinton, 452.

306 But as then secretary of defense Leon Panetta later pointed out: Panetta, *Worthy Fights*, 449.

306 She acknowledged the risks and shortcomings: Clinton, *Hard Choices*, 462–64.

314 After a number of calls to Yanukovych: Biden, *Promise Me, Dad*, 98.

314 According to Ben Rhodes: Rhodes, *World as It Is*, 270.

314 With regard to negotiations, the administration: Kerry, *Every Day Is Extra*, 437.

316 Obama told Putin we had no interest: Rhodes, *World as It Is*, 271.

316 Obama's strategy was to "thread a needle": Rhodes, 272.

316 He arranged the ouster of Russia from the G8: Baker, *Obama*, 267.

Chapter 11 NORTH KOREA: CRAZY LIKE A FOX

325 Available evidence suggests the North began pursuing the ability: Heinonen, "North Korea's Nuclear Enrichment."

326 Perry also said publicly that the United States: Clinton, *My Life*, 591.

326 As Clinton later wrote, "I believed that if North": Clinton, 591.

328 On November 12, 1998, Clinton asked: Clinton, 828.

329 Perry delivered a letter from Clinton: Clinton, 856.

330 The North Korean leader decided: Albright, *Madam Secretary*, 463.

331 With regard to verification of these commitments: Albright, 466–68.

331 The United States would not agree to full normalization: Albright, 471–72.

331 Clinton, immersed in a last-ditch effort: Clinton, *My Life*, 929.

331 Even though Clinton didn't make the trip: Clinton, 935.

332 According to most estimates, 2 million to 3 million: Natsios, *Politics of Famine*, 1.

332 According to a United States Institute of Peace report in 1999: Natsios, 10.

332 Presumably because of plotting against him: Natsios, 10.

334 Henceforth, North Korea "would have to change": Bush, *Decision Points*, 90.

334 Kim Dae-jung, as Condi Rice wrote: Rice, *No Higher Honor*, 36–37.

335 Rice, then the national security adviser, also believed in applying pressure: Rice, 158–59.

336 According to Rice, there was an "unbridgeable disagreement": Rice, 159–60.

336 Jiang responded that the North was Bush's problem: Bush, *Decision Points*, 424.

336 At this point in late 2002, Bush reaffirmed his strong tilt: Rice, *No Higher Honor*, 163.

336 Regarding Kim, Bush said: "The United States is through": Bush, *Decision Points*, 423.

337 He warned Jiang in February that if the problem couldn't be solved diplomatically: Bush, 424.

337 With the Six-Party Talks stalled, Secretary Rice visited Beijing: Rice, *No Higher Honor*, 401.

338 "However, our neighbor turned a deaf ear to our advice": Bush, *Decision Points*, 425.

339 She added that Bush might be willing: Rice, *No Higher Honor*, 530.

339 He warned that "some problems cannot be solved through negotiations": Rumsfeld, *Known and Unknown*, 637, 641–42.

340 She acknowledged that the North's uranium enrichment: Rice, *No Higher Honor*, 705–6.

340 He argued that the Six-Party Talks simply provided the North a way to hide: Cheney, *In My Time*, 481–82.

343 The only overture was from Secretary of State Clinton: Clinton, *Hard Choices*, 53–54.

Chapter 12 CHINA: COMPETITION, CONFLICT, OR SOMETHING NEW?

353 "The future is hard to predict in China": Reagan, *An American Life*, 373.

353 "If people have commercial incentives": Bush and Scowcroft, *World Transformed*, 89.

353 "Greater trade and involvement would bring": Clinton, *My Life*, 598.

353 "I believed that, over time, the freedom": Bush, *Decision Points*, 427.

353 "I believe in a future where China": Obama, "Remarks by President."

357 As one observer wrote: Mandelbaum, *Mission Failure*, 26.

358 Premier Li Peng bluntly told Christopher: Mandelbaum, 27.

358 As he later wrote, "Because our engagement": Clinton, *My Life*, 598.

358 His rationale? "The United States had a big stake": Clinton, 598.

361 Beginning in 2005, Chinese direct investment: Clinton, *Hard Choices*, 270–71.

361 As Secretary Clinton wrote, "hide and bide" had been supplanted: Clinton, 74.

363 Over the next twenty years, China's declared military budget: *Economist,* "Army Dreamers," 36.

367 Within five years of China's earliest: Blackwill and Harris, *War by Other Means,* 56.

367 As Secretary Clinton observed, "Few people": Clinton, *Hard Choices,* 538.

369 Compare that with the $590 billion in financing: Manuel, "China's Economic March," 129.

373 China has also asked major international: Perlez, "China Retools," A1.

373 Ahead of Xi's speech, the governor of the People's Bank: Wong and Areddy, "China's Xi Vows New Direction," A6.

373 A 2019 report counted forty Chinese debt: Gayou, "Who's Afraid of Belt and Road," A17.

375 The unit has stolen software source code, trade secrets: Siebel, *Digital Transformation,* 138–39.

375 They had committed an estimated $79 billion: Prasso, "China's Digital Silk Road."

376 China Central television (CCTV) has over seventy foreign bureaus: Custer et al., *Ties That Bind,* 8–9.

376 Its news pages in 2018: *Economist,* "Gaining Face," 81.

376 Globally, between 2004 and 2018, more than 525 CIs: Custer et al., *Ties That Bind,* 12.

377 By the time State shuttered the program: Perlez and Ding, "China Thwarts U.S. Effort," A9.

377 When the new law was enacted: Economy, "Problem with Xi's China Model."

378 Beijing has even created a scholarship program: Custer et al., *Ties That Bind,* 12–13.

378 State-owned Chinese media companies: Pomfret, "China's Meddling in Australia."

378 Other countries, including Britain, have also reported: *Economist,* "At the Sharp End," 20.

379 Between 2001 and 2014, China built: Emanuel, Gadsden, and Moore, "How U.S. Surrendered to China," C3.

380 By 2015, China was spending over $400 billion each year: Hu, "U.S. Is Overly Paranoid."

380 This, of course, does not count non–federally funded research: Emanuel, Gadsden, and Moore, "How U.S. Surrendered to China," C3.

381 As one expert wrote, "Interventionist government bureaucracy": Hu, "U.S. Is Overly Paranoid."

382 As one scholar put it, "Not since Mao Zedong had a Chinese leader": Economy, "China's New Revolution," 60.

384 Economic growth, the mainstay of Party rule: *Economist*, "Bitter Generation," 41–43.

Chapter 13 LESSONS LEARNED

394 In deciding whether a mission is appropriate: Hastings, *Vietnam*, 210.

399 Finally, presidents should always bear in mind: Perry, *Partners in Command*, 46.

Bibliography

Abbaszadeh, Nima, M. Crow, M. El-Khoury, J. Gandomi, D. Kuwayama, C. MacPherson, M. Nutting, N. Parker, and T. Weiss. *Provincial Reconstruction Teams: Lessons and Recommendations.* Princeton, NJ: Woodrow Wilson School of Public & International Affairs, January 2008.

Albright, Madeleine. *Madam Secretary.* New York: Harper Perennial, 2013.

Baker, James A. *The Politics of Diplomacy.* New York: G. P. Putnam's Sons, 1995.

Baker, Peter. *Obama: The Call of History.* New York: Calloway, 2019.

Biden, Joe. *Promise Me, Dad.* New York: Flatiron Books, 2017.

Blackwill, Robert D., and Jennifer M. Harris. *War by Other Means.* Cambridge, MA: Harvard University Press, 2016.

Blanchard, Christopher M. *Afghanistan: Narcotics and U.S. Policy.* Washington, DC: Congressional Research Service, August 12, 2009.

Boot, Max, and Richard Bennet. "The Colombian Miracle," *Weekly Standard,* December 14, 2009.

Brands, Hal. "Democracy vs Authoritarianism: How Ideology Shapes Great-Power Conflict." *Survival* 60, no. 5 (2018).

Bush, George, and Brent Scowcroft. *A World Transformed.* New York: Alfred A. Knopf, 1998.

Bush, George W. *Decision Points.* New York: Crown Publishers, 2010.

Chandrasekaran, Rajiv. *Little America.* New York: Alfred A. Knopf, 2012.

Cheney, Richard B. *In My Time.* New York: Threshold Editions, 2011.

Clinton, Bill. *My Life.* New York: Alfred A. Knopf, 2016.

Clinton, Hillary R. *Hard Choices*. New York: Simon & Schuster, 2014.

Cordesman, Anthony H. *The U.S. Cost of the Afghan War*. Washington, DC: Center for Strategic & International Studies, May 14, 2012.

Council on Foreign Relations and Milbank Memorial Fund. *Addressing the HIV/AIDS Pandemic*. New York: Council on Foreign Relations and Milbank Memorial Fund, 2004.

Custer, S., B. Russell, M. DiLorenzo, M. Cheng, S. Ghose, J. Sims, J. Turner, and H. Desai. *Ties That Bind: Quantifying China's Public Diplomacy and Its "Good Neighbor" Effect*. Williamsburg, VA: AidData at William & Mary, 2018.

Daschle, Tom, and Bill Frist. *Building Prosperity, Stability, and Security Through Strategic Health Diplomacy: A Study of 15 Years of PEPFAR*. Washington, DC: Bipartisan Policy Center, July 2018.

——. *The Case for Strategic Health Diplomacy: A Study of PEPFAR*. Washington, DC: Bipartisan Policy Center, November 2015.

Dillinger, Jessica. "Nobel Prize Winners by Country." WorldAtlas. October 23, 2019. https://www.worldatlas.com/articles/top-30-countries-with-nobel-prize-winners.html.

Economist. "Army Dreamers." *Economist*, June 29, 2019.

——. "At the Sharp End." *Economist*, December 14, 2017.

——. "The Bitter Generation." *Economist*, May 3, 2019.

——. "Gaining Face." *Economist*, April 20, 2019.

——. "The Nord Stream 2 Gas Pipeline Is a Russian Trap." *Economist*, February 16, 2019.

——. "Putin's Pipeline." *Economist*, February 16, 2019.

Economy, Elizabeth C. "China's New Revolution," *Foreign Affairs*, May/June 2018.

——. "The Problem with Xi's China Model," *Foreign Affairs*, March 6, 2019. https://www.foreignaffairs.com/articles/china/2019-03-06/problem-xis-china-model.

Emanuel, Ezekiel, Amy Gadsden, and Scott Moore. "How the U.S. Surrendered to China on Scientific Research." *Wall Street Journal*, April 20, 2019.

European Commission's Directorate-General for European Civil Protection and Humanitarian Aid Operations. "EU Development Aid: 15 Things You May Not Know About EU Development Cooperation in 2015." January 15, 2015. https://reliefweb.int/report/world/eu-development-aid-15-things-you-may-not-know-about-eu-development-cooperation-2015.

Faiola, Anthony, and Karen DeYoung. "Russia Sees Opportunity in Ailing Venezuela." *Washington Post,* December 25, 2018.

Fields, Mark, and Ramsha Ahmed. "A Review of the 2001 Bonn Conference and Application to the Road Ahead in Afghanistan." *Strategic Perspectives.* Washington, DC: National Defense University Press, November 2011.

Fox, James W., and Lex Rieffel. "Strengthen the Millennium Challenge Corporation: Better Results Are Possible." Brookings, December 10, 2008. http://www.brookings.edu/research/strengthen-the-millennium -challenge-corporation-better-results-are-possible.

Galbraith, Peter W. "Washington, Erdut and Dayton: Negotiating and Implementing Peace in Croatia and Bosnia-Herzegovina." *Cornell International Law Journal* 30, no. 3, art. 2 (1997).

Gayou, Gerard. "Who's Afraid of the Belt and Road." *Wall Street Journal,* June 10, 2019.

Gerami, Nina. "Nuclear Breakthrough Unlikely Under Rouhani." Washington Institute for Near East Policy, Policy Watch 2094, June 24, 2013.

Halberstam, David. *The Coldest Winter.* New York: Hyperion, 2007.

Hamid, Shadi. "Everyone Says the Libya Intervention Was a Failure. They're Wrong." Brookings, April 12, 2016. https://www.brookings.edu /blog/markaz/2016/04/12/everyone-says-the-libya-intervention-was-a -failure-theyre-wrong/.

Hastings, Max. *Vietnam.* New York: HarperCollins, 2018.

Heinonen, Olli. "North Korea's Nuclear Enrichment: Capabilities and Consequences." 38 North, June 22, 2011. https://www.38north.org/2011/06 /heinonen062211/.

Hu, Fred. "The U.S. Is Overly Paranoid About China's Tech Rise." *Washington Post,* August 22, 2018.

Kerry, John. *Every Day Is Extra.* New York: Simon & Schuster, 2018.

Machiavelli, Niccolo. *The Prince and The Discourses.* New York: Random House, 1950.

Manchester, William, and Paul Reid. *The Last Lion.* New York: Little, Brown, 2012.

Mandelbaum, Michael. *Mission Failure.* New York: Oxford University Press, 2016.

Manuel, Anja. "China's Economic March: Will It Undermine the Liberal World Order." Presented at the Aspen Strategy Group, Aspen, Colorado, August, 2017.

Matlock, Jack F. *Autopsy on an Empire*. New York: Random House, 1995.

McMeekin, Sean. *The Russian Revolution: A New History*. New York: Basic Books, 2017.

Meacham, Jon. *Destiny and Power*. New York: Random House, 2015.

Natsios, Andrew. *The Politics of Famine in North Korea*. Washington, DC: United States Institute of Peace, August 2, 1999.

Obama, Barack. "Remarks by the President at the U.S./China Strategic and Economic Dialogue." Speech, Ronald Reagan Building and International Trade Center, Washington, DC, July 27, 2009.

Odling-Smee, John. "The IMF and Russia in the 1990s." International Monetary Fund Staff Paper 53, no. 1, 2006.

Office of the U.S. Global AIDS Coordinator and Health Diplomacy. *PEPFAR 2018 Annual Report to Congress*. Washington, DC: United States Department of State, April 2018.

Panetta, Leon, with Jim Newton. *Worthy Fights: A Memoir of Leadership in War and Peace*. New York: Penguin, 2014.

Perlez, Jane. "China Retools Vast Global Building Push Criticized as Bloated and Predatory." *New York Times*, April 25, 2019.

———. "With Allies Feeling Choked, Xi Loosens His Grip on China's Global Building Push." *New York Times*, April 26, 2019.

Perlez, Jane, and Luz Ding. "China Thwarts U.S. Effort to Sustain Culture Centers." *New York Times*, December 30, 2018.

Perry, Mark. *Partners in Command*. New York: Penguin, 2007.

Pomfret, John. "China's Meddling in Australia." *Washington Post*, June 14, 2017. https://www.washingtonpost.com/news/global-opinions/wp/2017/06/14/how-should-the-u-s-deal-with-chinas-rise-look-to-australia/.

Prasso, Sheridan. "China's Digital Silk Road Is Looking More Like an Iron Curtain." *Bloomberg Businessweek*. January 9, 2019. https://www.bloomberg.com/news/features/2019-01-10/china-s-digital-silk-road-is-looking-more-like-an-iron-curtain.

Reagan, Ronald. *An American Life*. New York: Simon & Schuster, 1990.

Rhodes, Ben. *The World as It Is*. New York: Random House, 2018.

Rice, Condoleezza. *Democracy*. New York: Twelve, 2017.

———. *No Higher Honor*. New York: Crown Publishers, 2011.

Risen, James, and Doyle McManus. "U.S. OKd Iranian Arms for Bosnia, Officials Say." *Los Angeles Times*, April 5, 1996.

Rochlin, Jim, "Plan Colombia and the Revolution in Military Affairs: The Demise of the FARC." *Review of International Studies*, 2011.

Rumsfeld, Donald. *Known and Unknown.* New York: Sentinel, 2011.

Runde, Daniel. *The Millennium Challenge Corporation in the Trump Era.* Washington, DC: Center for Strategic & International Studies, February 2017.

Schmitt, Eric. "Russia's Military Mission Creep Advances to a New Front: Africa." *New York Times,* March 31, 2019.

Seib, Jerry. "A Regime Still Fighting Great Satan." *Wall Street Journal,* March 2–3, 2019.

Shultz, George P. *Turmoil and Triumph.* New York: Charles Scribner's Sons, 1993.

Siebel, Thomas M. *Digital Transformation: Survive and Thrive in an Era of Mass Extinction.* New York: RosettaBooks, 2019.

Smith, Jean E. *Eisenhower in War and Peace.* New York: Random House, 2012.

Statistic Brain. "Countries That Give the Most in Foreign Aid Statistics." Sources: OECD, The World Bank, Development Assistance Committee. September 26, 2017. https://www.statisticbrain.com.

Stent, Angela. "Putin's Big Move Back into the Middle East." *Wall Street Journal,* February 16, 2019.

Tarnoff, Curt. *Millennium Challenge Corporation.* Washington, DC: Congressional Research Service, April 18, 2018.

———. *U.S. Agency for International Development (USAID): Background, Operations, Issues.* Washington, DC: Congressional Research Service, July 21, 2015.

Taubman, William. *Gorbachev.* New York: W. W. Norton, 2017.

Tenet, George. *At the Center of the Storm.* New York: Harper Collins, 2007.

United Nations Office for the Coordination of Humanitarian Affairs Financial Tracking Service. "Donor Profile: United States in 2016." http://fts.unocha.org.

United States Department of Defense, Office of the Under Secretary for Personnel and Readiness. "Humanitarian Service Medal—Approved Operations." PDF accessed from https://prhome.defense.gov/M-RA/Inside-M-RA/MPP/OEPM/.

United States Department of State. *Plan Colombia Fact Sheet.* Washington, DC: Bureau of Western Hemisphere Affairs, March 14, 2001.

———. *United States Support for Colombia Fact Sheet.* Washington, DC: Bureau of Western Hemisphere Affairs, July 19, 2000.

United States Government Accountability Office. *Plan Colombia: Drug Reduction Goals Were Not Fully Met, but Security Has Improved; U.S. Agen-*

cies Need More Detailed Plans for Reducing Assistance. Washington, DC: USGAO, October 2008.

———. *Provincial Reconstruction Teams in Afghanistan and Iraq*. Washington, DC: USGAO, October 1, 2008.

Wellman, Phillip W. "Afghan Forces Struggling to Reclaim Lost Territory, Watchdog Says." *Stars and Stripes*. July 31, 2018. https://www.stripes.com/news/middle-east/afghan-forces-struggling-to-reclaim-lost-territory-watchdog-says-1.540237.

Wilson Center. "U.S. Assistance to Egypt, Tunisia and Libya." September 10, 2012. https://www.wilsoncenter.org/article/us-assistance-to-egypt-tunisia-and-libya.

Wong, Chun Han, and James T. Areddy. "China's Xi Vows New Direction for 'Belt and Road' After Criticism." *Wall Street Journal*, April 26, 2019.

Index

A Note About the Author

ROBERT M. GATES was appointed the twenty-second secretary of defense (2006–11) by President George W. Bush and is the only secretary of defense in U.S. history to be asked to remain in that office by a newly elected president. President Barack Obama was the eighth president Gates served. President Obama awarded him the Presidential Medal of Freedom, America's highest civilian honor, on Gates's last day in office. Before becoming secretary of defense, Gates was president of Texas A&M University. Prior to that, he served as interim dean of the George H. W. Bush School of Government and Public Service at the university from 1999 to 2001. Gates joined the Central Intelligence Agency in 1966. In 1967, he was commissioned a second lieutenant in the U.S. Air Force. He spent nearly nine years at the National Security Council, serving four presidents of both political parties. He served as deputy director of central intelligence from 1986 to 1989 and as assistant to the president and deputy national security adviser for President George H. W. Bush from 1989 to 1991. Gates served as director of central intelligence from 1991 to 1993. A native of Kansas, Gates received his bachelor's degree from the College of William & Mary, his master's degree from Indiana University, and his doctorate in Russian and Soviet History from Georgetown University. He was installed as chancellor of the College of William & Mary in 2012. He is the author of *From the Shadows: The Ultimate Insider's Story of Five Presidents and How They Won the Cold War; Duty: Memoirs of a Secretary at War;* and *A Passion for Leadership: Lessons on Change and Reform from Fifty Years of Public Service.*